THE CONSTITUTION
IN THE COURTS

D1567728

THE CONSTITUTION IN THE COURTS

Law or Politics?

MICHAEL J. PERRY

New York   Oxford
OXFORD UNIVERSITY PRESS

Oxford University Press

Oxford   New York
Athens   Auckland   Bangkok   Bombay
Calcutta   Cape Town   Dar es Salaam   Delhi
Florence   Hong Kong   Istanbul   Karachi
Kuala Lumpur   Madras   Madrid   Melbourne
Mexico City   Nairobi   Paris   Singapore
Taipei   Tokyo   Toronto

and associated companies in
Berlin   Ibadan

First published in 1994 by Oxford University Press, Inc.,
198 Madison Avenue, New York, New York 10016

First issued as an Oxford University Press paperback, 1996

Oxford is a registered trademark of Oxford University Press

Library of Congress Cataloging-in-Publication Data
Perry, Michael J.
The Constitution in the courts: law or politics?/
Michael J. Perry
p.   cm.   Includes bibliographical references and index.
ISBN 0-19-508347-4
ISBN 0-19-510464-1 (pbk.)
1. Judicial review—United States.
2. Political questions and judicial power—United States.
3. United States—Constitutional law—Interpretation
and construction.   I. Title.
KF4575.P47   1994   342.73'02—dc20
[347.3022]   93-18539

1 3 5 7 9 8 6 4 2

Printed in the United States of America
on acid-free paper

For my wife,
Sarah Anne O'Leary

ACKNOWLEDGMENTS

I discuss Robert Bork's book, *The Tempting of America: The Political Seduction of the Law* (1989), at various points in this book. In January 1990, when my family and I were beginning a semester's sojourn in New York City, my wife Sarah, not knowing that I had already acquired a copy of *The Tempting of America*, went to a nearby bookstore where Bork was autographing copies of the book. When her turn finally came, Sarah mentioned to Bork that she was my wife. (She knew that Bork and I were acquainted.) He smiled and then wrote in the copy of the book she purchased for me: "To Michael Perry, with best wishes for a conversion experience." Well, I haven't had quite the conversion experience Bork wished for me. But my views *have* changed in important ways over the years.

In particular, there are many important differences between this book and my first book in constitutional theory, *The Constitution, the Courts, and Human Rights: An Inquiry into the Legitimacy of Constitutional Policymaking by the Judiciary* (1982). (There are some important affinities, too.) *The Constitution, the Courts, and Human Rights* was blessed with a great deal of attention both in the United States and in Japan (where a Japanese language edition appeared in 1987). Much of that attention, especially here in the United States, was critical. I've learned a lot from the criticism—as I hope this book reflects. I'm reminded of the refrain from Bob Dylan's *My Back Pages*: "Ah, but I was so much older then, I'm younger than that now."

For critical comments on an earlier version of some or all of this book, I am indebted to many colleagues, both at the Northwestern University Law School and elsewhere. I am indebted, too, to the Northwestern law students who attended and often facilitated the gestation of this book. For special help, I am especially grateful to John Ely, Kent Greenawalt, Bob Nagel, Steve Smith, and Larry Solum. I am also grateful to Yasuji Nosaka, of Rikkyo University in Tokyo, for ongoing conversations both in Tokyo and subsequently by fax.

I owe a special word of thanks to Koichiro Fujikura of the University of Tokyo, who made it possible for me to present and discuss my work in constitutional theory at the University of Tokyo and elsewhere in Japan during the fall of 1991.

This book, as its title indicates, is about the Constitution in the courts. I want to acknowledge my longstanding debt to the two persons who gave me the privilege of serving them in the (federal) courts: Jack B. Weinstein and Shirley M. Hufstedler. I could not have been more fortunate than to have begun my career in the law as law clerk (in 1973–74) to Judge Weinstein and then (1974–75) to Judge Hufstedler. They remain for me a principal inspiration.

I also want to acknowledge a debt to Howard J. Trienens, chair of the executive committee of the law firm of Sidley and Austin. Since 1990, it has been my privilege to occupy the Howard J. Trienens Chair in Law at Northwestern—a chair made possible by the support of Mr. Trienens's friends and colleagues at Sidley. Some at Sidley claim that Howard Trienens is the greatest lawyer who ever lived, others merely that he is the greatest living lawyer. I have no right to expect that Mr. Trienens will be interested in all the work I do, much of which is quite marginal to his important concerns. But I do hope that *this* book will interest him: Howard Trienens served as law clerk to the Chief Justice of the U.S. Supreme Court, Fred M. Vinson. (Trienens and another now-famous lawyer were card-playing buddies during their year together as Supreme Court law clerks: William H. Rehnquist, who was then law clerk to Justice Robert H. Jackson.)

As I worked on this book, my boys, Daniel and Gabriel, were almost always nearby. Indeed, they were sometimes underfoot. Daniel was born in 1989; Gabriel followed two years later, after work on this book had begun. Everything I do these days is enriched beyond measure by their presence. I have dedicated this book to their mom, my dear wife, Sarah O'Leary.

Evanston, Illinois   M.J.P.
June 1993

CONTENTS

THE CONSTITUTION
IN THE COURTS

1

Constitutional Adjudication:
Law or Politics?

In the title of this book, "the Constitution" is the Constitution of the United States, and "the courts" are both the federal courts and the courts of the states. The court with which I am principally concerned in this book, however, is the Supreme Court of the United States: Among the federal courts and the courts of the states, the Supreme Court has the last word about the meaning of the Constitution and is therefore the most powerful court in the country. This book is about what approach to constitutional interpretation the Supreme Court should follow. It is also about what role the Court should play—in particular, about how large or active a role it should play, or how small or passive a role—in bringing the interpreted Constitution to bear in resolving constitutional conflicts. Although I focus on the Supreme Court, much of what I say in this book about constitutional adjudication—that is, about interpreting the constitutional text and bringing the interpreted Constitution to bear in resolving the conflict at hand—is applicable to every court, state as well as federal, charged with protecting the United States Constitution.

My focus in this book is on the parts of the Constitution concerned with the rights of persons (whether all persons or just citizens[1]) against government: rights to do, or not to do, something, which we sometimes call "liberties" or "privileges"; rights to have government do something for us, which we sometimes call "entitlements"; and rights to have government not do something to us, which we sometimes call "immunities". It is principally the parts of the Constitution concerned with such rights—especially the Bill of Rights and the Fourteenth Amendment—that in our time frame the great and perennial controversy over what role the Court should play in resolving constitutional conflicts. But much of what I say here about constitutional adjudication is applicable to other parts of the Constitution, including the parts concerned with allocating powers, first, between the federal government and the governments of the states and, second, among the three branches of the federal government.

The Constitution of the United States is not the only constitution in the United States. Each of the fifty states has its own constitution. Although I am concerned in this book mainly with the judicial protection of the United States Constitution, much of what I say is applicable to the protection by the courts of a state of the constitution of that state. Written constitutions were not common throughout the world in 1789, when the United States Constitution was ratified, but they are quite common today, and some of what I say is applicable even to the protection by the courts of another country of the constitution of that country.

I

The question "Law or Politics?" derives from the claim that constitutional adjudication is not law, but politics; more precisely, that the process of constitutional adjudication—the judicial process of interpreting the Constitution and then of bringing the interpreted Constitution to bear in resolving the conflict at hand—is not a legal process, but a political one. On the political right a variant of that claim is pressed most prominently, perhaps, by Robert Bork, according to whom constitutional adjudication should be mainly a legal process but has been, in the Supreme Court, especially in the modern period of American constitutional law, mainly a political process.[2] (The modern period began in 1954, when the Court decided *Brown v. Board of Education*,[3] ruling that the Fourteenth Amendment forbids state government to segregate public schools on the basis of race.[4]) On the political left a variant of the claim is pressed by "critical legal scholars", according to whom adjudication, including constitutional adjudication, can be only a political process.[5] I want to focus, in this introductory chapter, on Robert Bork's version of the claim: Bork's recent book about American constitutional law is a useful and prominent point of departure.

The title of Bork's book is *The Tempting of America*. What is America tempted by? Bork's answer—suggested by his book's subtitle, *The Political Seduction of the Law*—is that "the American people" are tempted by "the belief that nothing matters beyond politically desirable results, however achieved."[6] In particular, they are tempted by the belief that "politically desirable results" are a higher value, in constitutional adjudication, than constitutionally correct results.

The principal object of Bork's vigorous critique, however, is not the American people; it is the courts, particularly the federal courts, especially the United States Supreme Court. A more accurate title for Bork's book would be *The Tempting of the Supreme Court*; a more precise subtitle, *The Politicization of the Constitution*. According to Bork, constitutional adjudication, properly understood and practiced, is not politics and should not be politicized; his central concern is what he sees as a politicization—especially by the Supreme Court, aided and abetted by academic theorists—of constitutional adjudication. He writes:

> In law, the moment of temptation is the moment of choice, when a judge realizes that in the case before him his strongly held view of justice, his political and moral imperative, is not embodied . . . in any provision of the Constitution. He must choose between his version of justice and abiding by the American form of government [which requires that in constitutional adjudication he not substitute his own version of morality or justice for the Constitution's version]. Yet the desire to do justice, whose nature seems to him obvious, is compelling, while the concept of constitutional process is abstract, rather arid, and the abstinence it counsels is unsatisfying. To give in to temptation, this one time, solves an urgent human problem, and a faint crack appears in the American foundation. A judge has begun to rule where a legislator should.[7]

Bork continues: "The American people are tempted as well. Many of the results seem good, and they are told [by whom?] that the choice is between a cold, impersonal logic, on the one hand, and, on the other, morality and compassion. This has always been the song of the tempters, and now it is heard incessantly from those who would politicize the courts and the Constitution. . . ."[8]

The siren song of the tempters must be resisted, however, both by the American people and, especially, by judges, because, insists Bork, nothing less than "[t]he democratic integrity of law", including constitutional law, is at stake. That integrity "depends entirely upon the degree to which its processes are legitimate", and the "processes" of law are not "legitimate" unless "[a] judge who announces a decision [can] demonstrate that he began from recognized legal principles and reasoned in an intellectually coherent and politically neutral way to his result. Those who would politicize the law offer the public, and the judiciary, the temptation of results without regard to democratic legitimacy."[9]

The crucial phrase in the preceding passage is "politically neutral". To achieve "democratic legitimacy", argues Bork, constitutional adjudication must be "politically neutral".[10] His book is about "the clash of law and politics";[11] it is about, in particular, the frequent failure of constitutional adjudication to be politically neutral or, therefore, legitimate; it is about the frequent failure of the courts, especially the Court, to resist "the temptations of politics".[12] "The progression of political judging, judging unrelated to law, [is] recounted in this book. This progression has greatly accelerated in the past few decades and now we see the theorists of constitutional law urging judges on to still greater incursions into American's right to self-government."[13] Consequently, but regrettably, "Americans increasingly view the courts, and particularly the Supreme Court, as political rather than legal institutions."[14]

The mission of Bork's book is to reaffirm the orthodox view that because the Constitution is law—indeed, supreme law—the courts, including the Court, in constitutional adjudication, should act like the legal institutions they are supposed to be rather than like political institutions. What does Bork mean when he says that the Constitution is (supreme) law and that the Court should act like a "legal" institution? "Either the Constitution . . . [is] law, which means that [its] principles are known and control judges, or [it] is [a] malleable text that judges may rewrite to see that particular groups or political causes win."[15] The Constitution is law, then, because its "principles are known and control judges". What does Bork mean when he says that constitutional principles "control" judges? Or, as he puts it, "What does it mean to say that a judge is bound by law? It means that he is bound by the only thing that can be called law, the principles of the text, whether Constitution or statute, *as generally understood at the [time of] enactment*."[16] That tells us what Bork means by constitutional "law": the "principles of the [Constitution] as generally understood at the time of enactment". But what does he mean when he says that a judge is "bound" by constitutional law, that constitutional law "controls" judges? Bork means to challenge what he calls the "heresy" that "judges are [not] bound by law".[17] Bork proclaims that "[t]he intended function of the federal courts is to apply the law as it comes to them from the hands of others. . . . [In adjudicating constitutional issues, t]hey must not make or apply any policy not fairly to be found in the Constitution. . . ."[18] When Bork says that a court is "bound" by constitutional law he means that it is obligated to apply constitutional law "as it comes to them from the hands of others". A court acts like a "legal" institution, according to Bork, if and to the extent it confines itself to "apply[ing] the law as it comes . . . from the hands of others." A court acts like a "political" institution, however, if instead of merely "applying" the law it usurps the political function of making law (legislating). Although Bork acknowledges—he says "[it] is true of course"—"that judges to some extent must make law every time they decide a case," he claims that "it is minor, interstitial lawmaking. The ratifiers of the Constitution put in place the walls, roof, and beams; judges protect the major architectural features, adding only filigree."[19]

I discuss Bork's understanding of constitutional adjudication, including his approach to constitutional interpretation, at several points in this book. For now I want only to note that, as the foregoing passages suggest, the master distinction or opposition on which Bork relies in his book is "law" versus "politics". The functionally similar but verbally different distinction George Bush relied on in comments announcing his nomination of David Souter to the Supreme Court was "interpretation" versus "legislation": "Judge Souter is committed to interpreting, not making the law. . . . I have selected a person who will interpret the Constitution, and in my view not legislate from the Federal bench. . . . What I'm certain of is that he will interpret the Constitution, not legislate from the Federal bench."[20] In an op-ed piece supporting President Bush's nomination of Judge Souter, Bork relied both on Bush's distinction and on his own: "The Constitution is law. Like all law it is expressed in language. Language has meaning. Judges who depart from any plausible meaning of the language are not interpreting, they are legislating. . . . Mr. Bush seems determined to return the Court to its proper role as a legal rather than a political institution."[21] What Bork and Bush want to say is that legislatures are "political" institutions, in the sense that their job is to "make" law, to "legislate", whereas courts are supposed to be "legal" institutions: their proper job is to "apply" law and therefore to "interpret" it. (A court can't "apply" a law—it can't bring a law to bear in resolving a conflict—until it first "interprets" the law, in the sense of ascertaining what norm or norms the law represents.)

To the extent Bork's book contains truths about constitutional adjudication, they are half-truths and, like all half-truths, seriously misleading. In this book I explain why Bork's distinction between "law" and "politics", like President Bush's distinction between "interpreting" law and "making" or "legislating" it, is a deeply problematic way of trying to mark opposed positions about the nature of constitutional adjudication. At its best, constitutional adjudication comprises both the "legal" process of "interpreting" law and the "political" process of "making" law. Bork has conceded the point,[22] but, as I later explain, he has failed to understand how deeply the point cuts. The challenge is to understand, first, the respect in which constitutional adjudication is—or at least should be—a legal process, and, second, the respect in which it is—and must be—a political process.[23] I aim to meet that challenge in this book. Bork's and Bush's claim about constitutional adjudication—that it should be "law", not "politics", that it should involve "interpretation", not "legislation"—serves only to obscure the challenge.[24]

Regrettably—but perhaps inevitably, given the real-world political stakes—contemporary debate about constitutional adjudication is excessively polemical. Bork's book is a glaring example, but there are many others, and the problem emanates from the political left as well as from the political right. Polemical writing about constitutional adjudication, whether from the right or from the left, clarifies little and obscures much.

II

I said that Bork's book is a useful and prominent point of departure for this book.[25] But it is only a point of departure. The questions I address here range far beyond those Bork discusses in his book.

I want to identify, here at the outset, a set of related distinctions fundamental to my analysis in this book: (1) text versus norm, (2) the indeterminacy of a text versus the indeterminacy of a norm, and (3) the interpretation of a text versus the specification of a norm. It is not always clear what norm (or norms) a written legal text, such as a constitutional provision, represents. A legal text can be, in the political community whose text it is, opaque, vague, ambiguous, and so on. To interpret a legal text is to (try to) identify the norm the text represents. The aim of the interpretive inquiry is to translate or decode the text, to render the text intelligible by identifying the meaning of the text—by identifying, that is, the norm represented by the text. A legal text can be indeterminate, in the sense that given all the available relevant data, the members of the political community whose text it is can reasonably disagree about what norm the text represents.

But even if it is agreed—or, at least, even if it is not presently in question—that a legal text represents a particular norm, that norm can itself be indeterminate in the context of a particular case, in this sense: Persons who agree about (1) what the relevant facts are, (2) what the other relevant legal norms are, and (3) what the implications of those other norms for the case are, can nonetheless disagree—*reasonably* disagree—about how, given the norm, the case should be decided, the conflict resolved. A norm that governs a conflict—a norm that is relevant to the conflict, that is implicated in it—but that is indeterminate in the context of the conflict must be specified. To "specify" an indeterminate norm, in the special sense in which I use the term in this book, is to shape the norm, it is to render the norm determinate in the context of a conflict to which it is relevant but in which it is indeterminate. I elaborate the notion of "specifying" indeterminate constitutional norms in chapter 5.

These distinctions—or my presentation of them—may strike the reader as maddeningly abstract and even opaque. I hasten to add, therefore, that at appropriate points in this book I clarify the principal distinction, in part by using various concrete examples of (on the one hand) the interpretation—the translation, the decoding—of a text and (on the other) the specification of a norm represented, or thought to be represented, by a text. I also defend the distinction, in part by identifying, in chapter 3, a different, problematic distinction with which my distinction might be confused: the distinction between "understanding" a norm and then "applying" the norm in a particular context. Not only is that distinction not my distinction, but my distinction, as I later explain, presupposes that the understanding/application distinction is false.[26] Now, however, in part against the background of the distinction between the interpretation of a text and the specification of a norm, I want to provide an overview of this book and of some of its main arguments.

I begin, in chapter 2, with the question of the legitimacy of the practice known as "judicial review"; in chapter 3, I address the question of the approach to constitutional interpretation that should inform the practice of judicial review. Those two fundamental issues are inextricably linked, and chapters 2 and 3 are therefore connected: As I explain in chapter 3, the argument for judicial review I present in chapter 2 bears strongly on the argument I present in chapter 3 for the "originalist" approach to constitutional interpretation, according to which the "original" meaning of a constitutional provision, rather than some other meaning, is authoritative. In terms of the distinctions I identified above, "originalism"—the originalism I defend here—is a position about the proper judicial approach to the interpretive inquiry, the inquiry into what norms the constitutional text represents. It bears emphasis that originalism, properly conceived, is *not* a position about the proper judicial approach to the normative inquiry.

More than one religion marches under the banner of "originalism" (as I explain in chapter 3). I want to stress, therefore—before I am mistakenly praised by some for having saved my soul and condemned by others for having lost it—that the originalist approach I elaborate and defend in chapter 3 is *not* the originalist approach usually associated with "conservative" attacks on the modern Supreme Court. Far from it. Indeed, one of my principal aims, in this book, is to loosen the grip of conservative constitutional commentary on originalism and, while not to claim the originalist approach for "progressive" constitutional commentary, at least to show (in chapters 8 and 9) that originalism is an inadequate basis for criticizing many of the modern constitutional decisions that so aggrieve conservative originalist commentators like Robert Bork. Many constitutional commentators of both the right (like Bork) and the left (Geoffrey Stone and David Strauss, for example[27]) need not only to be set straight about what originalism, properly conceived, is and is not; they need to be disabused of the notion that originalism is a position necessarily congenial to constitutional conservatives and hostile to constitutional progressives. There are, of course, real and significant differences between constitutional conservatives and constitutional progressives—for what it's worth, I count myself a constitutional progressive—but it is a serious mistake to think that the originalist approach to constitutional interpretation is necessarily conservative.

It is important to distinguish between two fundamental issues that are often conflated: first, the question of the approach to constitutional interpretation—to the interpretation of the constitutional text—that should inform the practice of judicial review and, second, the question of the role the Court should play—primary or secondary, large or small, active or passive—in bringing the *interpreted* constitutional text to bear in resolving constitutional conflicts. In chapter 4, I begin to discuss judicial "minimalism", which comprises two positions. Although one of the positions, "interpretive minimalism", is, like originalism, about the proper judicial approach to the interpretive inquiry, the other minimalist position, "normative minimalism", is about the proper judicial approach to the normative inquiry, that is, to the specification of the indeterminate norms represented, or believed to be represented, by the constitutional text.

Many constitutional commentators, such as Bork, assume that originalism entails judicial minimalism; they assume, that is, that originalism is necessarily minimalist. Indeed, it is at least partly because they believe that originalism is necessarily minimalist that they find originalism as appealing as they do. But, as I explain in chapters 4 and 5, originalism does not entail minimalism, either interpretive minimalism or normative minimalism. To defend originalism, as I do in chapter 3, is not to defend minimalism. This is not to deny that one can be both an originalist and a minimalist; my point is simply that one can, consistently with originalism, reject the minimalist approach—whether the minimalist approach to the interpretation of the constitutional text, the minimalist approach to the specification of the indeterminate constitutional norms represented by the text, or both.

That originalism does not entail minimalism, however, is not an argument against minimalism. In chapter 6, I turn to the question of minimalism. Although I discuss both interpretive minimalism and normative minimalism in chapter 6, I focus on normative minimalism, which holds that the Supreme Court ought to play only a small or passive role, not a large or active one, in bringing the interpreted Constitution to bear in resolving constitutional conflicts. In particular, normative minimalism holds that the Court ought to assume, not the primary responsibility for specifying indeterminate constitutional norms, but only a secondary responsibility, deferring to any "reasonable" specification implicit in the governmental action under review. I explore, in chapter 6, the reasons both why one might accept normative minimalism and why one might reject it. Because the argument for normative minimalism is substantially the same as the argument for interpretive minimalism, to explore the former argument is to explore the latter.

In chapter 7, I inquire into the original meaning of section 1 of the Fourteenth Amendment so that, in chapters 8 and 9, I can pursue the implications both of originalism and of normative minimalism for two major areas of the modern Supreme Court's Fourteenth Amendment work product: the Court's "equal protection" doctrine (chapter 8) and its "substantive due process" doctrine (chapter 9). My principal general conclusion is that originalism, properly understood, is an inadequate basis for criticizing many of the modern Court's Fourteenth Amendment decisions.

Earlier I commented on the excessively polemical character of much writing—too much—about constitutional adjudication. I hope that by the end of this book Robert Bork's critique of the modern Supreme Court's Fourteenth Amendment work product[28]—a critique endorsed by many others, including many scholars—can be seen for what it is: a vigorous and engaging polemic, but ultimately a shallow effort, clarifying little, obscuring much, and likely to mislead the underinformed. The results of my inquiry in this book—in particular, of my inquiry in chapters 8 and 9—are a substantial vindication of Lawrence Solum's claim that originalists, like Robert Bork and Supreme Court Justice Antonin Scalia,[29] "have won a Pyrrhic victory [over nonoriginalists]. As originalism has been clarified in response to its critics, it has gradually become more and more evident that it has no force as a critique of the kind of constitutional interpretation practiced by the Warren Court."[30]

III

It is also evident, therefore, that the principal problem to which Bruce Ackerman's project *We the People*[31] is directed—the impossibility of defending important aspects of the modern Court's constitutional work product on the basis of a nonproblematic conception of what it means to "interpret" the Constitution—is simply an illusion. In particular, neither of the two main cases Ackerman discusses in the first volume of his project— each of them a Fourteenth Amendment case—poses that problem: *Brown v. Board of Education*[32] which I discuss in chapter 8, and *Griswold v. Connecticut*,[33] discussed in chapter 9.[34]

Is Ackerman's effort nonetheless an attractive alternative account of how the relevant aspects of the modern Court's constitutional work product might be justified? For important reasons well developed by others, I am deeply skeptical.[35] Even for one sympathetic to Ackerman's interesting and provocative project, however, a fundamental problems remains: For all its learning and ambition, Ackerman's *We the People*[36] disappoints by its failure to address a crucial issue. Jeremy Waldron's statement of the problem goes to the heart of the matter:

> Even if one concedes the superior authority of Ackerman's higher law making, one is left unsure why it should be the special function of the courts to interpret that legislation. Judicial review becomes politically most important in cases where citizens disagree among themselves about the best way of understanding some constitutional provision. . . . [W]e were all enthusiastically in favor of the free exercise of religion, [for example,] but now in the cold light of morning we have to work out how it is to fit in with public-education policy. Surely on Ackerman's account, this is a problem for normal politics—the phase of the democratic process that alone is capable of working out how various aspects of public policy fit together. . . . Once the people begin disagreeing among themselves about how to interpret their own past acts of higher law making, it is unclear why any particular interpretation of that heritage should be able to trump any other simply because it is endorsed by five judges out of nine. Ackerman asks, "Isn't it better for the Court to represent the *absent* People by forcing our elected politicians/statesmen to measure their statutory conclusions against the principles reached by those who have most successfully represented the People in the past?" But that game is up once there is disagreement about the meaning of those principles: then all we have is our present legislation, measured against two or more contrary interpretations of our past.[37]

Ackerman's failure to address the question highlighted by Waldron is all the more conspicuous, and all the more disappointing, when we recall that under Ackerman's approach, the Court is not merely to ascertain the meaning, in particular contexts, of written constitutional principles. The Court is also to ascertain whether, during some extraordinary political moment, the written Constitution has been modified by an *unwritten* "amendment"; if in the Court's view the Constitution has been so amended, the Court must also ascertain what the unwritten amendment "says" or provides. Let's assume, for the sake of argument, that as a theoretical matter there can be unwritten constitutional amendments of the sort Ackerman imagines (even though the assumption is in fundamental tension with the textualist sensibility of American constitutionalism,[38] which I discuss in chapter 3[39]). Just as there can be and often is disagreement about the contextual meaning of one or another written constitutional principle, there can be and surely would be disagreement both about whether, during some extraordinary political moment, the Constitution has been modified by an unwritten amendment and, if it has been so amended, about precisely what the unwritten amendment provides. Why should the Court's answers to such questions—the answers, at the limit, of five out of nine members of the Court—get to trump the competing answers of the electorally accountable representatives of the people?

Because the question Ackerman neglects—the question Waldron rightly highlights—is of fundamental importance, I address it at length in this book. Of course, not every norm represented by the constitutional text is indeterminate in every context in which the norm is implicated. But as I explain in chapter 5, in discussing the indeterminacy of constitutional morality, some constitutional norms are sometimes contextually indeterminate. Thus, the question of minimalism—in particular, the question of normative minimalism—arises: Should the Court play the primary role in specifying constitutional indeterminacy; that is, should it play the primary role in deciding what the concrete contextual meanings of indeterminate constitutional norms shall be? Or, in bringing contextually indeterminate constitutional norms to bear, should the Court play only a secondary or minimalist role of the sort espoused by James Bradley Thayer a little over a century ago? (I discuss Thayer's position mainly in chapter 6.)

IV

As the title of this book indicates, and as my comment on Ackerman's *We the People* underscores, I am principally engaged here by fundamental problems that attend constitutional adjudication—that attend, that is, the Constitution *in* the courts, especially the Constitution in *the* Court. Has there been, as Cass Sunstein (among others) has recently claimed, "far too much emphasis, in the last generation, on the role of the courts in the American constitutional system"?[40] Certainly much of the academic discussion of the role of the judiciary in constitutional cases has been, not merely in the last generation but throughout this entire century, repetitive, polemical, and worse.[41] The problems that attend constitutional adjudication, however, are not merely the obsession of some of us in the legal academy. They are real-world problems. They engage and divide us Americans far beyond the confines of the legal academy, and often they divide us quite deeply. The ways in which we as a people respond to the problems, or fail to respond to them, have profound consequences—even, sometimes, life-and-death consequences—for many people. Rather than try to marginalize the problems, we must continue to struggle with them. Closure has not been achieved, either in the academy or outside it.

There has not been "too much emphasis" on the question of the proper role of the courts in resolving constitutional conflicts. But this is not to deny that there should be more emphasis on the role of the Constitution—of constitutional morality—in the ordinary political deliberations, if not of "We the people", then at least of our political representatives. (More emphasis on the Constitution outside the courts does not mean less emphasis on the Constitution in the courts—as if we were playing a zero-sum game.) I share the "hope for newly reinvigorated deliberation about constitutional commitments—deliberation that will occasionally take place in the courtroom, but more often, and far more fundamentally, through democratic channels."[42] Indeed, in my concluding chapter, I offer a perhaps utopian suggestion for multiplying the occasions and enhancing the quality of political deliberations about matters of constitutional morality.[43] Of course, there is ample room for skepticism about the extent to which we or our representatives can or will, in our ordinary politics, which often seems so debased, deliberate seriously about controversial matters of constitutional morality. (I express some skepticism in chapter 6.) In any event, by addressing in the chapters that follow the still difficult problems that attend the Constitution in the Courts, I do not mean to deny that important issues also attend the Constitution outside the courts—issues we must not neglect.

If we don't need less attention to the problems of the Constitution in the courts, is it nonetheless the case that there has been inordinate emphasis in the last generation on the question of what it means, especially for a court, to "interpret" the Constitution? Suzanna Sherry has suggested as much with her exasperated plea: "Enough about interpretation! Let's talk about substance!"[44] The problem, of course, is that often our talk about "substance"—our talk about real-world issues of constitutional morality—leads inevitably to talk about interpretation. At least, often our talk—our arguments—about substance cannot go forward carefully and productively unless we take time to identify and address those issues of interpretation that are logically prior to the issues of substance that engage and divide us.

Our talk about substance makes claims about or at least presupposes what the relevant constitutional norms are; we claim or presuppose what norms the constitutional text represents. Your claim or presupposition that one or another provision of the constitutional text represents one or another norm may well be contested by some of us with whom you are talking about substance; moreover, that aspect of our disagreement may reflect that we challenge the conception of constitutional "interpretation" that underlies your claim/presupposition about what norm the constitutional provision represents. If so, our differences about what it means to interpret the constitutional text need to be discussed, not bracketed. Our failure to discuss those differences will prevent our primary talk—our talk about substance—from going forward in a careful, productive way. Moreover, because the courts, too, talk about substance—because the judiciary addresses issues of constitutional morality—we cannot avoid the further, fundamental question of the particular role the courts should play in talking about substance: Should they play the primary role in addressing issues of constitutional morality or should they play merely a secondary role of the sort Thayer espoused?

Yes, certainly, let's talk about substance. And so that we may do so in a way that is discerning of *all* the relevant issues that engage and divide us as we talk (argue) about substance, let's talk about interpretation, too. That, at any rate, is what I shall do in the chapters that follow: talk about interpretation as well as about substance—and about the question of the courts' role in talking about substance.

2

The Argument for Judicial Review

I address two fundamental questions in this book: the question of the approach to constitutional interpretation the Supreme Court should follow, and the question of the nature of the role the Court should play—how large or active, or how small or passive—in bringing the interpreted Constitution to bear in resolving constitutional conflicts. Neither question would arise but for the practice of judicial review, which involves, centrally, the Court interpreting the Constitution in the course of resolving constitutional conflicts. In this chapter, I inquire into the legitimacy of judicial review. I do so not because the legitimacy of the practice is at issue in the United States today; judicial review seems to enjoy virtually consensual support in contemporary American society.[1] I do so because it is useful to explain why a practice that yields persistent controversy about constitutional interpretation and proper judicial role not merely enjoys our support but merits it. Moreover, as I explain in chapter 3, the argument for judicial review—the particular argument I make in this chapter—bears strongly on the argument I make in chapter 3 for the approach to constitutional interpretation that should inform the practice of judicial review. As I said in chapter 1, the question of the legitimacy of the practice of judicial review and the question of the approach to constitutional interpretation that should inform the practice are inextricably linked. As this and the next chapter illustrate, one's response to the first question is an essential determinant of one's response to the second.

The "judicial review" whose legitimacy is under discussion in this chapter is the judicial practice of inquiring if a governmental act, or failure to act, violates the Constitution of the United States.[2] A governmental act whose constitutionality is in question may be, at the one extreme, a statute, or, at the other, a single action by a person in her capacity as an official or employee of the government, or it may be something in between. I am not concerned here or elsewhere in this book with the judicial practice of inquiring if a governmental act (or failure to act) violates a *state* constitution, although much of what I say in this book about judicial review for federal constitutionality, including what I say in this chapter about the legitimacy of the practice, is applicable to the distinct but analogous practice of judicial review for state constitutionality. I am principally concerned here and elsewhere in this book with judicial review (for federal constitutionality) by the Supreme Court of the United States, although much of what I say about judicial review, including what I say about the legitimacy of the practice, is applicable both to judicial review by a federal court other than the Supreme Court and to judicial review by a state court.

The legitimacy under discussion in this chapter is *not* the constitutional legitimacy—the constitutionality—of judicial review, but legitimacy in a different sense: Is judicial review a good practice for us Americans, one we should support, or is it, instead, a practice we would be better off without, one we should oppose? Even if the Constitution establishes the practice of judicial review, we can inquire if we should applaud that state of affairs or, instead, condemn it and try to do something about it. (At the end of this chapter, I address the question whether the Constitution establishes the practice of judicial review.)

I

The problem of the legitimacy of judicial review is rooted in what Alexander Bickel famously called "the counter-majoritarian difficulty":

> The root difficulty is that judicial review is a counter-majoritarian force in our system. There are various ways of sliding over this ineluctable reality. Marshall did so when he spoke of enforcing, in behalf of "the people," the limits that they have ordained for the institutions of a limited government. And it has been done ever since in much the same fashion by all too many commentators. Marshall himself followed Hamilton, who in the 78th *Federalist* denied that judicial review implied a superiority of the judicial over the legislative power—denied, in other words, that judicial review constituted control by an unrepresentative minority of an elected majority. "It only supposes," Hamilton went on, "that the power of the people is superior to both; and that where the will of the legislature, declared in its statutes, stands in opposition to that of the people, declared in the Constitution, the judges ought to be governed by the latter rather than the former." But the word "people" so used is an abstraction. Not necessarily a meaningless or a pernicious one by any means; always charged with emotion, but nonrepresentational—an abstraction obscuring the reality that when the Supreme Court declares unconstitutional a legislative act or the action of an elected executive, it thwarts the will of representatives of the actual people of the here and now; it exercises control, not in behalf of the prevailing majority, but against it. That, without mystic overtones, is what actually happens. . . . [I]t is the reason the charge can be made that judicial review is undemocratic.[3]

Although, as Bickel acknowledged at length, "no democracy operates by taking continuous nose counts on the broad range of daily governmental activities"[4] and "the process of reflecting the will of a popular majority in the legislature is deflected . . . by all sorts of institutional habits and characteristics, which perhaps tend most often in favor of inertia",[5] it is nonetheless true, as Bickel insisted, that "nothing in the . . . complexities and perplexities of the [American democratic] system . . . can alter the essential reality that judicial review is a deviant institution in the American democracy. . . . [N]othing can finally depreciate the central function that is assigned in democratic theory and practice to the electoral process; nor can it be denied that the policy-making power of representative institutions, born of the electoral process, is the distinguishing characteristic of the system. Judicial review works counter to this characteristic."[6]

Given the counter-majoritarian difficulty, the question arises whether judicial review is a practice we Americans should support. Does judicial review, which enjoys our support, merit our support?

II

Political communities can establish rights and liberties—that is, they can establish them as "law", accord them the status of "law"—by means of statutory law, and they often do. But political communities can also establish rights and liberties by means of constitutional law, and they sometimes do. Consider what it means for a democratic political community that wants to accord a right (or a liberty) the status of law to opt for the constitutional strategy rather than for—or merely for—the statutory strategy. Consider, that is, what it means, as a practical matter, for a democratic political community to name and then to seek to protect a right by means of constitutional law rather than (merely) by statutory law. (The constitutional strategy can be used to establish the various institutions of government, and to allocate power among them, as well as to establish limits, in the form of rights and liberties, on governmental power. But because my principal concern in this book is with those parts of the Constitution, like the Bill of Rights and the Fourteenth Amendment, that establish rights and liberties, I want to comment on the constitutional strategy mainly as a strategy for establishing rights and liberties.) Whereas statutory law typically may be revised or repealed by legislative majorities, national constitutions typically provide that constitutional provisions may be amended only by legislative and/or popular supermajorities. According to Article V of the United States Constitution, for example, "The Congress, whenever two thirds of both Houses shall deem it necessary, shall propose Amendments to this Constitution, or, on the Application of the Legislatures of two thirds of the several States, shall call a Convention for proposing Amendments, which, in either Case, shall be valid to all Intents and Purposes, as Part of this Constitution, when ratified by the Legislatures of three fourths of the several states, or by Conventions in three fourths thereof, as the one or the other Mode of Ratification may be proposed by the Congress. . . ." Article 96 of the Japanese Constitution, to cite another example, provides that "[a]mendments to this Constitution shall be initiated by the Diet, through a concurring vote of two-thirds or more of all the members of each House. . . ."[7]

Indeed, constitutions can and sometimes do provide that a particular provision or provisions may not be amended at all. Article V of the United States Constitution of the United States provides that "no State, without its Consent shall be deprived of its equal Suffrage in the Senate." The Japanese Constitution arguably immunizes some constitutional provisions against amendment in providing, in Article 11, that "[t]he people shall not be prevented from enjoying any of the fundamental human rights. These fundamental human rights guaranteed to the people by this Constitution shall be conferred upon the people of this and future generations as eternal and inviolate rights."[8]

For a democratic political community to opt for the constitutional strategy for establishing a right, then—for it to articulate a right and then to seek to protect it by means of judicially enforceable constitutional law rather than (merely) by judicially enforceable statutory law—is for the community to try to make it especially difficult, both for the present members of the community at a later time and, above all, for the future members at a much later time, to disestablish the right. (And, if and to the extent the community's constitution is taken seriously in the future, opting for the constitutional strategy is for the community not merely to try to make it especially difficult in the future to disestablish the right, but to succeed in doing so.) Opting for the constitutional strategy is for the community to decree, in effect, that the right may be disestablished, if at all, not by a legislative majority acting through the ordinary politics of legislative revision, but only by a legislative and/or a popular supermajority acting through the extraordinary politics of constitutional amendment. (The "may", of course, is the may of legality, not of politics or of morality.[9])

We might be tempted to think that the constitutional strategy for establishing a right differs from the statutory strategy in another basic respect, in that constitutions, unlike statutes, typically declare themselves to be "the supreme law"[10]—and that therefore for a democratic political community to opt for the constitutional strategy is for it to decree that the right is lexically prior to statutory and other nonconstitutional law, in particular to subsequently enacted law. But perhaps a legislature may decree in a statute establishing a right that the right is lexically prior to *subsequently enacted* statutory law in this sense and to this extent: "A court is not to give effect to any future statute enacted by this legislature to the extent the statute, in the court's judgment, violates the right established by this statute, *unless such future statute explicitly states that a court is to give it effect even if in the court's judgment the statute violates the right established by this statute.*"[11] Even if a legislature may, in one session, enact such a decree, however, the legislature presumably may, in a later session, repeal the decree.[12] What is most distinctive about the constitutional strategy, then, is less the supremacy of constitutional law than the extreme difficulty of amending a constitution.

Why, in any event, might a political community want to accord lexical priority to a right? The basic reason, presumably, is that the community deems the right to be especially important. But assuming that a democratic political community may accord lexical priority to a right it deems especially important by means of the kind of statutory strategy suggested in the preceding paragraph, why might the community opt for the constitutional strategy? Why, that is, might at least *some* members of the community want to make it so difficult to disestablish a right or a liberty? A basic reason, presumably, is that they are skeptical about the capacity of the ordinary, majoritarian politics of the community adequately to protect the right, especially during politically stressful times when the right may be most severely challenged. The reasons for their skepticism can be various: They may fear that at some points in the future, perhaps even at many points, they who are so enthusiastic about the right will no longer dominate the ordinary politics of the community, or dominate it to the extent they presently do; they may even fear that many of those who will dominate the ordinary politics of the community, at some points in the future, will be hostile to the right. They may also fear that even at those points when they (the enthusiasts of the right) continue to dominate ordinary politics, they will, for one reason or another, fail adequately to protect the right, or they may fear that their political representatives, over whom they exert imperfect control, will fail adequately to protect it. Whatever the precise reason or constellation of reasons for their skepticism,[13] the constitutional strategy for establishing a right, as distinct from the statutory strategy, presupposes a distrust, a lack of faith, in the (future) ordinary politics of the community.

Not that there aren't other basic reasons for pursuing the constitutional strategy, which, as I said, can be used to allocate governmental power as well as to establish limits on that power. For example, a political community may need to establish, or to reestablish, its basic institutions, institutional arrangements, and practices, so that an ordinary politics might then begin, or begin again, to operate. Or a community may want to remove certain issues from the agenda of ordinary politics, based less on a fear that its ordinary politics cannot be trusted to resolve the issues than on a fear that a contest about how they should be resolved might incapacitate or even destroy the ordinary politics of the community.[14] Even when a political community does not need to establish any basic institutions, institutional arrangements, or practices, however, and even when the community has little if any reason to fear that a contest about how a certain issue should be resolved might incapacitate, much less destroy, its ordinary politics, the community may be skeptical about the capacity of ordinary politics (especially during stressful times) adequately to protect a right the community deems particularly important.

In a federal political community, like the United States, such skepticism may focus, at a given time, less on the capacity of the ordinary politics of the states to protect a right than on the capacity of the ordinary politics of the national government. At another time, it may focus less on the capacity of the ordinary politics of the national government than on the capacity of the ordinary politics of the states, or of some of them. Whatever the particular case, such skepticism seems *a*, if not *the*, fundamental reason why the constitutional strategy exemplified by provisions like the Bill of Rights and the Fourteenth Amendment has been pursued in the United States.

Given such distrust, the constitutional strategy will include—and, to be effective, must include—an enforcement mechanism.[15] Judicial review is the principal such mechanism. Article VI of the Constitution of the United States, for example, provides not merely that "[t]his Constitution . . . shall be the supreme law of the land", but also that "the judges in every state shall be bound thereby, anything in the constitution or laws of any state to the contrary notwithstanding." Article 81 of the Constitution of Japan provides that "[t]he Supreme Court is the court of last resort with power to determine the constitutionality of any law, order, regulation or official act." Is it the case, then, that the constitutional strategy for establishing a right, which presupposes a distrust of ordinary politics, presupposes a trust in constitutional adjudication; does it presuppose that constitutional adjudication will be adequate to protect the right, even during those politically stressful times when the right may be most severely challenged? Not necessarily. Those who opt for the constitutional strategy for establishing a right may simply be, for whatever reason or reasons, less skeptical about the capacity, in general, of constitutional adjudication adequately to protect the right than about the capacity, in general, of ordinary politics adequately to do so.[16]

III

Thus far I have suggested why the members of a political community (or some of them) might opt for the constitutional strategy for establishing a right. I have suggested, that is, why some of the *present* members of a political community might want to try to make it especially difficult for the *future* members (or for themselves at a future time) to undo certain of their deeds. I have said nothing, however, in support of the proposition that when the future becomes the present, the present should acquiesce in the efforts of the past to tie its hands. In particular, I have not explained why we, the living members of the American political community, should support the constitutional strategy (including judicial review) for which long-dead members of the American political community opted when they were the living members of the community and we were not even born. The Constitution begins: "We the people of the United States . . . do ordain and establish this Constitution for the United States of America." Well, "We the people of the United States" *now living* did not, not even the oldest among us, establish the basic features of American government— its various basic institutions, institutional arrangements, and practices.[17] (This is not to deny that to some extent, of course, American government is continually being reestablished.) The question is not whether *they* (the past) had (what were for them) good reasons for opting for the constitutional strategy. The question, rather, is whether *we* (the present) have (what are for us) good reasons for maintaining, rather than disestablishing, what they bequeathed us. In particular, is judicial review, as it has come down to us,[18] a practice "We the people of the United States" *now living* should support; or is it, instead, a practice we should oppose?

Cass Sunstein has written that "[t]he precommitment strategy permits the people to protect democratic processes against their own potential excesses or misjudgments."[19] But the main point of the constitutional strategy is to tie the hands, not so much of the generation opting for the strategy, but of future generations. That it may not be morally problematic for us to tie our own hands to some end certainly does not entail that it is not morally problematic for us to tie someone else's hands, even to the same end. Thus, we must inquire not merely why the present generation of a political community might want to pursue the constitutional strategy; we must also inquire why a later generation of the community might want to acquiesce in that strategy.[20]

The argument for judicial review, the reason we should support the practice, is simple: Judicial review serves us well—not perfectly, but well —as a mechanism for protecting the Constitution of the United States; the obvious alternatives seem palpably inferior; and unless and until we identify and establish a better mechanism, we should continue to support the practice rather than oppose it. In his Hart Lecture at Oxford University, Justice William J. Brennan, Jr., said:

> One can imagine a variety of means for redressing violations of funda-
> mental legal rights. Individuals might appeal, for example, to some non-
> judicial branch of government authorized to discipline the alleged
> offender—complaining to the executive about legislative overreaching,
> for instance, or vice versa. Alternatively, coordinate branches of govern-
> ment could act on their own initiative. Or proposed legislation could be
> reviewed by a special constitutional court or commission, such as France's
> Constitutional Council. Or citizens themselves could initiate review by
> judges empowered to invalidate laws that trench upon protected rights,
> to halt official conduct that invades those rights, and to order relief for
> past injuries. In my view, America's experience with the last of these
> alternatives is the most sensible, effective device for protecting personal
> liberties. This is particularly true if judges may only be removed for

good cause and if their salaries may not be reduced, thus enhancing
their independence of decision. It is essential to the defense of liberty
that individuals be able to bring their own claims, rather than wait on the
decisions of officers of agencies that lack the same stake in the aggrieved
party's freedoms. And the importance of passing judgment on the propriety of legislation or government conduct in a concrete setting cannot
be overestimated; not all laws are meaningfully subject to challenge
before they have been placed in operation and their ramifications
become plain, which is all that an advisory body passing on legislation
could consider.[21]

The argument for judicial review has force, of course, only for those
who believe that the Constitution of the United States is worth protecting.
Is it? More precisely, is the constitutional strategy pursued by our political
ancestors worth maintaining; are the various constitutional directives they
issued worth protecting? In particular: (1) Are the various constitutional
directives our political ancestors issued—especially the various constitutional directives regarding rights and liberties and other limits on governmental power—so important (if important at all) that they merit their
status as "supreme law"? (2) Even if they are so important, should those
various directives be placed beyond the reach of ordinary politics?[22]

As evidence that for many constitutional directives issued by our political ancestors an affirmative answer to the question of their importance
is not controversial, consider this fact: The Charter of Paris for a New
Europe, signed in Paris on November 21, 1990, by the heads of state or
government of the thirty-four member nations of the Conference on Security and Cooperation in Europe, including many advanced industrial
nations with which the United States has a close political-moral affinity,
specifies the following rights and liberties as among the "[h]uman rights
and fundamental freedoms [that] are the birthright of all human beings,
. . . inalienable and . . . guaranteed by law":

> The right of every individual, without discrimination, to] freedom of
> thought, conscience, and religion or belief, freedom of expression, free-
> dom of association and peaceful assembly, freedom of movement, [free-
> dom from] arbitrary arrest or detention, [freedom from] torture or
> other cruel, inhuman or degrading treatment or punishment, [the right]
> to know and act upon his rights, to participate in free and fair elections,
> to fair and public trial if charged with an offense, to own property . . .
> and to exercise individual enterprise, to enjoy his economic, social, and
> cultural rights.

The Charter declares that "[f]ull respect for these precepts is the bedrock
on which we will seek to construct the new Europe."[23] The Charter's
"human rights and fundamental freedoms" are either identical or very
similar to many of the rights and liberties our political ancestors constitutionalized. (Because there can be disagreement, and often is, about precisely what right or liberty our political ancestors, in ratifying a particular
constitutional provision, constitutionalized,[24] I should say that the Char-

ter's rights and freedoms are identical or very similar to many of the rights and liberties our political ancestors constitutionalized *on any plausible account of what they constitutionalized.*)

However, that many of the constitutional directives issued by our political ancestors are of fundamental importance does not entail that every such directive should be placed beyond the reach of ordinary politics— does not entail, that is, that we should distrust the capacity of ordinary politics adequately to protect every such directive. Should we distrust the capacity of ordinary politics, whether the ordinary politics of the national government or that of the states (or both)? The fact that our political ancestors, now dead, did so does not conclude the question whether we, now living, should do so. As I argue later in this book, there are good reasons for being skeptical about the capacity of ordinary politics adequately to protect all of the most important constitutional directives issued by our political ancestors.[25] But it is not necessary to rely on such skepticism in making the argument for judicial review.

Assume that although we (the living) would and should place beyond the reach of ordinary politics many constitutional directives issued by our political ancestors, we neither would nor should place beyond the reach of ordinary politics every constitutional directive of fundamental importance they (the dead) placed beyond its reach. Assume, too, that not every constitutional directive issued by our political ancestors is so important, if important at all, that it merits its status as supreme law, much less its immunization against ordinary politics. It does not follow that because we would/should not place beyond the reach of ordinary politics a directive they placed beyond its reach, we should not acquiesce in their strategy to constitutionalize the directive. Even if we should be much less skeptical about the capacity of ordinary politics adequately to protect the directive than they were, we should want the Court to continue to protect the directive as a constitutional directive—a directive beyond the reach of ordinary politics—*unless and until we can disestablish the directive in a way that is less problematic than the Court continuing to protect the directive.* Some ways of disestablishing a directive, after all—the president of the United States unilaterally picking and choosing which constitutional directives he will respect, for example, or the Supreme Court unilaterally picking and choosing which constitutional directives it will protect—may well be much more problematic, all things considered, than simply continuing to live with the directive until it can be disestablished in a relatively unproblematic way.

I do not mean to deny the possibility that, depending both on the nature of a constitutional directive issued by our political ancestors and on the relevant particularities of context, it is less problematic, all things considered, for the Court unilaterally to discontinue protecting the directive, or for the president unilaterally to discontinue respecting it, than for the Court to continue protecting the directive, or for the president to continue respecting it, until the directive can be disestablished in a relatively unproblematic way. But that possibility seems marginal. Who among us would be comfortable with the politically unaccountable Court,[26] or even the politically accountable president, exercising such a large power—the power to pick and choose which constitutional directives will be protected or respected—even if in some imaginable, if unlikely, circumstance we might be willing to concede that, all things considered, a judicial or a presidential nullification of a directive constitutionalized by our political ancestors is the lesser or least of evils?

One unproblematic way of disestablishing a constitutional directive issued by our political ancestors, of course, is the amendment process specified by Article V of the Constitution. Whether the Article V process is the only unproblematic way to disestablish a constitutional directive is a separate question. The Article V process is surely the least problematic way. It seems implausible that the Article V process is the only *morally* legitimate way to alter the Constitution,[27] even if it is the only *constitutionally* legitimate way. (Whether the Article V process is the only constitutionally legitimate way to amend the Constitution is a matter of controversy.[28]) In the conclusion to this book (chapter 10), I suggest a modification in the practice of judicial review under which the Congress and the president, acting together in their legislative capacity, would play a larger role, not in amending the Constitution, but in giving shape, in particular contexts, to indeterminate constitutional values.[29] Perhaps they should play a larger role, too, in amending the Constitution, as Bruce Ackerman has recently suggested.[30]

To say that the various constitutional directives issued by our political ancestors are worth protecting is not to deny that some of those directives may be worth protecting only until they can be disestablished in a relatively unproblematic way. The argument for judicial review, which presupposes that the various directives constitutionalized by our political ancestors are worth protecting, is simply that the practice serves us well as a mechanism for protecting those directives, and that unless and until we alter the practice by establishing a better mechanism, we should continue to abide the practice.

IV

Does the Constitution of the United States—whether as ratified in 1789, as amended by ratification of the Bill of Rights in 1791, or as subsequently amended, for example, by ratification of the Fourteenth Amendment in 1866–68—establish the practice of judicial review? More specifically, does it establish judicial review (1) by *state* courts, of acts of *state* government; (2) by *federal* courts, in particular by the Supreme Court, of acts of *state* government; (3) by *state* courts, of acts of the *federal* government; or (4) by *federal* courts, in particular by the Supreme Court, of acts of the *federal* government? (Again, we're talking here about judicial review for federal constitutionality, not judicial review for state constitutionality. The United States Constitution does not speak to the question of judicial review, whether by state courts or by federal courts, of state acts under the constitution of a state.)

Judicial review of the first sort is mandated by the supremacy clause of Article VI of the (1789) Constitution, which provides: "This Constitution . . . shall be the supreme law of the land; and the judges in every state shall be bound thereby, anything in the constitution or laws of any state to the contrary notwithstanding." Judicial review of the second sort—in particular, appellate review by the United States Supreme Court of state court decisions about the federal constitutionality of state acts—"is not compelled by the language of the [1789] Constitution; it is implied from desirable ends ["uniform construction and application of the Constitution as against inconsistent state law throughout the country"] that are attributed to the entire [constitutional] scheme. But most assuredly there is nothing in the language that forbids it. And Congress has . . . provided [for such appellate review]—consistently, from the first Judiciary Act of the first Congress onward—and it has done so unambiguously."[31] Moreover, at least by 1868, when the Fourteenth Amendment became a part of the Constitution, it was taken for granted—indeed, it was a basic presupposition of the Fourteenth Amendment—that the Constitution establishes, in the form of appellate review of state court decisions, judicial review by the Supreme Court of states acts.

What about judicial review of state acts by federal courts other than the Supreme Court? That practice, too, is well established—and it does not seem problematic, given that federal court decisions about the federal constitutionality of state acts are subject to appellate review by the Supreme Court, which, in consequence of its power to review state court decisions about the federal constitutionality of state acts, already has the power to review state acts.

The constitutional pedigree of judicial review of the third and fourth sorts—judicial review of federal acts—is more controversial. Some have argued that the Constitution, as ratified in 1789, establishes such review, but others have disagreed.[32] Even if by itself the constitutional text (as of 1789) is not clear, it is possible that, as some historians have argued, those who, during 1787–89, voted to ratify the Constitution understood and meant it to establish judicial review of federal acts; other historians, however, have argued that the ratifiers did not so understand the Constitution, or that the evidence that they did so understand it is weak.[33] Whatever the understanding of the ratifiers, Leonard Levy and others have argued that the practice of judicial review of federal acts was for the founding generation of Americans a strong and eventually inescapable inference from the nature and structure of the national government established by the Constitution.[34] Moreover, by 1791, when the Bill of Rights became a part of the Constitution, it was almost certainly taken for granted that the Constitution establishes judicial review of federal acts. Indeed, such review is almost certainly a basic presupposition of the Bill of Rights. Recall, in that regard, that Hamilton's argument for such review, in *The Federalist* No. 78, was published in 1788.[35] Recall, too, that "[i]n introducing the Bill of Rights . . . to the First Congress, Madison declared that 'independent tribunals of justice will consider themselves in a peculiar manner the guardians of those rights; they will be an impenetrable bulwark against every assumption of power in the legislative or the executive.'"[36]

Even if we accept one or more of the arguments for the constitutionality of judicial review of federal acts, this problem remains: Recent scholarship suggests that the practice of judicial review of federal acts that was (arguably) established by the Constitution at the end of the eighteenth century was not as broad as the practice that was subsequently established by the Supreme Court, in the late nineteenth century, and that prevails today.[37] To credit that scholarship is to conclude that if the Constitution—whether as ratified in 1789 or as amended by ratification of the Bill of Rights in 1791—established *a* practice of judicial review of federal acts, it did not establish the broad modern practice, according to which "courts are entitled to overturn any act of Congress [or of the president] they find to be unconstitutional, as long as a relevant case is brought before them. Moreover, such a finding by the Supreme Court of the United States is final, not subject to further action by any other agency of government, except in conformity with the Court's decision."[38] According to the narrower practice established by the Constitution at the end of the eighteenth century, however, "federal courts are entitled to invalidate acts of Congress and the president with finality only when to let such acts stand would violate the constitutional restrictions on judicial power."[39] However, doesn't Madison's statement to the First Congress, quoted in the preceding paragraph, imply that the judicial review that is a basic presupposition of the Bill of Rights is a broader practice than that?

The debate about whether the Constitution establishes judicial review has limited relevance today. The practice of judicial review, including the modern practice of judicial review of federal acts, has indisputably become a definitive feature of American government—indeed, a feature we unreservedly hold out as a model to the world. Any argument that judicial review was not established by the Constitution and is, in that sense, "unconstitutional", however plausible the argument may be as an historical matter, is, at this point in the development of American political institutions and practices, antiquarian. In the sense that judicial review is now a definitive feature of American government—a *constitutive* feature—judicial review is constitutional.[40]

My concern in this chapter, in any event, has been not with the legal question of the constitutionality of judicial review but with the political-moral question of its legitimacy. The force of the argument for judicial review I have presented in this chapter does not depend on whether the judicial review is of state acts or, instead, of federal acts. This is not to deny, however, that the overall case for judicial review by federal courts of state acts—which case includes the practical considerations rehearsed by Alexander Bickel ("uniform construction and application of the Constitution as against inconsistent state law throughout the country") —is stronger than the overall case for judicial review, whether by state courts or by federal courts, of federal acts.[41]

The question of the legitimacy of the practice of judicial review is fundamental one for constitutional theory. The practice gives rise to two further such questions: the question of the approach to constitutional interpretation the Supreme Court should follow, and the question of the role the Court should play—how small/passive, or how large/active—in bringing the interpreted Constitution to bear in resolving constitutional conflicts. I address the first of those questions in the next chapter.

3

The Argument for the Originalist Approach to Judicial Review

The practice of judicial review involves, centrally, the Court interpreting the Constitution in the course of resolving constitutional conflicts. What approach to the interpretation of the constitutional text, among the approaches that have been recommended to it, should the Supreme Court follow? What approach to constitutional interpretation should inform the practice of judicial review?

As I emphasized in chapter 1, the question of the proper judicial approach to constitutional *interpretation*—to the interpretation of the constitutional text—should not be confused with the different question, addressed in subsequent chapters, of the proper judicial approach to constitutional *specification*—to the specification of indeterminate constitutional norms or directives represented by the constitutional text. (I elaborate the idea of constitutional "specification" in chapters 5 and 6.) Constitutional adjudication comprises two distinct inquiries. The question addressed in this chapter concerns the proper judicial approach to the first of those inquiries: the *interpretive* inquiry, the inquiry into what directive or directives a particular provision of the constitutional text represents. The position I defend in this chapter—"originalism"—is a position about the proper judicial approach to the interpretive inquiry. It bears emphasis that originalism is not a position about the proper judicial approach to the second of those inquiries: the *normative* inquiry, the inquiry into what shape to give, in a particular context, an indeterminate directive represented, or believed to be represented, by a particular provision of the constitutional text. Originalism—the originalism I defend here—is a position about constitutional interpretation, not about constitutional specification. Originalism must not be confused with judicial "minimalism", which comprises two positions, one of which, like originalism, is about constitutional interpretation ("interpretive minimalism"), the other of which is about constitutional specification ("normative minimalism"). In subsequent chapters, in discussing minimalism, I explicate the relation between originalism and minimalism.

I

The directives constitution makers issue are typically about what the institutions of government are to be and how power is to be allocated among them, or about how governmental power is to be limited.[1] What directives is it legitimate, as a matter of democratic political morality, for the Supreme Court to enforce as *constitutional* directives—directives that are part of "the supreme law of the land"[2] and that, as a legal matter,[3] may not be repealed except by means of the Article V amendment process?[4] The "textualist" answer is that the Court may enforce as constitutional only directives represented by the text of the Constitution. The "nontextualist" answer is that the Court may enforce as constitutional, not only directives represented by the constitutional text, but also some directives not so represented.

It is difficult, in the context of modern American political-legal culture, to discern a persuasive case for nontextualism. The argument for judicial review, presented in the preceding chapter, presupposes the importance of protecting the Constitution of the United States—the Constitution that begins with the words "We the people of the United States" and ends, as of now, with the Twenty-seventh Amendment.[5] What justification can there be, therefore, for the Court enforcing, as constitutional, directives not represented by the Constitution? Recalling that Chief Justice John Marshall's justification for the practice of judicial review, in *Marbury v. Madison*, appealed to the writtenness of the Constitution,[6] Michael Moore has commented that "[j]udicial review is easier to justify if it is exercised with reference only to the written document. . . . By now, the object of [constitutional] interpretation should be clear: it is the written document. Hugo Black was right, at least, about this. Black's Constitution—the one he was so fond of pulling out of his pocket—is our only Constitution."[7]

Samuel Freeman has asserted that "[o]ur written Constitution is . . . only a part of our constitution. It plays a significant though non-exclusive role in constitutional interpretation. It is not, and is not generally understood to be, the complete representation or embodiment of all constitutional conditions and institutions."[8] As Freeman has developed the point:

> There is . . . a sense of the term "constitution" that designates an institution. . . . In its institutional sense, the political constitution of any regime is that system of publicly recognized and commonly accepted rules for making and applying those social rules that are laws. This system of highest-order rules constitutes a political system in that it defines offices and positions of political authority, with their respective qualifications, rights, powers, duties, immunities, liabilities, and so on, and the procedures officials are to observe for making, applying, and enforcing valid laws. As such, the constitution itself cannot be law in an ordinary sense, for what is law within the legal system is ultimately identified by reference to its constitution.[9]

There is no a priori reason why a political community cannot put its constitution (in what Freeman calls the term's "institutional sense") in writing. And, indeed, the constitution of the American political community has been put in writing, to *some* extent at least. The United States Constitution—that is, the written Constitution—is, whatever else it is, a "system of publicly recognized and commonly accepted rules for making and applying those social rules that are laws. This system of highest-order rules constitutes a political system in that it defines offices and positions of political authority, . . . and the procedures officials are to observe for making, applying, and enforcing valid laws." There can be little doubt, therefore, that the written Constitution is a substantial part, at least, of our constitution. The serious question is whether the written Constitution exhausts our constitution, or whether, as Freeman has asserted, "[o]ur written Constitution is . . . only a part of our constitution."

I do not claim that the written Constitution exhausts our constitution (in the "institutional sense" of the term). For example, I suggested in chapter 2 that the practice of judicial review, as a constitutive feature of American government, is "constitutional" even if the written Constitution does not establish the practice. But even if the written Constitution does not exhaust our constitution, the fact remains that *insofar as the practice of judicial review is concerned*, Freeman is wrong and Moore is right: Our written Constitution is our only constitution; it is the whole, and not merely a part, of our constitution. (To say that the written Constitution is our only constitution is not to prejudge the question of the meaning of the written Constitution; for example, it is not to prejudge the question whether the written Constitution, or some part of it, has a "natural rights" meaning.[10]) Freeman to the contrary notwithstanding, the written Constitution is "generally understood to be the complete representation or embodiment of all constitutional conditions and institutions" *the Supreme Court may enforce or protect*. Indeed, we may even say that according to our (unwritten) constitution, the (written) Constitution is our only constitution insofar as the practice of judicial review is concerned.[11] Freeman may want to make an argument in support of the nontextualist approach to constitutional adjudication, but it is difficult to imagine any such argument that would have wide appeal in the context of modern American political-legal culture.[12]

Do at least some modern constitutional decisions presuppose that the written Constitution is *not* our only constitution insofar as the practice of judicial review is concerned? I think not: I argue, in chapters 8 and 9, that even the most controversial modern decisions can be defended on an originalist basis; a fortiori, they can be defended on a textualist basis. (Originalism, as I explain later in this chapter, is a species of textualism.[13]) Of course, to say that a constitutional decision can be defended on a textualist basis is not to say that it *was* defended, by the Supreme Court justices who made the decision, on a textualist rather than on a nontextualist basis. However, it is difficult in the modern period of American constitutional law to identify a Supreme Court justice who is not a textualist.

"[J]udges sometimes admit that constitutional interpretation is sensitive to historical evolution and that history adds a 'gloss' on the text. But they never admit to deriving the authority for their decisions from outside the constitutional text. . . . Instead, any new result is unfailingly presented as a new and better *interpretation* of the text itself. . . . This behavior of judges is very significant because it expresses their belief that purely noninterpretive [that is, nontextualist] review would constitute an abuse of their power and undermine the legitimacy of judicial review. In this belief, moreover, they are very likely to be right."[14]

Consider, for example, retired Justice William J. Brennan, Jr., who is conventionally understood to have followed an "activist" approach to constitutional adjudication. Even if an activist, Justice Brennan is clearly not a nontextualist:

> But if America's experience demonstrates that paper protections are not a sufficient guarantor of liberty, it also suggests that they are a necessary one, particularly in times of crisis. Without a textual anchor for their decisions, judges would have to rely on some theory of natural right, or some allegedly shared standard of the ends and limits of government, to strike down invasive legislation. But an appeal to normative ideals that lack any mooring in the written law . . . would in societies like ours be suspect, because it would represent so profound an aberration from majoritarian principles. . . . A text . . . helps tether [judges'] discretion. I would be the last to cabin judges' power to keep the law vital, to ensure that it remains abreast of the progress in man's intellect and sensibilities. Unbounded freedom is, however, another matter. One can imagine a system of governance that accorded judges almost unlimited discretion, but it would be one reminiscent of the rule by Platonic Guardians that Judge Learned Hand so feared. It is not one, I think, that would gain allegiance in either of our countries.[15]

To reject nontextualism—as Justice Brennan, for example, has done—is not to deny that in enforcing, and therefore in specifying, an indeterminate directive represented by the constitutional text, a judge must rely on premises, including normative premises, not represented by the constitutional text. In chapter 6, I discuss the judicial process of specifying indeterminate constitutional directives.[16]

II

Even if we accept, as I think we should, that the Supreme Court may enforce as constitutional only directives represented by the text of the Constitution, a fundamental problem remains: It is not always clear what directive (or directives) a provision of the constitutional text represents. Moreover, because any text can be, and in particular because constitutional provisions often are, understood in different ways by different people—whether different people at the same time or different people at different times—the question "What directive does this constitutional provision represent?" must be met by the question "This constitutional provision *as understood by whom?*" As I am about to explain, the question "Which approach to constitutional interpretation should the Court follow?" is substantially the question "Whose understanding of the constitutional text should be deemed authoritative—whose understanding should be 'privileged'—for purposes of constitutional adjudication?"

Whose understanding should be privileged? The "originalist" answer is that the "original" understanding should be privileged: The constitutional text *as originally understood* should be deemed authoritative for purposes of constitutional adjudication. More precisely and ideally, the understanding of a constitutional provision by "the people" at the time the provision was constitutionalized should be privileged. The Constitution begins: "We the people of the United States . . . do ordain and establish this Constitution for the United States of America." According to originalism, the ratification of a proposed constitutional provision by the representatives of the people should be taken to presuppose the people's understanding of the provision—the people who, through their representatives, did "ordain and establish" the provision.[17] Surely it should not be taken to presuppose a secret understanding not shared with, or by, the people.[18]

The point can be put in terms of original "meaning" as well as of original "understanding": The meaning of a constitutional provision to the people at the time the provision was constitutionalized should, according to originalism, be privileged. To speak of *how* a text is *understood by* someone is to speak of *what* the text *means to* her, and vice versa.

Not all the people invariably pay attention, however, and not all who do pay attention, or try to, invariably achieve access to all the relevant information. It is a reasonable working hypothesis that the understanding of a constitutional provision by those who represented the people in the constitutional process is a close approximation to how the provision was understood by the people, *or would have been understood by them* had they been paying attention and had they achieved access to all the relevant information. Therefore, the understanding of a constitutional provision by those who represented the people in the constitutional process—in particular, the ratifiers' understanding—may, according to originalism, be privileged. Moreover, with respect to constitutional amendments proposed by the Congress[19]—as, so far, all the constitutional amendments have been—the congressional understanding may fairly be taken to indicate the ratifiers' understanding. In writing about the original understanding of the Fourteenth Amendment, Alexander Bickel observed:

> [T]he debates of the Congress which submitted, and the journals and documents of the legislatures which ratified, the amendment provide the most direct and unimpeachable indication of original purpose and understanding. . . . Of these two sets of materials, the Congressional

debates . . . rank . . . first in importance. It may perhaps be said that whatever they establish constitutes a rebuttable presumption. For it is not unrealistic, in the main, to assume notice of Congressional purpose in the state legislatures. A showing of ratification on the basis of an understanding different from that revealed by Congressional materials must carry the burden of proof. And, of course, the ratifying states are a chorus of voices; a discordant one among them proves little.[20]

The "nonoriginalist" answer to the question of the understanding that should be privileged, by contrast, is that the understanding of some person or persons other than the understanding of the people at the time the provision was constitutionalized, or of their representatives, should be deemed authoritative for purposes of judicial review. The understanding of what person or persons? The understanding of the judge enforcing the provision? The understanding of the present generation of the people— or, if no one understanding of the provision is shared by all members of the present generation of the people, the understanding of some members of the present generation? Which members? Or perhaps the understanding of a combination of different groups of persons? Which groups?[21] ("[T]he central practical defect of nonoriginalism is fundamental and irreparable: the impossibility of achieving any consensus on what, precisely, is to replace original meaning, once that is abandoned."[22]) Whatever a particular nonoriginalist's response, nonoriginalism does not presuppose that the understanding of a constitutional provision by the people at the time the provision was constitutionalized, or of their representatives, is different from the understanding that, according to nonoriginalism, should be privileged. Nonoriginalism holds only that whether or not—and, therefore, even if—the original understanding is different from the latter, the latter understanding, not the former, should be deemed authoritative for purposes of judicial review.

According to originalism, then, the relevant question about a constitutional provision is "What directive does this provision, as originally understood, represent?" An equivalent inquiry is "What constitutional directive did the people—or those who represented them, in particular the ratifiers—understand this provision to communicate? What constitutional directive did our political ancestors mean to issue, in ratifying this provision?" According to nonoriginalism, however, the relevant question is "What directive does this provision, as understood by X, represent?" (Who X is depends, of course, on how a nonoriginalist responds to the question in the preceding paragraph: "The understanding of what person or persons?") An equivalent inquiry: "What directive does X understand this provision to represent?"

Which approach to constitutional interpretation—originalism or nonoriginalism—should the Court follow; which approach should inform the practice of judicial review? What should the object of the Court's interpretive inquiry be: the original understanding or a nonoriginal understanding? That is, in enforcing a constitutional provision, should the

Court be concerned to enforce the directive represented by the provision as originally understood, the constitutional directive our political ancestors meant to issue in ratifying the provision—or, instead, should it be concerned to enforce the directive represented by the provision as understood by X? The question is far from merely an academic one. The directive represented by a constitutional provision as originally understood may well be different from the directive represented by the provision as understood by X (whether X is the judge enforcing the provision, all or some members of the present generation of the eople, a combination of different groups of persons, etc.).

Consider, for example, the free exercise clause of the First Amendment, which provides that "Congress shall make no law . . . prohibiting the free exercise [of religion]. . . ." Does the free exercise clause represent only the directive that Congress is not to discriminate against one or more religions, or does it represent the directive that Congress is not only not to discriminate against one or more religions, but that even when regulating behavior in a nondiscriminatory way, Congress is to tread as lightly around religious practice as it practically can.[23] Does the assistance of counsel clause of the Sixth Amendment ("[i]n all criminal prosecutions, the accused shall enjoy the right . . . to have the assistance of counsel for his defense") represent only the directive that government is not to prevent the accused from having a lawyer, or does it represent the directive that government is not only not to prevent the accused from having a lawyer, but that when the accused is unable to procure a lawyer for himself, government is to provide one? Does the privileges or immunities clause of the Fourteenth Amendment ("[n]o State shall make or enforce any law which shall abridge the privileges or immunities of citizens of the United States") represent only the directive that states are not to regulate protected privileges or immunities in a discriminatory way (on the basis of race, for example), or does it represent the directive that states are not to regulate protected privileges or immunities in a discriminatory *or otherwise unreasonable* way.[24] The answer to such questions may well depend on whether one is asking about a constitutional provision as originally understood or, instead, about the provision as understood by some person or persons other than the people, or their representatives, at the time the provision was constitutionalized.

Ronald Dworkin has suggested that the originalist conception of constitutional interpretation is fundamentally confused: "The problem a judge 'committed' to original understanding has is not deciding what an abstract provision says—it says something as abstract as the words it uses—but deciding what impact it has in concrete cases. He is trying to *establish* the Constitution's meaning in that sense, and it is no help to tell him that he must *first* discover its meaning."[25] Originalists, like Robert Bork (whose position Dworkin was criticizing in the quoted passage), do not suggest, however, nor does their advice presuppose or entail, that the problem an originalist judge faces is deciding what a constitutional provision—a piece of the constitutional text—abstractly worded or otherwise, *says*. They understand that the problem is deciding what the piece of text *means*. In particular, the problem is deciding what the text means in two senses: first, deciding what directive the text, as originally understood, represents, and, second, deciding what that directive means, what it requires, in the context of the conflict to be resolved. An originalist judge—indeed, any judge, originalist or not—must *first* "discover" the meaning of the *text*, she must first identify the directive represented by the text, *before* she can address the question of the meaning of the *directive* represented by the text—before, that is, she can decide what the directive means for the conflict at hand and therefore what it *shall* mean for relevantly similar conflicts thereafter, before she can, in that sense, "establish" the meaning, the *contextual* meaning, of the directive. A judge simply cannot do the latter until she has first done the former.

Perhaps Dworkin believes that the question of a constitutional provision's meaning is a nonquestion. Perhaps he believes, for example, that the question "What does the free exercise clause of the First Amendment, as originally understood, mean, what directive does it represent?" is not a serious question. Perhaps he wants to try to minimize the question by answering (impatiently?) "It means what it says, that 'Congress shall make no law . . . prohibiting the free exercise [of religion]. . . .'; *that* is the directive the text, as originally understood, represents; our political ancestors meant what they said and said what they meant, no more, no less!" Such a response, however, is conspicuously unhelpful. *We* do not always succeed in communicating precisely what we mean to communicate, even when we succeed in saying precisely what we meant to say, and there is certainly no reason to assume a priori that in saying what they did, in writing a constitutional provision as they did, our political ancestors invariably succeeded in communicating precisely what they meant to communicate (even if they invariably succeeded in saying what they meant to say), that they invariably succeeded in communicating precisely the directive they meant to communicate. And, indeed, with respect to the free exercise clause, they did not succeed in communicating precisely the directive they meant to communicate: In the American political community, there is no widely shared agreement about the meaning of what they said, about what directive they meant to communicate by saying what they did. According to some scholars, the free exercise clause (as originally understood) represents only the directive that Congress is not to discriminate against one or more religions; according to others, it represents the directive that Congress is not only not to discriminate against one or more religions, but that even when regulating behavior in a nondiscriminatory way, Congress is to tread as lightly around religious practice as it practically can.[26]

It is not surprising that sometimes in the American political community there is no widely shared understanding of the meaning of something our political ancestors said (wrote) in the Constitution, of the directive they meant to communicate by saying (writing) what they did. Sometimes texts—not least, old texts—are or become, in the life of the community, opaque, vague, ambiguous, and so on. Sometimes, therefore, a text must undergo a serious interpretive effort—a serious effort at translation or decoding—if the message it was meant to communicate is to be received. Constitutional texts are no exception: Some constitutional provisions are opaque, vague, or ambiguous, and some constitutional provisions must therefore undergo a serious interpretive effort if the directives they were meant to communicate are to be received. It is not true of every constitutional provision, even if it is true of some, that the question of its meaning, of what directive it represents, can usefully be answered by a statement of what the provision says. Referring to Article II of the Constitution, which provides in relevant part that "[n]o person except a natural born citizen . . . shall be eligible to the office of the President", John Ely has observed that "[u]nless we know whether 'natural born' meant born to American parents on the one hand or born to married parents on the other, we don't know what the ratifiers thought they were ratifying and thus what we should recognize as the constitutional command."[27]

The question of the meaning of *a constitutional provision* can be a serious question, therefore, and almost certainly is a serious question in the absence of a widely shared understanding of the meaning of the provision—in the absence, that is, of a widely shared understanding of what directive the provision represents. A judge must first answer that question before "establishing", in the context of the case at hand, the meaning of *the directive represented by the provision*. Even in the presence of a widely shared contemporary understanding of the meaning of a constitutional provision, the question of the *original* meaning of the provision—of what directive the provision, as originally understood, represents—can be a serious question: The widely shared present understanding may diverge radically from the original understanding.

Of course, the question of the meaning of a constitutional provision is not invariably a serious one. If there is, in a community, a widely shared understanding of the meaning of a text, the question "What does it mean?", if posed by a member of the community, may elicit the impatient reply "It means what it says!" Consider, for example, section 3 of Article I of the Constitution, which provides, inter alia, that "[t]he Senate of the United States shall be composed of two Senators from each State. . . ." Because there is a widely shared understanding of the meaning of the provision in the American political community, the question "What does the provision mean?" (if posed by a member of the community) would seem strange. (If posed by someone not a member of the community, the question would not seem strange, or as strange. That there is in a community a widely shared understanding of the meaning of any provision or text is, of course, a contingent fact, not a necessary one. The situation could be otherwise.) We might be tempted to reply—even though the object of the question is not what the provision says but what it means—"It means what it says, that there shall be two senators—no more, no less—from each state." This is not to deny that to say of a text "It means what it says!" is to interpret the text; it is just to emphasize that the question "What does it mean?" may seem strange in the presence of a widely shared understanding of the meaning of the text. But the question "What does the free exercise clause mean?" does not seem strange. Given the absence of a shared understanding of the clause, the (Dworkinian?) reply "The free exercise clause means what it says!" *would* seem, not merely strange, but perverse.[28]

In responding to Dworkin, and indeed throughout this book, I have relied on the distinction between, on the one hand, the interpretive inquiry (which, for the originalist, is an historical inquiry)—*interpreting* the constitutional *text*, in the sense of identifying the directive represented by a piece of the text—and, on the other, the normative inquiry—*establishing* the contextual meaning of a directive represented by the text (if the directive is contextually indeterminate) by means of the process I call "specification". I can anticipate two objections to my distinction. The first objection—challenging the familiar dichotomy between "understanding" a law and then "applying" the law, now understood, to resolve a case—insists, with Hans-Georg Gadamer, that "[u]nderstanding . . . is always application."[29] This objection misconceives my distinction. My distinction is not—nor does it presuppose, entail, or even track—the problematic dichotomy Gadamer rightly challenged: the distinction between, on the one hand, understanding a legal norm or directive and, on the other, "applying" the norm—in the sense of "bringing it to bear"—in adjudicating a particular conflict. That distinction is not my distinction. Indeed, the second part of my distinction—what I call the normative inquiry—presupposes that Gadamer is right. It presupposes that there is no difference between understanding the *contextual* meaning of a legal norm or directive and "applying" the norm, bringing it to bear, in the case at hand; to do the latter is to establish the contextual meaning of the norm (by specifying the norm). The first part of my distinction simply recognizes that some legal texts—not all, but some—are, to the Court, initially unintelligible (opaque, vague, ambiguous, etc.), in the sense that it is not initially clear to the Court what norm or directive the text represents or, pace originalism, was meant to represent. If it is not clear to the Court what directive a legal text was meant to represent, the Court must translate or decode the text: The Court must identify, or try to, the directive the text was meant to represent. *Before* the directive the text was meant to represent can be "understood"/"applied"—which, pace Gadamer, is not two moves, but one—the directive the text was meant to represent must be identified. Before the normative inquiry, the interpretive inquiry. (In many cases, of course—perhaps in most cases—the interpretive inquiry will be unnecessary: The Court will already have identified, in an earlier case now deemed authoritative, the directive the text was meant to represent.)

The second objection goes like this:

The Court's identification of the directive a particular constitutional provision (the "first" text) represents constitutes a further text (the "second"
text): the Court's statement of the directive. But the second text, no less
than the first, may be, to the Court, unintelligible (opaque, etc.) and thus
necessitate the Court's translating/decoding it before the Court can
begin the process of specification. Therefore, after the interpretive
inquiry, there may be only more interpretive inquiry, and so on, ad
infinitum. Alternatively, if the second text is intelligible to the Court and
therefore does not necessitate translation before the Court can begin the
process of specification, why can't the first text be intelligible to the
Court and therefore not necessitate translation before the Court can
begin the process of specification?[30]

I want to respond to this objection, in two steps, from the perspective of
originalism. First, a particular constitutional provision *can* be initially
intelligible, rather than unintelligible, to the Court, in the sense that it is
clear to the Court from the outset what directive the provision was meant
to represent. (Consider, again, this provision: "The Senate of the United
States shall be composed of two Senators from each State. . . .") In that
case, the Court need not translate the provision—it need not try to identify the directive the provision was meant to represent. But with respect to
some constitutional provisions it is not clear to the Court from the outset
what directive the provision was meant to represent, in which case the
Court must identify the directive that, in its view, the provision was meant
to represent. Second, the Court's identification of the directive that, in
its view, a particular constitutional provision was meant to represent does
indeed constitute a further text: the Court's statement of the directive.
But, for reasons I give in the next section of this chapter, the possibility
seems more hypothetical than real that after exhausting the interpretive inquiry the Court will end up only with a translation, a reading, of
the provision that is itself unintelligible to the Court—a statement, like
"Plot the knot", that because of its unintelligibility prevents the Court
from getting on with the business of deciding if the provision has been
violated.

In the remainder of this chapter, I want to elaborate the originalist position more fully—the position that in enforcing a constitutional provision,
the Court should be concerned to enforce the directive represented by
the provision as originally understood, the directive the people at the time
the provision was constitutionalized, or their representatives, understood
the provision to communicate, the directive they meant to issue. And then
I want to explain why the originalist position—the originalist approach to
constitutional interpretation—is much stronger, in the context of modern American political-legal culture, than nonoriginalism.

III

According to the originalist approach to the interpretation of a constitutional provision, the object of the Supreme Court's interpretive inquiry should be the directive (or directives) represented by the provision as originally understood: the directive the people at the time the provision was constitutionalized, or their representatives, understood the provision to communicate, the directive they meant to issue. A common objection to originalism is that there may well be no single directive a sufficiently large number of the people, or of their representatives in the constitutional process, understood a constitutional provision to communicate; there may well be, in that sense, no single original understanding, no single directive a sufficiently large number of our political ancestors meant to issue.

That possibility is extremely unlikely. Constitutional provisions do not emerge out of thin air. They are efforts to deal with real problems. Consider, for example, the important second sentence of section 1 of the Fourteenth Amendment: "No State shall make or enforce any law which shall abridge the privileges or immunities of citizens of the United States; nor shall any State deprive any person of life, liberty, or property, without due process of law; nor deny to any person within its jurisdiction the equal protection of the laws." As I explain in chapter 7, there is no serious question whether that sentence was understood, by all the persons who constitutionalized it, to communicate at least a set of directives about discrimination against persons "of African descent".[31] As the Supreme Court said in the *Slaughter-House Cases*, "The most cursory glance at [the three post–Civil War amendments] discloses a unity of purpose, when taken in connection with the history of the times, which cannot fail to have an important bearing on any question of doubt concerning their true meaning. . . . [T]he one pervading purpose found in them all, lying at the foundation of each, and without which none of them would have been even suggested[, is] the freedom of the slave race, the security and firm establishment of that freedom, and the protection of the newly-made freeman and citizen from the oppressions of those who had formerly exercised unlimited dominion over him."[32] There is no serious question, either, whether the second sentence of section 1 was meant to communicate a set of directives not just about discrimination against persons of African descent, but about discrimination based on race. "We do not say that no one else but the negro can share in this protection. . . . Undoubtedly while negro slavery alone was in the mind of the Congress which proposed the thirteenth [amendment], it forbids any other kind of slavery, now or hereafter. If Mexican peonage or the Chinese coolie labor system shall develop slavery of the Mexican or Chinese race within our territory, this amendment may safely be trusted to make it void. And so if other rights are assailed by the States which properly and necessarily fall within the protection of these [amendments], that protection will apply, though the party interested may not be of African descent."[33] Similarly, in 1880 the Court wrote: "Nor if a law should be passed excluding all naturalized Celtic Irishmen, would there be any doubt of its inconsistency with the spirit of the [fourteenth] amendment."[34] The serious, and disputed, question is whether the sentence was understood, by a sufficiently large number of those who constitutionalized it, to communicate any directives about matters other than discrimination based on race[35]—even, perhaps, about matters other than discrimination. In any event, the objection that there is no single directive our political ancestors meant to issue in ratifying a particular constitutional provision is best tested by scrutinizing the available relevant historical materials.

Consider this statement by Robert Bork: "The judge who cannot make out the meaning of a provision is in exactly the same circumstance as a judge who has no Constitution to work with. There being nothing to work with, the judge should refrain from working. A provision whose meaning cannot be ascertained is precisely like a provision that . . . is obliterated past deciphering by an ink blot. No judge is entitled to interpret an ink blot on the ground that there must be something under it."[36] Bork then adds: "Oddly enough, the people who relish agnosticism about the [original] meaning of our most basic compact do not explore the consequences of their notion. They view the impossibility of knowing what the Constitution means as justification for saying that it means anything they would prefer it to mean. But they too easily glide over a difficulty fatal to their conclusion. If the meaning of the Constitution is unknowable, if, so far as we can tell, it is written in undecipherable hieroglyphics, the conclusion is not that the judge may write his own Constitution. The conclusion is that judges must stand aside and let current democratic majorities rule, because there is no law superior to theirs."[37] However, if because the Court could not reach a plausible conclusion about the original meaning of many constitutional provisions the originalist approach to constitutional interpretation would lead to treating a significant portion of the Constitution as a dead letter, that consequence would surely count as a powerful argument against the claim that the originalist approach is the proper approach. But, again, there is no reason to think that the Court is usually unable to reach a plausible conclusion about original meaning. (And so, in any event, Bork's statement, whatever its theoretical force, has little practical relevance.)

Another common objection to originalism—similar to the first objection and, indeed, perhaps merely a variation on it—is that originalism is unable to deal with what is probably the most fundamental interpretive problem, namely, identifying the level of generality of the directive represented by a constitutional provision. For example, a judge cannot determine, pursuant to the originalist approach, whether the directive the people, or their representatives, understood the privileges or immunities clause of the Fourteenth Amendment to communicate is only about discrimination based on race or whether it is about discrimination more generally, of which racial discrimination is simply an instance,[38] or even whether it is about more than discrimination. This objection seems mistaken. As Bork has explained: "The role of a judge committed to the philosophy of original understanding is . . . to find the meaning of a text—a process which includes finding its degree of generality, which is part of its meaning. . . . [A] judge should state the principle at the level of generality that the text and historical evidence warrant. . . . [Originalism] avoids the problem of the level of generality . . . by finding the level of generality that interpretation of the words, structure, and history of the [constitutional provision] fairly supports."[39] According to originalism, then, a judge should try not to articulate the directive represented by a constitutional provision (as originally understood) at a level of generality any broader— or any narrower—than the relevant materials ("words, structure, and history") warrant. Of course, deciding what level of generality the relevant materials warrant may often be a difficult task.

Of course, the Court will not always be able to identify easily, or with certainty, the directive represented by a constitutional provision as originally understood, including the correct level of generality. (It is a mistake—for some, it is wishful thinking—to suppose that the originalist approach to constitutional interpretation is always or even often easy.) Nonetheless, there is no reason to doubt that the Court will usually be able to reach a plausible conclusion about original meaning, if in no other way, then by constructing an original understanding on the basis of what we might think of as a hypothetical conversation with those in the past whose understanding counts: The effort must be to discern, on the basis of the available historical materials, which directive *they* most likely would have chosen, in the conversation, confronted by the various possibilities—the various candidate directives, some of them broader, some narrower—as being the one that best captures the purpose or point or meaning of what they did.[40] That counterfactual project, though difficult, is hardly impossible. That sometimes the best the Court can do is to construct an original understanding is, for purposes of the originalist approach, good enough. That sometimes the Court can do no more hardly counts as an argument for a nonoriginalist approach. There is no denying that the counterfactual project sketched here will often leave a judge ample room for "discretionary" judgments about original meaning; as I explain in the next chapter, "the indeterminacy of history" is one reason why, the view of some originalists to the contrary notwithstanding, originalism does not entail judicial minimalism.

In his more polemical moods, Bork complains about the tendency of some "liberals"—both liberal judges and liberal scholars—to "overgeneralize" the original meaning of constitutional provisions. For example: "[Although not all] the theorists of liberal constitutional revisionism"— Bork kindly includes me in that group[41]—"would agree that they have rejected the original understanding, . . . I think it can be shown that they have generalized that understanding so greatly, stated it at such a high level of abstraction, that virtually no one who voted to ratify the document would recognize the principles of the theorists as his own."[42] It would make just as much sense, however, to complain about the tendency of some ("conservative"?) judges and scholars to "undergeneralize". Indeed, the complaint that some judges tend to undergeneralize seems the more plausible one with respect to constitutional provisions, like the three clauses of the second sentence of section 1 of the Fourteenth Amendment (the privileges or immunities, equal protection, and due process clauses), the language of which is relatively broad.[43] (At least, as it is or probably would be used today, the language of those clauses is relatively broad.) After all, the generality of the language of a constitutional provision is some evidence that the original meaning of the provision—the directive represented by the provision as originally understood—is similarly general (and, therefore, relatively indeterminate, because, as I later explain, indeterminacy often, though not necessarily, accompanies generality[44]). Something "seems invariably to get lost in excursions into the intent of the framers, namely, that *the most important datum bearing on what was intended is the constitutional language itself.*"[45] "Interpreters who emphasize extrinsic evidence of the founders' intent tend to ignore the generality of the text and to substitute much narrower conceptions of intent. The founders focused on the specific problems most salient to their lives, but they constitutionalized general principles that seem designed to cover whole classes of similar problems. What they left a record of having specifically and consciously intended is often a small subset of the text they proposed and ratified. Interpretation limited to specific and provable intentions thus tends to be fatally inconsistent with the constitutional text."[46] Of course, it is always possible that—and sometimes merits inquiry whether— language that appears general to us in the present appeared much less general, if not specific, to them in the past.[47] Nonetheless, "[c]ertainly when most readers agree that a particular clause or phrase means one thing, the burden of persuasion ought to be on the advocate of some other meaning. Such a presumption is fully consistent with [the originalist approach to constitutional interpretation] and a convenient rule of administration."[48]

In any event, the commitment of an originalist judge is to retrieve the original meaning of constitutional provisions as accurately as possible and, therefore, neither to overgeneralize nor undergeneralize original meaning.[49]

It is important not to confuse the originalist approach I am presenting here with another version often the target of critics of originalism.[50] Assume that the directive represented by the privileges or immunities clause as originally understood is that states are not to regulate the protected privileges or immunities on the basis of race—in particular, that they are not to deny them to any person on the basis of race. Assume further that the ratifiers of the privileges or immunities clause (whose understanding of the clause we are accepting as a proxy for the understanding of the people they represented) happened not to believe that the clause proscribed racially segregated public schools. According to a problematic version of originalism, segregated schools therefore do not violate the clause and may not legitimately be disestablished in the name of the clause.[51] According to the originalism I am presenting here, however, the question whether segregated schools violate the clause—the clause *as originally understood*—is not to be referred to the past; it is a question for the present; in particular, it is a question for the court charged with determining whether such schools violate the clause. What is authoritative, for originalism, is the directive the ratifiers understood a constitutional provision to communicate, the directive they meant to issue. That the ratifiers may not have believed that this or that practice (law, etc.) with which they were familiar violated a constitutional directive they were issuing—even that they believed that the practice did not violate the directive—is not determinative. (I elaborate and defend the point in chapter 5.) If in the court's view a practice does in fact violate a constitutional directive the ratifiers issued, the court's duty is to invalidate the practice. Of course, that the ratifiers believed that a practice with which they were familiar did not violate a constitutional provision they were ratifying is some evidence of what directive the ratifiers understood the provision to communicate, of what directive they meant to issue in ratifying the provision; in particular, it may suggest that the directive the ratifiers meant to issue does not have precisely the shape—for example, the breadth—we might otherwise have been inclined to conclude.

A fortiori, that a practice is one with which the ratifiers were not familiar—one they did not foresee and perhaps could not have foreseen—and therefore one they could not have believed violated a constitutional directive they were issuing is beside the point. The court's duty, according to originalism, is to invalidate a practice—whether or not it was foreseen or even foreseeable by the ratifiers—if in the court's view the practice violates a constitutional directive issued by the ratifiers. As Bork puts it:

> [A]ll that a judge committed to [the philosophy of] original understanding requires is that the text, structure, and history of the Constitution provide him not with a conclusion but with a major premise. That major premise is a principle or . . . value that the ratifiers wanted to protect against hostile legislation or executive action. The judge must then see whether that principle or value is threatened by the statute or action challenged in the case before him. The answer to that question provides his minor premise, and the conclusion follows. It does not follow without difficulty, and two judges equally devoted to the original purpose may disagree about the reach or application of the principle at stake and so arrive at different results, but that in no way distinguishes the task from the difficulties of applying any other legal writing.
>
> This version of [originalism] certainly does not mean that judges will invariably decide cases the way the men of the ratifying conventions

would if they could be resurrected to sit as courts. Indeed, the various ratifying conventions would surely have split within themselves and with one another in the application of the principles they adopted to particular fact situations. That tells us nothing other than that the ratifiers were like other legislators. Any modern congressional majority would divide over particular applications of a statute its members had just enacted. That does not destroy the value of seeking the best understanding of the principle enacted in the case either of the statute or of the Constitution.[52]

As the foregoing passage confirms, some originalists, like Bork, understand that the specification of a constitutional directive—that is, the development of the concrete, contextual meaning of a constitutional directive—is not only not precluded by the originalist approach but is, indeed, necessitated by it. For example, Bork writes: "When there is a known [constitutional] principle to be explicated the evolution of doctrine is inevitable. Judges given stewardship of a constitutional provision . . . whose core is known but whose outer reach and contours are ill-defined, face the never-ending task of discerning the meaning of the provision from one case to the next. There would be little need for judges . . . if the boundaries of every constitutional provision were self-evident. . . . It is the task of the judge in this generation to discern how the [ratifiers'] values . . . apply to the world we know. . . . [Judges may] refine and evolve doctrine . . . , so long as one is faithful to the basic meaning of the [constitutional provision]. . . . To say that such adjustments must be left to the legislature is . . . gradually to render constitutional guarantees meaningless."[53] Near the end of his book Bork emphasizes that "[t]he provisions of the Constitution state profound but simple and general ideas. The law laid down in those provisions gradually gains body, substance, doctrines, and distinctions as judges, equipped at first with only those ideas, are forced to confront new situations and changing circumstances."[54] Commenting on the Supreme Court's decision in *Brown v. Board of Education* outlawing racially segregated public schooling,[55] Bork says: "[I]t became evident over time that the racial separation the ratifiers of the fourteenth amendment assumed"—the racial separation, that is, that they took for granted—"was completely inconsistent with the equal protection of the laws they mandated."[56]

It is not difficult to understand why Bork and some other originalists have moved toward what Gregory Bassham calls "moderate intentionalism" originalism and away from what he calls "strict intentionalism" originalism:[57] The former "recognizes the importance of striking a balance between the values of predictability and stability on the one hand, and those of flexibility and adaptability on the other. . . . Moderate intentionalism enjoys the significant advantage of being able to respond, as strict intentionalism does not, both to originalism's traditional concern with the values of certainty, stability, and judicial restraint, and to the perennial complaint of originalism's critics that the theory is hopelessly at odds with the need to treat the Constitution as a living, flexible document."[58] Even more important, argues Bassham, is moderate intentionalism's "capacity to recognize that constitutional provisions, in principle, may signify aspirations and values that transcend the framers' temporally bounded conceptions of the scope of those provisions."[59] Bassham concludes: "Moderate intentionalism thus seem[s] an attractive half-way house between two unacceptable extremes: a jurisprudence that constitutionalized the repellent prejudices of former generations on the one hand, and a jurisprudence of open-ended judicial policymaking on the other."[60]

John Ely has written to much the same effect: "The language and legislative history of our Constitution seldom suggest an intent to invalidate only a small set of historically understood practices. (If that had been the point the practices could simply have been listed.) More often the Constitution proceeds by briefly indicating certain fundamental principles whose specific implications for each age must be determined in contemporary context."[61] Consider, in that regard, Tom McAffee's criticism of Raoul Berger's brand of originalism:

> [I]n a book-length treatment of the scope of the "exceptions clause" of Article III using his own "original intent" approach,[62] Berger clearly confused the meaning of the generally worded provision with particular contemplated applications of the provision as revealed by statements in the "legislative" history. Berger simply failed to grasp that the intended meaning of a provision is not necessarily limited to its contemplated specific applications. This approach to discovering binding "intent" reflects what has been described as the "pointer theory of meaning," which incorrectly assumes that we use words to describe specific things that we are thinking about rather than general ideas. In practice, reliance on this assumption amounts to a form of strict construction that fails to implement the policy established by the statute or constitution in favor of giving effect only to the specific, known intentions (read specifically intended applications) of the adopters.[63]

McAffee—himself a committed originalist—goes on to make the same criticism of Berger's analogous mistake in arguing as Berger does[64] about the original meaning of the equal protection clause of the Fourteenth Amendment.[65]

In chapter 5, I explain how an originalist judge (of Bassham's "moderate intentionalist" variety"), in specifying an indeterminate constitutional directive, should deal with (1) particular practices that they who issued the directive specifically meant the directive to ban, (2) particular practices that they did not understand, or would not have understood, the directive to ban, and (3) particular practices that they specifically meant the directive not to ban.[66] For now I want only to note that Bork's insistence that the cruel and unusual punishments clause of the Eighth Amendment ("cruel and unusual punishments [shall not be] inflicted") cannot be interpreted to prohibit imposition of the death penalty, because the ratifiers of the Constitution and Bill of Rights presupposed the existence of the death penalty and, elsewhere in the Constitution and Bill of

Rights, regulated imposition of the death penalty,[67] is difficult to square with Bork's paean to evolving constitutional doctrine. The ratifiers' expectation that reliance on the death penalty would persist into the future and their decision, given that expectation, to regulate imposition of the penalty do not constitute a decision to authorize reliance on the death penalty, to *constitutionalize* the death penalty—in that sense, they do not constitute a decision to exempt the death penalty from possible prohibition by the Eighth Amendment. Of course, that the ratifiers expected a practice, like the death penalty or segregated public schooling, to persist into the future is evidence that they did not believe that they were prohibiting the practice. But that they did not believe that they were prohibiting a practice does not mean that the constitutional directive they issued is not best specified to prohibit the practice. Bork understands that he cannot rule out, on the basis of the originalist approach to constitutional interpretation, the possibility that racially segregated public schooling does indeed violate a directive represented by section 1 of the Fourteenth Amendment as section 1 was originally understood—the possibility, in that sense, that such schooling is *really* a violation of section 1—notwithstanding that the ratifiers of section 1 did not so think. It is therefore curious that Bork fails to see that, absent evidence that the ratifiers meant to constitutionalize the death penalty—Bork points to no such evidence, and I am aware of none—he cannot rule out, on the basis of the originalist approach, the possibility that the death penalty does indeed violate the directive represented by the cruel and unusual punishments clause as the clause was originally understood—the possibility, that is, that the death penalty is *truly* a cruel or unusual punishment—notwithstanding that the ratifiers of the clause did not so believe.[68]

Many criticisms of the originalist approach to constitutional interpretation have force if directed against (what Bassham calls) "strict intentionalism" originalism.[69] If directed against the originalism presented here, however, as such criticisms sometimes are,[70] they have much less force, if indeed they have any. Richard Kay has effectively rebutted the principal practical and conceptual criticisms of originalism—criticisms to the effect that it is virtually impossible to discern the original understanding of a constitutional provision or even to know what "the original understanding" means, what it refers to. The reader concerned with such criticisms could do no better, in my view, than to consult Kay's work.[71] That today some critics of originalism trot out the frayed claims to which Kay has elaborately responded without even citing his work, much less attending to it, is dismaying.[72] That *Bork* failed to rely on or even mention Kay's work is startling as well as dismaying, since Bork does not respond to the relevant criticisms, or even identify them, nearly so well as Kay.[73] Not that Kay minimizes the practical difficulties that attend the originalist approach to constitutional adjudication; Kay is at least as sensitive to those difficulties as the critics whose arguments he so effectively parries.

The serious question concerns not the possibility but the legitimacy of the originalist approach to constitutional interpretation; the serious question is not whether originalism *can* inform the practice of judicial review— it can—but whether it *should* inform the practice.

IV

Originalism, then—or nonoriginalism? In the context of American political-legal culture, which is the more defensible approach to constitutional interpretation?

The argument for originalism begins with the observation that the United States Constitution is the yield of an effort—actually, the yield of many efforts over many years—to communicate, by means of a written text, various directives. Those directives are mainly of two types: (1) directives about what the institutions of the national government are to be and about how power is to be allocated, both horizontally, among the (legislative, executive, and judicial) institutions of the national government, and vertically, between the national government and the governments of the states; and (2) directives about how the power of government—the power of the national government or of state government or of both—is to be limited.[74] The argument for originalism—the argument that the originalist approach to constitutional interpretation should inform the practice of judicial review—continues by emphasizing the basic point of judicial review, which, as I explained in the preceding chapter, is to protect the various directives constitutionalized by our political ancestors: the various directives the constitutional text was understood to communicate by the people at the time the text was constitutionalized, or by their representatives. Because it is not always clear what directive(s) a particular piece of the text, a particular constitutional provision, was originally understood to communicate, however, the Court must "interpret" the provision: It must identify, or try to, the directive the provision was understood, by the people at the time the provision was constitutionalized or by their representatives, to communicate.

Recall that, as I said at the beginning of chapter 2, the question of the legitimacy of the practice of judicial review and the question of the approach to constitutional interpretation that should inform the practice of judicial review are inextricably linked: One's response to the first question is an essential determinant of one's response to the second. To (attempt to) justify the practice of judicial review, after all, is not to justify an abstraction; it is to justify the practice understood as protecting the Constitution not just in any sense of "the Constitution" but in a particular sense—and understood as well, therefore, as consisting not just of any conception of, or approach to, constitutional "interpretation" but of a particular conception, namely, the conception entailed by the particular sense of "the Constitution" in play. The argument for judicial review I made in chapter 2, therefore, bears strongly on the argument I make in this chapter for the approach to constitutional interpretation that should inform the practice of judicial review.

"The Constitution", in each and all of its various parts, is an intentional political act of a certain sort: an act intended to establish, not merely particular configurations of words, but particular directives, namely, the directives the particular configurations of words were understood to communicate.[75] The fundamental reason any part of the Constitution—any provision of the constitutional text—was ratified is that the ratifiers wanted to issue, and thought that in ratifying the provision they were issuing, a particular directive: the directive that they understood, and that the public they represented understood, or would have understood, the provision to communicate. (Does anyone really believe that were *we* to amend the Constitution in our day, it might be an intentional political act of a different sort: an act intended to establish, not particular directives, but merely particular configurations of words? If not, why would anyone believe that when *they* established or amended the Constitution in their day, they acted to establish merely particular configurations of words?) It is difficult to discern any justification, therefore, for the Court privileging any understanding of a constitutional provision other than the original understanding—for privileging, that is, any directive other than the directive the provision was originally understood to communicate, the directive the provision was ratified to establish.

Richard Kay has argued, in a series of essays, that nonoriginalism, which would have the Court privilege some understanding other than the original understanding, is divided against itself: "There may be plausible theories of government and judicial review which demote the authority of both intention and text, but it is hard to see what the political rationale would be for a theory that elevates a text for reasons unrelated to the people and circumstances which created it."[76] "[T]o the extent we would bind ourselves, in whole or in part, to rules inferred from mere marks and letters on paper without reference to the will of the human beings who selected those marks and letters, we enter a regime very foreign to our ordinary assumptions about the nature of law."[77] To deem authoritative the words of a constitutional provision "independently of the intentional act which created them", suggests Kay, "is to disregard exactly that which makes the text demand our attention in the first place. That the words will bear some different meaning is purely happenstance. Without their political history, the words of the Constitution have no more claim on us than those of any other text."[78] Steven Smith has made much the same point: "[I]t is hard to think of any recommendation for a regime of law created by the 'interpretation' of disembodied words that have been methodically severed from the acts of mind that produced them."[79]

It misses the point to say of constitutional provisions what Cass Sunstein has said of federal statutes: "The words were enacted; the original understanding was not. . . . Words have passed through the constitution-ally specified mechanisms for enactment of laws; intentions have not, and they are therefore not binding."[80] Yes, the words were enacted. But, as I pointed earlier in this chapter, in the absence of a widely shared under-standing of the meaning of words—especially, in the presence of compet-ing understandings (intertemporal, intratemporal, or both) of their mean-ing—there arises the question of *whose* understanding of the words, the meaning of the words *to whom*, is authoritative. I have presented an argu-ment for answering that the original understanding/meaning is authorita-tive. The ball is in the court of those who do not like that answer to present an argument for answering that some nonoriginal understanding/mean-ing is authoritative. Saying that "the words were enacted, the original understanding was not" does not constitute such an argument, it does not tell us why we should privilege some present meaning (for example) over the original meaning.[81] Sunstein's comment that "[i]n the end, Congress enacts laws, not its own views about what those laws mean"[82] is best under-stood not as a point against the originalism I have presented here. Adapted to the context of constitutional (not statutory) adjudication, the point, which the originalism I have presented here not only accepts but insists on, is that "in the end, the ratifiers (on behalf of the people, whom they represent) establish directives, not their own views about what those directives mean in particular contexts."

In view of a recent critique of originalism by Samuel Freeman, it bears emphasis that the connected arguments for judicial review and for the originalist approach to judicial review, presented in this and in the pre-ceding chapter, do not partake of ancestor worship, whether of a Burkean or of some other variety.[83] I have not said the constitutional directives our political ancestors bequeathed us should be protected, in part by means of judicial review, just because our political ancestors bequeathed them to us. (Who makes such a silly argument?) The point, rather, as I explained in the preceding chapter, is that "we the people" now living—who, after all, unlike our dead political ancestors, are now politically sovereign—should protect the constitutional directives they bequeathed us for one of two reasons: First, some of the directives they bequeathed us are good directives, directives that were we drafting a con-stitution from scratch, we should want to include. Second, even if some of the directives they bequeathed us are not directives that were we drafting a constitution from scratch, we should want to include—indeed, even if some of them are directives that we should want *not* to include—we should nonetheless protect such a directive *unless and until we can disestab-lish the directive in a way that is less problematic than the Court continuing to pro-tect the directive*.[84] Therefore, Samuel Freeman to the contrary notwith-standing, "affirming the Constitution as sovereign citizens, and not as subjects of someone else's will," does *not* "require that we reject the doc-trine of original meaning."[85] (Not that there may not be any *other* reasons for rejecting originalism.)

It bears emphasis, too, that the argument presented here for the originalist approach is not itself originalist. An originalist argument for the originalist approach to constitutional interpretation—in particular, the argument that the judicial review established by the Constitution *as originally understood* is originalist review—would be question-begging: The argument would presuppose the authority of the very thing at issue—the originalist approach to constitutional interpretation.[86]

The question whether the founders' approach to legal interpretation was originalist is nonetheless relevant. If the founders' approach was not originalist even in the "moderate intentionalism" sense, the argument for originalism presented in this chapter would be undermined to this extent: We could no longer say, as I have, that the Constitution, in each and all of its various parts, is an intentional political act of a certain sort— an act intended to establish, not merely particular configurations of words, but particular directives, namely, the directives the particular configurations of words were understood to communicate. We would have to say, instead, that in some of its parts—the parts ratified at the founding— the Constitution is an act intended to canonize merely particular configurations of words. So, was the founders' approach to legal interpretation originalist? Not in the "strict intentionalism" sense of originalism.[87] But to the extent "the framers collectively intended judges to employ any particular theory of constitutional interpretation, there can be little doubt that this interpretive theory was some variety of originalism. For during the founding era and indeed for much of the succeeding century, originalism was not simply the dominant theory of constitutional hermeneutics; with unimportant exceptions it was the only such theory."[88]

Of course, a judge purporting to follow the originalist approach to constitutional interpretation can act in bad faith.[89] But so can a judge purporting to follow any other approach to constitutional interpretation. The more significant point concerns the relation between the originalist approach and the exercise of judicial "discretion".[90] The argument presented here does not presuppose that the originalist approach always or even often constrains judicial discretion to a significant extent. (Nor does it presuppose that a nonoriginalist approach *fails to* constrain judicial discretion.[91]) As Bork[92] and many other enthusiasts of originalism (for example, former Attorney General Edwin Meese)[93] seem not, or not always, to understand, originalism does not entail—it does not necessarily eventuate in—judicial minimalism. I develop the point, at length, in chapters 4 and 5.

V

The polemical character of much academic constitutional discourse in the United States is evident in the tendency of many scholars to roll their eyes, if not sneer, when someone defends the originalist approach to constitutional interpretation. Sometimes the originalist approach is derisively waved away with epithets like "authoritarian".[94] It would be more productive were critics of originalism to take the time and spend the effort to present and defend an alternative, nonoriginalist approach.

What might a nonoriginalist approach to constitutional interpretation and the argument for it look like? Suppose (1) that the Supreme Court believes that a particular constitutional provision as originally understood represents directive D, but (2) that there is a very widespread belief, perhaps even a consensus, among the present generation of the people of the United States—at least, among those members of the present generation who think about such matters—that D is, for some reason or reasons, not morally acceptable, or, at least, that it no longer deserves constitutional status. Might one then plausibly contend for the legitimacy of the Supreme Court refusing to enforce D? Even if so, the argument would not support the Court enforcing, in the name of the provision, a directive not represented by the provision as originally understood; it would support merely the Court refusing to enforce D. Moreover, about what existing constitutional provision (or provisions) can it fairly be said that there is widespread agreement, in the American political community (among those citizens who think about such matters), that the directive represented or arguably represented by the provision, as originally understood, is no longer acceptable? (If one believes that with respect to some constitutional provision such a sentiment is widely, if not consensually, held, why not test the claimed "widespread agreement" by mounting an effort to amend the provision?)

Suppose, instead, (1) that there is a widespread belief, perhaps even a consensus, among the present generation of the people of the United States (or among those citizens who think about such matters) both that the meaning of a particular constitutional provision—the directive represented by the provision—is E and that E is not merely acceptable but morally compelling, but (2) that the Court believes, perhaps correctly, that E is not the directive represented by the provision *as originally understood.* Should the Court enforce E? The supposition is probably counterfactual: For any right- or liberty-regarding provision of the Constitution the subject of a significant amount of litigation, there is almost certainly a significant dissensus (among those citizens who think about such matters) about the meaning of the provision—about, that is, whether the provision represents this or, instead, that directive.[95] What is needed, therefore, is an argument that the Court may enforce as constitutional a directive represented by a constitutional provision *neither* (in the Court's view) as originally understood *nor* even (given the dissensus) as understood by some significant segment of those among the present generation of the People who think about such matters.

Let us vary the preceding hypothetical. Suppose (1) that some citizens—not all, and perhaps not even most, but some—believe that the directive represented by a particular constitutional provision is F, but (2) that the Court believes, perhaps correctly, that F is not the directive represented by the provision *as originally understood.* Suppose further, however, (3) that it is widely and perhaps even consensually held, even by those who do *not* believe that the provision represents F, that F is a morally compelling imperative and deserves constitutional status. Consider, for example, this provision of the Sixth Amendment: "In all criminal prosecutions, the accused shall enjoy the right . . . to have the assistance of counsel for his defense." This language will—and to some of us does— bear this meaning, or something like it: "Government should insure that an accused person unable to afford the assistance of counsel for his defense shall have it." Let us assume, for the sake of argument, that as originally understood the assistance of counsel provision does not represent any such directive[96] but that today there is widespread agreement that the directive is morally compelling and deserves constitutional status, at least with respect to felony prosecutions.[97] The existence of such a state of affairs constitutes what is probably the strongest basis for a nonoriginalist approach—and perhaps the Court should enforce F. But those who want to argue that the Court should enforce F should be prepared to explain why a different path should not be preferred: a political effort, pursuant to the Article V amendment process, to constitutionalize F. Such an effort would probably succeed—if F is indeed widely, and perhaps even consensually, held to be both morally compelling and deserving of constitutional status. Moreover, it is difficult for anyone—including a majority of the Court—to know, and could be self-serving for anyone— including a majority of the Court—to insist, that some F is widely held to be both morally compelling and deserving of constitutional status.

I doubt that in the context of American political-legal culture—a culture in which there is a healthy skepticism about placing too great an unchecked power in any political elite's hands—any argument for a nonoriginalist approach to constitutional interpretation (at least, any such argument I can imagine) is likely to gain widespread popular support, or even much professional support (from judges and lawyers).[98] In what context, if any, might such an argument gain significant support? Imagine a country, J, whose constitution was imposed on it by another country that had recently defeated it in war. Imagine, too, that (1) although after a time many citizens of J have come to embrace the constitution, many others oppose it, and that (2) the party that has been in power since the end of the war, and that has appointed all the judges to the country's constitutional court, came to power partly on the basis of a platform of opposition to the constitution. Imagine, finally, that for various practical reasons, involving both domestic and international politics, the party in power no longer seeks to repeal the constitution but chooses, instead, to pay it lip service.[99] One can see how, in such a political-legal context, the originalist approach to the interpretation of the constitution might have little appeal and a nonoriginalist approach that marginalized the constitution—by ignoring the directives it was originally understood to represent and, instead, imputing to it thin, inconsequential directives—might have considerable appeal. Notice, however, that the nonoriginalist approach contemplated in this scenario involves a judicial role that is relatively small/passive, vis à vis the other institutions of government, rather than large/active. "Nonoriginalism . . . is a two-way street that handles traffic both to and from individual rights."[100]

It is not impossible, therefore, to imagine the outlines of a coherent argument for a nonoriginalist approach to constitutional interpretation. But the context in which that argument might be credible is worlds removed from the political-legal context of the United States. In the absence of an argument for nonoriginalism that is persuasive, or even plausible, in the context of American political-legal culture, the serious question, in my view, is not whether the originalist approach should inform the practice of judicial review (it should) but what follows from that fact—and what does not follow from it. I explain, in the next two chapters, that pursuing the originalist approach does not necessarily involve a "minimalist" judicial practice—a practice in which the exercise of significant judicial "discretion" is negligible. Nor, as I explain, does accepting the argument for originalism commit one to accepting a minimalist practice.

4

Originalism Does Not Entail Minimalism, I: The Indeterminacy of History

As I said at the beginning of the preceding chapter, originalism is a position about constitutional interpretation, not about constitutional specification. Judicial "minimalism", as I shall call it, comprises two distinct but complementary positions. The first position, which we may call "interpretive minimalism", is about the Court's proper role in interpreting the constitutional text. The second position—"normative minimalism"—is about the Court's proper role in specifying the indeterminate directives represented by the text. I discuss the two positions—their complementarity, the considerations supporting or opposing them, and related matters—in chapter 6. For now suffice it to say that grounding each of the two positions is the view that there should be relatively little opportunity for a judge's own "subjectivity"—for her own political-moral values, her own "tastes," "preferences," etc.—to influence her resolution of the constitutional conflicts with which she must deal. As Robert Bork has put the point: "In a constitutional democracy the moral content of law must [never] be given . . . by the morality of the judge. . . . That abstinence from giving his own desires free play, that continuous and self-conscious renunciation of power, that is the morality of the jurist."[1]

Many people—judges and others—who find originalism an attractive approach to constitutional interpretation do so, like Bork, at least partly because, and some of them principally because, they believe that originalism entails a minimalist judicial role. They believe that the originalist approach, if properly understood and followed, entails—that it necessarily eventuates in—a relatively small or passive judicial role in constitutional adjudication, rather than in a relatively large or active role; they believe that originalism entails a process of constitutional adjudication that is more "legal" than "political". Relatedly, many critics of the modern Supreme Court's "activism," which they see as illegitimately political—

most prominently, perhaps, Robert Bork—think that originalism gives them the needed constitutional-theoretical ground from which to mount a fundamental assault on the legitimacy of much of the modern Court's work product.

There *is* a sense in which the judicial role under originalism is smaller or more passive than the judicial role under some imaginable nonoriginalist positions. Under originalism the Court is to enforce as constitutional only directives with a particular pedigree: directives represented by the constitutional text as originally understood. Under an imaginable nonoriginalism, by contrast, the Court may enforce directives represented by the constitutional text as it, the Court, understands the text, even if the directives are not represented by the text as originally understood. Nonetheless, as I begin to explain in this chapter, the originalist approach to constitutional interpretation does not entail—it does not necessarily eventuate in—a small or passive judicial role; the originalist approach is not necessarily inconsistent with a judicial role as large or active as any apostle of "the Warren Court" (I count myself one) could reasonably want. Relatedly, and as I illustrate in chapters 8 and 9, it is a mistake to think that originalism is an adequate basis for challenging the legitimacy of most, or even many, of the "activist" decisions that have so exercised the modern Court's fiercest critics, like Bork.

I

There are circumstances under which the originalist approach would entail a minimalist judicial role—a role in which the exercise of significant judicial "discretion" is negligible—but those circumstances rarely exist with respect to the constitutional provisions that ground most constitutional decision making. If there were invariably, or almost invariably, only one conclusion to the historical inquiry constitutive of the originalist approach to constitutional interpretation—the inquiry into the original meaning of a constitutional provision—that one could plausibly reach, and if the directive represented by the provision as originally understood were invariably, or almost invariably, a relatively determinate one, then originalism would, in that sense, "entail" a minimalist judicial role. An originalist judge could plausibly reach only one conclusion about the original understanding of the provision, and the directive represented by the provision as originally understood would, because determinate, leave negligible room for judicial discretion.

By "room for judicial discretion", I mean simply room for the kind of contestable judgments a court must make in the process of specifying indeterminate legal materials: judgments about which judges can reasonably disagree. I discuss the indeterminacy of (some) constitutional directives—what I call "the indeterminacy of (constitutional) morality"—in the next chapter; I also discuss, in the next chapter, the matter of specifying constitutional indeterminacy; in chapter 6, I discuss the judicial process of specification. For present purposes it suffices to say that a constitutional directive is determinate in the context of a conflict to which it is relevant, a conflict in which it is implicated, if and to the extent persons who agree about (1) what the relevant facts are, (2) what the other relevant norms are, and (3) what the implications of those other norms for the conflict are, cannot reasonably disagree with one another about how, given the directive, the conflict should be resolved; a directive is indeterminate in the context of a conflict to which it is relevant, by contrast, if and to the extent persons (who agree about what the relevant facts are, etc.) can reasonably disagree about how, given the directive, the conflict should be resolved.[2]

The originalist approach does not entail a minimalist judicial role because, as I illustrate in this chapter (and also in chapter 7, in discussing the ongoing controversy about the original meaning of the Fourteenth Amendment), (1) there is often more than one plausible conclusion to the inquiry into the original meaning of a constitutional provision, more than one conclusion an originalist judge can plausibly reach; in that sense, the historical inquiry constitutive of the originalist approach is often indeterminate; and (2) according to at least one of those conclusions the directive represented by the provision as originally understood is often relatively indeterminate in the context of the conflicts, or of many of them, to which it is relevant.

A reading of the original meaning of a constitutional provision is plausible if, based on the available historical data, a person could reasonably speculate that the reading more likely than not captures the original meaning of the provision. To say that more than one reading of original meaning is plausible is to say that persons can reasonably disagree about which reading more likely than not captures the original meaning.[3]

What is an originalist judge to do, or likely to do, when confronted by the indeterminacy of constitutional history? (In the next chapter, I ask what she is likely to do when confronted by the indeterminacy of constitutional morality.) Her conception of proper judicial role is one of the principal factors that influences an originalist judge to embrace one plausible conclusion about the original meaning of a constitutional provision rather than another plausible conclusion when there is more than one plausible conclusion to the inquiry and when according to at least one of those conclusions the directive represented by the provision as originally understood is relatively indeterminate. (Of course, judges differ in their self-awareness. Some judges may be very aware of the various influences on them; others may be only dimly aware, if aware at all.) As I illustrate in this chapter, an originalist judge with a minimalist conception of proper judicial role (like Antonin Scalia) is more likely to embrace a plausible conclusion according to which the directive represented by a constitutional provision as originally understood is relatively determinate than she is to

embrace a competing plausible conclusion according to which the directive represented by the provision is relatively indeterminate, because a
determinate directive leaves less room for judicial discretion than does an
indeterminate one. By contrast, an originalist judge less troubled by the
exercise of judicial discretion is less likely to shy away from a plausible
conclusion according to which the directive represented by a constitutional provision as originally understood is relatively indeterminate. In
short, the institutional consequences of embracing one plausible conclusion about the original meaning of a constitutional provision rather than
another plausible conclusion—as a judge sees and, in terms of her conception of judicial role, evaluates those consequences—incline the judge
to embrace one conclusion rather than another.

Apart from the likelihood that a judge's conception of proper judicial
role will dispose her to see one plausible conclusion about the original
meaning of a constitutional provision as at least somewhat more plausible, all things considered, than another plausible conclusion, a judge may
have a rule of thumb, based on her conception of proper judicial role, for
choosing between what seem to her to be equally plausible conclusions
about the original meaning of a constitutional provision.[4] The more likely
scenario, however, is surely the one in which a judge's conception of
proper judicial role influences her actually to see one plausible conclusion
about original meaning as at least somewhat more plausible than another
plausible conclusion: After all, perfect equipoise at the end of an historical
inquiry is as rare among individual judges as it is among individual historians. (This is not to deny that there is sometimes room, at the end of an
historical inquiry, for reasonable disagreement among judges [and histo-
rians] about which conclusion is more plausible.) So, my basic point here
is not about a judge self-consciously choosing, on the basis of her conception of proper judicial role, between what seem to her to be equally plausible conclusions about original meaning; instead, my point is about a
judge being influenced by her conception of judicial role to see one plausible conclusion as somewhat more plausible than another plausible conclusion—than another conclusion, that is, that a different judge could
reasonably believe to be the more plausible conclusion about original
meaning.

One might be tempted to argue that even if the circumstances under
which the originalist approach would clearly entail a minimalist judicial
role rarely exist, originalism nonetheless entails a minimalist judicial role,
because the originalist approach to constitutional interpretation calls for a
judge to resolve indeterminate historical inquiries into original meaning
in favor of the more determinate reading—the reading of original meaning according to which the directive represented by a provision is more
determinate or, equivalently, less indeterminate—rather than in favor of
the more indeterminate one. However, the originalist approach (as distinct from the minimalist approach) to constitutional interpretation does
not require that a judge resolve indeterminate historical inquiries into

original meaning in favor of the more determinate reading. The originalist approach, presented at length in the preceding chapter, leaves ample
room for the play of competing views about how the Court should resolve
indeterminate inquiries into original meaning.

Persisting, one might argue that even if the originalist approach to
constitutional interpretation does not itself call for a judge to resolve indeterminate historical inquiries into original meaning in favor of the more
determinate reading, the argument for the originalist approach, as distinct from the approach itself, somehow commits one who accepts the
argument to accept as well the interpretive-minimalist approach. Put
another way, one might insist that, at bottom, the argument for the originalist approach is also an argument for the interpretive-minimalist
approach. The argument for the originalist approach, however, is not such
an argument; indeed, it is quite distinct from the argument for the interpretive-minimalist approach.

Interpretive minimalism (i.e., the argument for the interpretive-minimalist approach) holds that in interpreting a provision of the constitutional text, and given a choice between two or more readings of the meaning of the provision, one of which is more determinate than the other, a
judge should opt for the more determinate reading—the reading according to which the directive reresents the more determinate directive—if
each of the readings has substantially equal plausibility for the judge. One
can be both an originalist and an interpretive minimalist. Originalism
(i.e., the argument for the originalist approach) holds that in interpreting
a constitutional provision, a judge should privilege the original meaning
of the provision. Minimalist originalism holds that given a choice between
two or more readings of the original meaning, one of which is more determinate than the other, a judge should opt for the more determinate reading if each of the readings has substantially equal historical plausibility for
the judge. Thus, as positions about constitutional interpretation (rather
than about constitutional specification), interpretive minimalism and originalism do not compete with, but complement, one another. But that they
complement one another should not obscure the fact that nowhere does
originalism either presuppose or entail any premise that requires the
embrace of the interpretive-minimalist approach.

Interpretive minimalism, as I explain in chapter 6, is fundamentally
an argument about the importance of limiting the discretion, in constitutional cases, of a politically unaccountable judiciary. By contrast, originalism, as the preceding chapter confirms, is fundamentally an argument
about what "the Constitution" is and what it should mean, therefore, for
any institution (and not just a court) charged with protecting the Constitution—including the Congress, the president, and a state legislature—to
"interpret" the constitutional text. The argument for the interpretive-minimalist approach, *but not the argument for the originalist approach,* is focused
just on the judiciary: on its proper constitutional-adjudicatory role in relation to the other branches and agencies of government. Although the argu-

ment *about* the originalist approach understandably arises principally in the context of debates about proper *judicial* role, the argument *for* the originalist approach is an argument for a particular approach to the interpretation of the constitutional text not just by the judiciary, but by any institution charged with protecting the Constitution. Like the originalist approach itself, the argument for the originalist approach leaves ample room for the play of competing views about how the Court—or any other institution charged with protecting the Constitution—should resolve indeterminate historical inquiries into original meaning.

Although, again, a judge can be both an originalist and an interpretive minimalist, a judge can also be both an originalist and an interpretive non-minimalist, that is, a judge who, given a choice between two or more readings of the original meaning of a constitutional provision, one of which is more determinate than the other, does not necessarily opt for the more determinate reading when each of the readings has substantially equal historical plausibility for her. (Of course, for an originalist judge to opt against the reading that has substantially more historical plausibility for her, whether that reading be the more determinate one or the less determinate one, is obviously for her to compromise her originalism.) In short, while one can be both an originalist and an interpretive minimalist, one can also, without acting inconsistently, accept originalism but reject interpretive minimalism. Originalism simply does not hold that indeterminate historical inquiries into original meaning should invariably be resolved in favor of the more determinate reading and against the more indeterminate reading.

Consider, as an illustration of how an originalist judge's conception of proper judicial role influences her reading of the original meaning of a constitutional provision, the case of Justice Scalia and the free exercise clause. The First Amendment provides, in relevant part, that "Congress shall make no law . . . prohibiting the free exercise [of religion]". Does the free exercise clause as originally understood represent merely the directive that government is not to discriminate against one or more religions, that it is not to enact any *discriminatory* prohibitions on the free exercise of religion? Or does the clause (as originally understood) represent the directive that government is not only not to enact any discriminatory prohibitions, but that government is to exempt religious practices even from *nondiscriminatory* prohibitions when not impracticable for government to do so? If a law forbids only the drinking of wine at Mass, the law violates the first, or antidiscrimination, directive. If a law forbids the drinking of wine in any and all circumstances, the law does not violate the first directive,[5] but it may violate the second, or antidiscrimination-plus-exemption, directive if the law fails to exempt the drinking of wine at Mass.

Antonin Scalia is a prominent proponent of originalism.[6] So is Michael McConnell.[7] Justice Scalia and Professor McConnell disagree about the original meaning of the free exercise clause. McConnell has mounted a strong argument that the directive represented by the free exercise clause as originally understood is the antidiscrimination-plus-exemption directive and not (merely) the antidiscrimination directive.[8] McConnell acknowledges, however, that the historical record does not speak unequivocally;[9] and, indeed, one could plausibly conclude, as some other scholars have, that the clause as originally understood probably represented no more than the antidiscrimination directive.[10] McConnell's reading of the original meaning of the free exercise clause has clear implications for judicial role. If an aspect of the original meaning of the clause is that government must sometimes (namely, when not impracticable) exempt a religious practice, then the courts' role in enforcing the clause is, to that extent, larger and somewhat more "discretionary": The courts must guard against not only discriminatory prohibitions, which today are rare; they must, as well, decide when government must exempt from nondiscriminatory prohibitions religious activity that, for whatever reason, government has declined to exempt. That institutional consequence of McConnell's reading is troubling for Justice Scalia, who, after all, is a prominent proponent, not only of originalism, but also of a very small role for courts—a role involving minimal judicial discretion—in adjudicating constitutional issues.[11]

And, indeed, Scalia's minimalist conception of proper judicial role certainly seems to have influenced his conclusion, in *Employment Division v. Smith*, that the free exercise clause represents, not the antidiscrimination-plus-exemption directive, but only the antidiscrimination directive.[12] McConnell has observed that, "[i]nterestingly, the Court did not pause to consider whether the historical context surrounding the adoption of the Free Exercise Clause might have a bearing on the two permissible [i.e., linguistically plausible] readings of the text. This is particularly surprising because the author of the majority opinion, Justice Scalia, has been one of the Court's foremost exponents of the view that the Constitution should be interpreted in light of its original meaning."[13]

That Justice Scalia's minimalist conception of proper judicial role almost certainly dictated his reading of the free exercise clause is consistent with what Scalia himself has said about the influence of his conception of judicial role on his interpretive practice. Scalia's essay "The Rule of Law as the Law of Rules"[14] is largely an argument for the interpretive-minimalist approach; allied with originalism, the argument holds that given a choice between two or more plausible readings of the original meaning, a judge should opt for the more determinate reading. Scalia announced, in the essay, that he was "inclined to disfavor" a reading of a statute or of a constitutional provision according to which the Court has a relatively indeterminate principle to enforce:

> In the area of the negative Commerce Clause, for example, it seems to me one thing to undertake uninvited judicial enforcement of the principle (never enunciated by Congress) that a state cannot overtly discriminate against interstate commerce. That is a general principle clear in

itself, and there can be little variation in applying it to the facts. It is quite something else, however, to recognize a cause of action to challenge state laws that do not overtly discriminate against interstate commerce, but affect it to an excessive degree, given the value of the state interests thereby protected. The latter can only be adjudged by a standardless balancing, and so I am not inclined to find an invitation for such judicial enforcement within Article I of the Constitution.[15]

Nor, for much the same reason, was Justice Scalia inclined to read the free exercise clause the way his fellow originalist Michael McConnell has argued, powerfully, that an originalist judge should read it. Given Scalia's studied inattention, in *Employment Division v. Smith*, to the history of the free exercise clause, could it be that in cases of conflict Justice Scalia's minimalist conception of proper judicial role trumps, or sometimes trumps, his commitment to the originalist conception of constitutional interpretation?[16] The point is not that Scalia failed to embrace McConnell's reading, but that he, a self-proclaimed originalist, failed even to address the question of original meaning.

Be that as it may, it does seem clear that an originalist judge's conception of proper judicial role may well influence the outcome of her inquiry into original meaning when the available historical materials render plausible, as they often do, more than one conclusion about original meaning. Indeed, an originalist judge's conception of judicial role may influence the outcome of her inquiry even when, to an impartial observer, the available historical materials render plausible only one conclusion about original meaning: a conclusion the judge, given her conception of proper judicial role, finds uncongenial. Of course, that might be true of an originalist judge with a nonminimalist conception of proper judicial role no less than of an originalist judge with a minimalist conception.

I have just been emphasizing that which of the available readings of the original meaning of a constitutional provision an originalist judge is inclined to see, or to choose, as the most plausible will almost certainly, if not inevitably, be influenced by her conception of proper judicial role. Depending on how much discretion her conception of judicial role commends to her, which of the available readings a judge is inclined to see/choose as the most plausible—a more determinate reading, or a more indeterminate one[17]—will almost certainly be influenced, as well, by her political-moral values: Given her political morality, one of the historically plausible conclusions may be more congenial to her—may make the constitutional provision whose original meaning is in question more attractive to her—than any of the other historically plausible conclusions. Earlier I said that a judge's evaluation (in terms of her conception of proper judicial role) of what she believes to be the likely institutional consequences of embracing one or another plausible conclusion about original meaning may well influence her to embrace one conclusion rather than another. Similarly, a judge's evaluation (in terms of her political morality) of what she believes to be the likely consequences for the well-being of the political community may well influence her to embrace one conclusion about original meaning rather than another.[18]

It would be a mistake to understand the process of influence described here—the influence of a judge's conception of proper judicial role, and perhaps (depending on her conception of judicial role) of her political morality, on her inquiry into the original meaning of a constitutional provision—simply as a forward-looking, "result-oriented" process. To an extent, the process is result-oriented, in this sense: As between two (or more) plausible conclusions about the original meaning of a constitutional provision, a judge is likely inclined to favor the conclusion that, in her view, has the better consequences as measured by her conception of judicial role or by her political morality (or by both) rather than the conclusion that, in her view, has the worse institutional or political-moral consequences. That a judge is likely so inclined seems quite natural and altogether unproblematic. Should she favor the conclusion that, in her view, has the worse consequences? Should she try to ignore—to "bracket"—her conception of judicial role and/or her political morality in reaching a conclusion? By hypothesis we are talking about a situation in which there are at least two plausible conclusions about original meaning. In that case, "the decision to read the Constitution narrowly, and thereby 'restrain' judicial interpretation, is not a decision that can be read directly from the text. The Constitution does not say, 'Read me broadly,' or 'Read me narrowly.' That decision must be made as a matter of political theory, and will depend on such things as one's view of the springs of judicial legitimacy and of the relative competence of courts and legislatures in dealing with particular types of issues."[19] None of this is to deny that a particular judge's conception of proper judicial role, or her political morality, or both, may be deeply problematic. (I argue later in this book that a minimalist conception of proper judicial role is indeed problematic in some contexts.)

To an extent, however, the process is not forward-looking or result-oriented, but backward-looking, in this sense: As between two plausible conclusions about the original meaning of a constitutional provision, a judge is likely inclined to favor, as somewhat more plausible, the conclusion that speculatively imputes to our political ancestors a position, whether about proper judicial role or about some political-moral issue, that seems quite sensible to the judge rather than the conclusion that imputes to them a position that seems to her decidedly less sensible, if not downright silly. That a judge is likely so inclined seems not only natural, but charitable. "As between any two logically, linguistically, and historically permissible interpretations, if one of them conforms to what the instant judge can accept as a correct or reasonable view of constitutional policy and value, and the other does not, the judge hardly can refrain from preferring the conforming interpretation; that is merely interpretive charity."[20]

II

I now want to examine the controversy about the original meaning of the Ninth Amendment, which nicely illustrates that historical inquiry into the original meaning of a constitutional provision does not always yield just a single plausible conclusion about the directive represented by the provision as originally understood; the relevant historical materials sometimes render plausible more than one conclusion. Moreover, the controversy illustrates that which of the available readings of the original meaning of a constitutional provision an originalist judge is inclined to see, or to choose, as the most plausible will almost certainly be influenced by her conception of judicial role. Although I focus here on the Ninth Amendment, it bears emphasis that one could focus, to the very same effect, on any of a number of other important constitutional provisions, especially provisions, like the free exercise clause, regarding rights or liberties. And, indeed, the controversy about the original meaning of section 1 of the Fourteenth Amendment—a controversy I discuss in chapter 7—strongly confirms that the available historical materials sometimes render plausible more than one conclusion about the original meaning of constitutional provisions regarding rights or liberties.

According to the Ninth Amendment, "The enumeration in the Constitution, of certain rights, shall not be construed to deny or disparage others retained by the people."[21] The Constitution, in the first eight amendments of the Bill of Rights and elsewhere, enumerates "certain rights"—certain *constitutional* rights—for example, the right (or, more precisely, the privilege) that is the correlative of government's duty under the First Amendment to refrain from enacting laws prohibiting the free exercise of religion. The Ninth Amendment is addressed to the possibility that someone—in particular, presumably, some part of the national government, whose powers the Bill of Rights was meant to limit[22]—might infer from the fact of the Constitution's enumerating certain constitutional rights that the people did not retain other, unenumerated constitutional rights.[23] The Ninth Amendment delegitimates that inference; it directs that the fact that certain rights are enumerated in the Constitution is not to be used to support the claim that the people have ("retain") no other, unenumerated constitutional rights.

The Ninth Amendment does not state that the people have other, unenumerated constitutional rights. But it does, on any plausible reading, presuppose that they do: Absent the presupposition that the people retain other, unenumerated constitutional rights, there would be no reason to delegitimate the inference (from the fact of the Constitution's enumerating certain rights) that they do not retain them.[24] And, indeed, in the view of many scholars, the relevant historical materials amply support the conclusion that the Ninth Amendment was meant to protect, against the national government, unenumerated constitutional rights by delegitimating the inference that they have no such rights.[25] The serious question concerns the nature of the rights meant to be protected by the Amendment.

In 1990, in an impressive dissent from the conclusion of many other scholars,[26] Thomas McAffee argued that the unenumerated rights meant to be protected, as constitutional rights of "the people" (both collectively and individually) against the national government, are simply "residual" rights: rights entailed by the fact that the national government is not a government of general powers, but only one of delegated powers; in particular, the protected unenumerated rights are not, in McAffee's view, "affirmative" rights: rights in the form of affirmative constitutional limitations on the delegated national powers.

> [The] residual rights reading sees the ninth amendment as designed to preserve the scheme of limited powers for securing interests that include, but are not necessarily limited to, traditional sorts of individual rights.
>
> The [affirmative rights reading], on the other hand, holds that the ninth amendment refers to constitutional rights as we generally think of them today—legally enforceable, affirmatively defined limitations on governmental power on behalf of individual claimants. . . . [The rights the adherents of the affirmative rights reading] conceive of are to be defined independently of, and may serve to limit the scope of, powers granted to the national government by the Constitution.[27]

A basic problem with McAffee's skillfully defended reading of the Ninth Amendment—a reading that scholars before McAffee had tendered,[28] but none, perhaps, so ably as McAffee—is that it seems to make the Ninth functionally equivalent to the Tenth, which provides: "The powers not delegated to the United States by the Constitution, nor prohibited by it to the States, are reserved to the States respectively, or to the people." Given McAffee's reading, the Ninth Amendment seems to bear no weight in constitutional analysis not already born by the Tenth. Out of fear that the inference might arise, from the fact that there was nothing in the Constitution explicitly to the contrary, that the national government is one of general powers, the Tenth Amendment, which makes explicit that it is a government only of delegated powers—thereby delegitimating the feared inference—was proposed and eventually ratified. According to McAffee, there was also a fear that the very same inference might arise from a different fact, namely, the fact of the Constitution enumerating, in the Bill of Rights, certain affirmative limitations on the national government. The reason for that fear (according to McAffee) is that at the time the Bill of Rights was proposed, Bill of Rights-type provisions were devices for limiting governments of general powers; some therefore feared that in enumerating affirmative limitations on the national government the Bill of Rights might be taken to imply that the national government is one of general powers. In McAffee's view, the Ninth Amendment, as distinct from the Tenth, was meant to prohibit "an inference that the Constitution's general reservation of rights was undermined by inclusion of specific limitations on governmental power. . . . [The] purpose [of the Ninth Amendment] was to prevent the inference of a government of general powers from the provision in a bill of rights for specific limitations on behalf of individual rights."[29]

The problem with McAffee's argument, however, is that whether the inference that the national government is one of general powers might have arisen from (1) the fact that prior to the Tenth Amendment the Constitution did not make explicit that the national government was one only of delegated powers, or (2) the fact of the Bill of Rights enumerating certain affirmative limitations on the national government, or both, the Tenth Amendment delegitimates the inference. It is difficult to see, therefore, the point of a Ninth Amendment that does only what the Tenth Amendment does and nothing more, namely, delegitimates the inference.[30]

A great strength of the affirmative rights reading of the Ninth Amendment, relative to McAffee's residual rights reading, is that it makes the Ninth complement rather than duplicate the Tenth Amendment. Whereas the Tenth Amendment emphasizes, by making explicit, the fundamental principle that the powers not delegated by the Constitution to the national government ("nor prohibited by it to the States") are reserved by the Constitution to the governments of the states "or to the people", the Ninth Amendment (according to the affirmative rights reading) emphasizes, by making explicit, the different, further principle that the delegated national powers—the powers *not* reserved to the states or to the people—are not only limited in character, but more limited than one might have been tempted, but for the Ninth Amendment, to think; they are limited not only by the constitutional rights—the *affirmative* constitutional rights—enumerated in the Constitution, especially in the Bill of Rights; they are limited also by "other rights retained by the people"— other, unenumerated affirmative constitutional rights. According to the affirmative rights reading, the power of the national government—the national government that was born in 1789 and that was understandably threatening to some of those present at its birth—was deliberately limited in two basic ways: First, the United States does not possess any powers not delegated to it by the Constitution, powers not delegated are reserved to the states or to the people (the Tenth Amendment); second, powers delegated to the United States by the Constitution are limited both by affirmative rights enumerated in the Constitution and by other, unenumerated affirmative constitutional rights (the Ninth Amendment).[31]

The charge of functional equivalence, however, as McAffee understands, is not fatal: "[T]he ninth and tenth amendments are widely recognized as provisions that were both intended to play a largely redundant, clarifying role. Madison, for one, believed that the tenth amendment was intentionally redundant."[32] Assuming that McAffee's historical reconstruction, though undeniably controversial,[33] is plausible[34]—McAffee's essay *is* impressive—the debate about the original meaning of the Ninth

Amendment confirms that historical inquiry does not always yield just a single plausible conclusion about the original meaning of a constitutional provision; the relevant historical materials often render plausible more than one conclusion. And where more than one conclusion is plausible, it seems altogether likely, as I explained earlier in this chapter, that a judge will be inclined to credit as more (or most) plausible the conclusion whose institutional implications are more congenial to her conception of proper judicial role. (It is also possible that even when only one conclusion is plausible a judge will be inclined to credit as more plausible a conclusion that is in fact inferior, if the institutional implications of the conclusion are more congenial to her conception of judicial role. It is even possible that in doing so the judge is acting in good faith.)

An originalist judge with a minimalist's aversion to the exercise of (significant) judicial discretion (former Judge Bork, for example, or Justice Scalia) has an obvious and strong practical incentive to embrace McAffee's version—the residual rights version—of the original meaning of the Ninth Amendment, because then she will never have to decide whether an affirmative right allegedly violated by the national government in the exercise of one of its delegated powers is a right "retained by the people" within the (original) meaning of the Ninth Amendment. That the national government is exercising one of its delegated powers—that it is not acting ultra vires—logically entails, given McAffee's reading of the Ninth Amendment, that the national government is not violating any right "retained by the people" within the meaning of the Ninth Amendment. By contrast, an originalist judge with minimalist proclivities who happens to accept that the Ninth Amendment was meant to protect affirmative constitutional limitations on governmental power is in a bind: Either she must explain why courts should not enforce any affirmative rights "retained by the people" within the meaning of the Ninth Amendment or she must articulate, and follow, a minimalist way of identifying such rights—a way that minimizes, that leaves minimal room for, the exercise of judicial discretion. Of course, any judge, minimalist or not, who accepts that the Ninth Amendment was meant to protect affirmative rights in the form of affirmative limitations on governmental power faces the problem of articulating a way of identifying such rights.[35] In chapter 8, I present two complementary strategies for identifying the rights in question. As it happens, the strategies I present are relatively minimalist; they involve the exercise of minimal judicial discretion.[36]

Assuming the Ninth Amendment was meant to protect affirmative and not merely residual rights, it is difficult to discern a credible justification for courts declining to enforce them (whatever they are).[37] I am inclined to agree with John Ely: "There is a difference between ignoring a provision, such as the First Amendment, because you don't like its specific substantive implications and ignoring a provision, such as the Ninth Amendment, because you don't like its institutional implications. But it's hard to make it a difference that should count."[38] An originalist judge who is also a minimalist and who accepts that the Ninth Amendment was meant to protect affirmative constitutional rights might say that although she would enforce such rights—the other, unenumerated rights retained by the people—if she could locate them, she cannot locate them, at least not with any confidence. But even that stance seems to require that in particular cases she entertain the possibility that an affirmative right allegedly violated by the government is one of the other, unenumerated rights "retained by the people" within the meaning of the Ninth Amendment. There is, moreover, Judge Morris Arnold's sensible point, which is in no way inconsistent with the premises of originalism (although in no way entailed by them either):

> [W]e can give meaning to the ninth amendment, without giving it any particular content, by ascribing to it a kind of supplementary role. The ninth amendment can usefully serve as a directive that rights ought to be taken seriously. It is altogether plausible to take the position that the ninth amendment serves as a direction to us to adopt a broad view and liberal construction of the first eight amendments and to regard the personal liberties enumerated there as deserving the most meticulous, fastidious, and expansive protection. At the very least, this would mean that in doubtful cases the balance ought to be struck against the existence of governmental power. A judicious use of the amendment in this way could create a constitutional jurisprudence which sees government powers "as islands surrounded by a sea of individual rights" rather than seeing "rights as islands surrounded by a sea of government powers." Such a role for the ninth amendment could radically alter the outcome of many cases. It at least satisfies the need to give meaning to everything in the Constitution, not to mention the duty to defend freedom.[39]

The practical incentive for an originalist judge hostile to the exercise of judicial discretion is clear and strong, therefore, to embrace McAffee's version of the original meaning of the Ninth Amendment—and thereby avoid even Judge Arnold's modest proposal for "giving meaning" to the Ninth Amendment—even though according to another plausible version the Amendment was meant to protect affirmative rights (though not necessarily only affirmative rights): "As a critique internal to originalism, . . . establishment of the affirmative rights reading would undercut the claim of many that originalism can significantly constrain constitutional decision makers. If originalists are to take their own theory seriously, it is difficult to see how they could ignore a constitutional provision prohibiting an inference against denying or disparaging unwritten affirmative limitations on governmental power."[40] What, then, is an originalist-minimalist judge to do, short of ignoring the Ninth Amendment? McAffee's counsel to such a judge is congenial to my argument about the influence of conceptions of proper judicial role on indeterminate inquiries into original meaning: "If . . . the evidence as to the original meaning of the ninth amendment is simply indeterminate, Bork and Meese would not contradict their professed commitment to originalism by deciding in favor of an

interpretation that renders the Constitution the most meaningful in originalist terms."[41]

What McAffee meant to say, I think—and in any event what one
should say—is not "most meaningful in originalist terms" but "most
meaningful in minimalist terms", most meaningful in terms of Bork's and
Meese's minimalist (hostile to judicial discretion) conception of proper
judicial role. McAffee mistakenly conflated originalism and judicial minimalism. But, again, both the originalist approach and the argument for
the approach leave ample room for the play of competing views about
how the Court should resolve indeterminate historical inquiries into original meaning—and about how deferentially or nondeferentially the Court
should specify indeterminate constitutional directives. One can be both
an originalist and a minimalist (both interpretive and normative), but one
need not be.

An originalist judge need not accept a minimalist conception of proper
judicial role, and indeed not every originalist judge does accept such a
conception. McAffee's counsel therefore speaks to originalist judges with
an other than minimalist conception—a Judge Morris Arnold, for example—no less than it speaks to a Judge Bork or a Justice Scalia: If the historical evidence of the original meaning of the Ninth Amendment is indeterminate,[42] an originalist judge with a nonminimalist conception of
judicial role would not contradict her professed commitment to originalism by deciding in favor of an interpretation—a plausible interpretation—that renders the Ninth Amendment most meaningful in terms of
her nonminimalist conception of proper judicial role. (Of course, an originalist judge who on the basis of her conception of proper judicial role—
whether that conception is minimalist or nonminimalist—decides in favor
of an interpretation of a constitutional provision that seems to her less
plausible, even if only slightly less, than a competing interpretation is not
unqualifiedly committed to the originalist approach. For the reason I gave
earlier in this chapter, in discussing Justice Scalia's curious performance in
Employment Division v. Smith—his studied inattention to the relevant history—it is a fair question whether Justice Scalia is not such a judge.)

The relevant historical materials permit, even if they do not require, an
originalist judge to conclude that the Ninth Amendment was meant to
protect unenumerated affirmative constitutional limitations. (Indeed, they
arguably permit that conclusion more easily than they permit the conclusion that the Amendment was not meant to protect such limitations—that,
instead, it was meant to protect *only* residual rights.[43]) Because an originalist judge can, in good faith, so conclude, it should be clear why, as I
said at the beginning of this chapter and elaborate in succeeding chapters, originalism is a much less promising ground from which to mount
an assault on the legitimacy of the modern Supreme Court's constitutional
work product than many of the Court's severest critics, like Robert Bork,
have seemed to understand. It should be clear, too, why the principal

focus of constitutional-theoretical debate should be not the competing approaches to constitutional interpretation—originalism, as elaborated in the preceding chapter, is a compelling position—but the competing conceptions of the role courts should play, especially the Supreme Court, both in resolving indeterminate historical inquiries into original meaning and, then, in specifying indeterminate constitutional directives. I hope it will be clear by the end of this book that the differences that explain most of the real-world debate about the legitimacy of this or that aspect of modern constitutional doctrine are differences, not about originalism versus nonoriginalism (much less about textualism versus nontextualism), but about the role the Court should play in confronting the indeterminacy both of constitutional history and of constitutional morality.

5

Originalism Does Not Entail Minimalism, II: The Indeterminacy of Morality

An originalist approach to the interpretation of the constitutional text does not entail a minimalist judicial role—a role in which the exercise of judicial discretion is negligible—because, as I explained in the preceding chapter, (1) there is often more than one plausible conclusion to the inquiry into the original meaning of a constitutional provision, more than one conclusion an originalist judge can plausibly reach; in that sense, the historical inquiry constitutive of the originalist approach is often indeterminate; and (2) according to at least one of those conclusions the directive represented by the provision as originally understood is often relatively indeterminate in the context of the conflicts, or of many of them, to which it is relevant. In the preceding chapter, I asked what an originalist judge is likely to do when confronted by the indeterminacy of constitutional history—the indeterminacy of historical inquiry into original meaning. Now the question is what an originalist judge is likely to do when confronted by the indeterminacy of constitutional morality—the indeterminacy of a constitutional directive.

I

The process of constitutional adjudication comprises two basic inquiries. The first inquiry—the "interpretive" inquiry—is focused on a provision of the constitutional text, which, in the political community, may be opaque, vague, ambiguous, and so on. The aim of the interpretive inquiry is to translate or decode the text, it is to render the text intelligible by identifying the directive or directives represented by the text. For an originalist judge, the interpretive inquiry is an historical inquiry, the object of which is the directive represented by the text as originally understood. The second basic inquiry—the "normative" inquiry—is focused on an indeterminate directive represented by the constitutional text. The aim of the normative inquiry is to specify or shape the directive, it is to render the directive determinate in a particular context—the context of the particular conflict to be resolved—by establishing the concrete meaning of the directive in that context. Hans-Georg Gadamer insisted that "[a] law is not there to be understood historically, but to be made concretely valid through being interpreted."[1] The aim of the normative inquiry, pace Gadamer, is to make the indeterminate directive believed to be represented by the constitutional text "concretely valid" in the context of the conflict to be resolved. I have defended the distinction between the interpretive inquiry and the normative inquiry—and I have emphasized the difference between that distinction and the different, problematic distinction Gadamer rightly criticized (between "understanding" a norm and "applying" the norm)—in chapter 3.[2]

I explained in the preceding chapter that an originalist judge's conception of proper judicial role can exert an important influence on her as she pursues the interpretive inquiry into the original meaning of a constitutional provision. And, if and to the extent her conception of proper judicial role leaves room for it, a judge's political morality—that part of it other than her conception of proper judicial role—can exert an important influence on her as she pursues the interpretive inquiry. Both her conception of judicial role and her political morality can incline her to resolve an indeterminate inquiry into original meaning one way rather than another. It is similarly the case that a judge's conception of judicial role and her political morality can each exert an important influence on the judge as she pursues the normative inquiry. A judge with a minimalist conception of proper judicial role—a judge who wants to minimize the exercise of significant judicial discretion—will want to defer to any reasonable (i.e., not unreasonable) specification implicit in a law or other governmental action claimed to violate an indeterminate constitutional directive. (If according to one specification of an indeterminate constitutional directive, a challenged law violates the directive, but according to another specification, the law does not violate the directive, the latter specification is, in that sense, implicit in the law.) Normative minimalism holds that a judge should minimize the exercise of judicial discretion by deferring to any reasonable specification implicit in the governmental action under review.[3] A judge with a nonminimalist conception of judicial role—a Justice Brennan—will want to resolve the conflict at hand, the case before her, on the basis of the particular specification that seems best to her even if the specification implicit in the challenged governmental action is not so beyond the pale as to be unreasonable.

Much of the discussion in the preceding chapter about the relation between originalism and interpretive minimalism is relevant to the question of the relation between originalism and normative minimalism. Three points bear emphasis here. First, it would be a mistake—a confusion—to think that after the interpretive inquiry is finished and the normative inquiry has begun, the originalist approach calls for a judge to defer to any reasonable specification implicit in the governmental act under review. The originalist approach is an approach to, and only to, constitutional inter-petation; it is not an approach to constitutional specification. The second point concerns not the originalist approach itself, but the argument for the approach: As I explained in the preceding chapter, the argument for the originalist approach to constitutional interpretation neither presupposes nor entails any premise that requires the embrace of the minimalist approach; that is no less true of the normative-minimalist approach than it is of the interpretive-minimalist approach discussed in the preceding chapter. The argument for originalism leaves ample room for the play of competing views, not only about how the Court should resolve indeterminate historical inquiries into original meaning, but also about how deferentially or nondeferentially the Court should specify indeterminate constitutional directives. One can be both an originalist and a minimalist (interpretive and normative) but one need not be. Third, like the process of influence described in the preceding chapter, and for the reason given there, the process of influence under discussion here—the influence of a judge's conception of proper judicial role, and of her political morality, on her normative inquiry—seems both natural and unproblematic.

II

In the preceding chapter, I said that a constitutional directive is indeterminate in the context of a conflict to which it is relevant, a conflict in which it is implicated, if and to the extent persons who agree about (1) what the relevant facts are, (2) what the other relevant legal norms are, and (3) what the implications of those other norms for the conflict are, can nonetheless disagree with one another—*reasonably* disagree—about how, given the directive, the conflict should be resolved. I now want to say more about the indeterminacy of constitutional directives[4]—and about the matter of "specifying" them.

The legal materials relevant to a court's resolution of a conflict are sometimes indeterminate: Judges can reasonably disagree with one another about how, given the relevant legal materials, the conflict should be resolved; more than one judgment—by which I mean result plus supporting rationale—is consistent (i.e., not inconsistent) with the relevant legal materials.[5] By "legal materials" I mean simply directives and other norms authoritative for a judge qua judge (as distinct from norms author-itative for her qua the particular person she is—Catholic, socialist, feminist, whatever). The relevant legal materials include both primary legal materials in the form of directives, which courts are charged with enforcing, and secondary legal materials in the form of norms about proper judicial role that, even if not codified as directives, are nonetheless axiomatic in our political-legal culture, and which courts are therefore expected to respect.[6] Of course, many norms about judicial role are, in our political-legal culture, contested rather than axiomatic. As Kent Greenawalt has commented, "No doubt there is room for much argument about the best conception of a judge's role, and no doubt this conception can shift significantly over time. A judge may self-consciously act upon a conception that is in some respects accepted only by a minority." But, as Greenawalt cautions, "there are limits."[7]

It is not true that the relevant legal materials are always indeterminate: Sometimes only one judgment (result plus rationale) is consistent with the relevant legal materials.[8] Nor is it true that the relevant legal materials are never indeterminate: Sometimes more than one judgment is consistent.[9] The relevant legal materials are *sometimes* indeterminate.[10]

It is important not to confuse the indeterminacy of a legal *text* with the indeterminacy of a *norm* represented by a legal text. A legal text—for example, a statute, a constitutional provision, or a prior judicial opinion—may be indeterminate in the sense that in the political community whose text it is, and given all the available relevant data, the members of the political community can reasonably disagree about what directive the text represents; more than one conclusion about what directive the text represents is plausible. The preceding chapter was addressed to such indeterminacy: the indeterminacy of legal texts ("textual indeterminacy"). (For the originalist, the indeterminacy of legal texts is "the indeterminacy of history": the indeterminacy of the inquiry into their original meaning.) A directive represented by a legal text may be indeterminate in the sense that more than one conclusion about what the directive requires in the context of the conflict to be resolved is plausible, even among persons who agree about what the relevant facts are, about what the other relevant legal norms are, including norms about judicial role axiomatic in the political-legal culture, and about what the implications of those other norms for the conflict are. This chapter is addressed to such indeterminacy: the indeterminacy of legal directives ("normative indeterminacy").[11] Textual determinacy/indeterminacy and normative determinacy/indeterminacy are independent: A legal text can be determinate in the sense that there is only one plausible conclusion about what directive the text represents, but the directive can be indeterminate in the context of the conflict to be resolved; or a legal text can be indeterminate in the sense that there is more than one plausible conclusion about what directive it represents, but one or more of the candidate directives, or even all of them, can be determinate in the context of the conflict to be resolved.

The process of "specifying", in a particular context, a norm relevant to but indeterminate in that context is the process of deciding what the norm shall mean, what it shall require, in that context. It is the process of "shaping" the norm, of rendering the norm determinate in a context to which it is relevant but in which it is (until specified) indeterminate. In adjudication the process of specification is the process of deciding what a legal directive relevant to but indeterminate in the context of the conflict to be resolved shall mean in that context, what resolution of the conflict the directive, in conjunction with all the other relevant legal norms, shall require.

An indeterminate legal directive of the sort with which I am primarily concerned here—a constitutional directive regarding a right or a liberty—represents a decision by those who constitutionalized the directive, who issued it, to privilege, against government, some political-moral value or values (or to deprivilege some disvalue). An indeterminate constitutional directive represents, that is, a decision to privilege some (indeterminate) aspect of a conception of human good—in particular, of the good or fitting way for the members of the political community to live their collective life, their life in common. Examples of such values from the Bill of Rights of the United States Constitution include: "the free exercise of religion" (First Amendment), "the freedom of speech" (same), "the freedom of the press" (same), and "due process of law" (Fifth Amendment). The United States Constitution is not distinctive among national constitutions in comprising indeterminate constitutional directives. The Japanese Constitution, to cite a foreign example, speaks of "freedom of thought and conscience" (Article 19), "freedom of religion" (Article 20), "freedom of assembly and association as well as speech, press and all other forms of expression" (Article 21); such values are "not to be violated" (Article 19) or are "guaranteed to all" (Article 21). Such examples could easily be multiplied. The Basic Law of Israel, for example, states that "[t]he . . . dignity of any person shall not be violated."[12] The challenge of specifying an indeterminate constitutional directive, then, is the challenge of deciding how best to achieve, how best to "instantiate", in a particular context, the political-moral value—the aspect of human good—embedded in the directive; it is the challenge of deciding how government can achieve the relevant political-moral value in the way that best serves all the various and sometimes competing interests of the political community at stake in the context.[13]

In *The Federalist* No. 37, James Madison commented on the need, in adjudication, for such specification: "All new laws, though penned with the greatest technical skill and passed on the fullest and most mature deliberation, are considered as more or less obscure and equivocal, until their meaning be liquidated and ascertained by a series of particular discussions and adjudications."[14] In *Truth and Method*, Hans-Georg Gadamer commented on the process of specification both in law and in theology:

> In both legal and theological hermeneutics there is the essential tension between the text set down—of the law or of the proclamation—on the one hand and, on the other, the sense arrived at by its application in the particular moment of interpretation, either in judgment or in preaching. A law is not there to be understood historically, but to be made con-

cretely valid through being interpreted. Similarly, a religious proclamation is not there to be understood as a merely historical document, but to
be taken in a way in which it exercises its saving effect. This includes the
fact that the text, whether law or gospel, if it is to be understood properly, i.e., according to the claim it makes, must be understood at every
moment, in every particular situation, in a new and different way.
Understanding here is always application.[15]

"Applying", in a particular context, a directive relevant to and determinate in that context should not be confused with "specifying", in a particular context, a directive relevant to but indeterminate in that context.
To rule that an ordinance that by its terms governs "automobiles" governs "Honda Accords" is, as I am using the terms, to "apply" the ordinance, not to "specify" it. By contrast, to construe a directive that forbids
government to prohibit any religious practice absent a compelling justification, to forbid government to prohibit the sacramental use of wine at
Mass is to "specify" the principle. Whereas the process of applying a determinate directive is essentially deductive, the process of specifying an indeterminate directive is essentially nondeductive. A specification "of a principle for a specific class of cases is not a deduction from it, nor a discovery
of some implicit meaning; it is the act of setting a more concrete and cate-
gorical requirement in the spirit of the principle, and guided both by a
sense of what is practically realizable (or enforceable), and by a recognition of the risk of conflict with other principles or values. . . ."[16] What
Anthony Kronman has said of the process of "judgment" accurately
describes the process of specifying an indeterminate directive. Such specification is a species of judgment.

> Good judgment, and its opposite, are in fact most clearly revealed in
> just those situations where the method of deduction is least applicable,
> where the ambiguities are greatest and the demand for proof most obvi-
> ously misplaced. To show good judgment in such situations is to do
> something more than merely apply a general rule with special care and
> thoroughness, or follow out its consequences to a greater level of detail.
> Judgment often requires such analytic refinement but does not consist in
> it alone. That this is so is to be explained by the fact that we are most
> dependent on our judgment, most in need of *good* judgment, in just
> those situations that pose genuine dilemmas by forcing us to choose
> between, or otherwise accommodate, conflicting interests and obliga-
> tions whose conflict is not itself amenable to resolution by the application
> of some higher-order rule. It is here that the quality of a person's judg-
> ment comes most clearly into view and here, too, that his or her deduc-
> tive powers alone are least likely to prove adequate to the task.[17]

Because the challenge of achieving one or more other important political-moral values implicated in a particular context—even one or more
other values of constitutional dimension—often competes in that context
with the challenge of achieving the value privileged by indeterminate
directive to be specified, the challenge of specifying the directive is often

quite difficult: The challenge is not merely that of making an "instrumental" choice about the most efficient means to an agreed-upon end; as Neil MacCormick's comments about specifications (or, to use MacCormick's terms, *"determinationes* or concretizations")[18] and Anthony Kronman's comments about judgment suggest, the challenge is that of making what we may call a "constitutive" choice: a choice about which value or values among two or more contextually competing values to achieve and/or about the extent to which to achieve it or them. (The most efficient means to an agreed-upon end may disserve an important value to a much greater extent than a much less efficient means; or, a much less efficient means may serve an important value to a much greater extent than the most efficient means. Whether to pursue the most efficient means or, instead, the much less efficient means is a question about which value or values to achieve and to what extent.) Such a choice is "constitutive" in the sense that it "constitutes" an aspect of the "moral identity" of the person or community who makes the choice, or on whose behalf it is made: It constitutes the person or community as *this* sort of person or community rather than *that* sort—as a person or community who, in some contexts at least, values *this* more highly than *that*.[19] Choices made in the course of specifying indeterminate constitutional directives are always at least partly constitutive in that sense rather than merely instrumental, because there are always contextually competing values at stake. "[A] court asked to apply a rule must decide in light of information not available to the promulgators of the rule, what the rule should mean in its new setting. That is a creative decision, involving discretion, the weighing of consequences, and, in short, a kind of legislative judgment. . . ."[20]

III

The fact of legal indeterminacy—and the need, therefore, for specification—is one thing, its value another: Why might a political community, or its elected representatives, want to issue an indeterminate directive? Why not issue only determinate directives? Discussing the matter of rules—in particular legal rules—H.L.A. Hart has emphasized that "a feature of the human predicament . . . that we labour under . . . whenever we seek to regulate, unambiguously and in advance, some sphere of conduct by means of general standards to be used without further official directions on particular occasions . . . is our relative ignorance of fact . . . [and] our relative indeterminacy of aim."[21] Given that "feature of the human predicament", it is sensible that many legal (and other) directives be relatively indeterminate. "If the world in which we live were characterized only by a finite number of features, and these together with all the modes in which they could combine were known to us, then provision could be made in advance for every possibility. We could make rules, the application of which to particular cases never called for a further choice. Everything could be known, and for everything, since it could be known, something could be done and specified in advance by rule. Plainly this world is not our world. . . . This inability to anticipate brings with it a relative indeterminacy of aim."[22] The point is not that (relatively) determinate directives cannot be achieved. (They can. One way to do so, writes Hart, "is to freeze the meaning of the rule so that its general terms must have the same meaning in every case where its application is in question. To secure this we may fasten on certain features present in the plain case and insist that these are both necessary and sufficient to bring anything which has them within the scope of the rule, whatever other features it may have or lack, and whatever may be the social consequences of applying the rule in this way."[23]) The point, rather, is that determinacy ought not always to be a goal.[24] To achieve determinacy is sometimes "to secure a measure of certainty or predictability at the cost of blindly prejudging what is to be done in a range of future cases, about whose composition we are ignorant. We shall thus succeed in settling in advance, but also in the dark, issues which can only reasonably be settled when they arise and are identified."[25]

We can distinguish legal (and other) norms along two dimensions: the dimension of (relative) determinacy/indeterminacy and the dimension of (relative) particularity/generality. The particularity/generality of a norm—which feature is, of course, a matter of degree and, so, "relative"—concerns the number of contexts to which the norm is relevant. The norm's determinacy/indeterminacy—also a matter of degree—concerns the specificity of the guidance provided by the norm in the contexts to which it is relevant. Generality and indeterminacy ought not to be confused. A relatively general norm—a norm relevant "to a wide variety of cases and circumstances", in that sense a "relatively context-free" norm[26]—can be quite determinate: for example, "Never lie to anyone." And a relatively particular imperative can be quite indeterminate: "Never lie to your spouse without good reason." Of course, generality (or "breadth") and indeterminacy often go together, because the larger the number of contexts to which a norm is addressed, the greater the likelihood that the guidance the norm offers for those many contexts will lack a high degree of specificity. Similarly, particularity (or "narrowness") and determinacy often go together: The smaller the number of contexts to which a norm is addressed, the greater the likelihood that the guidance the norm offers for those few contexts will have a high degree of specificity. But, again, a relatively general norm can be quite determinate, and a relatively particular norm can be quite indeterminate.

Consider four classes of legal directives: (1) determinate particulars, (2) determinate generals, (3) indeterminate particulars, and (4) indeterminate generals. Sometimes it makes sense for society to issue a determinate particular—a legal directive that is relevant to a relatively small number of contexts (even, at the limit, one context) and provides quite specific guidance in those contexts—because sometimes a problem (or an opportunity) arises in a relatively small number of contexts and society knows just how it wants to meet the problem (or exploit the opportunity) in those few contexts: for example, "No person . . . shall be eligible to the office of the President . . . who shall not have attained to the age of thirty-five years" (U.S. Const., art. II, § 1). Sometimes it makes sense to issue a determinate general—a legal directive that is relevant to a relatively large number of contexts (even an indefinitely large number) but that provides quite specific guidance—because sometimes a problem arises in a relatively large number of contexts, and society knows just how it wants to meet the problem in each and every one of those many contexts.

Sometimes, however, it makes sense to issue a legal directive that, whether particular or general, is indeterminate, because sometimes society values something that may well be or become implicated (e.g., imperiled) in a number of various contexts, including contexts unforeseeable from the perspective of those issuing the norm, without knowing or being able to know in advance just how it wants to achieve (e.g., protect) the value privileged by and embedded in the directive in each and every one of those various contexts, even if it does know just how it wants to achieve the value in some of the contexts. (It is also possible that although there is a virtual consensus in society about how to achieve the value in some contexts, there is dissensus about how to achieve it in some, even many, other contexts.) In the enterprise of constitution making or constitution amending at least as much as in any other law-making enterprise, a society often does not and cannot know in advance just how to achieve what it values in each and every context in which the value may become implicated. Thus, constitutional provisions often "state not rules for the passing hour," as Cardozo put it, "but principles for an expanding future. Insofar as it deviates from that standard, and descends into details and particulars, [a constitution] loses its flexibility, the scope of interpretation contracts, the meaning hardens. While it is true to its function, it maintains its power of adaptation, its suppleness, its play."[27]

I said that the fact of legal indeterminacy is one thing, its value another. Well, the value of the indeterminacy of ordinary legal directives is one thing, the value of the indeterminacy of *constitutional* directives is another. In the next chapter, I address the question why a political community might want to issue, not merely indeterminate statutory directives, but indeterminate constitutional directives as well—why, that is, the community might want to entrust to *the courts* for specification, not merely indeterminate statutory directives, but indeterminate constitutional directives as well. Whatever one thinks about the value (or disvalue) of entrusting indeterminate statutory directives to the courts for specification, one might be skeptical, or especially skeptical, about the wisdom of entrusting indeterminate constitutional directives to the courts for specification—least of all, perhaps, to the electorally unaccountable federal courts. After all, the choices made in the course of specifying such directives, unlike the choices made in the course of specifying statutory directives or in the course of developing the common law, are immune to revision or repeal by means of ordinary, majoritarian politics.[28] No court, not even the Supreme Court, need be the institution of government charged with the primary responsibility for specifying constitutional indeterminacy. According to normative minimalism, the Court should exercise only a secondary responsibility.

IV

There are, however, limits to what specifications of an indeterminate constitutional directive an originalist judge, no matter what her conception of proper judicial role or what her political morality, should credit as "not unreasonable", much less adopt as her own. In chapter 3, I said that I would later explain how an originalist judge, in specifying an indeterminate constitutional directive, should deal with (1) particular practices that they who issued the directive specifically meant the directive to ban, (2) particular practices that they did not understand, or would not have understood, the directive to ban, and (3) particular practices that they specifically meant the directive not to ban. I now want to offer that explanation.

The Supreme Court should not tolerate, much less adopt as its own, an implicit legislative specification of a constitutional directive if according to the specification a particular practice (law, etc.) they who issued the directive specifically meant to ban, and indeed thought that in ratifying the constitutional provision at issue they were banning, does not violate the directive. Instead, the Court should deem the directive determinate with respect to the question of the constitutionality of such a practice and rule that the practice violates the directive. To do otherwise is almost certainly, if not necessarily, to misconceive the precise character of the directive they issued.[29] The proper approach, for an originalist judge, is to presume that a specific aspect of the (complex) directive they issued is that the practice in question is forbidden.[30]

The Supreme Court should conclude, therefore, that the antidiscrimination directive represented by section 1 of the Fourteenth Amendment—that is, by section 1 as originally understood—is not simple, but complex. As I explain in chapter 7, where I discuss the original meaning of the Fourteenth Amendment, the antidiscrimination directive represented by section 1 forbids government to make political choices based on the view that the members of a group are inferior, as human beings, to persons not members of the group, if the group is defined in terms of a trait irrelevant to their status as human beings. But we should also conclude, because of the considerations presented in the preceding paragraph, that in a different aspect—a more specific and concrete (determinate) aspect—the directive also proscribes political choices based on the view that the members of a group are morally inferior to others *by virtue of race*. The presupposition of this more specific/concrete aspect of the antidiscrimination directive is the premise that connects the more specific aspect to the more general, indeterminate aspect of the directive, namely, that a person's race is not relevant to the question of her status or worth as a human being.

Should the Court ever adopt a specification of an indeterminate constitutional directive if according to the specification a particular practice they who issued the directive did not think they were banning—or, in the case of a practice they did not foresee and perhaps could not have foreseen, would not have thought they were banning if they had foreseen it—violates the directive? For example, should the Court specify, should it shape, the general/indeterminate aspect of the antidiscrimination directive represented by section one of the Fourteenth Amendment by ruling that sex is not relevant to a person's status or worth as a human being? Certainly the folks who gave us the Fourteenth Amendment did not believe that sex is irrelevant to a person's status as a human being.[31] Therefore, it is not a specific/concrete aspect of the original meaning of section one that political choices may not be based on the view that sex is a determinant of a person's moral worth.

Or, instead, should the Court deem the directive determinate with respect to the question of the constitutionality of such a practice—a practice they who issued the directive did not think they were banning—and rule that the practice does not violate the directive? It is possible, of course, that to conclude that a directive, properly specified, does not tolerate a practice they who issued the directive did not think, or would not have thought, they were banning may be to misconceive the character of the directive they issued.[32] But it is also true that to insist that "the directive they issued" must be understood so as to tolerate any practice they who issued the directive did not think, or would not have thought, they were banning may be to misconceive the character of the directive they issued. "A principle does not exist wholly independently of its author's subjective, or his society's conventional exemplary applications, and is always limited to some extent by the applications they found conceivable"; nonetheless, "[w]ithin these fairly broad limits, . . . [they who constitutionalized the principle] may have intended their examples to constrain more or less."[33] Relatedly, to say that whatever "the directive they issued" is, it *necessarily* tolerates any practice they who issued it did not think, or would not have thought, they were banning is at odds with the originalist approach defended in chapter 3, which "recognize[s] that constitutional provisions, in principle, may signify aspirations and values that transcend the framers' temporally bounded conceptions of the scope of those provisions. . . . Moderate intentionalism thus seem[s] an attractive half-way house between two unacceptable extremes: a jurisprudence that constitutionalized the repellent prejudices of former generations on the one hand, and a jurisprudence of open-ended judicial policymaking on the other."[34]

(My discussion, in chapter 3, of capital punishment as an issue under the cruel or unusual punishments clause is relevant here[35]—as is my discussion, in chapter 8, of modern constitutional doctrine regarding sex-based discrimination.[36])

But what if they who issued a directive not only did not think, or would not have thought, that in issuing the directive they were banning a particular practice, but specifically meant not to ban it; what if they specifically meant to allow the practice? If their specific intention to disallow a particular practice should be deemed determinative, why not also their specific intention to allow a practice? Even if their specific intention to allow a particular practice should be deemed determinative, about what provisions of the United States Constitution, provisions regarding a right or a liberty, is it the case that they who voted to ratify the provision specifically meant, not only to disallow a particular practice (or practices), but also to allow a particular practice? Is it true, for example—do the relevant historical materials support the claim—that they who voted to ratify the Fourteenth Amendment specifically meant, not only to disallow discrimination based on race, but also to allow discrimination based on sex? That they did not think they were banning discrimination based on sex is beside the point: The question is whether they specifically meant to allow it. (Similarly, that in constitutionalizing the cruel or unusual punishments clause our political ancestors did not think that they were banning capital punishment is beside the point: The question is whether they specifically meant to allow it.) Who among those who voted to ratify the Fourteenth Amendment, and how many, specifically meant to allow such discrimination? It seems that it would be quite difficult, with respect to constitutional provisions regarding rights or liberties, to support a historical claim, not merely of a specific intention to disallow, but of a specific intention to allow alongside a specific intention to disallow. Indeed, it seems quite doubtful that such claims could often (ever?) be sustained.[37] But maybe I am flat wrong about that. If, in any event, such a claim of a specific intention to allow *can* be sustained,[38] then the better approach, for an originalist judge—and certainly the consistent approach, given what I said earlier about a specific intention to disallow—is to presume that a specific aspect of the (complex) directive they issued is that the practice in question is permitted.

V

If, and only if, both history and morality—constitutional history and constitutional morality—were invariably determinate would the originalist approach entail a minimalist judicial role. But neither constitutional history nor constitutional morality is invariably determinate, and, so, originalism does not entail minimalism. As both this chapter and the preceding one suggest, the interesting relation between originalism and minimalism runs in the other direction: If an originalist judge happens to be a judicial minimalist—if, for whatever reason or reasons, she happens to be averse to the exercise of judicial "discretion"—her minimalist conception of proper judicial role is very likely a principal factor influencing her, as she pursues the interpretive inquiry, to embrace one plausible conclusion about the original meaning of a constitutional provision, about what directive the provision (as originally understood) represents, rather than another plausible conclusion. And her minimalist conception is also very likely a principal factor influencing her as she pursues the normative inquiry, as she engages in the process of specifying an indeterminate constitutional directive.

The most important questions for contemporary constitutional-theoretical debate do not concern originalism versus nonoriginalism, much less textualism versus nontextualism. Given the appeal of originalism, but given, too, the indeterminacy both of constitutional history and of constitutional morality—and given, finally, the influence a judge's conception of proper judicial role and her political morality very likely exert on her as she pursues both the interpretive inquiry and then the normative inquiry—the most important questions concern the role the Supreme Court (and other courts) should play when confronted either by the indeterminacy of constitutional history or by the indeterminacy of constitutional morality, or by both. Whether or not this or that judge is a judicial minimalist—whether or not she is averse to the exercise of judicial discretion—*should* she be? Regardless of how this or that member of the Supreme Court (or of another court) is very likely inclined, because of her minimalist or nonminimalist sensibilities, to resolve indeterminate historical inquiries into original meaning, how *should* she resolve such inquiries? Interpretive minimalism is one answer. Regardless of the role—large or small, active or passive—this or that member of the Court is very likely inclined to play in bringing indeterminate constitutional directives to bear (by specifying them) in resolving constitutional conflicts, what role *should* she play? Normative minimalism is one answer.

I turn, in the next chapter, to the question of minimalism, both interpretive minimalism and normative minimalism.

6

Skepticism about Minimalism — and about Nonminimalism, Too

The search must be for a function which might (indeed, must) involve the making of policy, yet which differs from the legislative and executive functions; which is peculiarly suited to the capabilities of the courts; which will not likely be performed elsewhere if the courts do not assume it; which can be so exercised as to be acceptable in a society that generally shares Judge [Learned] Hand's satisfaction in a "sense of common venture"; which will be effective when needed; and whose discharge by the courts will not lower the quality of the other departments' performance by denuding them of the dignity and burden of their own responsibility.[1]

I have argued in the two preceding chapters that originalism does not entail minimalism: either interpretive minimalism or normative minimalism. More precisely, the originalist approach does not necessarily involve a minimalist judicial practice—a practice in which the exercise of significant judicial discretion is negligible; nor does the argument for originalism support a minimalist practice. To defend originalism, as I did in chapter 3, is not to defend minimalism.[2] This is not to deny that one can be an originalist *and* a minimalist: both an interpretive minimalist and a normative minimalist. My point is simply that one can, consistently with originalism, reject the minimalist approach both to the interpretation of the constitutional text and to the specification of indeterminate directives represented by the text.

That originalism does not entail minimalism, however, is not an argument against minimalism (though it *is* an argument against a particular argument for minimalism: the argument that because originalism entails minimalism, originalists should be minimalists). Should the Supreme Court follow the minimalist approach, either in pursuing the interpretive inquiry (i.e., in interpreting the constitutional text) or in pursuing

the normative inquiry (in specifying indeterminate constitutional directives)? I have argued, in chapter 3, that the originalist approach to the
interpretive inquiry is more defensible in the context of American political-legal culture than any nonoriginalist approach. But interpretive minimalism, and not just originalism, is a position about which approach to
the interpretive inquiry the Court should follow; as a position about the
proper approach to the interpretive inquiry, interpretive minimalism
complements, rather than competes with, originalism: Should the Court
follow the minimalist originalist approach in resolving indeterminate historical inquiries into original meaning? Normative minimalism is a position about the approach to the normative inquiry the Court should follow: Should the Court follow the minimalist approach in specifying
constitutional indeterminacy?

I. Interpretive Minimalism

According to minimalist originalism (i.e., originalism supplemented by
interpretive minimalism), a judge, given two or more readings of the
original meaning of a constitutional provision that have, for her, substantially equal historical plausibility, should favor the reading according to
which the directive represented by the provision is, if not determinate, at
least more determinate (or, equivalently, less indeterminate) than the
directive(s) represented by the provision according to the other plausible
reading(s). Minimalist originalism is consistent with the general point of
judicial minimalism, which, as I indicated at the beginning of chapter 4, is
to afford relatively little opportunity for a judge's own political-moral values, for her own "tastes", "preferences", and so on, to influence her resolution of the conflict at hand. The minimalist originalist approach favors,
as the original meaning of a constitutional provision, the directive the
judicial enforcement of which affords the least opportunity for a judge's
own political-moral values to influence the outcome of particular cases.

Thus, as Justice Scalia's position in the Oregon peyote case illustrates,
minimalist originalism favors the reading of (the original meaning of) the
free exercise clause according to which the directive represented by the
clause is merely the antidiscrimination directive and not the antidiscrimination-plus-exemption directive.[3] (That is, minimalist originalism holds
that a judge should favor that reading if the reading has, for her, an historical plausibility substantially equal to the plausibility of the reading
according to which the directive represented by the clause is the antidiscrimination-plus-exemption directive. For an originalist judge to favor a
more determinate reading over a less determinate one when the less
determinate reading has more historical plausibility for her is obviously
for the judge to compromise her originalism. An originalist judge with
strong minimalist inclinations will not often be tempted to compromise

her originalism, however, because, as I suggested in chapter 4, she will be disposed to see the more determinate reading—the reading according to which the provision represents the more determinate directive—as having more historical plausibility than the less determinate reading.) Similarly, the approach favors the reading of the Ninth Amendment according to which the rights protected by the Amendment are merely (what Thomas McAffee has called) "residual" rights and not also "affirmative" rights.[4] The approach also favors the reading of the privileges or immunities clause of the Fourteenth Amendment according to which the clause is directed not against any nondiscriminatory state legislation, but only against (some) discriminatory laws or policies.[5] The approach would favor a reading according to which the clause is directed only against *racially* discriminatory laws or policies were such a limited reading historically plausible.[6]

The minimalist approach to the interpretive inquiry minimizes the opportunity for a judge's own political-moral values to influence her resolution of the conflict at hand. The argument for that approach is a way of responding to "the counter-majoritarian difficulty": Interpretive minimalism minimizes the role of judicial "subjectivity" in the adjudicative process, principally on the ground that the authoritative subjectivity (values, tastes, preferences, etc.) is that of the people, who are sovereign. The people's subjectivity—as mediated, for better or for worse, by their representatives—operates in the domain of ordinary politics, which is majoritarian; by contrast, the judges' subjectivity operates, when it operates, in the domain of constitutional adjudication, which is counter-majoritarian. The Thayerian argument for normative minimalism, presented in the next section of this chapter, more fully develops the case for depriveleging judicial subjectivity in the adjudicative process. Because that argument supports confining judicial subjectivity at the interpretive stage of the inquiry as well as at the normative stage, it may be incorporated by reference here.

Justice Scalia, who has written in defense of originalism,[7] has also written in defense of interpretive minimalism. Indeed, he has been the principal proponent of interpretive minimalism. Scalia wants to minimize the role of judicial subjectivity, in individual cases, by making adjudication as "rule bound" as possible. In an essay defending his inclination to impute to the Constitution relatively determinate (rather than relatively indeterminate) norms, which he calls "rules", Scalia has explained: "[W]hen, in writing for the majority of the Court, I adopt a general rule, and say, 'This is the basis for our decision,' I not only constrain lower courts, I constrain myself as well. If the next case should have such different facts that my political or policy preferences regarding the outcome are quite the opposite, I will be unable to indulge those preferences; I have committed myself to the governing principle. In the real world of appellate judging, it displays more judicial restraint to adopt such a course than to announce that, 'on balance,' we think the law was violated here—leaving ourselves free to say in the next case that, 'on balance,' it was not."[8]

The thoroughgoing judicial minimalist, intent on minimizing the role
of judicial "subjectivity" in the adjudicative process, will embrace both
interpretive minimalism and normative minimalism. Like Scalia, she will
pursue the minimalist approach to the interpretive inquiry: She will coax
the context of the text to yield a relatively determinate directive ("rule")
to enforce. The originalist judge will coax the history of the text to yield
such a directive. But if in the end history resists and yields only a relatively indeterminate directive, she will then pursue the minimalist
approach to the normative inquiry. She will assume only a secondary
responsibility for specifying the indeterminate directive: She will defer to
any "not unreasonable" specification, implicit in the governmental action
under review, according to which the action is not unconstitutional. Interpretive minimalism and normative minimalism thus complement one
another.

II. Normative Minimalism

One searches in vain through the contemporary literature of constitutional theory for a thoughtful presentation and defense of the minimalist
approach to the normative inquiry. (Justice Scalia has defended the minimalist approach to the interpretive inquiry.) Because contemporary minimalists have tended to believe, mistakenly, that originalism entails minimalism, including what I am here calling "normative minimalism", they
have tended to think, mistakenly, that in presenting and defending originalism they were presenting and defending minimalism. As I have
already explained, however, originalism does not entail minimalism.
Moreover, whereas originalism is a position wholly about the interpretive
inquiry—wholly about what it means, or should mean, to "interpret" the
constitutional text—the minimalism we now need to consider, normative
minimalism, is a position wholly about the normative inquiry; it is a
response to the question of the Court's proper role in specifying constitutional indeterminacy.

We do not search in vain, however, if we look past the contemporary
literature of constitutional theory—specifically, about one hundred
years past, to an article by James Bradley Thayer. According to Leonard
Levy:

> Felix Frankfurter described [Thayer], his teacher, as "our great mas-
> ter of constitutional law." Thayer, said Frankfurter, "influenced Holmes,
> Brandeis, the Hands (Learned and Augustus) . . . and so forth. I am of
> the view that if I were to name one piece of writing on American Consti-
> tutional Law—a silly test maybe—I would pick an essay by James
> Bradley Thayer in the *Harvard Law Review*, consisting of 26 pages, pub-
> lished in October, 1893, called 'The Origin and Scope of the American
> Doctrine of Constitutional Law' . . . . Why would I do that? Because

from my point of view it's a great guide for judges and therefore, the great guide for understanding by non-judges of what the place of the judiciary is in relation to constitutional questions."[9]

Thayer's article is the locus classicus of the minimalist response to the question of the role the courts, including the Court, should play in specifying indeterminate constitutional directives:

> If their duty were in truth merely and nakedly to ascertain the meaning of the text of the constitution and of the impeached Act of the legislature, and to determine, as an academic question, whether in the court's judgment the two were in conflict, it would, to be sure, be an elevated and important office, one dealing with great matters, involving large public considerations, but yet a function far simpler than it really is. Having ascertained all this, yet there remains a question—the really momentous question—whether, after all, the court can disregard the Act. It cannot do this as a mere matter of course—merely because it is concluded that upon a just and true construction the law is unconstitutional. . . . It can only disregard the Act when those who have the right to make laws have not merely made a mistake, but have made a very clear one—so clear that it is not open to rational question. That is the standard of duty to which the courts bring legislative Acts; that is the test which they apply—not merely their own judgment as to constitutionality, but their conclusion as to what judgment is permissible to another department which the constitution has charged with the duty of making it. This rule recognizes that, having regard to the great, complex, ever unfolding exigencies of government, much which will seem unconstitutional to one man, or body of men, may reasonably not seem so to another; that the constitution often admits of different interpretations; that there is often a range of choice and judgment; that in such cases the constitution does not impose upon the legislature any one specific opinion, but leaves open this range of choice; and that whatever choice is rational is constitutional.
>
>   . . . .
>
> [A] court cannot always . . . say that there is but one right and permissible way of construing the constitution. When a court is interpreting a writing merely to ascertain or apply its true meaning, then, indeed, there is but one meaning allowable; namely, what the court adjudges to be its true meaning. But when the ultimate question is not that, but whether certain acts of another department, officer, or individual are legal or permissible, then this is not true. In the class of cases which we have been considering, *the ultimate question is not what is the true meaning of the constitution, but whether legislation is sustainable or not.*[10]

The Thayerian response to the question of the role the Court should play in pursuing the normative inquiry is the minimalist response: The Court should resolve the constitutional conflict, it should decide the case, not on the basis of its own view about how the relevant constitutional directive should be specified, but, instead, on the basis of the specification implicit in the legislative action—or (to extend Thayer's range of reference) in the governmental action—whose constitutionality is in question, so long as that implicit specification is reasonable (or, as Thayer put it, "rational"). As Thayer's most prominent judicial disciple, Felix Frankfurter, wrote in his dissenting opinion in *West Virginia State Board of Education v. Barnette* (in which the Court invalidated a public school regulation, challenged by a Jehovah's Witness, that compelled students to salute the flag and recite the Pledge of Allegiance): "Only if there be no doubt that any reasonable mind could entertain can we deny to the states the right to resolve doubts their way and not ours. . . . I think I appreciate fully the objections to the law before us. But to deny that it presents a question upon which men might reasonably differ appears to me to be intolerance. And since men may so reasonably differ, I deem it beyond my constitutional power to assert my view of the wisdom of this law against the view of the State of West Virginia."[11] As Justice Frankfurter understood, the minimalist approach to the normative inquiry—to the specification of constitutional indeterminacy—affords relatively little opportunity for a judge's own values (tastes, preferences, etc.) to influence her resolution of the conflict at hand.

Of course, to afford relatively little opportunity is not to afford no opportunity. Even the minimalist approach leaves room for reasonable differences *among reviewing judges*. (Any approach, including the minimalist approach, leaves room for unreasonable differences among reviewing judges.) As a contemporary proponent of Thayer's approach has acknowledged: ". . . Thayer's rule, like all guideposts, is not self-applying. Even limited by the rule of administration, judges, like criminal juries, might differ over what constitutes a reasonable doubt; the possibilities, the stuff of which reasonable doubts are made, do not always strike all men, however reasonable, alike. Even under Thayer's rule of administration, then, the freedom and the burden of decisionmaking remain. But that freedom is narrowed, and that was Thayer's aim. He sought to reduce the scope of judicial freedom without diminishing the judicial duty and burden of judging."[12]

The Thayerian account of judicial minimalism suggests the nonminimalist response to the question of the Court's proper role—the response of a Justice Brennan, for example. Justice Brennan has rejected Thayer's minimalist approach as "much too crimped to be desirable in a society such as ours."[13] According to the nonminimalist response, the Court should exercise the primary responsibility, not merely a secondary one, for specifying constitutional indeterminacy: The Court should decide the case on the basis of its own independent view about how the relevant directive should be specified—its own view about the correct, or the best, specification of the directive.[14]

As a preliminary matter, note that the question at hand is not whether the Court should play a minimalist role in specifying indeterminate constitutional directives. As it stands, that question is too general and, so, properly elicits this response: Indeterminate constitutional directives *of what sort?* Directives regarding the (vertical) allocation of power between the national government and the governments of the states ("federalism" directives)? Directives regarding the (horizontal) allocation of power among the three departments (legislative, executive, and judicial) of the national government ("separation of powers" directives)? Or directives regarding rights or liberties (or both): the rights and the liberties of citizens and others against government? The question at hand is whether the Court should play a minimalist role in specifying indeterminate constitutional directives regarding rights or liberties. Even that question is insufficiently focused: As I explain later in this book, in responding to the question of the Court's proper role in specifying indeterminate directives regarding rights or liberties, we need to distinguish between or among different kinds of directives regarding rights or liberties.[15]

In the past I joined others in arguing that the minimalist approach to constitutional adjudication is fitting with respect to claims that the Congress, to the detriment of the states, is acting in excess of its delegated power under a federalism directive.[16] I also argued in support of the minimalist approach to the adjudication of some (but not all) claims that the Congress or the president, to the detriment of a co-ordinate branch of the federal government, is acting in excess of its power under a separation-of-powers directive.[17] But that the minimalist approach may be fitting with respect to either sort of claim, or even with respect to both sorts, does not entail that the minimalist approach is fitting with respect to claims that the national government or a state government, to the detriment of an individual qua citizen or simply qua person, is acting in violation of a directive regarding a right or a liberty of the people.[18]

Neglect of the question of normative minimalism has led contemporary commentators on constitutional adjudication to underestimate, and therefore to understate, the complexity of their subject matter. At the beginning of *The Tempting of America*, for example, Robert Bork insists that judges, in adjudicating constitutional issues, must not "make or apply any policy not fairly to be found in the Constitution. . . ." Bork then acknowledges: "It is of course true that judges to some extent must make law every time they decide a case. . . ." But, cautions Bork, "it is minor, interstitial lawmaking. The ratifiers of the Constitution put in place the walls, roofs, and beams; judges preserve the major architectural features, adding only filigree."[19] Near the end of his book, Bork sounds a similar note: "The principles of the actual Constitution make the judge's major moral choices for him."[20] By neglecting the question of minimalism, Bork overlooks, in these passages, two related things Thayer well understood: (1) some "principles of the actual Constitution" are quite indeterminate and therefore require significant specification; in that sense, some constitutional principles not merely leave room for, but necessitate significant moral choices; and (2) whether the courts (and, finally, the Supreme Court) exercise the primary responsibility for making those choices, or whether, instead, the Congress or a state legislature (or, in the executive

domain, the president or a state governor) exercises that responsibility—
with the courts exercising only the secondary responsibility of reviewing,
in the extremely deferential manner recommended by Thayer, the Congress's or a state legislature's exercise of that responsibility—depends on
whether the courts choose to follow the minimalist approach to the normative inquiry.

Consider, as another example of how neglect of the question of normative minimalism can lead one to underestimate/understate the complexity of the subject matter, Justice Brennan's H.L.A. Hart Lecture at
Oxford in 1989, "Why Have a Bill of Rights?" Justice Brennan supported,
in the lecture,

> couch[ing Bill-of-Rights-type guarantees] in *general* terms, their specifi-
> cation left to adjudicative bodies reviewing official conduct or legisla-
> tion. So long as they are not unduly vague, as I believe [the American
> Bill of Rights is] not, broad formulations of personal rights are a virtue,
> because they permit judges to adapt canons of right to situations not
> envisaged by those who framed them, thereby facilitating their evolu-
> tion and preserving their vitality. As Justice Brandeis . . . once said of the
> American Constitution, it "is not a strait-jacket. It is a living organism. As
> such it is capable of growth—of expansion and of adaptation to new
> conditions. . . . Because our Constitution possesses the capacity of adap-
> tation, it has endured as the fundamental law of an ever-developing
> people". What Justice Brandeis said of the Constitution is equally true of
> a bill of rights painted with a flat brush rather than etched with a jew-
> eller's pin.[21]

What Justice Brennan's statement obscures, by neglecting the question of
minimalism, is that the importance of having a constitution that is not a
"strait-jacket"—a constitution that is a "living organism . . . capable of
growth . . . of expansion and of adaptation to new conditions"—is one
thing, and perhaps undisputed; the wisdom of entrusting to "adjudicative bodies reviewing official conduct or legislation" the primary responsibility for specifying such a constitution, for "expanding" and "adapting"
such a constitution "to new conditions", is quite something else, and
deeply disputed. Even if a constitutional bill of rights should be "painted
with a flat brush rather than etched with a jeweller's pin," the question
remains whether the primary responsibility for specifying the rights
should be entrusted to the courts—whether, that is, the courts should follow the minimalist approach, or, instead, Justice Brennan's nonminimalist approach, in specifying the rights.

A final example is this statement by Richard Posner: "To banish all discretion from the judicial process would indeed reduce the scope of constitutional rights. The framers of a constitution who want to make it a
charter of liberties and not just a set of constitutive rules face a difficult
choice. They can write specific provisions, and thereby doom their work
to rapid obsolescence or irrelevance; or they can write general provisions,
thereby delegating substantial discretion to the authoritative interpreters,

who in our system are the judges."[22] By neglecting the question of normative minimalism, Judge Posner, like Justice Brennan and former Judge Bork, misleads (or is misled): For "the framers" to "write general provisions" is for them to "delegat[e] substantial discretion to . . . the judges" only if the framers direct, implicitly if not explicitly, the judges to follow the nonminimalist approach in enforcing the general provisions. But the mere writing of a general provision—the mere issuing of an indeterminate directive—does not entail such a direction, and if, pace Thayer, the judges follow the minimalist approach, they do not exercise "substantial discretion" in specifying the provision.

Why might a judge think she should not exercise substantial discretion in specifying constitutional indeterminacy? Thayer's minimalism—his understanding of the proper role role of the courts vis à vis the other, electorally accountable departments of government—was not rooted in a faith in the capacity of those other departments to resolve constitutional questions responsibly. Indeed, as Paul Kahn has reminded us, Thayer "describe[d] the reality of Congress in harsh words: '[T]he question is not merely what persons may rationally do who are such as we often see, in point of fact, in our legislative bodies, persons untaught it may be, indocile, thoughtless, reckless, incompetent.'"[23] Thayer's minimalism (according to Kahn) was not even rooted in a belief that the electorally accountable departments of government are truly representative of the people.[24] Thayer's minimalism was rooted, instead, in a democratic conviction that "We the people"—who are, after all, the ultimate sovereign—must learn to take final responsibility for resolving constitutional questions ourselves, rather than have an external sovereign, or even an unrepresentative legislature, do it for us. He feared that the nonminimalist approach would impede that democratic project. As Thayer later wrote:

> [T]he exercise of judicial review, even when unavoidable, is always attended with a serious evil, namely, that the correction of legislative mistakes comes from the outside, and the people thus lose the political experience, and the moral education and stimulus that comes from fighting the question out in the ordinary way, and correcting their own errors. The tendency of a common and easy resort to this great function, now lamentably too common, is to dwarf the political capacity of the people, and to deaden its sense of moral responsibility.
> . . . .
> And if it be true that the holders of legislative power are careless or evil, yet the constitutional duty of the court remains untouched; it cannot rightly attempt to protect the people by undertaking a function not its own. On the other hand, by adhering rigidly to its own duty, the court will help, as nothing else can, to fix the spot where responsibility lies, and to bring down on that precise locality the thunderbolt of popular condemnation. . . . For that course—the true course of judicial duty

always—will powerfully help to bring the people and their representatives to a sense of their own responsibility.[25]

Like Thayer, a judge might believe that "We the people" must learn to take final responsibility for resolving constitutional questions ourselves, rather than have someone else do it for us, and, again like Thayer, she might fear that the nonminimalist approach will impede that democratic project. A contemporary Thayerian, the Canadian legal scholar Allan Hutchinson, has written that "[b]y endlessly waiting for Coraf[[26]], we place ourselves *in waiting*; it inculcates a servile and sycophantic attitude in people. Such a practised posture of dependence is anathema to the democratic spirit. It is infinitely better to run the unfamiliar risks of genuinely popular rule than to succumb to the commonplace security of distant authority."[27]

A judge might even believe that the people must learn to struggle with difficult political-moral issues less as issues of constitutional legality and more as political-moral issues, and she might fear, once more like Thayer, that the nonminimalist approach will impede that project, too. "No doubt our doctrine of constitutional law has had a tendency to drive out questions of justice and right, and to fill the mind of legislators with thoughts of mere legality, of what the constitution allows. . . . [N]ot being thrown back on themselves, on the responsible exercise of their own prudence, moral sense, and honor, [the people] lose much of what is best in the political experience of any nation."[28] As Kahn has encapsulated Thayer's point, "the more the Court tries to represent the people, the more the people cease to function as the popular sovereign."[29]

We can imagine a variation on Thayer's argument—a neo-Thayerian argument that is both self-consciously epistemological in its wariness about the notion of "the reasonable" and (more importantly) skeptical about the possibility, in a highly complex and highly bureaucratized advanced industrial society like ours, of turning "We the people" into a locus of serious constitutional—or, more broadly, of serious political-moral—reflection. At least, the neo-Thayerian argument is skeptical either about the extent to which that can be done or about how often it can be done—or about both. The argument contemplates, therefore, the electorally accountable representatives of the people (acting in the domain of ordinary politics) rather than the people themselves (acting collectively in a domain of extraordinary politics) as the relevant possible locus of serious constitutional reflection.

The argument begins with the claim that once we have excluded unreasonable answers to the question of how an indeterminate constitutional directive should be specified, there are, among the remaining, reasonable answers, no better or worse answers, only preferences for one or another specification, and the choice of one or another (reasonable) specification should therefore be left, not to the extraordinary processes of constitutional adjudication, which is counter-majoritarian, but to the ordinary processes of majoritarian politics. We are, after all, democrats (with a small *d*).[30] A claim "in the alternative" is that even if there are, among the reasonable answers, better and worse answers, there is no reason to think that the Supreme Court is more likely (or even as likely) to identify the better answers than are the electorally accountable representatives of the people in the Congress or perhaps even in a state legislature (or, in the executive domain, than is the president or a state governor). Yet another claim "in the alternative"—indeed, perhaps this is the principal claim—is that even if we assume *arguendo* that the Court is in general more likely to identify the better answers, our commitment to majoritarian ("democratic") policy making demands that the electorally accountable representatives of the people be charged with the primary responsibility for choosing one or another reasonable specification. This last claim might be joined with a Thayerian insistence that in the long run the capacity of ordinary politics to deliberate well about constitutional questions, and then to choose well, will be bolstered if ordinary politics, rather than constitutional adjudication, is the primary matrix of choice with respect to the specification of indeterminate constitutional directives.

These, then, emerge as some of the central inquiries in evaluating the appeal of the minimalist approach to the specification of constitutional indeterminacy (in cases involving directives regarding rights or liberties):

- Is the process of specifying indeterminate constitutional directives a "rational" one? Are there, among the reasonable answers to the question of how an indeterminate constitutional directive should be specified, better and worse answers, such that one can reasonably choose among the reasonable answers; or are such choices merely a matter of "taste" or "preference"?
- Even if there are (among the reasonable answers) better and worse answers, is there any reason to think that the Court is in general more likely (or even as likely) to identify the better answers than are the electorally accountable representatives of the people?[31]
- Even if there is reason to think that the Court is generally more likely to identify the better answers, does our commitment to majoritarian policy making demand that the electorally accountable representatives of the people be charged with the primary responsibility for choosing one or another reasonable specification? Relatedly, is there reason to believe that the capacity of ordinary politics to deliberate well about constitutional questions, and then to choose well, will eventually be bolstered if ordinary politics, not constitutional adjudication, is the primary matrix of specifications of indeterminate constitutional directives?

Whether constitutional adjudication, rather than ordinary politics, should be the primary matrix of specifications of indeterminate constitutional directives—in particular, whether the Supreme Court should have the primary responsibility for specifying such directives—is a more difficult question than whether judges should have the primary responsibility for specifying indeterminate *statutory* directives. If the elected and electorally accountable representatives of the people conclude that a court's specification of a statutory norm is problematic, they can, pursuant to the ordinary processes of majoritarian politics, revise, even to the point of reversing, what the court has done. In that sense, in their statutory mode courts can fairly be understood as political inferiors—as delegates—of the electorally accountable representatives of the people. (This is not to deny that as a practical matter it may sometimes be quite difficult for a legislature to reverse what a court has done in its statutory mode, especially if the executive branch of government, armed with a veto, is sympathetic to what the court has done—or, at least, unsympathetic to what the legislature is trying to do.) By contrast, even if both the Congress and the president conclude that the Supreme Court's specification of a constitutional directive is deeply problematic, they cannot, pursuant to the ordinary processes of majoritarian politics—as distinct from the extraordinary processes of supermajoritarian politics: the processes of constitutional amendment— revise what the Court has done. Nor can a simple majority of "We the people" threaten the Court with political retribution, much less revise what the Court has done. In its constitutional mode, therefore, the Supreme Court can fairly be understood as a political superior of the electorally accountable representatives of the people—and, moreover, as a politically unaccountable superior.[32] That is why the issue of "the counter-majoritarian difficulty"[33] arises in the context of constitutional adjudication but not in the context of statutory adjudication (or in the context of common law adjudication). "[I]n nonconstitutional contexts, the court's decisions are subject to overrule or alteration by ordinary statute. The court is standing in for the legislature, and if it has done so in a way the legislature does not approve, it can soon be corrected. When a court invalidates an act of the political branches on constitutional grounds, however, it is overruling their judgment, and normally doing so in a way that is not subject to 'correction' by the ordinary lawmaking process. Thus the central function, and it is at the same time the central problem, of judicial review. . . ."[34]

In chapter 2, I argued that notwithstanding the counter-majoritarian difficulty, the practice of judicial review, which enjoys our support, merits our support. Now we face a related, but different, question: Which kind of judicial review merits our support: minimalist judicial review or nonminimalist review? Given the counter-majoritarian difficulty, should we— the American political community—entrust the primary responsibility for specifying indeterminate constitutional directives to our courts, and finally to the Supreme Court, rather than to our electorally accountable representatives? Or, instead, should we embrace judicial minimalism and entrust the primary responsibility for specifying constitutional indeterminacy to ordinary politics, with the Court exercising only the secondary responsibility of deferential, Thayerian review?[35]

I should pause here, to try to head off a possible misunderstanding. In *The Hollow Hope: Can Courts Bring about Social Change?* Gerald Rosenberg argues that in constitutional (and in other) cases, courts, contrary to what many judicial "liberals" have hoped and many judicial "conservatives" have feared, do not and cannot produce significant political or social change. In the conclusion to his study, Rosenberg declares: "American courts are not all-powerful institutions. They were designed with severe limitations and placed in a political system of divided powers. To ask them to produce significant social reform is to forget their history and ignore their constraints. It is to cloud our vision with a naive and romantic belief in the triumph of rights over politics. And while romance and even naivete have their charms, they are not best exhibited in courtrooms."[36] It bears emphasis, against the background of Rosenberg's study, that the nonminimalist approach to the judicial specification of constitutional indeterminacy does *not* presuppose—falsely presuppose, *if* Rosenberg is right[37]— that courts do or can produce significant political or social reform.

To favor the nonminimalist approach is to favor the courts exercising the primary responsibility for deciding what indeterminate constitutional directives shall mean in the various particular contexts in which they are implicated. There is no reason to think that the courts' specifications of constitutional indeterminacy are always meant to produce significant political or social change, though, of course, they are sometimes meant to produce it; at least, it is sometimes hoped that they might help to produce it. But whether the courts' specifications of constitutional indeterminacy actually succeed in producing any political or social change, significant or otherwise, is a question distinct from the question whether the courts should follow the minimalist approach in specifying constitutional indeterminacy. That the courts' specifications of constitutional indeterminacy may not (often) succeed in producing significant change does not entail that the courts should follow the minimalist approach. That entailment would exist only if the principal reason for wanting the courts to follow the nonminimalist rather than the minimalist approach were the belief that in following the nonminimalist approach the courts would produce significant political or social reform. But the principal reason for wanting the courts to follow the nonminimalist approach is *not* that belief; the principal reason, rather, is simply skepticism about the extent to which ordinary, majoritarian politics is the appropriate institutional locus of the primary responsibility for deciding what the concrete contextual meanings of an indeterminate constitutional directive shall be.

But, why the skepticism?

III. Is the Process of Specification Rational?

Was there ever such a profession as ours, anyhow? We speak of ourselves as practicing law, as teaching it, as deciding it; and not one of us can say what law means. Start a discussion as to its meaning, try to tell how it is born, whence it comes, out of what we manufacture it, and

> before the dispute is fairly under way, the vociferous disputants will be
> springing at each other's throats. Their inability to agree about the basic
> implications of their calling has in it elements of comedy when at the
> end of the dispute they are seen to be peacefully engaged in the manu-
> facture of the finished products—out of what, they cannot tell you, and
> by a formula they cannot state.
>
> How much of the process is to be classified as reasoning and how
> much as mere emotion, the students of juristic method are unable to
> agree. That is disconcerting enough, but even more disconcerting it is to
> learn that neither jurists nor philosophers can explain the rationality of
> reasoning, can set the process on its feet, and justify our faith in it.[38]

Let's put aside, for a moment, the question whether the primary responsibility for specifying constitutional indeterminacy should be in the hands
of the Court or, instead, in the hands of the Congress or of some other
actual or imaginable institution of government, and ask simply whether
the process of specifying constitutional indeterminacy is a rational one—
and, if so, in what sense of "rational"? Or is the process fundamentally
"arbitrary"? Specifications of indeterminate constitutional directives are a
species of political-moral judgment, and political-moral judgment is one
kind of moral judgment. Is moral judgment a matter of justification? Or
does such judgment lie outside the domain of rationality, outside the
domain of the reasonable and the unreasonable, or of the more reasonable and the less reasonable? Is moral judgment finally a matter, not of
justification or reasonableness, but merely of "taste" or "preference"?
("De gustibus non disputandum est.") Does moral judgment, including
political-moral judgment, of which the specification of constitutional
indeterminacy is a species, lie inside the domain of the merely "arbitrary",
the merely "subjective", the merely "willful"? "[A]ll evaluation is the
expression of subjective preferences or desires. Everything is up for
grabs, and the transaction we benightedly think of as reasoned argument
is really nothing more than a game in which one party tries to influence
another."[39]

The relevance of this inquiry into the rationality *vel non* of the process
of specifying constitutional indeterminacy should be obvious. One's position about how large or how small a role courts should play, vis à vis the
other branches and institutions of government, in specifying indeterminate legal materials—how "activist" or how "restrained" a role—is typically based at least partly on one's position about what the process of specification or adjudication can be, at its best: "principled" or merely
"arbitrary", "deliberative" or merely "willful", and so on. For example,
one who believes that there is no such thing as adjudication "at its best",
that all that adjudication ever is or can be is (relatively) arbitrary, willful,
and the like, may well embrace, because of that belief, a minimalist conception of judicial role, one according to which courts, in adjudicating
issues, should play a relatively small, restrained role, engaging at most
only in what Robert Bork has called "minor, interstitial lawmaking".[40]

One who believes that adjudication can be (relatively) principled, deliberative, and so on—and who believes that such adjudication is a realistic possibility for courts in her society—may well support a conception of judicial role according to which courts should play a more significant role, engaging sometimes (not always, but sometimes) in lawmaking in a "major" rather than in a "minor" key. In any event, if the process of specifying constitutional indeterminacy were a fundamentally arbitrary one, the case for allocating the primary responsibility, or indeed any responsibility, for specifying constitutional indeterminacy to the Supreme Court, rather than to ordinary, majoritarian politics, would not be at all obvious.

If we accept the holistic account of justification, political-moral judgment, including the specification of constitutional indeterminacy, *is* a matter of justification: The specification of constitutional indeterminacy lies inside the domain of the more reasonable and the less reasonable; such judgment lies outside the domain of the merely arbitrary/subjective/willful. I have sketched the holistic account of justification elsewhere.[41] The holistic model of justification has replaced what Bernard Williams has called "the linear model", which, as Williams explains, "is wrong. No process of reason-giving fits this picture, in the sciences or elsewhere. . . . [T]he foundationalist [epistemological] enterprise, of resting the structure of knowledge on some favored class of statements, has now generally been displaced in favor of a holistic type of model, in which some beliefs can be questioned, justified, or adjusted while others are kept constant, but there is no process by which they can all be questioned at once, or all justified in terms of (almost) nothing. In von Neurath's famous image, we repair the ship while we are on the sea."[42] Catherine Elgin's spare but articulate portrayal of holistic justification merits quotation:

> Support for a conclusion comes, not from a single line of argument, but from a host of considerations of varying degrees of strength and relevance. What justifies the categories we construct is the cognitive and practical utility of the truths they enable us to formulate, the elegance and informativeness of the accounts they engender, the value of the ends they promote. We engage in system-building when we find the resources at hand inadequate. We have projects they do not serve, questions they do not answer, values they do not realize. Something new is required. But the measure of the adequacy of a novelty is its fit with what we think we already know. If the finding is at all surprising, the background of accepted beliefs is apt to require modification to make room for it, and the finding may require revision to be fitted into place. A process of delicate adjustments occurs, its goal being a system in wide reflective equilibrium.[43]

What is true of justification generally, including scientific justification, is true of moral justification in particular, including political-moral justification (of which the specification of constitutional indeterminacy is a species): "For the holist . . . the justification of moral knowledge neither depends upon independently known foundations nor is called into question by the impossibility of placing any given moral judgment beyond doubt. Practical justification is a dialectical affair, intelligible only in relation to the simultaneously social and intellectual setting of a particular time and place."[44]

The implications of the holistic account of justification, for present purposes, are that there are not only reasonable and unreasonable answers to the question of how an indeterminate constitutional directive should be specified, but that even among reasonable answers there are better and worse answers, such that one, including a judge, can reasonably choose among the reasonable answers; such choices not merely matters of "taste" or "preference". Let me elaborate, with particular reference to the *judicial* specification of constitutional indeterminacy—to constitutional specification *by a judge*.

I have written elsewhere, at length, about the moral pluralism—including, indeed especially, the religious-moral pluralism—of the American political community.[45] Given, first, the holistic account of justification and, second, the moral pluralism of the political community, and assuming the nonminimalist approach to the normative inquiry, this question arises: On what basis—on the basis of what, or whose, premises—should a judge specify, in the context of the conflict to be resolved, a constitutional directive relevant to but indeterminate in that context—including a directive that, though it has previously been (in Madison's words) "liquidated and ascertained by a series of particular discussions and adjudications",[46] nonetheless remains indeterminate in the context of the conflict to be resolved? On what basis should a judge try to make an indeterminate constitutional directive (what Gadamer has called) "concretely valid"[47] in the context of the conflict at hand? On the basis of what or whose premises should a judge decide how best to achieve, in the context at hand, the political-moral value privileged by the directive?

The heart of the judge's responsibility, of course, is to decide on the basis of "legal" premises (to the extent there are relevant legal premises): premises authoritative for her qua judge.[48] Assuming that the relevant legal premises do not conclude the question, it seems fitting for a judge to decide on the basis of premises that, although not authoritative for her qua judge, are nonetheless the object of widespread consensus in American society—even, perhaps, part of the society's "common sense"—unless the consensus/common sense is, in her view, either contrary to legal premises or mistaken;[49] conversely, it seems problematic for her to decide on the basis of premises widely rejected in American society. According to Justice Brennan, "[E]ven high court judges are constrained in issuing rulings[,] . . . not just by precedent and the texts they are interpreting, but also, *on any attractive political and jurisprudential theory*, by a decent regard for public opinion. . . ."[50]

Assuming, however, that legal premises and/or consensual/commonsensical premises, even if they rule out some answers to the "how best to achieve the value question", do not yield a single answer, presumably the judge should decide on the basis of premises she accepts, premises authoritative for her qua the particular person she is—unless, of course, an axiomatic (for the political-legal culture) norm about judicial role requires her to forsake reliance on one or more premises she accepts[51] (or unless one or more premises she accepts is widely rejected in American society). What sense would it make to suggest that when legal premises and consensual/commonsensical premises do not together yield an answer, a judge should decide on the basis of premises she rejects, premises not authoritative for her qua the particular person she is? (To say that an axiomatic norm about judicial role may require her to rely on one or more premises she rejects is just to say that one or more premises she rejects may be authoritative for her qua judge—that, in other words, one or more such premises may be legal premises.) In an essay titled "The Catholic Public Servant", U.S. Circuit Judge James L. Buckley has written: "When faced with ambiguities, or with problems that fall within the interstices that inevitably exist within and between laws, a judge is necessarily called upon to exercise a large measure of discretion. In doing so, he will inevitably bring to that task everything that he is—the books he has read; his experience as spouse, parent, and public official; his understanding of the nature of man and the responsibilities of citizenship; his sense of justice; even his sense of humor. A judge is not a machine, and the judicial function cannot be displaced by a formula or measured by an equation."[52]

To say, as I did a moment ago, that a judge should not rely on premises widely rejected in American society is not to say that she should never rely on premises not widely accepted in American society; it is not to say that she should "never be the first person to bring a new value, a new political or ethical insight, into the law."[53] As Justice Brennan has said, "High court judges interpreting a bill of rights may at times lead public opinion".[54] Justice Brennan quickly added, however, that "in a democratic society they cannot do so often, or by very much."[55]

If a judge should decide on the basis of premises she accepts (as well as on the basis of legal premises and consensual/commonsensical premises), pursuant to what process should she do so? She should decide pursuant to a process that is "dialogic", rather than monologic, in this sense:[56] a process in which she publicizes rather than conceals her real premises— the premises on which she is inclined to rely—thereby inviting challenges to her premises; and in which she cultivates a genuinely deliberative rather than dismissive stance, prepared to take seriously (rather than ignore) a challenge to her premises, and also to take seriously the competing premises of others. It is always better to address difficult issues dialogically rather than monologically. ("It matters relatively little whether the dialogue is through person-to-person dialogue or through that peculiar form of dialogue we call serious reading of texts, rituals, or events."[57]) But there is a special, practical reason why the process of specifying indeterminate constitutional directives should be dialogic: Even if decreed by a single judge at the trial stage, a particular specification cannot be maintained beyond the trial stage, and no specification can be decreed at the appellate stage, unless it enjoys the support of several judges. Specifying constitutional indeterminacy is an instance of collective, not individual, political-moral judgment.

I doubt that anyone wants to contend for an adjudicative process that is *not* dialogic (in the sense indicated): a process in which judges conceal their real premises and take seriously neither challenges to their premises nor the competing premises of others.[58] The much more likely contention is that the contested specifications yielded by the adjudicative process—even the adjudicative process at its dialogic best—are, like political-moral judgments generally, fundamentally matters of "taste" or "preference" rather than of "deliberation" and "justification". I have suggested that that argument trips, inter alia, on the holistic account of justification. ("Here we see a conspicuous gap in the argument: for showing that a fixed extrahistorical structure is not there [for us to use as a basis] to adjudicate disagreements is a long way from showing that we have no rational and principled ways of adjudicating disagreements."[59]) But this is not to deny that the contested specifications yielded by the adjudicative process are often based at least in part on premises—in particular, on political-moral premises, premises about what, as a political-moral matter, is better or best—that, though accepted by enough judges to get the specifications established, are neither "legal" nor "consensual"/"commonsensical".

An alternative likely contention is that among reasonable specifications of an indeterminate constitutional directive, one is as good as another, insofar as the strength of its justification is concerned. But relative *to whom* is one specification as reasonable as every other? It is simply not true that it is always or even often the case that the justification of every (reasonable) specification is a strong as the justification of every other one *from the perspective or vantage point of a particular judge evaluating the specifications, or even from the vantage point of the political community*. The strength of any justification, in a particular context, is a function of the strength, in that context, of the various premises on which it relies. Some premises not the object of consensus in American society are nonetheless more widely shared throughout American society than others; some premises are more widely rejected. Given certain premises widely shared throughout American society, some other premises, not the object of consensus in American society and perhaps not even widely shared—both nonnormative premises (about the way things were, are, or likely will be, or about the likely consequences of a choice) and normative ones (about what is morally good or fitting)—are nonetheless more plausible in the context of American society than other premises; and some premises are more implausible than others. In a dialogic process a consensus will sometimes emerge precisely because one position is supported by a justification the interlocutors eventually accept as stronger than the justification(s) that supports the competitor position(s). But that a consensus does not emerge—that a (diminished?) dissensus persists—does not entail that no justification can be stronger than another.

Of course, this is not to deny that judges may "reasonably" disagree among themselves about the best specification of an indeterminate directive. After all, judges do not all accept all the same relevant premises. Sometimes speculative premises about consequences are relevant, but judges, like the rest of us, do not all accept the same speculative premises, and often it is virtually impossible to confirm or disconfirm competing speculative premises. (Observing that "so little is known about the consequences of legal decisions", Richard Posner has written that "[n]ot only are the usual methods of scientific verification unavailable but so are the commonplace observations and experiences that enable us to correct our everyday behavior, whether in riding a bicycle, changing a fuse, or assembling a piece of equipment. Common sense cannot answer the question whether the preservation of political or religious freedom requires a broad reading of the First Amendment, or whether the exclusionary rule is needed as an adjunct to the tort remedies against unreasonable police searches."[60]) More importantly, judges do not all accept the same relevant normative premises: premises about what is good or fitting or valuable or right. And even if two or more judges in a case do accept the same relevant "values", they may not all rank them precisely the same way. The normative pluralism that characterizes citizens in general also characterizes those who represent them, including judges.

Nonetheless, the vocabulary of "objective" justification, "subjective" moral "preferences", and the like, is not at all helpful in thinking about the nature (and the limits) of moral justification. The specification of constitutional indeterminacy *is* a matter of justification, even though it is often the case, in the morally pluralistic American political community, that a particular specification cannot be justified across the entire community. To accept that the specification of constitutional indeterminacy is a matter of deliberation and justification—and that some political institutions might therefore be better suited for it than others, because some political institutions possess a richer deliberative capacity, or a more fitting kind of deliberative capacity—is to take a middle path between two extremes: the extreme of a nihilism according to which moral choice is merely an aesthetic (or perhaps a culinary) matter[61] and the extreme of a dogmatism according to which moral choice is algorithmic and one and only one algorithm is right. We can say about the specification of constitutional indeterminacy, including judicial specification, what Judge Posner has said about judicial decisions in the face of legal indeterminacy— that they "are not easily determined to be 'right' or 'wrong'; the vocabulary of apodictic certainty is misplaced. Perhaps the highest aspiration of the judge is reasonableness in adjudication."[62] The process of specifying constitutional indeterminacy is not an "arbitrary" one; such specification is a matter of justification, it lies inside the domain of the more reasonable and the less reasonable.

IV. A Digression on "The Rule of Law"

But, while not arbitrary, the process is nonetheless political: The specification of constitutional indeterminacy is, as I have indicated, a species of political-moral judgment. I want to digress from the main course of our inquiry to pursue the implications, for the ideal of "the rule of law", of conceding to the courts, in constitutional adjudication, the primary responsibility for making the relevant sort of political-moral judgments, for specifying indeterminate constitutional directives: Is it consistent with the rule of law for judges to exercise the primary responsibility for specifying constitutional indeterminacy? The answer depends, of course, on how we conceive the ideal. ("The rule of law is a notoriously contested concept. . . ."[63]) The rule of law is typically distinguished from rule that is "arbitrary". The phrase "a government of laws, not of men", although usually meant to track the difference between a government under the rule of law and an arbitrary government, is obviously misleading, since even a government of laws—a government under the rule of law—is a government of men and women. The relevant difference is between a government (of men and women) that respects the rule of law—government *by* law and *under* law—and one that does not, one that is, in that sense, arbitrary.[64]

The ideal of the rule of law governs legislation (law making) and administration (law enforcement) as well as adjudication. On any plausible account of the ideal it requires, with respect to legislation, "that new laws should be publicly promulgated, reasonably clear, and prospective".[65] With respect to administration it requires that the law be enforced against everyone (everyone, that is, to whom the law applies, everyone the law restrains or constrains), even the most powerful members of society, including the highest government officials, and that the equal protection of the law be extended to everyone, even the most marginal members of society, including the poor and the unpopular. With respect to adjudication—which is our principal concern here—the rule of law (on any plausible account) requires "that judicial decisions should be in accordance with law, issued after a fair and public hearing by an independent and impartial court, and that they should be reasoned and available to the public".[66] The important element, for present purposes, is that judicial decision making be "in accordance with law". The answer to the question about the consistency, with the ideal of the rule of law, of entrusting the primary responsibility to the courts for specifying constitutional indeterminacy depends on what it means for judicial decision making to be "according to law".

A preliminary, conceptual problem merits attention. Is the requirement that judicial decision making be "according to law" really a rule-of-law requirement at all—or is it, instead, a separation-of-powers requirement? Isn't it the separation of powers that grounds the according-to-law requirement? "The job of the elected and electorally accountable Congress, in conjunction with the president, is to make the laws; the job of the electorally unaccountable federal judiciary is to decide cases according to the laws that have been made." Is it a conceptual confusion, then, to refer the according-to-law requirement to the ideal of the rule of law? The answer, it seems to me, is that the according-to-law requirement is really two distinct but complementary requirements, one of which is indeed referable to the separation of powers, but the other of which is properly understood as grounded on the ideal of the rule of law.

The separation-of-powers requirement is that judicial decision making — other than judicial decision making in common law cases, which is a kind of legislation — be "according to law" in the sense of "according to the relevant law that has been established extrajudicially", whether that law be statutory or constitutional. The rule-of-law requirement is that judicial decision making — including judicial decision making in common law cases — be "according to law" in the sense of "according to the exercise of reason", where "the exercise of reason" is opposed to "the mere imposition of will".[67] A judicial decision complies with the separation-of-powers requirement if it is not ruled out by the relevant law that has been established extrajudicially. But because the relevant law that has been established extrajudicially is sometimes indeterminate, that a decision is not ruled *out* by the relevant law does not entail that only one decision is ruled *in* by the relevant law. In a case in which the relevant law that has been established extrajudicially is indeterminate, the rule-of-law requirement is that among the various possible decisions not ruled out by the relevant legal materials, the court choose "reasonably" rather than merely "arbitrarily" (in the sense of "willfully"). Similarly, in a case in which the relevant law ("precedent") has been established judicially, not extrajudicially — which includes many statutory and constitutional cases, of course, as well as, by definition, all common law cases — and in which the court is therefore not prevented by the separation of powers from "amending" the relevant law, the rule-of-law requirement is that the court decide reasonably rather than arbitrarily.[68] There seems to be no reason for confining that rule-of-law requirement to adjudication: Surely the ideal of the rule of law — which is concerned, after all, with the problem of arbitrary governance — requires that legislation, too, should be according to law rather than merely according to will. Legislation that is not according to law — in the rule-of-law sense of "according to law" — is arbitrary.

The crucial question about the rule-of-law variant of the according-to-law requirement, then, is this: In what sense of "reason" should judicial decision making be according to reason rather than merely according to will? If a judicial decision is according to reason if and only if the decision is determined by the relevant legal materials — only if, that is, the materials are determinate in the context of the conflict to be resolved — then obviously judicial decisions are often not according to reason or, therefore, consistent with the rule of law: The relevant legal materials are sometimes indeterminate. Because the relevant legal materials are sometimes indeterminate, the so-called formalist conception of adjudication and, relatedly, of the rule of law[69] is implausible. According to the formalist conception, adjudication proceeds, or should proceed, only by the "application" of determinate legal norms to the case at hand, understood as a largely "deductive" act; it does not, or should not, ever proceed by the "specification" of indeterminate legal norms, understood as a largely "nondeductive" process. A judicial decision is "according to law", according to the formalist conception, only if it is the conclusion of a deductive application of the relevant, determinate legal materials. Such judicial decision making is thought to conform to the rule of law, according to the formalist conception, because there is no room in such decision making for the kind of "discretion"—and therefore for the kind of "arbitrariness" or "willfullness"—that characterizes nondeductive specification of legal indeterminacy. According to "the traditional conviction that the Rule of Law demands that judges 'apply' rather than 'make' the law", writes Margaret Radin, "[i]f rules do not tie judges' hands with their logical or analytic application, . . . judges will have personal discretion in how to apply the law. This will . . . confer on judges a realm of 'arbitrary power'. . . ."[70]

The rule of law, properly conceived, does not require judicial "decisionmaking according to opaque legal rules".[71] It requires, not the "heavy use of outcome-determining rules laid down in advance, but . . . the use of procedures designed to ensure that legal decisionmaking is not merely the ad hoc imposition of personal will or the practice of politics."[72] Relatedly, and especially, the rule of law requires that a judge specify legal indeterminacy pursuant to a process of justification ("reason") that is dialogic rather than monologic: a process in which she publicizes rather than conceals her real premises—the premises on which she is inclined to rely—thereby inviting challenges to her premises; and in which she cultivates a genuinely deliberative rather than dismissive stance, prepared to take seriously (rather than to ignore) a challenge to her premises, and also to take seriously the competing premises of others.

Moreover, if they are to exercise the primary responsibility for specifying constitutional indeterminacy, the courts should, to the extent possible, aim at the *common* good—the good *of the (political) community*—rather than at the good merely of some part of the community, much less the good merely of the judge; and proceed, as much as possible, on the basis of premises, including moral premises about the good of the community, *widely shared in the community*, but in any event not on the basis of premises widely rejected there. (Again, Justice Brennan: "When Justices interpret the Constitution, they speak for their community, not for themselves alone. The act of interpretation must be understood with full consciousness that it is, in a very real sense, the community's interpretation that is sought."[73]) Each of those two imperatives opposes a kind of "arbitrariness": arbitrariness in the sense of privileging "I" or "mine" over "we" or "ours". Each element merits assimilation to the rule-of-law ideal of "a government of laws, not of men": a government of men and women, not qua individuals—out for themselves or for their groups—but qua citizens, engaged in the communal enterprise of trying both to maintain fidelity to, and to develop, the conception of human good, of the good or fitting way to live the life in common, to which the political (constitutional) tradition is committed.

Indeed, even if they are to exercise only secondary responsibility for specifying constitutional indeterminacy, the courts should accept as "reasonable" only those implicit specifications that aim at the *common* good rather than at the good merely of some part of the community. (Of course, one way to aim at the common good may be to aim at the good of some part of the community—for example, the poorest part. But then the aim is not "merely" at the good of some part.) Because the ideal of the rule of law governs legislation as well as adjudication—and, in particular, because the ideal requires that legislation as well as adjudication be according to "law" in the sense of "reason" rather than merely according to "will"—legislation, too, should aim at a good that is in some sense "common", a good of the entire community and not merely of some part—some "faction"—of it. It has even been argued that various rights provisions of the Constitution entail, or have been interpreted to support, such a requirement.[74]

Rejecting the formalist conception of ideal of the rule of law is not rejecting the ideal itself—though accepting the ideal while rejecting the formalist conception does require reconceiving the ideal.[75] The ideal of the rule of law is properly conceived to require, not that judges never engage in the nondeductive process of specifying indeterminate constitutional directives, but that when they engage in that process, they do so dialogically, in the sense I indicated above, and in a way that is doubly representative of the community: representative both of the community's good and of the community's conception of its good. If, and to the extent that, judicial specification of constitutional indeterminacy proceeds within the confines suggested here—and if and to the extent the specification is "issued after a fair and public hearing by an independent and impartial court,"[76] which "give[s] public reasons for [its] decision"[77]—then, and to that extent, constitutional adjudication is a constituent of government under the rule of law rather than a constituent of arbitrary government. It is neither "the ad hoc imposition of personal will" nor "the practice of [ordinary] politics". Judicial specification of constitutional indeterminacy can be (though, of course, in particular instances of it might not be) according to law—"law" in the sense of "reason", and "reason" in the sense of a re-presentative and dialogic practice of justification. In that respect at least, entrusting the primary responsibility for the specification of constitutional indeterminacy to the courts can be consistent with the ideal of the rule of law. Acceptance of the practice of judicial specification of constitutional indeterminacy entails "a way of understanding what the rule of law is, not a way of rejecting that ideal."[78]

V. Should the Court Play the Primary Role?
Herein of "Ordinary Politics"

However, that it is not inconsistent with the rule of law for judges to exercise the primary responsibility for specifying constitutional indeterminacy
does not by itself mean that they should exercise the primary responsibility—that they should follow the nonminimalist approach. I now want to
return to the main course of our inquiry to address the remaining basic
issues I identified earlier in this chapter: Even if there are, among the
reasonable specifications of a constitutional directive, better and worse
specifications, is there any reason to think that the Court (and the courts)
is in general more likely, or even as likely, to identify the better specifications than are the electorally accountable representatives of the people in
the Congress or in a state legislature (or, in the executive domain, than is
the president or a state governor)? And even if there is some reason to
think that the Court is generally more likely to identify the better specifications, does our commitment to majoritarian policy making demand
that the electorally accountable representatives of the people be charged
with the primary responsibility for choosing one or another reasonable
specification? And is there reason to believe, with Thayer, that the capacity of ordinary politics to deliberate well about constitutional questions,
and then to choose well, will eventually be bolstered if ordinary politics,
not constitutional adjudication, is the primary matrix of specifications of
indeterminate constitutional directives?

The principal reason for doubting that ordinary politics can generally
do a good job of specifying constitutional indeterminacy is that for most
members of the Congress, incumbency is a very important, if not overriding, value.[79] (Is there any reason to doubt that the same is true for
most persons who occupy the presidency of the United States? For most
state legislators? For most state governors?) That state of affairs has been
widely, if sadly, reported. From a 1989 *Newsweek* cover story on the Congress: "Congressmen are obsessed with . . . losing an election. . . . 'Every-
body here checks their spines in the cloakroom,' says Rep. Patricia
Schroeder. Shorn of significant party connections, each member is his
own political and policy operator. But these legislators are the world's
only entrepreneurs devoted to shunning risk. Among the favorite words
in everyday Capitol Hill conversation is 'cover'; it's a noun meaning a
position on an issue that is structured so as to avoid any political cost."[80]
From a 1990 *Business Week* cover story: "Nothing motivates members of
Congress like the fear of doing something that might be criticized. So all
too often they do nothing."[81]

The point is not that incumbency is, for each and every member of
the Congress, or even for most members, the only important value
(though surely for some members, if only a few, it does sometimes seem to
be the overriding value). Other important values include achieving a

position of influence in the Congress and participating in the making of (what a member believes to be) good public policy. Indeed, I am inclined to believe (perhaps naively) that for many members of the Congress, perhaps most, participating in the making of good public policy is the fundamental role value. "[T]he main reward of being a legislator lies in shaping public policy. When we say that legislators seek power, this is typically the power that they seek. Getting elected or re-elected is of course the precondition to this power, but control of public policy is its real substance."[82] Is it the case, however, as proponents of the public choice conception of legislative politics are inclined to claim, "that the motivation to be re-elected will dominate all others"?[83]

> [P]ublic choice [theory] commits the error of equating electoral defeat with death. Many legislators can live perfectly happy lives after they are defeated, making more money, exercising more personal power, or simply not working as hard. Some can even return to the legislature in a subsequent election. Since re-election is not an absolute precondition for a rewarding life experience, we must inquire into the legislator's desire for re-election. This inquiry brings us to the same ideological considerations that motivated the legislator to seek office in the first place.[84]

Nonetheless, incumbency is undeniably a fundamental value for most members of the Congress. Members of the Congress are therefore more likely to cater to the interests and views of their constituents—and of their contributors—than they otherwise would. Responsiveness to constituent interests and views is not always a bad thing; it is often, though not always, a good thing.[85] The point is simply that a regime in which incumbency is (inevitably?) a fundamental value seems often ill suited, in a politically heterogeneous society like the United States, to a truly deliberative, truly dialogic specification of indeterminate constitutional norms.

Perhaps I underestimate the severity of the problem. Perhaps it is not an exaggeration to see the concern with maintaining incumbency as a near-obsession and to conclude that this concern, coupled with the increased and increasing influence of the mass media—especially television—has in our time (de)generated a politics in which, as Mary Ann Glendon has put it, "it has become increasingly difficult even to define critical questions, let alone debate and resolve them."[86]

> While the nations of Eastern Europe are taking their first risk-laden and faltering steps toward democracy, the historic American experiment in ordered liberty is . . . undergoing a less dramatic, but equally fateful, crisis of its own. It is a crisis at the very heart of the American experiment in self-government, for it concerns the state of public deliberation about the right ordering of our lives together. In the home of free speech, genuine exchange of ideas about matters of high public importance has come to a virtual standstill.[87]

Glendon adds that "it [is not] readily apparent how the public forum, dominated as it is by images rather than ideas, could be reclaimed for genuine political discourse."[88]

The estimate of America's ordinary politics offered by George Will in his recent, book-length argument for term limits for those who serve in the Congress is no less dire than Professor Glendon's.[89] What Glendon and Will and an increasing number of others are saying about ordinary politics deserves our serious attention and consideration. But even if one is inclined to reject estimates like Glendon's and Will's as exaggerated, presumably there are *some* questions we want to lift at least somewhat above the fray of ordinary politics—above, for example, the distortions of thirty-second or even ten-second "sound bites" and political ads.[90] (Do you want Jane Doe to represent you in the Congress? She voted in favor of desecrating the flag! "When the main question in a member's mind every time he votes is, 'What kind of thirty-second spot are they going to make out of this vote?' then truly the ability of the political system to make complicated and tough decisions in the long-range interest of the United States is atomized."[91]) We lift constitutional questions above the political fray principally by entrusting the questions—entrusting them not wholly, but mainly and finally—to a politically insulated ("independent") judiciary. Thus, one reason one might have been sympathetic to the proposition that the Congress (or a state legislature) would be a better institution (and that, in the executive domain, the office of the presidency or of a state governor would be a better institution) than the Court for purposes of specifying indeterminate constitutional norms—namely, that the Congress, unlike the Court, is a politically accountable institution—turns out, on reflection, to be a reason for rejecting the proposition, not accepting it. And, indeed, I cannot fathom how anyone familiar with recent, extensive analyses of the character of America's ordinary politics[92] can even take seriously the claim, much less accept it, that ordinary politics is an unproblematic locus of the primary responsibility for deciding what the concrete contextual meanings of indeterminate constitutional norms shall be. A kindred claim seems equally doubtful: the claim that ordinary politics could be transformed into an unproblematic locus of the primary responsibility, if only the Court would help by following Thayer's advice and forsaking the nonminimalist approach.[93] But, again, we must distinguish among different genres of constitutional norms. Even if not every indeterminate constitutional norm would likely fare poorly in the hands of ordinary politics, surely *some* such norms would: norms "unusually vulnerable to majority sentiment."[94] (I return to the point—about the unusual vulnerability of some constitutional norms to majority sentiment—in chapter 10.)

Those persons who believe, with Justice Brennan, that "[the role of] reason and reflection . . . in moral judgment and constitutional adjudication . . . is considerable",[95] but who doubt that there is often ample room in ordinary politics for such reason and reflection, will be skeptical that ordinary politics can generally do a good job of specifying constitutional indeterminacy; they will be skeptical, therefore, about the capacity of ordinary politics for mature, informed deliberation about the specification of constitutional norms regarding rights or liberties; they will be skeptical about the Thayerian, minimalist approach to constitutional adjudication. They may even be inclined to follow Justice Brennan in supporting the nonminimalist approach; they may be inclined to support entrusting the primary responsibility for specifying indeterminate constitutional directives, not to ordinary politics, but to the courts—and, finally, to the Court. (It bears repeating, at this point, that we are discussing indeterminate constitutional directives regarding rights or liberties, not indeterminate directives regarding the horizontal allocation of power among the three parts of the national government or the vertical allocation of power between the national government and the governments of the states.)

With respect to the demands of specifying, in various particular contexts, indeterminate constitutional values, the processes of adjudication may be, in some respects at least, generally superior to the processes of legislation or policymaking. According to Henry Hart and Herbert Wechsler, "Both Congress and the President can obviously contribute to the sound interpretation of the Constitution. But are they, or can they be, so organized and manned as to be able, without aid from the courts, to build up a body of coherent and intelligible constitutional principle, and to carry public conviction that these principles are being observed? In respect of experience and temperament of personnel? Of procedure for decision? Of means of recording grounds of decision? Of opportunity for close examination of particular questions?"[96] Alexander Bickel pressed a complementary point: "[An] advantage that courts have is that questions of principle never carry the same aspect for them as they did for the legislature or the executive. Statutes, after all, deal typically with abstract or dimly foreseen problems. The courts are concerned with the flesh and blood of an actual case. This tends to modify, perhaps to lengthen, everyone's view. It also provides an extremely salutary proving ground for all abstractions; it is conducive, in a phrase of Holmes, to thinking things, not words, and thus to the evolution of principle by a process that tests as it creates."[97] So, the goal of a sensible division of political labor—a division sensitive to different institutions' relative strengths and weaknesses— offers some support for allocating to the judiciary, and finally to the Supreme Court, significant responsibility for deciding what the concrete contextual meanings of indeterminate constitutional norms shall be.[98]

If the minimalist approach to the (judicial) specification of constitutional indeterminacy is appropriately described as Thayerian, the nonminimalist approach is appropriately associated with the early position of Alexander Bickel: Over thirty years ago, Bickel presented a view, much like the one I have sketched here, about the relative strengths and weaknesses of ordinary politics and constitutional adjudication as matrices of mature deliberation about the contextual meaning of the indeterminate constituents of the American constitutional tradition. Because of its relevance here, a central passage of Bickel's argument merits full quotation:

> [M]any actions of government have two aspects: their immediate, necessarily intended, practical effects, and their perhaps unintended or unappreciated bearing on values we hold to have more general and permanent interest. It is a premise we deduce not merely from the fact of a written constitution but from the history of the race, and ultimately as a moral judgment of the good society, that government should serve not only what we conceive from time to time to be our immediate material needs but also certain enduring values. This in part is what is meant by government under law. But such values do not present themselves ready-made. They have a past always, to be sure, but they must be continually derived, enunciated, and seen in relevant application. And it remains to ask which institution of our government—if any single one in particular—should be the pronouncer and guardian of such values.
>
> Men in all walks of public life are able occasionally to perceive this second aspect of public questions. Sometimes they are also able to base their decisions on it; that is one of the things we like to call acting on principle. Often they do not do so, however, particularly when they sit in legislative assemblies. There, when the pressure for immediate results is strong enough and emotions ride high enough, men will ordinarily prefer to act on expediency rather than take the long view. Possibly legislators—everything else being equal—are as capable as other men of following the path of principle, where the path is clear or at any rate discernible. Our system, however, like all secular systems, calls for the evolution of principle in novel circumstances, rather than only for its mechanical application. Not merely respect for the rule of established principles but the creative establishment and renewal of a coherent body of principled rules—that is what our legislatures have proven themselves ill equipped to give us.[99]

VI. Skepticism about Nonminimalism

I said in the preceding section that those who are skeptical that ordinary politics can often serve as a matrix of mature deliberation about the contextual meaning of indeterminate constitutional directives may be inclined to follow Justice Brennan in supporting the nonminimalist approach. It is also possible, however, that such a skeptic may be disinclined to support the nonminimalist approach. After all, skepticism about the constitutional-deliberative capacity of ordinary politics neither presupposes nor entails faith in the nonminimalist approach of a Justice Brennan. There may be good reasons for doubting that either the Thayerian approach or Brennan's approach can serve us well. Put another way, skepticism about the capacity of ordinary politics to specify constitutional indeterminacy does not necessarily translate into faith in the capacity of judges—in particular, in the capacity of Supreme Court justices—to specify constitutional indeterminacy. ("The comparative independence of judges frees them from the potentially distorting influence of public will but offers no particular affirmative promise that, so freed, judges will reach good outcomes on their own; nor, taken alone, does it offer any reason for supposing that popular politics will stray from the oath of political justice more often than judicial judgment of that the net result of judicial intervention will be more, rather than less, political justice overall."[100]) Justice Brennan's faith in constitutional adjudication may be just as problematic as Professor Thayer's faith in ordinary politics. If so, and if one has an all-else-being-equal preference for ordinary, majoritarian politics, then one will be inclined to conclude that Thayer's minimalist approach prevails by default. What good democrat (small *d*) does not have such a preference? Indeed, one might have an even-if-all-else-is-not-equal preference for ordinary, majoritarian politics. But if all else is apparently not equal—in particular, if one perceives the capacity of courts to specify constitutional indeterminacy to be significantly superior to the capacity of ordinary politics to do so—surely that counts for something, even for a good democrat.

As I noted earlier, specifications of indeterminate constitutional directives are a species of political-moral judgment. Skepticism about the capacity of judges to specify constitutional indeterminacy is skepticism about their capacity for making sound political-moral judgments. "To possess good judgment . . . is not merely to possess great learning or intelligence, but to be a person of a certain sort, to have a certain character, as well."[101] A dialogic capacity is an important element of the capacity for good judgment. I have emphasized, in this chapter, the importance of specifying constitutional indeterminacy in a dialogic, not monologic, way. Dialogic capacity, however, is in short supply. "For however often the word is bandied about, dialogue remains a rare phenomenon in anyone's experience. Dialogue demands the intellectual, moral, and, at the limit, religious ability to struggle to hear another and to respond. To respond critically, and even suspiciously when necessary, but to respond only in dialogical relationship to a real, not a projected other."[102] If one doubts that more than a (relatively) few judges, or more than an occasional justice of the Supreme Court, have, or will have, the requisite qualities of mind and character—and, in particular, the requisite dialogic capacity—then one will be skeptical that constitutional adjudication can generally be a matrix of mature deliberation about the concrete meaning, in various particular contexts, of indeterminate constitutional directives. It is understandable that some of us, perhaps many of us, harbor such skepticism, that we do not expect much of our courts—including (especially?) the Supreme Court of the United States. There is, after all, the Court's often depressing history and the fact that ideologues—often mediocre ideologues—have sometimes sat on the Court.[103]

Do we now have the judges and justices the nonminimalist approach requires? Even if such judges and justices are, alas, in depressingly short supply, it does not follow that we should not want—or, therefore, that we should not spend time and energy pursuing—the appointment of more such judges and justices. Our (understandable) skepticism about the capacity for good judgment of many of the judges and justices we now have, unless that skepticism is dogmatic, can coexist with an aspiration for more judges and justices who embody the requisite qualities of mind and character; it can coexist, too, with various practical efforts to achieve the appointment of such judges and justices. That some of us cannot bring ourselves to expect much of our courts does not mean that we should not ask much of them either.[104]

In thinking about what we should ask of our courts, about what kind of judges and judiciary we should aspire to—in thinking, in particular, about what role courts can usefully play in American society, in cases involving questions of constitutional rights or liberties—it might be clarifying to turn our attention away from American society to Eastern Europe,[105] for example, or to the international legal order. What kind of judges and judiciary do we think that the self-transforming societies of Eastern Europe should aspire to, especially in connection with the protection of human rights?[106] What kind of judges and judiciary do we think that the international legal order should aspire to, as it seeks to protect human rights and to develop their concrete meaning in and for various particular contexts? Those of us who have lofty ambitions for courts in other parts of the world, or for international courts, have some explaining to do if simultaneously we insist that our own courts—even the Supreme Court as it confronts questions of constitutional human rights—should play only a relatively small, almost ministerial role.

It bears emphasis that the point about the importance of the judicial capacity for good judgment is not a partisan political one. I am not suggesting, for example, that we need more judges from the left side of the political spectrum. There are (or have been) good and even great judges whose politics is (or was) of the right—just as there are (or have been) good and even great judges whose politics is (or was) of the left. So also there are (and have been) poor judges—judges bereft of the requisite qualities of mind and character—of the left as well as of the right. The point is not that our judges and justices should all be in the grip of the very same "subjectivity", the very same political-moral convictions and sensibilities, though surely some political-moral convictions and sensibilities are antithetical to and subversive of basic constitutional principles. We members of the political community from which our judges and justices come and which they represent are not all in the grip of the same political-moral convictions and sensibilities. The American political community is pluralistic. The political-moral culture of our judiciary is very unlikely to be monistic while the larger political-moral culture is pluralistic. My point, however, is normative: The political-moral culture of our judiciary should not be monistic even if somehow it could be. "Some lawyers and judges believe that a diverse judiciary is bad, because it makes law uncertain, unpredictable. They have a point. But from the standpoint not of order but of knowledge, they are wrong. A diverse judiciary exposes— yet at the same time reduces—the intellectual poverty of law, viewed as a method not just of settling disputes authoritatively but also of generating cogent answers to social questions."[107]

In the end, whether and to what extent one finds it an appealing prospect to have our judges and justices actually follow the nonminimalist approach to the specification of constitutional indeterminacy depends at least partly on whether and to what extent one believes that, in general, our judges and justices have a better capacity for sound political-moral judgment than, in general, do our legislators. (The cynic will say that whether one believes that our judges and justices have such a capacity depends simply on whether and to what extent one believes that our judges and justices are deciding constitutional cases, on balance, the way one believes they ought to be decided.) Earlier, and relatedly, I suggested that the absence of the capacity for good judgment among those who populate our ordinary politics diminishes the appeal of the Thayerian, minimalist approach. The question arises, therefore, should we be more sanguine about the possibility of populating our courts with persons who have the capacity for sound political-moral judgment than we are about the possibility of populating our politics with such persons? Of course, we should certainly be at least as insistent that those who populate our ordinary politics be persons with the capacity for good judgment as we are that those who populate our courts be persons with that capacity. We should demand too that, given their political vulnerability, the persons who populate our ordinary politics have not merely the capacity for good judgment but also the complementary, enabling capacity for relatively fearless judgment. (Edmund Burke said that "[y]our representative owes you, not his industry only, but his judgment; and he betrays, instead of serving you, if he sacrifices it to your opinion."[108]) Life-tenured judges don't need that enabling capacity nearly as much.

If and to the extent our demand that the persons who populate our ordinary politics be persons of good (and fearless) judgment were eventually satisfied, the need for and therefore the appeal of the nonminimalist judicial approach would be diminished. If and to the extent that demand is unfulfilled, however, the need for the nonminimalist judicial approach persists. But if and to the extent our demand that the judges and justices who populate our courts be persons of good judgment is unfulfilled, the appeal of our judges and justices actually following the nonminimalist approach is doubtful. Indeed, to those who are skeptical that our courts are now or ever will be more than haphazardly populated with persons who have the requisite capacity for sound political-moral judgment, the appeal even of promoting, as a kind of ideal, the nonminimalist approach to the normative inquiry is doubtful. Consider, in that regard, this sobering observation—sobering to me, at any rate—by Martin Shapiro:

Imagine . . . a [Supreme Court] justice with strong tendencies toward imprudence that had, in the past, been held partially in check by qualms about the democratic deficit of the Court and the political and moral legitimacy of justices forcing their own particular moral conclusions down the throats of the American people. Reading Perry should send such a justice to the Crusades as a prophet armed. Nothing is easier for any human being than to imagine himself a moral deliberator when he is really only asserting a self-serving ideology. Among human beings none is more likely to fall into this vice than a Supreme Court justice who has just been awarded the mantle and crown of philosopher king. . . . [Perry's] teachings will powerfully arm the worst as well as the best of our Supreme Court justices.[109]

I said earlier that the thoroughgoing judicial minimalist, intent on minimizing the role of judicial "subjectivity" in the adjudicative process, will embrace both interpretive minimalism and normative minimalism, which are complementary positions. Although I have discussed interpretive minimalism in this chapter, my focus has been on normative minimalism: why one might embrace it, why one might reject it, and why one, tempted to reject it, might be wary about doing so. Unless one accepts the case for normative minimalism—in particular, unless one accepts that the judicial process of specifying constitutional indeterminacy is seriously problematic (and therefore wants to tame the process, which is the aim of normative minimalism)—one has little reason to embrace interpretive minimalism. Interpretive minimalism, after all, is basically just a strategy for diminishing the occasions on which a judge will have to specify (whether deferentially or not) constitutional indeterminacy—for diminishing, that is, conclusions about original meaning according to which a constitutional provision represents an indeterminate directive. It is difficult to see why a judge would deploy the strategy if she did not think it seriously problematic for judges to specify constitutional indeterminacy. Because the argument for normative minimalism is substantially the same as the argument for interpretive minimalism, nothing is lost by focusing, as I have in this chapter and as I continue to do in subsequent chapters, on normative minimalism.

Up to now, I have proceeded acontextually: I have addressed, in chapter 3, the question of originalism and, in this chapter, the question of minimalism—especially the question of normative minimalism—outside the context of any particular area of constitutional doctrine. It is now time to contextualize the inquiry. In chapters 8 and 9, I inquire into the extent to which modern equal protection doctrine and modern substantive due process doctrine are consistent with the originalist approach to constitutional interpretation. Moreover, I inquire into the extent to which they are—and also into the extent to which they should be—consistent with the minimalist (Thayerian) approach to constitutional specification. Contextualizing the inquiry has a special payoff with respect to the question of normative minimalism: I hope it will be clear, by the end of chapter 9, why in responding to the question of the Court's proper role in specifying indeterminate directives regarding rights or liberties, it is difficult to reach any confident conclusions—as this chapter demonstrates—without distinguishing between or among different kinds of directives regarding rights or liberties.

7

The Original Meaning of the Fourteenth Amendment

I want to inquire into the implications both of originalism and of normative minimalism for the constitutional doctrine the modern Supreme Court has fashioned in the name of "equal protection" and also for the doctrine it has fashioned in the name of "substantive due process". We cannot begin that inquiry, however, until we ascertain the original meaning of the relevant part of the Fourteenth Amendment, the second sentence of section 1, which provides: "No State shall make or enforce any law which shall abridge the privileges or immunities of citizens of the United States; nor shall any State deprive any person of life, liberty, or property, without due process of law; nor deny to any person within its jurisdiction the equal protection of the laws."

There are various questions one can ask about the original meaning of that sentence: What privileges and immunities were meant to be protected; that is, how was the phrase "the privileges or immunities of citizens of the United States" originally understood? How was "abridge" originally understood; that is, what were the privileges and immunities that were meant to be protected meant to be protected from? Were they meant to be protected from more than racial discrimination? From more than discrimination? Was the privileges or immunities clause, or some other part of the second sentence, meant to make the privileges and immunities of the Bill of Rights applicable to the states? Were the three clauses of the second sentence each meant to serve a distinct function? If so, what function was each clause meant to serve? And so on.

If the voluminous historical scholarship about the Fourteenth Amendment is any indication, there is room for reasonable disagreement about the answers to at least some of those questions. Against the background of my discussion in chapter 4 of the indeterminacy of history, my aim in this chapter is limited: to identify, not the putative right answer to each of the various relevant questions about the original meaning of the second sentence of section 1, but the plausible answer or answers—the answer or answers one can reasonably endorse. I base my conclusions in this chapter less on my own exploration of the relevant historical materials than on the arguments of several scholars who have recently explored those materials. My assumption is that one good way to identify the answers one can reasonably endorse, if not indeed the best way, is to look at the answers that have actually been endorsed by such credible analysts of the historical record as Michael Kent Curtis, William Nelson, Akhil Amar, John Harrison, and some others. Of course, these scholars—whose work I cite at various points in this chapter—do not always agree with one another. But that's the point: the indeterminacy of history. There is room for reasonable disagreement about the original meaning of the second sentence of section 1.

I

The basic features of the historical background of the Fourteenth Amendment are neither disputed nor unfamiliar.[1] For present purposes, a bare sketch is sufficient.

In 1863, during the Civil War, President Abraham Lincoln issued the Emancipation Proclamation,[2] declaring an end to slavery in the United States. In 1865, after the Civil War, the Thirteenth Amendment proclaimed that "[n]either slavery nor involuntary servitude, except as a punishment for crime whereof the party shall have been duly convicted, shall exist within the United States, or any place subject to their jurisdiction."[3]

In the American South, however, the subordinated position of the freed slaves was maintained by the infamous Black Codes. In Mississippi, for example, an 1865 law provided:

> Every civil officer shall, and every person may, arrest and carry back to his or her legal employer any freedman, free negro, or mulatto who shall have quit the service of his or her employer before the expiration of his or her term of service without good cause. . . .
>
> . . . If any freedman, free negro or mulatto, convicted of any of the misdemeanors provided against in this act, shall fail or refuse for the space of five days after conviction, to pay the fine and costs imposed, such person shall be hired out by the sheriff or other officer, at the public outcry, to any white person who will pay said fine and all costs, and take the convict for the shortest time.[4]

"Other provisions of some of the Black Codes barred Blacks from any business except 'husbandry' without obtaining a special license, or forbad them from renting or leasing land except in towns and cities."[5] In 1872, in the *Slaughter-House Cases*, the Supreme Court recounted the story of the Black Codes:

Among the first acts of legislation adopted by several of the States [were] laws which imposed upon the colored race onerous disabilities and burdens, and curtailed their rights in the pursuit of life, liberty, and property to such an extent that their freedom was of little value, while they had lost the protection which they had received from their former owners from motives both of interest and humanity.

They were in some States forbidden to appear in the towns in any other character than menial servants. They were required to reside on and cultivate the soil without the right to purchase or own it. They were excluded from many occupations of gain, and were not permitted to give testimony in the courts in any case where a white man was a party. It was said that their lives were at the mercy of bad men, either because the laws for their protection were insufficient or were not enforced.[6]

The Civil Rights Act of 1866[7] was directed against the Black Codes. Section 1 of the Act provided, in relevant part:

[A]ll persons born in the United States and not subject to any foreign power, excluding Indians not taxed, are hereby declared to be citizens of the United States; and such citizens, of every race and color, without regard to any previous condition of slavery or involuntary servitude, except as punishment for a crime whereof the party shall have been duly convicted, shall have the same right, in every State and Territory of the United States, to make and embrace contracts, to sue, be parties, and give evidence, to inherit, purchase, lease, sell, hold, and convey real and personal property, and to full and equal benefit of all laws and proceedings for the security of person and property, as is enjoyed by white citizens, and shall be subject to like punishment, pains, and penalties, and to none other, any law, statute, ordinance, regulation, or custom, to the contrary notwithstanding.

President Andrew Johnson had vetoed the 1866 Civil Rights Act partly on the ground that the Congress lacked the constitutional power to enact it.[8] The Congress—the 39th Congress—overrode the veto and then, leaving nothing to chance, proposed the Fourteenth Amendment, which, when the process of ratification was completed two years later, in 1868, removed any doubt about congressional power to enact legislation like the 1866 Act.[9]

The relevant provisions of the Fourteenth Amendment, for present purposes, are sections 1 and 5. Section 1 consists of two sentences, the first of which states: "All persons born or naturalized in the United States, and subject to the jurisdiction thereof, are citizens of the United States and of the State wherein they reside." The principal point of that sentence was to "overturn the Dred Scott decision by making *all persons* born within the United States and subject to its jurisdiction citizens of the United States."[10] Whatever else it does, the second sentence of section 1 constitutionalizes the 1866 Act.[11] Section 5 of the Amendment speaks specifically to the question of the Congress' power to enact, not merely the 1866 Act, but other, kindred acts the Congress might (and did) in the future want to enact: "The Congress shall have power to enforce, by appropriate legislation, the provisions of this article."

II

What are the plausible answers to the various relevant questions about the original meaning of the second sentence of section 1 of the Fourteenth Amendment? Let's consider the three clauses in the order in which they appear in the second sentence.

The Privileges or Immunities Clause. As a *textual* matter—that is, reading the words of the text in the sense in which we would likely use them[12]— the privileges or immunities clause is a limitation both on *legislation* and on *administration*; the clause limits the laws a state may "enact" (legislate) or "enforce" (administer): No state may enact or enforce laws that abridge certain privileges or immunities, namely, "the privileges or immunities of citizens of the United States". (I address below the question of the original meaning of "the privileges or immunities of the citizens of the United States".) Thus read, the clause speaks to all the principal institutions of state government, both those that play a role in the process of enacting legislation—primarily the legislative branch of government, but also the executive branch, which often proposes legislation and which has the power of veto—and those, like the police, that administer the laws.

As a *contextual* matter, the privileges or immunities clause was meant to prohibit (both enactment and enforcement of) laws that "abridge" any of the protected privileges or immunities, in the sense of denying to non-white citizens any of the protected privileges or immunities granted to white citizens, or of otherwise diminishing nonwhite citizens' enjoyment, relative to white citizens' enjoyment, of any such privilege or immunity.[13] Was the clause meant to prohibit only such laws? The words of the clause, at least as we would likely use them, do not preclude the possibility that the clause was meant to prohibit discriminatory laws beyond just racially discriminatory laws—or even the possibility that it was meant to prohibit more than just discriminatory laws.

(By "racially discriminatory" laws, I mean, in the present context, laws, enacted by a political establishment wholly or largely white, discriminating against nonwhites. Similarly, but more generally, by "racial discrimination", I mean discrimination by whites against nonwhites. To conclude, as I later do, that, in addition to whatever else it was meant to prohibit, the privileges or immunities clause was meant to prohibit laws, enacted wholly or largely by whites, discriminating against some (other) whites—in particular, against Southern whites who had remained loyal to the Union during the Civil War or Northern whites migrating to the South after the Civil War[14]—is to conclude that the clause was meant to prohibit discriminatory laws beyond just racially discriminatory laws.)

The Equal Protection Clause. As a *textual* matter, the equal protection clause is a limitation on *administration*—on a state's administration of the laws. Thus read, the clause speaks principally to the institutions of state government, like the police, charged with administering or enforcing the laws. (The clause also speaks to the legislative branch of state government to the extent the legislature wants to prescribe rules authorizing the discriminatory administration or enforcement of the laws.) That a state has not enacted and is not enforcing any law that abridges a protected privilege or immunity does not entail that the state is not administering any of its laws in a discriminatory fashion, denying the protection of the laws to some persons, to the detriment of their life, liberty, or property. The privileges or immunities clause, as I said, limits both legislation and administration, in that it limits the laws a state may "enact" (legislate) or "enforce" (administer); the equal protection clause, too, limits administration. But whereas the privileges or immunities clause speaks to the *administration of unconstitutional laws* (laws that "abridge" protected privileges or immunities), the equal protection clause, as a textual matter, speaks to the *unconstitutional administration of laws* (administration that denies the equal protection of the laws).[15]

As a *contextual* matter, the equal protection clause was meant to prohibit principally racially discriminatory administration: Law enforcement officers in the American South often did not investigate, much less prosecute, lawless acts of violence against the person or property of freed slaves, of other Americans of African ancestry, or even of white persons who sympathized with the plight of the freed slaves. ("[T]he wave of Klan lynchings and private violence undeterred and unpunished by the state that characterized the post–Civil War era is the paradigmatic equal protection violation, not Jim Crow laws and segregated schools."[16]) Was the equal protection clause meant to prohibit only racially discriminatory administration? The words of the clause (as we would likely use them) do not preclude the possibility that the clause was meant to prohibit discrimination more broadly.

It is possible, too, that the equal protection clause was meant to govern discriminatory legislation as well as discriminatory administration. The position of the Supreme Court, which has construed "the equal protection of the laws" to mean, in part, "the protection of equal laws",[17] has been that the clause was meant to govern, inter alia, discriminatory legislation. (I discuss the relevant constitutional doctrine in chapter 8.) There is significant support in the historical record for the Court's position, in particular Senator Jacob Howard's important and now famous speech in the Congress on May 23, 1866. Howard said, in the part of that speech relevant here,

> [The equal protection clause] abolishes all class legislation in the States and does away with the injustice of subjecting one caste of persons to a code not applicable to another. It prohibits the hanging of a black man for a crime for which the white man is not to be hanged. It protects the

black man in his fundamental rights as a citizen with the same shield which it throws over the white man. Is it not time, Mr. President, that we extend to the black man, I had almost called it the poor privilege of the equal protection of the law? Ought not the time to be now passed when one measure of justice is to be meted out to a member of one caste while another and a different measure is meted out to the member of another caste, both castes being alike citizens of the United States, both bound to obey the same laws, to sustain the burdens of the same Government, and both equally responsible to justice and to God for the deeds done in the body?[18]

So, perhaps as a contextual matter the equal protection clause and the privileges or immunities clause overlap in governing discriminatory legislation. The important point, for present purposes, is that although the privileges or immunities clause governs, inter alia, the administration (as well as the enactment) of discriminatory laws, only the equal protection clause governs the discriminatory administration of laws—laws that, as written, are nondiscriminatory—even if, like the privileges or immunities clause, it also governs the enactment and enforcement (administration) of discriminatory laws. In any event, section 1 as a whole governs, whatever else it governs, both the enactment and enforcement of discriminatory laws and the discriminatory enforcement of nondiscriminatory laws.[19]

The Due Process Clause. As a *textual* matter, the due process clause is a limitation on *adjudication*—on a state's adjudication of cases under the relevant laws, whether its own laws or applicable national laws (statutory or constitutional). Thus read, the clause speaks principally to the institutions of state government charged either with adjudicating cases—the courts—or with developing and presenting cases, especially the investigative and prosecutorial arms of government. (The clause also speaks to the legislative branch of state government to the extent the legislature wants to prescribe rules for the investigation, prosecution, or adjudication of cases.[20]) That a state has not enacted and is not enforcing any law that abridges a protected privilege or immunity does not entail that the state is not prosecuting or adjudicating any cases in a problematic fashion, to the detriment of the life, liberty, or property of the persons against whom the state is acting. One can easily imagine, for example, the prosecution of constitutionally valid rules principally against just a particular class of persons.

As a *contextual* matter, the due process clause was meant to prohibit principally racially discriminatory action (prosecution or adjudication). Was it meant to prohibit only racially discriminatory action? Like the words of the equal protection clause, the words of the due process clause do not preclude the possibility that it was meant to prohibit discrimination more broadly. There is no reason to conclude that the due process clause was meant to prohibit discrimination *less* broadly than the equal protection clause. Indeed, if the relation between the two clauses is, as both the text and the historical context of section 1 suggest, at least partly complementary, it is implausible to conclude that one clause was meant to prohibit discrimination less, or more, broadly than the other: Each clause was meant to protect, in a distinctive but complementary way, a person's life, liberty, and property, the equal protection clause by prohibiting (principally, if not only) discriminatory *inaction* constituting the denial of the equal *protection* of the laws, the due process clause by prohibiting discriminatory *action* constituting the imposition of the unequal *burden* of the laws.[21] But was the due process clause meant to prohibit only discriminatory action? The words of the due process clause, unlike those of the equal protection clause, strongly suggest that it was meant to prohibit, in addition to discriminatory action, action that, though not discriminatory, is problematic in some other way.

   The Citizen/Person Distinction. As a *textual* matter, there is an interesting difference between, on the one side, the privileges or immunities clause and, on the other, the equal protection clause and the due process clause: Whereas the latter two clauses speak of "persons", the former clause speaks of "citizens"—"citizens of the United States". As a *contextual* matter, are the intended beneficiaries of the privileges or immunities clause all persons or, instead, only citizens? The privileges or immunities clause was unquestionably meant to be limited, and by its language is limited, to the privileges and immunities *of* citizens (whatever those privileges and immunities are). But the language of the clause does not preclude the possibility that the clause was not meant to be limited *to* citizens. As John Ely has put the point: "'No State shall make or enforce any law which shall abridge the privileges or immunities of citizens of the United States' *could* mean that only citizens are protected in their privileges or immunities, but it surely doesn't have to. It could just as easily mean that there is a set of entitlements, 'the privileges and immunities of citizens of the United States,' which states are not to deny to anyone. In other words, the reference to citizens may define the class of rights rather than limit the class of beneficiaries."[22] Ely's conclusion: "Since everyone seems to agree that such a construction would better reflect what we know of the purpose, and since it is one the language will bear comfortably, it is hard to imagine why it shouldn't be followed."[23]

   Note Ely's "everyone seems to agree". He also says that "[i]t seems to be generally agreed that no conscious intention to limit the protection of the [privileges or immunities] clause to citizens appears in the historical records."[24] Ely to the contrary notwithstanding, however, it is *not* generally agreed that "no conscious intention . . . appears in the historical records."[25] In particular, Earl Maltz and John Harrison, in separate articles, have recently presented an impressive argument that whereas the intended beneficiaries both of the equal protection clause and of the due process clause are all persons, aliens as well as citizens, the intended beneficiaries of the privileges or immunities clause are only citizens.[26] The Maltz/Harrison reading imputes to the original meaning of section 1 the position that although with respect to life, liberty, and property everyone, aliens included, merits both the same "protection of the laws" citizens have and the same "process of law" due citizens, not everyone merits *all* the same privileges and immunities citizens have—in particular, and for example, aliens do not merit precisely the same privileges of buying, owning, and selling real property citizens have. (This is not to say that a state may not extend to aliens precisely the same such privileges its citizens have.) "The framers clearly believed that aliens were entitled to *some* rights; at the same time, however, they carefully noted and preserved the distinction between aliens and citizens. . . . The absolute right to real property . . . derived from citizenship; thus, the rights of aliens in this regard were often restricted by the states."[27]

Even if we were to conclude, with Maltz and Harrison and against Ely, that the intended beneficiaries of the privileges or immunities clause are only citizens, it is not clear what the implications would be—or, indeed, whether there would be any serious implications—for modern constitutional law: As I have explained elsewhere, the modern Supreme Court's solicitude for aliens is better justified, neither on the basis of the equal protection clause, on which the Court has tended to rely, nor on the basis of any other part of section 1, but on the basis of the supremacy clause of Article VI of the Constitution.[28]

It is not surprising, then, that the bulk of the controversy about the original meaning of the second sentence of section 1 of the Fourteenth Amendment has focused, not on the "all persons or only citizens" question, but on three other inquiries, the answers to which *do* have significant implications for modern constitutional law:

First, what is the original meaning of the phrase "the privileges or immunities of citizens of the United States"? What category or categories of privileges and immunities were meant to be protected?

Second, what were the privileges and immunities that were meant to be protected meant to be protected from? Does the privileges or immunities clause, as originally understood—and perhaps the equal protection clause, too, if we read it as overlapping, to an extent, the privileges or immunities clause—represent only the directive that states are neither to enact nor to enforce laws that deny to nonwhite citizens any of the protected privileges or immunities granted to white citizens, or that otherwise diminish nonwhite citizens' enjoyment, relative to white citizens' enjoyment, of any such privilege or immunity? Or does it represent a broader antidiscrimination directive—and, if so, what directive? Does it represent a directive that prohibits, in addition to (some) discriminatory laws, even (some) laws that abridge protected privileges or immunities in a nondiscriminatory way? (As a matter both of text and of context, it is implausible to think that the equal protection clause, which arguably overlaps the privileges or immunities clause to an extent, governs more than discriminatory state action.) Put another way, does a law "abridge" a protected privilege or immunity, within the original meaning of the privileges or immunities clause, only if the law discriminates against a class of persons?[29] Or does "abridge", as originally understood, have a broader meaning: a meaning that includes but is not limited to discrimination?

Third, do the equal protection clause and the due process clause, as originally understood, represent only the directive that states are not to discriminate on the basis of race in administering the laws (equal protection)[30] or in prosecuting or adjudicating cases (due process)? Or do they represent a broader antidiscrimination directive? Does the due process clause represent a directive that prohibits, in addition to (some) discriminatory prosecution/adjudication, even (some) nondiscriminatory prosecution/adjudication?

The First Inquiry: What Privileges and Immunities Were Meant to Be Protected?

What privileges and immunities were meant to be protected, against state government, by the privileges or immunities clause—what privileges and immunities are they that, according to the original understanding, "no state shall abridge"? What is the original meaning of "the privileges or immunities of citizens of the United States"?

Scholars agree that, contrary to the position of the majority in the *Slaughter-House Cases*,[31] "the privileges or immunities of citizens of the United States"—that is, the privileges and immunities of persons who are citizens of the United States, all of whom are also, under the first sentence of section 1 of the Fourteenth Amendment, citizens "of the State wherein they reside"—was meant to include all the privileges and immunities citizens enjoy under state law. They agree that the privileges and immunities meant to be protected include, for example, both (1) the fundamental rights to life and to liberty ("liberty" in the traditional, Blackstonian sense of the absence of any legal restraint on one's ability to go where one wants[32]) and (2) basic rights of property and of contract. "No one who sat in Congress or in the state legislatures that dealt with the Fourteenth Amendment doubted that section 1 was designed to put to rest any doubt about the power of the national government to protect basic common law rights of property and contract. While there were doubts about the extent to which the section protected basic rights, there was no doubt that it extended some protection to them."[33]

As the 1866 Civil Rights Act attests, the folks who gave us the Fourteenth Amendment were obviously and understandably focused on particular privileges and immunities, especially the fundamental rights to life and to liberty and basic rights of property and of contract. But the privileges or immunities clause was meant to protect, against state government, each and every privilege or immunity citizens enjoy under the laws of the state.[34] Just as state law may not deny, to nonwhite citizens, some particular right of contract or of property white citizens enjoy under the laws of the state, neither may it deny, for example, access to some particular benefit—public schools, say, or public beaches—to which white citizens enjoy access under state law. Nor, of course, may a state diminish the quantity or quality of one's access to such a benefit. (Of course, racially segregated public schools diminished a nonwhite student's access to the benefit of a public education.) That in 1868, when the Fourteenth Amendment became a part of the Constitution, there were, compared to today, relatively few privileges and immunities citizens enjoyed under state law, whereas today, in the age of the welfare state, there are (compared to 1868) relatively many such privileges and immunities, is beside the point: The privileges or immunities clause was meant to protect, not merely *some* of the privileges and immunities citizens enjoy under state law, but *all* of them. Even on its face, after all, the clause forbids states to abridge, not just some of the privileges and immunities of citizens, but any of them (including any they enjoy under state law).

Indeed, it seems that the clause was probably meant to protect, by forbidding the states to abridge, each and every privilege (or "freedom to") and immunity ("freedom from") befitting the citizens of a "free" society—each and every freedom of a citizen to do, or to refrain from doing, as he wants. (Recall that the intended beneficiaries of the clause were probably only citizens and not all persons.) As Senator Howard put it in his speech in the Congress on May 23, 1866 (quoting Justice Bushrod Washington's opinion in *Corfield v. Coryell*[35]): [The protected privileges and immunities include] those privileges and immunities . . . *which belong of right to the citizens of all free Governments. . . .* They may . . . be all comprehended under the following general heads: protection by the Government, the enjoyment of life and liberty, with the right to acquire and possess property of every kind, *and to pursue and obtain happiness and safety*, subject nevertheless to such restraints as the Government may justly prescribe for the general good of the whole."[36] (Senator Howard was not merely a member of the Joint Committee on Reconstruction of the 39th Congress; he was the person principally responsible for explaining the text of the proposed Fourteenth Amendment—section 1 of which had been drafted by Howard's ally in the House, Representative John A. Bingham—to the Senate during the congressional debates.) Anyone who thinks that Senator Howard's (or Judge Washington's) construal of the privileges and immunities of the citizens of a free society is implausible may need a refresher course in American history: The Declaration of Independence proclaims as a "self-evident" truth that "all men . . . are endowed by their Creator with certain unalienable Rights, that among these are Life, Liberty, and *the pursuit of Happiness.*" The Declaration continues: "[T]o secure these rights, Governments are instituted among Men. . . ." Senator Howard could have cited, in addition to the Declaration, Blackstone: "Civil liberty, the great end of all human society and government, is that state in which each individual has the power to pursue his own happiness according to his own views of his interest, and the dictates of his conscience, unrestrained, except by equal, just, and impartial laws."[37]

Whether or not one accepts that the category of privileges and immunities of (persons who are) citizens of the United States is as broad as Senator Howard said—and as the Declaration and Blackstone suggest—a
difficult question arises, concerning the original meaning of "abridge",
that I will address later in this chapter: However broad (or narrow) the
category or protected privileges and immunities may be, what were the
protected privileges and immunities meant to be protected from—
merely from (some) discriminatory state laws, or even from (some)
nondiscriminatory state laws?

Even if one does not accept that the category of protected privileges
and immunities is so broad, there is another set of privileges and immunities undeniably meant to be protected by the privileges or immunities
clause: all the privileges and immunities citizens enjoy, against either the
national government or state government, under federal law, including
federal constitutional law. The protected privileges or immunities
include, therefore, the privileges and immunities citizens enjoy under
the Bill of Rights; they include, for example, as the Supreme Court put
it in the *Slaughter-House Cases*, the "right to peaceably assemble and petition for redress of grievances",[38] which citizens enjoy under the First
Amendment. But agreement on that point is merely prelude to an important disagreement.

The privileges and immunities citizens enjoy under the Bill of Rights
are privileges and immunities *against the national government*, not against
state government.[39] There has been disagreement about whether the
privileges or immunities clause was meant merely to forbid the states to
interfere with a citizen's exercise, vis à vis the national government, of any
of her Bill of Rights (or other federal constitutional) privileges against the
national government (or with her invocation of any of her Bill of Rights
immunities against the national government), or whether, in addition, the
clause was meant to transform the Bill of Rights privileges and immunities of citizens against the national government into privileges and immunities against state government as well. That the privileges or immunities
clause was meant to transform the Bill of Rights privileges and immunities of individual citizens against the national government into privileges
and immunities against state government does not entail that the clause
was meant to transform every Bill of Rights privilege and immunity into
a privilege and immunity against state government: Arguably, not every
Bill of Rights privilege or immunity is a privilege and immunity of individual citizens; some are, arguably, privileges and immunities (so to
speak) of the states against the national government.[40]

Even if there were no Fourteenth Amendment, no state would be acting consistently with the Constitution that interfered with a citizen's exercise, vis à vis the national government, of any of her federal constitutional
privileges (or even with her exercise of any of her federal statutory privileges) against the national government. (Nor, of course, would a state be
acting constitutionally, even absent the Fourteenth Amendment, if it vio

lated any of its own federal constitutional duties, including its duties vis à vis citizens—for example, its duty not to "impair the obligation of contracts".[41]) Therefore, the position that, with respect to the Bill of Rights privileges and immunities, the privileges or immunities clause was meant only to forbid the states to interfere with a citizen's exercise, vis à vis the national government, of any of her Bill of Rights privileges against the national government makes the clause, in that respect, superfluous.[42] Moreover, some very credible historical work—most notably, perhaps, Michael Kent Curtis' *No State Shall Abridge: The Fourteenth Amendment and the Bill of Rights* (1986), which has recently been described as "the leading scholarly work" on the subject[43]—supports the position that the privileges or immunities clause was meant to transform the privileges and immunities citizens enjoy against the national government under the Bill of Rights into privileges and immunities they enjoy against state government as well, protecting the transformed privileges and immunities from the same threats from which they are protected (against the national government) by the Bill of Rights.[44]

What is the original meaning of phrase "the privileges or immunities of citizens of the United States"? The privileges and immunities meant to be protected (against state government) by the privileges or immunities clause include all the privileges and immunities citizens enjoy under both federal law and state law. That much seems clear. That they include, as well, each and every freedom of a citizen to do, or to refrain from doing, as he or she wants, in the "pursuit" (as the Declaration says) of his or her "happiness", certainly seems to be a plausible further conclusion about the breadth of the original meaning of "the privileges or immunities of citizens of the United States". Whether or not one accepts that further conclusion, a difficult questions awaits: What were the protected privileges and immunities meant to be protected from? Put another way: What is the original meaning of "abridge"?

The Second Inquiry: What Were the Protected Privileges and Immunities Meant to Be Protected From?

Let us assume that the privileges or immunities clause was meant to transform the privileges and immunities citizens enjoy against the national government under the Bill of Rights into privileges and immunities they enjoy against state government as well, protecting the transformed privileges and immunities from the same threats from which they are protected (against the national government) by the Bill of Rights. It follows, then, that a state law "abridges" a transformed privilege or immunity, within the meaning of section 1, if the law, were it a federal law, would be unconstitutional. (There is, however, this proviso: As Akhil Amar has recently suggested, "Various rules and subdoctrines associated with the original Bill [of Rights] may not incorporate jot for jot . . .

[because] they may reflect federalism and other structural concerns unique to the central government. For example, to the extent the First Amendment freedom of speech is read as an absolute, not as a matter of free speech doctrine, but for reasons of federalism rooted in a lack of enumerated congressional power in Article I, Section 8 [of the Constitution]—to *that* extent, the clause does not sensibly incorporate jot for jot."[45]) But what about all the protected privileges and immunities that do not derive from the Bill of Rights or from any other federal source of law: What were these other protected privileges and immunities meant to be protected from? What constitutes an "abridgment" of these other privileges and immunities? Were they meant to be protected only from (enactment and enforcement of) racially discriminatory legislation? (That they were meant to be protected, not just from legislation discriminating against persons "of African descent",[46] but from racially discriminatory legislation generally—legislation, enacted wholly or largely by whites, discriminating against nonwhites, whether or not of African descent—is clear.) Or were they meant to be protected from discrimination more broadly? Were they meant to be protected even from some nondiscriminatory legislation?

As I noted earlier, nothing in the language of the privileges or immunities clause, or of section 1 generally—the language as we would likely use it—precludes the possibility that the clause, and section 1 generally, were meant to prohibit, in addition to racial discrimination, discrimination defined more broadly. (The language of the 1866 Civil Rights Act, by contrast, does seem to preclude the possibility that the Act was meant to prohibit discrimination more broadly.[47]) Moreover, it seems clear, as a contextual matter, that section 1 of the Fourteenth Amendment, including the privileges or immunities clause, was meant to prohibit discriminatory state action more broadly.[48] William Nelson's recent, exhaustive, and acclaimed work on the history of the Fourteenth Amendment seems conclusive on that point.[49] "While equality for blacks was surely the central concern of the [fourteenth] amendment's framers and ratifiers, it was never their sole and exclusive concern. Those who discussed the amendment were aware of its implications for other groups, such as Chinese, Indians, women, and religious minorities. Moreover, there is no doubt that the proponents of the amendment meant to protect yet another group—namely, Northern whites who were migrating to the South after the Civil War and were threatened with potentially discriminatory legislation at the hands of Southern states and localities."[50]

Nelson neglects to mention, in the foregoing passage, that proponents of the Fourteenth Amendment also meant to protect yet another group of whites: the returning Southern whites often called "refugees—that is to say the loyal white men who have fled their homes because of the rebellion".[51] As Alfred Avins concluded: "If the first section [of the Fourteenth Amendment] had been confined to racial discrimination, one of the major objects of congressional solicitude in submitting the fourteenth amendment [namely, the Southern whites who had been loyal to the Union] would have been left out. It is therefore clear once again that if racial discrimination were deemed to have a special condemnation, under the fourteenth amendment, an important group, of equal concern with Negroes to the framers, could not benefit from it. This is strong evidence that no such primacy was given to racial discrimination."[52]

The following interchange during congressional discussion of the proposed Fourteenth Amendment is additional evidence that the privileges or immunities clause and section 1 generally were meant to prohibit discrimination more broadly than just racial discrimination:

> On February 27, [1866,] Robert Hale of New York asked whether the amendment would remove all legal disabilities that most states then imposed on married women. No, replied Thaddeus Stevens, not if all wives were treated alike; "where all of the same class are dealt with in the same way, there is no pretense of inequality." Hale did not hesitate to close the trap into which Stevens had fallen. "Then by parity of reasoning it would be sufficient if you extended to one negro the same rights you do to another, but not those you extend to a white man." Hale voted for the amendment anyway, in spite of the fact that he never got a convincing answer to his objections.[53]

The most significant thing about this interchange, for present purposes, is what Hale's question to Stevens did *not* presuppose and what Stevens's answer to Hale did *not* assert: namely, that the amendment governs only discrimination based on race (i.e., discrimination against nonwhites), and that, therefore, discrimination based on sex (discrimination against women, whether women generally or some subset, such as married women) does not even implicate, much less violate, the amendment. (That the privileges or immunities clause and section 1 generally were meant to prohibit discrimination more broadly than just racial discrimination does not entail, nor am I suggesting, that they who gave us the Fourteenth Amendment believed it to prohibit sex-based discrimination. In the next chapter, I present the originalist case for concluding that discrimination based on sex implicates, and sometimes violates, section 1 of the Fourteenth Amendment notwithstanding the implausibility of concluding that more than a few, if indeed any, of those who proposed or ratified the Fourteenth Amendment, or of those they represented, believed that sex-based discrimination violates the Amendment.)

There is little serious question, then, that the privileges or immunities clause, and section 1 generally, were meant to prohibit discrimination more broadly than just racial discrimination. But how broadly? How broad or general an antidiscrimination directive was section 1 of the Fourteenth Amendment originally understood to represent?

> A theory that the state should treat all people equally cannot mean that the state may never treat two people differently, for such a theory would mean the end of all law. In order to sustain a principle of equality under

law—the principle for which the framers of the Fourteenth Amendment
were striving, it is necessary to have some theory about when discrimination is appropriate and when it is not.

In their efforts to elaborate a theory of equality, statesmen of the
generation which framed and ratified the Fourteenth Amendment faced
[a difficult issue] that continue[s] to plague Fourteenth Amendment
analysis today. [The issue], once they moved beyond obviously defective
racial criteria, was to distinguish classifications that would be reasonable
under the amendment from those that would be arbitrary. . . .

In dealing with the . . . issue, the congressional proponents of the
Fourteenth Amendment were always able to specify whether a particular
classification was reasonable or arbitrary. But they were persistently
unable to elaborate how their conclusions were derived from or compelled by their more general theory; they simply knew an arbitrary
exercise of power when they saw one.[54]

The challenge for the originalist judge, then, is to construct, or to
reconstruct, "their more general theory"—and to (re)construct it neither
more narrowly nor more broadly than necessary to account for what the
available historical materials disclose. The historical materials that Nelson
and others have presented support the conclusion that the antidiscrimination directive the privileges or immunities clause (and, to the extent it
overlaps the privileges or immunites clause, the equal protection clause)
was originally meant to represent has two basic aspects:

First, the directive forbids states to enact or enforce laws that deny
protected privileges or immunities to a group (or that otherwise diminish a group's enjoyment of protected privileges or immunities) on the
ground that the members of the group are inferior, as human beings, to
persons not members of the group, *if the group is defined, explicitly or
implicitly, in terms of a trait irrelevant to their status as human beings*.[55] A law
that denies protected privileges or immunities to a racial group on
white-supremacist grounds is the prototypical example of a law that violates this first aspect of the directive. The Congress that proposed the
Fourteenth Amendment (which was, after all, the Congress that enacted
the Civil Rights Act of 1866) meant the privileges or immunities clause to
forbid the states to deny to *nonwhite citizens*—in particular, though not
exclusively, citizens of African ancestry—"the same right . . . to make and
enforce contracts, to sue, be parties, and give evidence, to inherit, purchase, lease, sell, hold, and convey real and personal property, . . . as is
enjoyed by *white citizens*".[56] (Similarly, it meant the equal protection
clause to forbid the states to deny to nonwhite citizens the "full and equal
benefit of all laws and proceedings for the security or person and property, as is enjoyed by white citizens".[57]) The construction of "their more
general theory" I am presenting here accounts for their position in that
regard: The conclusion is not merely reasonable but, as a real-world
matter, inescapable that any law denying to nonwhite citizens the same
right to make and enforce contracts, and so on, as is enjoyed by white citizens, is indeed grounded in white-supremacist ideology and thus vio-

lates the privileges or immunities clause; in particular, any such law violates the first aspect of the antidiscrimination directive represented by the clause.

Second, the directive also forbids states to enact or enforce laws that deny protected privileges or immunities to a group on the basis of hostility towards the members of the group, *if the group is defined, explicitly or implicitly, in terms of an activity, a way of life, or a set of beliefs—whether that activity, way of life, or set of beliefs be religious, political, cultural, etc.— towards which no state may, as a constitutional matter, express hostility.* A law that denied protected privileges or immunities to Southern whites ("refugees") who had remained loyal to the Union during the Civil War, or to Northern whites who had migrated to the South after the Civil War, would not have violated the first aspect of the directive, but it would have violated this second aspect. Such a law would have been premised, not on an ideology that some persons (e.g., white persons) belong to a higher order of humanity—that they are, in that sense, more fully human—than some other persons (e.g., persons of African ancestry); such a law would have been premised, rather, on hostility to the way of life and to the underlying beliefs—in particular, the anti-Confederacy, if not antislavery, beliefs— that many in the post–Civil War South surely, and reasonably, associated with such white persons.

The foregoing (re)construction of the original meaning of the privileges or immunities clause—the foregoing conclusion about the breadth or generality of the complex antidiscrimination directive the clause was originally understood to represent—certainly seems to be a plausible one, if not, indeed, the only plausible one. I have more to say, in the next chapter, in support of this construction of the original meaning of the privileges or immunities clause—and in opposition to a competitor construction congenial to opponents of "affirmative action". I do not mean to suggest, however, either here or in the next chapter, that the historical record leaves no room for reasonable disagreement about the precise shape or contours of the "general theory" of equality that informs the original meaning of the privileges or immunities clause and of section 1 generally.

A more difficult question—and also a more contested one—is whether "the privileges or immunities of citizens of the United States" were meant to be protected even from some nondiscriminatory laws. Was the privileges or immunities clause, unlike the equal protection clause, originally understood to represent more than just an antidiscrimination directive—and if so, what directive?

[The proponents of the Fourteenth did not effectively] explain how national enforcement of principles designed to affect nearly every aspect of human endeavor could be limited so as not to undermine the plenary lawmaking power of the states. The most cogent explanation was that the Fourteenth Amendment would not, in and of itself, create rights, but would leave that task to state law; the amendment's sole restriction on state legislative freedom would lie in its requirement that the states confer equal rights on all.

But not all of the amendment's proponents accepted this view. Consistently with their antislavery heritage, some Republicans claimed that the amendment did more than protect rights equally; it protected absolutely certain fundamental rights such as those specified in the Bill of Rights and those given by common law to enter contracts and to own property. This absolute rights interpretation involved the Republican proponents of the amendment in a serious difficulty, however, because congressional assumption of plenary legislative jurisdiction over basic rights threatened to deprive state legislatures of their authority over the rights. Republicans protested, of course, that they did not intend the Fourteenth Amendment to have this effect, and a few tried to explain why it would not. They urged that, although section 1 would prohibit states from impairing the enjoyment of fundamental rights, states would remain free to regulate those rights *for the public good in a reasonable fashion*.[58]

What, then, are we to conclude? Were the protected privileges and immunities meant to be protected, not only from some discriminatory laws, but also from some nondiscriminatory laws: in particular, from laws that fail to regulate a protected privilege or immunity "for the public good in a reasonable fashion"? After a painstaking review of the historical record, Nelson has concluded:

> Only one historical conclusion can . . . be drawn: namely, that Congress and the state legislatures never specified whether section 1 was intended to be simply an equality provision or a provision protecting [even from some nondiscriminatory legislation] as well. Historical analysis of the framing and ratification of the Fourteenth Amendment cannot, by itself, resolve the dilemma created by the conflicting commitments of those who participated in the process. Judges and lawyers wishing to be guided only by the original intention cannot know whether to construe the amendment as a guarantor [merely of equal legislation or of reasonable legislation as well].[59]

It seems, then, that an originalist judge can plausibly reach either of two conclusions about the original meaning of the privileges or immunities clause—that is, about the aspect of the original meaning at issue here—because, if Nelson's presentation of the historical record is credited, the record underdetermines the choice between the conclusions. Two originalist judges, each with a different conception of proper judicial role, or with a different political morality, can reasonably disagree with each other, on the basis of their different conceptions of judicial role, or of their different political moralities, about which of these two conclusions more likely captures the original meaning: (1) The protected privileges and immunities—the privileges and immunities of citizens of the United States—were meant to be protected from, and only from, legislation that discriminates on certain prohibited bases.[60] (2) The protected privileges and immunities were meant to be protected, not only from such legislation, but also from some nondiscriminatory legislation, namely, legislation that fails to regulate for the public good in a reasonable fashion.

There is no serious doubt that the privileges or immunities clause was meant to protect the privileges and immunities of citizens of the United States from legislation that discriminates on certain prohibited bases. The serious question is whether it was meant to do more than that. Writing about the privileges or immunities clause in particular, John Ely has said: "But that equality for blacks, or even equality more broadly conceived, was the only relevant purpose . . . is a proposition much more difficult to defend."[61] That the privileges or immunities clause was meant to protect the privileges and immunities of citizens of the United States even from some nondiscriminatory legislation gains support from a passage, quoted earlier, in Senator Howard's speech in the Congress on May 23, 1866: "[The protected privileges and immunities include] the enjoyment of life and liberty, with the right to acquire and possess property of every kind, and to pursue and obtain happiness and safety, subject nevertheless to such restraints as the Government may justly prescribe *for the general good of the whole*."[62] I have italicized what are, for present purposes, the crucial words. According to the broader reading of the original meaning, the privileges or immunities clause forbids states to enact or enforce laws that "abridge" protected privileges or immunities in either of two ways: first, by denying protected privileges or immunities (or by otherwise diminishing the enjoyment of protected privileges or immunities) on certain prohibited bases; or, second, by otherwise unreasonably regulating protected privileges or immunities—that is, by failing to regulate them "for the public good" (or "for general good of the whole") "in a reasonable fashion". Denying protected privileges or immunities on certain prohibited bases is one way—and, for purposes of the Fourteenth Amendment, the exemplary way—of unreasonably regulating protected privileges or immunities, but, according to the broader reading, it is not the only way. I address, in the next chapter, the question what counts, or should count, as an "otherwise reasonable" regulation of a protected privilege or immunity.

The Third Inquiry: The Equal Protection Clause and the Due Process Clause

Do the equal protection clause and the due process clause of section 1, as originally understood, represent just the directive that states are neither to administer the laws (equal protection) nor to prosecute/adjudicate cases (due process) in a racially discriminatory way? Or do they represent a broader antidiscrimination directive? What I said about the privileges or immunities clause applies with equal force both to the equal protection clause and to the due process clause: In particular, an originalist judge may plausibly conclude, if not indeed *most* plausibly conclude, that together those clauses represent the directive that neither in administering the law nor in prosecuting/adjudicating cases may a state discriminate against a group, or against a person qua member of a group, either (1) on the ground that the members of the group are inferior, as human beings, to persons not members of the group, if the group is defined in terms of a trait irrelevant to their status as human beings, or (2) on the basis of hostility towards members of the group, if the group is defined in terms of a trait toward which no state may express hostility.

Does the due process clause represent, in addition to an antidiscrimination directive, a directive that governs even nondiscriminatory prosecution/adjudication? As I noted before, the language of the due process clause (as we would use the language), unlike the language of the equal protection clause, strongly suggests that the clause was meant to prohibit even some nondiscriminatory state action—just as the due process clause of the Fifth Amendment[63] prohibits some nondiscriminatory federal action. The presumption should surely be that the due process clause of the Fourteenth Amendment was meant to limit state prosecutorial/adjudicatory practices and procedures to the same extent the identically worded due process clause of the Fifth Amendment limits federal prosecutorial/adjudicatory practices and procedures.[64] I am aware of no argument about the original meaning of the due process clause of the Fourteenth Amendment that challenges, much less rebuts, that presumption. The conclusion seems more than plausible, then, that the due process clause of the Fourteenth Amendment was meant to apply to state prosecutorial/adjudicatory practices and procedures the very norms applicable to federal prosecutorial/adjudicatory practices and procedures under the Fifth Amendment due process clause.[65]

III

As I explained in chapter 4, historical inquiry does not always yield just a single plausible conclusion about the original meaning of a constitutional provision; the available historical materials often render plausible more than one conclusion. The voluminous scholarship about the original meaning of the second sentence of section 1 of the Fourteenth Amendment provides a particularly confirmatory illustration of the indeterminacy of history, because that scholarship comprises such great and persistent dissensus. In particular, and as I have recounted in this chapter:

* One can plausibly conclude, though it would be an exaggeration to say that the relevant materials compel the conclusion,[66] that the privileges and immunities meant to be protected by section 1 of the Fourteenth Amendment include each and every freedom of a citizen to do, or to refrain from doing, as he or she wants, in the "pursuit" (as the Declaration says) of his or her "happiness".

- Scholars disagree about whether section 1 was meant merely to forbid state government to interfere with a citizen's exercise, vis à vis the national government, of any of her Bill of Rights privileges against the national government, or whether, in addition, it was meant to transform the Bill of Rights privileges and immunities into privileges and immunities against state government as well.
- There can be, and is, reasonable disagreement about whether the privileges and immunities meant to be protected by section 1 (other than those that derive from the Bill of Rights or from some other federal source) were meant to be protected, not only from some discriminatory legislation—namely, legislation that discriminates on certain prohibited bases—but also from some nondiscriminatory legislation: legislation that fails to regulate for the public good ("for the general good of the whole") in a reasonable fashion.
- One can reasonably disagree about the precise shape of the "general theory" of equality that informs the original understanding of section 1.

In her probing, thoughtful review of William Nelson's book on the Fourteenth Amendment, Judith A. Baer, a participant in the historical controversy about the original meaning of the Fourteenth Amendment, has written: "To say that we fourteenth amendment mavens disagree among ourselves about the framers' meaning is a considerable understatement. The extremes of opinion are represented on the right by Raoul Berger's insistence that section 1 of the amendment had only the 'clearly understood and narrow' purpose of putting the Civil Rights Act of 1866 beyond the reach of presidential veto; and on the left by those of us who assert that 'the amendment both applies the Bill of Rights to the states and guarantees equality together with other unspecified rights.'"[67] Baer concludes her review by observing that, "[l]ooking for a balanced, moderate interpretation of the fourteenth amendment, Nelson finds it. It is there to be found among the rich, copious records, just as the broad and narrow readings are there to be found."[68]

8

The Supreme Court and the
Fourteenth Amendment, I:
Equal Protection

We are now in a position to pursue the implications both of originalism and of normative minimalism for the constitutional doctrine the modern Supreme Court has fashioned in the name of "equal protection" and for the doctrine it has fashioned in the name of "substantive due process". No modern constitutional doctrines are more controversial. To what extent are modern equal protection doctrine and modern substantive due process doctrine consistent with the originalist approach to constitutional interpretation? And to what extent are they consistent with the minimalist, or Thayerian, approach to the constitutional specification? Although I do not discuss, in this or in the next chapter, every doctrinal development the modern Court has fashioned in the name either of equal protection or of substantive due process, I do discuss the most important doctrinal developments, including the two that are probably the most controversial: those concerning affirmative action and abortion. My concern here is not with every detail of the developments I discuss, but only with the basic features of those developments: I want to inquire into the implications of originalism and of normative minimalism for the basic features of the most important doctrinal developments the modern Court has fashioned in the name either of equal protection or of substantive due process. In surveying the basic features both of the Supreme Court's modern equal protection doctrine and of its modern substantive due process doctrine, I aim to determine the extent to which, if any, Robert Bork is right in asserting that "[o]f the [Fourteenth A]mendment's three clauses, two have been pressed into the service of judicial imperialism—the due process and equal protection clauses. . . ."[1]

My concern here is not with formal, as distinct from substantive, matters. Traditionally, the Court has invoked the due process clause to support decisions (results)—that is, decisions invalidating governmental action—that, strictly speaking, are supported, if at all, by the privileges or immunities clause: decisions striking down state action in the form, not of prosecutorial or adjudicatory practices or procedures, which the due process clause governs,[2] but of legislation, which the privileges or immunities clause governs.[3] That practice presents a minor formal problem, not a major substantive one: The fundamental legitimacy of a constitutional result invalidating governmental action is not undermined if the Court mistakenly invokes the wrong clause in its support, for that legitimacy depends, not on the Court invoking the right clause, but on the result being supported by *some* clause—by some provision of the constitutional text. More precisely, it depends on sound analysis grounded by some clause, if not necessarily by the clause the Court invoked. (From the perspective of originalism, which is the principal perspective of this and of the next chapter, the fundamental legitimacy of a constitutional result depends, finally, on its being supported by some constitutional provision *as originally understood*.) Moreover, when it mistakenly invokes the due process clause, the Court's error is especially minor: Wrong clause, but not the wrong sentence. The right clause—the privileges or immunities clause—is a part of the very sentence that contains the due process clause.

If it is one's position that, as originally understood, the equal protection clause, unlike the privileges or immunities clause, does not govern discriminatory legislation—if it is one's position that the equal protection clause governs only discriminatory administration[4]—one can make the same point about the Court's traditional practice of invoking the equal protection clause to support results that (according to the stated position) are supported, if at all, by the privileges or immunities clause: that the practice presents a minor formal problem, not a major substantive one.[5]

I. The Fourteenth Amendment and the Bill of Rights

Before I begin the principal inquiry—which concerns modern "equal protection" doctrine and modern "substantive due process" doctrine—I want to comment briefly on a controversial doctrinal development of fundamental importance, the earliest stages of which predate the modern era of American constitutional law.

As I explained in the preceding chapter, although scholars agree that "the privileges or immunities of citizens of the United States" include, inter alia, the privileges and immunities citizens enjoy against the national government under the Bill of Rights, there is disagreement about whether the privileges or immunities clause was meant only to forbid state government to interfere with a citizen's exercise, vis à vis the national government, of any of her Bill of Rights privileges against the national government (or with her invocation, vis à vis the national government, of any of her Bill of Rights immunities against the national government), or whether, in addition, the clause was meant to transform the privileges and immunities citizens enjoy against the national government under the Bill of Rights into privileges and immunities they enjoy against state government as well, protecting the transformed privileges and immunities from the same threats from which they are protected (against the national government) by the Bill of Rights. (As I remarked in the preceding chapter, to say that the privileges or immunities clause was meant to transform the Bill of Rights privileges and immunities of individual citizens against the national government into privileges and immunities against state government is not to say that the clause was meant to transform every Bill of Rights privilege and immunity into a privilege and immunity against state government, because arguably not every Bill of Rights privilege or immunity is a privilege and immunity of individual citizens; some may be privileges and immunities (so to speak) of the states against the national government.[6]) There is disagreement, for example, about whether the privileges or immunities clause was meant only to forbid a state to interfere with a citizen's exercise of her privilege "peaceably to assemble, and to petition the [national] Government for a redress of grievances", which is protected by the Bill of Rights—specifically, by the First Amendment—or whether, in addition, the clause was meant to forbid state government to interfere with a citizen's effort peaceably to assemble, and to petition the government *of the state* for a redress of grievances.

In a series of cases dating back to the end of the nineteenth century,[7] the Supreme Court has ruled that many of the privileges and immunities citizens enjoy against the national government under the Bill of Rights—in particular, most of the privileges and immunities protected by the First, Fourth, Fifth, Sixth, and Eighth Amendments—are transformed by section 1 of the Fourteenth Amendment into privileges and immunities they enjoy against state government.[8] Those rulings are consistent with what is probably the most plausible conclusion about the relevant aspect of the original meaning of the privileges or immunities clause, namely, that the clause was meant to transform the Bill of Rights privileges and immunities of citizens against the national government into privileges and immunities against state government as well.

But, as I emphasized in chapter 4, more than one conclusion about the original meaning of some constitutional provisions can be plausible. Let us assume, for the sake of argument, that the following conclusion, too, is plausible: that the privileges or immunities clause was meant only to forbid state government to interfere with a citizen's exercise, vis à vis the national government, of any of her Bill of Rights privileges against the national government (or with her invocation, against the national government, of any of her Bill of Rights immunities against the national government). That conclusion, even if (counterfactually?[9]) we assume it to be plausible, is by no standard of historical judgment a *better* conclusion about the original meaning of the privileges or immunities clause, insofar as the available historical materials are concerned—it is by no standard more likely accurate—than the competing conclusion for which the Court, in effect, has substantially opted.[10]

What nonhistorical reasons, then, might influence an originalist judge to incline in favor of that conclusion rather than in favor of the competitor conclusion? The political-moral reasons for so inclining are less than obvious: Who would suggest—and why—that it is better, as a matter of political morality, that state government *not* be subject to the provisions regarding religious liberty, or those regarding the freedoms of speech and of the press, to which the national government is subject under the First Amendment? Or that it not be subject to the just compensation provision to which the national government is subject under the Fifth Amendment? (And so on.) One might be tempted to think that if a state is to be subjected to such limitations, it is better that it be subjected to them not by the national Constitution, but by the state constitution. Charles Black, in his inimitably elegant way, has made the decisive objection to that position: "[W]ithout such a corpus of national human rights law good against the States, we ought to stop saying, 'One nation indivisible, with liberty and justice for all,' and speak instead of, 'One nation divisible and divided into fifty zones of political morality, with liberty and justice in such kind and measure as these good things may from time to time be granted by each of these fifty political subdivisions.'"[11]

If there are no good political-moral reasons, are there institutional reasons—reasons in the form of a minimalist conception of proper judicial role—for inclining against the conclusion for which the Court has substantially opted? It seems unlikely. In cases challenging, on the basis of a Bill of Rights provision, the constitutionality of some action of the national government, it is already the case that the Court must enforce the provision and therefore must interpret the provision and, if the interpreted provision is indeterminate, must specify it. Why, then, would one think it problematic, as a matter of proper judicial role, for the Court to perform the very same function—not a larger or a smaller one—in the context of cases challenging, on the basis of a Bill of Rights provision as "incorporated" against the states by the Fourteenth Amendment, the constitutionality of some action of a state government? I suspect that the institutional reasons one might be tempted to conjure up at this point, or to cobble together, would be reasons, not for resisting the conclusion for which the Court has substantially opted, but only for insisting that, in cases challenging, on the basis of an incorporated Bill of Rights provision, the constitutionality of some state action, the Court pursue the originalist approach—even, perhaps, the minimalist originalist approach[12]—to the interpretation of the Bill of Rights provision, or that it pursue the minimalist approach to the specification of the interpreted provision. It bears emphasis, at this point, that a Supreme Court Justice can pursue the originalist approach—even, pace Justice Scalia, the minimalist originalist approach—to the interpretation of Bill of Rights provisions, or, pace Thayer, the minimalist approach to the specification of interpreted Bill of

Rights provisions, in cases challenging state action no less than in those challenging federal action.

The Supreme Court's conclusion that the privileges and immunities of citizens against the national government protected by the Bill of Rights are transformed by section 1 of the Fourteenth Amendment into privileges and immunities against state government is a fixed feature of American constitutional law; indeed, it has become a constitutive feature of modern American government. (Look again at Charles Black's statement.) The Court's conclusion, moreover, seems not only quite plausible as a matter of history, but relatively unproblematic as a matter both of political morality and of proper judicial role.[13] It is not surprising, therefore, that today few persons are interested in challenging the application to the states of those Bill of Rights provisions the Court has ruled applicable to the states under the Fourteenth Amendment. Of course, this is not to suggest that everyone agrees with all of the Court's interpretations (or with all of its specifications) of the Bill of Rights provisions on which it has relied in striking down state action. But to disagree with the Court's interpretation of a Bill of Rights provision is not to challenge the application of the provision to the states.

II. The Protected "Privileges" and "Immunities"

Now, on to our principal inquiry. Let's begin with the question whether all or virtually all the privileges and immunities protected by the modern Court in the name of section 1 of the Fourteenth Amendment are privileges and immunities protected by section 1 as originally understood. It is clear that the privileges and immunities meant to be protected, against state government, by the privileges or immunities clause include all the privileges and immunities citizens enjoy under both federal law and state law. As I explained in the preceding chapter, it is a quite plausible further conclusion about the breadth of the original meaning of "the privileges or immunities of citizens of the United States" that the privileges and immunities meant to be protected also include each and every freedom of a citizen to do, or to refrain from doing, as he or she wants, in the "pursuit" (as the Declaration says) of his or her "happiness". (The harder question, as I said, concerns what those protected privileges and immunities — including those protected "citizen freedoms" — were meant to be protected from.) It would be difficult, therefore, to conclude that the Court had protected a privilege or immunity in the name of section 1 that was not meant to be protected. The modern Court has not erred in following its predecessors in protecting, under section 1, a wide range of citizen freedoms.

As the Court stated in 1897, the freedoms protected by section 1 of the Fourteenth Amendment include "not only the right of the citizen to be free from the mere physical restraint of his person, as by incarceration, but . . . the right of the citizen to be free in the enjoyment of all his faculties; to be free to use them in all lawful ways; to live and work where he will; to earn his livelihood by any lawful calling; to pursue any livelihood or avocation. . . ."[14] Later, in 1923, the Court wrote that the protected freedoms include "not merely freedom from bodily restraint but also the right of the individual to contract, to engage in any of the common occupations of life, to acquire useful knowledge, to marry, establish a home and bring up children, to worship God according to the dictates of his own conscience, and generally to enjoy those privileges long recognized at common law as essential to the orderly pursuit of happiness by free men."[15] Still later, in 1961, Justice Harlan wrote that the freedoms protected by section 1 are "not a series of isolated points pricked out in terms of [such specific gurantees as speech and religion]. [They constitute] a rational continuum which, broadly speaking, includes a freedom from all arbitrary impositions and purposeless restraints. . . ."[16] All these statements are generally congruent with Senator Howard's statement in the Congress on May 23, 1866, quoted in the preceding chapter, that "[the protected privileges and immunities include] those privileges and immunities . . . *which belong of right to the citizens of all free Governments.* . . . They may . . . be all comprehended under the following general heads: protection by the Government, the enjoyment of life and liberty, with the right to acquire and possess property of every kind, and to pursue and obtain happiness and safety, subject nevertheless to such restraints as the Government may justly prescribe for the general good of the whole."[17] They are also congruent, as I noted in the preceding chapter, with the Declaration of Independence, which speaks of "the pursuit of Happiness", and with Blackstone: "Civil liberty, the great end of all human society and government, is that state in which each individual has the power to pursue his own happiness according to his own views of his interest, and the dictates of his conscience, unrestrained, except by equal, just, and impartial laws."[18]

I said that, given the breadth of the citizen freedoms arguably meant to be protected, it would be difficult to conclude that the Court had protected, in the name of section 1, a privilege or immunity—a citizen freedom—not meant to be protected. Let's consider a set of related constitutional decisions in which, according to the conventional wisdom, the modern Court has protected, in the name of section 1 of the Fourteenth Amendment, a privilege not originally understood to be protected by section 1. Because the folks who gave us the Fourteenth Amendment did not believe that the right to vote, much less the right to appear on a ballot, was a privilege, a freedom, of a person simply qua citizen—women who were citizens could not vote—they did not think that the privileges or immunities clause protected the right.[19] (The Fourteenth Amendment did not extend the right of suffrage to freedmen. It took the Fifteenth Amendment, two years after ratification of the Fourteenth, to do that.) Yet, many laws the modern Court has invalidated in the name of section 1 abridged the right to vote, or the right to appear on a ballot. Consider, for example, the Court's decisions in *Reynolds v. Sims*[20] and in its many progeny (the "one person, one vote" decisions). Consider, too, the Court's decisions in cases like *Harper v. Virginia Board of Elections*[21] (invalidating a poll tax), *Kramer v. Union Free School District No. 15*[22] (invalidating restrictions on the ability of residents to vote in school district elections), and *Williams v. Rhodes*[23] (invalidating restrictions on the ability of third-party candidates to appear on the presidential ballot). Must we conclude, then, that these and similar decisions are inconsistent with the originalist approach to interpretation of the privileges or immunities clause, that in these decisions the Court has protected a privilege not meant to be protected?

That the folks who gave us the Fourteenth Amendment did not believe that the right to vote is a privilege of persons qua citizens—even that they believed that it was not such a privilege—is not determinative for an originalist judge. The right to vote is *now* a privilege of (adult) citizens and, therefore, protected by the privileges or immunities clause. The Fifteenth Amendment (1870) and the Nineteenth Amendment (1920) both speak of "the right of citizens of the United States to vote"—as does an amendment, the Twenty-sixth (1971), that postdates some of the modern decisions in question. According to the Fifteenth Amendment, that right "shall not be denied or abridged by the United States or by any State on account of race, color, or previous condition of servitude"; according to the Nineteenth, the right "shall not be denied or abridged . . . on account of sex"; and according to the Twenty-sixth, "The right of citizens of the United States, who are eighteen years of age or older, to vote shall not be denied or abridged . . . on account of age." What clearer indication could there possibly be that the right to vote is now a "citizen freedom"—a privilege "of citizens of the United States"?[24] ("Excluding the Eighteenth and Twenty-first Amendments—the latter repealed the former—six of our last ten constitutional amendments have been concerned precisely with increasing popular control of government. And five of those six—the exception being the . . . Seventeenth—have extended the franchise to persons who had previously been denied it."[25]) If it is such a freedom/privilege, then it is protected by the privileges or immunities clause. (Because restrictions on a person's right to appear on a ballot are restrictions on the right to vote, in the sense that they limit the persons for whom one may vote, the right to appear on a ballot can fairly be understood to derive from the right to vote, even if it can also be understood to stand independently of the right to vote.)

Thus, the originalist approach to constitutional interpretation leaves room even for the decisions cited in the preceding paragraph; those decisions are not inconsistent with the originalist approach. As a strategy for limiting the jurisdiction of section 1 of the Fourteenth Amendment over the kinds of laws states may enact and enforce, insisting that originalism requires that the category of protected privileges and immunities—of protected citizen freedoms—be construed narrowly is a weak one. In construing broadly, rather than narrowly, the freedoms protected by section 1, the American constitutional tradition has not acted inconsistently with the originalist approach. In the next chapter, I consider a different strategy for limiting the jurisdiction of section 1 over the kinds of laws states may enact and enforce, namely, insisting that originalism requires that "any law which shall abridge" be construed to include, not laws that regulate protected privileges or immunities in a nondiscriminatory way, but only (some) laws that regulate protected privileges or immunities in a discriminatory way (e.g., on the basis of race).

There is little doubt that in Justice Scalia's view, section 1 governs, not laws that regulate protected freedoms (privileges and immunities) in a nondiscriminatory way, but only (some) laws that regulate protected freedoms in a discriminatory way.[26] But, because a majority of the Supreme Court does not share that view, Scalia has pursued an alternative strategy in his determined effort to limit the jurisdiction of section 1 over the kinds of laws states may enact and enforce: In several recent cases he has construed the category of protected freedoms very narrowly, arguing, in effect, that the laws at issue in those cases, because they did not regulate a protected liberty, did not even implicate, much less violate, section 1.[27] Scalia is not the only member of the modern Court who has swum against the constitutional tradition by construing narrowly, rather than broadly, the freedoms protected by section 1,[28] but he is the member of the present Court doing so with the fiercest determination. Here, too, Scalia's doctrinal position—his "crabbed construction" of the freedoms protected by section 1[29]—may be animated more by his minimalist conception of proper judicial role[30] than by his professed commitment to originalism.[31]

III. The Fourteenth Amendment and Racial Discrimination

As I said in the preceding chapter, the Congress that proposed the Fourteenth Amendment (which was, after all, the Congress that enacted the Civil Rights Act of 1866) meant section 1 to forbid the states to deny to *nonwhite* citizens—in particular, though not exclusively, to those of African ancestry—"the same right . . . to make and enforce contracts, to sue, be parties, and give evidence, to inherit, purchase, lease, sell, hold, and convey real and personal property," or to deny to them the "full and equal benefit of all laws and proceedings for the security or person and property, as is enjoyed by *white* citizens".[32] To the extent the Court has acted consistently with that (original) understanding of section 1, the Court has acted unobjectionably.

Moreover, the Court has acted consistently with the original meaning of section 1 in ruling, as it began to in the mid 1940s,[33] that some instances of racially discriminatory state action (or inaction)—in the sense of action, by a wholly or largely white political establishment, discriminating against nonwhites—violate section 1, not necessarily or always, but only if and when the action is not "necessary to serve a compelling governmental interest".[34] As I argued in the preceding chapter, according to the most plausible (re)construction of the original meaning of section 1, the antidiscrimination directive of section 1 has two basic dimensions, the relevant one of which, for present purposes, is that no state may discriminate against a group on the ground that the members of the group are inferior, as human beings, to persons not members of the group, *if the group is defined, explicitly or implicitly, in terms of a trait, like race, irrelevant to their status as human beings*.[35] (In 1967, the Supreme Court stated: "The clear and central purpose of the Fourteenth Amendment was to eliminate all official state sources of invidious racial discrimination in the States."[36]) There is no reason to doubt that this part of the antidiscrimination directive is violated by state action denying to nonwhites "the same right . . . to make and enforce contracts, to sue, be parties, and give evidence, to inherit, purchase, lease, sell, hold, and convey real and personal property," or denying to them the "full and equal benefit of all laws and proceedings for the security or person and property, as is enjoyed by white citizens". As the Court said in *Strauder v. West Virginia*, for example: "The very fact that colored people are singled out and expressly denied by a statute all right to participate in the administration of the law, as jurors, because of their color . . . is practically a brand upon them, affixed by the law, an assertion of their inferiority. . . ."[37] There is no reason to believe, however, that *every* imaginable instance of governmental action that singles out nonwhites for worse treatment than whites is necessarily predicated on the view that the nonwhites are inferior, as human beings, to whites. Therefore, it does not make sense for the Court to rule that every instance of governmental action singling out nonwhites for worse treatment necessarily or invariably violates section 1 of the Fourteenth Amendment.[38] It *does* make sense for the Court to rule that some instances of governmental action singling out nonwhites for worse treatment are conspicuously unconstitutional, such as governmental action denying to nonwhites "the same right . . . to make and enforce contracts, to sue, be parties, and give evidence, to inherit, purchase, lease, sell, hold, and convey real and personal property," or denying to them the "full and equal benefit of all laws and proceedings for the security or person and property, as is enjoyed by white citizens".[39] But not every instance of governmental action singling out nonwhites for worse treatment is conspicuously unconstitutional. What is the Court to do when it is not sure whether a particular instance of such governmental action is predicated on the view that nonwhites are inferior, as human beings, to whites?

Given the practical difficulty sometimes of separating the wheat from the chaff—of discerning if a particular instance of governmental action singling out nonwhites for worse treatment is in fact predicated on the view that the nonwhites are inferior—but given, too, the persistent prevalence of racism in American society[40] and the importance, therefore, of a healthy suspicion about the real, as distinct from the asserted, predicate of any governmental action whereby whites single out nonwhites for worse treatment than the whites themselves receive—it makes good sense for the Court to do just what it does: treat such governmental action (action not conspicuously unconstitutional) as presumptively unconstitutional and abandon the presumption of unconstitutionality if, but only if, the Court is persuaded that the action is necessary to serve a governmental interest that is not merely constitutionally legitimate, but compelling. (Obviously, an interest that presupposes that nonwhites are inferior to whites is not constitutionally legitimate, much less compelling.) The Court's appropiate suspicion about the real (versus the asserted) predicate of such governmental action should be, and is, dissipated if, but only if, the Court is persuaded that the action is necessary to serve a compelling governmental interest. Happily, the Court has almost never been so persuaded. The most prominent case in which a majority of the Court was so persuaded—the Japanese-American Exclusion Case, *Korematsu v. United States*[41]—is now almost universally discredited.[42]

In what is perhaps the most famous American constitutional case of the twentieth century, *Brown v. Board of Education*,[43] the Supreme Court ruled that it is a violation of section 1 of the Fourteenth Amendment for states to segregate public schools on the basis of race. Thirteen years later, in 1967, in a case aptly named *Loving v. Virginia*,[44] the Court ruled that it is a violation of section 1 for states to forbid persons of one race to marry persons of another race. It is sometimes said that the folks who gave us the Fourteenth Amendment would have been surprised by those decisions—that they did not believe either segregated public schools or antimiscegenation laws to be inconsistent with the Fourteenth Amendment. "The same Congress that passed the Fourteenth Amendment almost immediately thereafter enacted legislation establishing racially segregated public schools in the District of Columbia."[45] Nonetheless, pursuant to the originalist approach to constitutional interpretation I elaborated in chapter 3,[46] both *Brown* and *Loving* were rightly decided:[47] There is, finally, no blinking the fact that the laws and practices at issue in *Brown* (and in its extensive progeny[48]) and in *Loving* were rooted in white-supremacist ideology; they were predicated on the view that nonwhites—in particular, persons of African ancestry—are inferior, as human beings, to whites. In their ridiculous and shameful opinion in *Plessy v. Ferguson*,[49] in which they rejected a challenge to a Louisiana law that required "equal but separate accommodations" for "white" and "colored" railroad passengers, a majority of the Court purported to deny that undeniable fact. Justice John Marshall Harlan, in one of the most prophetic dissents ever penned by a Supreme Court justice, protested: "We boast of the freedom enjoyed by our people above all other peoples. But it is difficult to reconcile that boast with a state of the law which, practically, puts the brand of servitude and degradation upon a large class of our fellow-citizens, our equals before the law. The thin disguise of 'equal' accommodations . . . will not mislead anyone, nor atone for the wrong this day done."[50] Chief Justice Earl Warren, speaking for the Court in *Loving*, was much more honest than the majority in *Plessy* had been seventy years earlier: "The fact that Virginia prohibits only interracial marriages involving white persons demonstrates that the racial classifications must stand on their own justification, as measures designed to maintain White Supremacy."[51]

The companion case to *Brown, Bolling v. Sharpe*,[52] presents a special problem. The racially segregated public schooling the Court ruled unconstitutional in *Bolling*, unlike that it ruled unconstitutional in *Brown*, was schooling, in the District of Columbia, maintained by the national government, not by a state government. But the Fourteenth Amendment, on which the Court relied in *Brown*, limits the action of state government, not that of the federal government. The relevant (second) sentence of section 1 of the Fourteenth Amendment begins: "No State shall. . . ." In *Bolling*, therefore, the Court relied, not on the Fourteenth Amendment, but on a provision that limits the action of the national government: the due process clause of the Fifth Amendment ("nor shall any person . . . be deprived of life, liberty, or property, without due process of law"). (Similarly, both in *Hirabayashi v. United States*[53] and in the related, and notorious, case of *Korematsu v. United States*,[54] the Court relied on the Fifth Amendment due process clause in assessing the constitutionality of action of the national government discriminating against Americans of Japanese ancestry.) The problem with the Court's strategy in *Bolling* (and in other, relevantly similar cases, like *Korematsu*), at least for an originalist Justice, is that there is no reason to think that the Fifth Amendment due process clause, as originally understood, is even implicated, much less violated, by racially segregated public schooling. The most plausible reading of the original meaning of the due process clause of the Fifth Amendment is one according to which the clause governs the prosecution and adjudication of cases.[55] Must an originalist conclude, then, as the originalist Robert Bork has, that *Bolling* was wrongly decided?[56]

The result in *Bolling* can be defended, in originalist terms, on the basis of the Ninth Amendment, which provides: "The enumeration, in the Constitution, of certain rights, shall not be construed to deny or disparage others retained by the people." As I explained in chapter 4: According to the most plausible reading of its original meaning, the Ninth Amendment protects, against the national government, unenumerated "affirmative" constitutional rights.[57] The challenge for the originalist judge who accepts that reading is to develop an appropriately constrained strategy for identifying (specifying) the unenumerated rights so protected, whether rights-as-privileges ("freedom to") or rights-as-immunities ("freedom from"). The challenge for the originalist judge committed to the minimalist approach to the specification of constitutional indeterminacy is to develop a strategy that will yield conclusions about what unenumerated rights are protected by the Ninth Amendment—that is, about what unenumerated rights are protected by the Ninth Amendment, *assuming that some unenumerated rights are protected by it*—so sound that the Congress and the president cannot reasonably dispute them.

One such strategy is to say that if the constitutional text, as originally understood, protects a basic right against state government, and if no one can reasonably conclude that the right, if already protected against state government, ought not also to be protected against the national government, that right should be deemed to be one of those unenumerated rights protected against the national government by the Ninth Amendment. This strategy for identifying the rights protected by the Ninth Amendment has the great advantage of constraining judges to such an extent that even a committed normative minimalist should be satisfied: A judge may not identify a right as protected by the Ninth Amendment unless (1) the right is already protected, against state government, by the constitutional text as originally understood, and (2) no one can reasonably conclude that the right ought not also to be protected against the national government. If a right is already protected, against state government, by the constitutional text as originally understood, and if no one— which includes the members of Congress and the president—can reasonably conclude that the right, if already protected against state government, ought not also to be protected against the national government, then not even a Thayerian minimalist need resist the conclusion that the right is protected against the national government by the Ninth Amendment. This strategy is a far cry from one in which a judge identifies a right as protected by the Ninth Amendment simply because she finds the right appealing or "fundamental".

There would probably be, at most, only a few occasions on which this strategy for identifying unenumerated Ninth Amendment rights could in good faith be used to challenge action by the national government. (If so, that should please anyone wary of multiplying the occasions of constitutional adjudication.) But *Bolling v. Sharpe*, at least, was one such occasion: From the perspective of originalism, the Ninth Amendment is a much more plausible basis for attacking racially segregated public schooling maintained by the national government—or, more generally, for attacking *any* discriminatory treatment by the national government that, if practiced by a state government, would violate section 1 of the Fourteenth Amendment—than is the due process clause of the Fifth Amendment. John Ely, too, has suggested that "[h]ope for responsible application of an equal protection concept to the federal government may . . . lie, if anywhere, in that old constitutional jester, the Ninth Amendment. . . ."[58]

Another strategy—a similar and complementary strategy—for dealing with the Ninth Amendment, for making it meaningful and for enforcing it, is for the judiciary to rule that if the constitutional text, as originally understood, protects a basic right against one part of the national government (e.g., the Congress), and if no one can reasonably conclude that the right, if already protected against the one part of the national government, ought not also to be protected against another part (e.g., the executive), that right should be deemed to be one of those unenumerated rights protected against the national government—that is, against that other branch—by the Ninth Amendment. This strategy for taking the Ninth Amendment seriously, like the one discussed in connection with *Bolling v. Sharpe*, has the great advantage of constraining judges to such an extent that even a normative minimalist should be satisfied. (Note the affinity between this strategy and Judge Arnold's approach to the Ninth Amendment, reported in chapter 4.[59]) The principal effect—and point—of this strategy is to ground a feature of American constitutional law the practical wisdom of which few persons today, if any, would challenge: By its terms, the First Amendment protects the free exercise of religion, the freedoms of speech and of the press, and "the right of the people peaceably to assemble, to petition the government for a redress of grievances", only against *Congress*—and even then only against congressional *legislation*. The Amendment states: "Congress shall make no law. . . ." Yet the norms of the First Amendment have been applied against both the executive branch and the judicial branch of the federal government. "'Congress' does not on its face refer to the president, the courts, or the legions that manage the Executive Branch, and 'law' only arguably includes administrative orders or congressional investigations. Freedom of political association, which (without serious controversy) has been held to be fully protected, is not even mentioned in the document; and of course the states are not directly covered by the First Amendment. It requires a theory to get us where the courts have gone."[60]

Just as it is not always obvious whether a law or other governmental action that singles out nonwhites for worse treatment than whites is predicated on the view that nonwhites are inferior as human beings to whites, it is not always obvious whether a law alleged to single out nonwhites for worse treatment in fact does so. That a law sweeps up some whites in its net may suggest that the law does not single out nonwhites, but it does not preclude the possibility that the law does single out nonwhites for worse treatment. Imagine a decision not to fund an effort to find a cure for sickle-cell anemia. If that decision would not have been made but for the fact that the disease afflicts primarily nonwhites—if, instead, a decision to fund such research would have been made—the decision not to fund singles out nonwhites for worse treatment (notwithstanding that some whites are victimized by the decision, namely, those who are or will be afflicted by sickle-cell anemia) in this important sense: To say that the decision not to fund would not have been made but for the fact that the disease afflicts primarily nonwhites is to say that if sickle-cell anemia afflicted only or even primarily whites, the decision would not have been made. Perhaps we should say that such a decision singles out nonwhites for worse treatment than whites *would* receive if whites were in the position (with respect to sickle-cell anemia) that nonwhites are in. The fact remains, however, that even if the better description is "would receive", at a minimum such a race-based decision disadvantaging nonwhites is appropriately suspected of being predicated on the view that nonwhites are inferior to whites and dealt with accordingly.

The examples can easily be multiplied. Imagine the use of a particular test to screen applicants for a job.[61] If no test, or a different test, would have been used but for the fact that a larger proportion of nonwhite than white applicants fail the test, use of the test singles out nonwhites for worse treatment than whites (would) receive (notwithstanding that some whites are victimized, namely, those who fail the test): If a larger proportion of white job applicants than of nonwhite job applicants would fail the test, the decision would not have been made. Similarly, imagine a refusal to permit low-income housing to be built in the community.[62] If permission would have granted made but for the fact that many nonwhites would be occupants of the housing, the refusal singles out nonwhites for worse treatment (notwithstanding that some white are victimized, namely, those who would occupy the housing): If whites would be the only, or almost the only, occupants of the housing, permission would have been granted.

How the Court should determine whether in fact a law singles out nonwhites (or women[63]) for worse treatment—how the Court should go about ferreting out covert race-based (or sex-based) "singling out for worse treatment"—is an important question.[64] The question arises with particular urgency in the context of racially imbalanced public schools.[65] But because the issue does not implicate the (originalist and normative-minimalist) concerns of this chapter, I do not address it here.[66] (The issue does not implicate normative minimalism, because normative minimalism counsels judicial deference, not in answering questions of fact, like the question whether in fact a law singles out nonwhites for worse treatment, but in making normative judgments, in specifying constitutional indeterminacy.)

IV. Discrimination beyond Racial Discrimination

One of the more controversial doctrinal developments in modern constitutional law—one that engaged Robert Bork in his confirmation proceedings and that, in engaging him, tripped him up[67]—concerns discrimination based on sex. Since 1971,[68] the Supreme Court has invalidated, in the name of section 1 of the Fourteenth Amendment—specifically, in the name of the equal protection clause—a number of laws singling out, either women for worse treatment than men receive or men for worse treatment than women receive.[69] Is this doctrinal state of affairs consistent with the originalist approach to constitutional interpretation?

Clearly, legislative and other governmental distinctions based on sex were not thought constitutionally problematic by many persons in the generation that gave us the Fourteenth Amendment. In the *Slaughter-House Cases*, the Court wrote: "To [citizens of the United States], everywhere, all pursuits, all professions, and all avocations are open without other restrictions than such are imposed equally upon all others of the same age, *sex*, and condition."[70] In *Strauder v. West Virginia*, in striking down as racially discriminatory a law that restricted jury service to "white male persons who are twenty-one years of age [or older] and who are citizens of this State", the Court said: "We do not say [that] a State may not prescribe the qualifications of its jurors, and in so doing make discriminations. It may confine the selection to *males*, to freeholders, to citizens, to persons within certain ages, or to persons having educational qualifications."[71] But it is also clear, as I explained in the preceding chapter, that section 1 was not meant to apply only to discrimination (by a wholly or largely white political establishment) against nonwhites: The antidiscrimination directive that the privileges or immunities clause and section 1 generally were meant to represent proscribes, as a predicate for governmental action, the view that the members of a group are inferior, as human beings, to persons not members of the group, *if the group is defined, explicitly or implicitly, in terms of a trait irrelevant to their status as human beings*.

In 1868, when the Fourteenth Amendment became part of the Constitution, many persons would not have thought that a person's sex was irrelevant to his or her status as a human being. Indeed, even today there are persons who do not think that sex is irrelevant to a person's status as a human being. An ideology implicit in much of contemporary American culture—and sometimes explicit—is "that the man is the 'norm' for being human while the woman is an 'auxiliary,' someone defined exclusively by her relationships to men."[72] The "erroneous conviction 'that the one sex . . . is superior to the other in the very order of creation or by the very nature of things'"[73] is prevalent even today.[74] But the question for an originalist judge, charged with enforcing the antidiscrimination directive represented by section 1 of the Fourteenth Amendment, is not whether in 1868 a person's sex would or would not have been thought relevant to his or her status as a human being. The question, rather, is whether sex is in fact relevant to a person's status as a human being.

The Nineteenth Amendment strongly buttresses the Court's conclusion that not only race, but sex too, is irrelevant to a person's status as a human being. (Surely it makes sense for the Court, in specifying an indeterminate constitutional directive, to be guided by normative judgments explicit or implicit elsewhere in the Constitution. To do otherwise would be for the Court to act, not less "subjectively", but more so—which is something no apostle of judicial minimalism will want to encourage.) The Nineteenth Amendment provides: "The right of citizens of the United States to vote shall not be denied or abridged by the United States or by any State on account of sex."[75] The Amendment indisputably represents at least a partial subversion of the view that "a man is the norm for being human", that "the male sex is superior to the female in the very order of creation or by the very nature of things".

Not every law or other governmental action singling out women (or men) for worse treatment than men (or women) is predicated on the view that sex is relevant to a person's status as a human being. Therefore, it does not make sense for the Court to rule that every such action necessarily or invariably violates section 1 of the Fourteenth Amendment. But much such action has presupposed, has been predicated on, some such view.[76] Moreover, even a law (or other governmental action) singling out *men* for worse treatment than women receive may be rooted in a sexist ideology according to which men and women should, "by nature", play different roles in life and occupy different spheres. Men's gender-assigned roles have invariably complemented—that is, reinforced—women's gender-assigned roles. Moreover, the Court is properly (if implicitly) wary about the claim that what often explains sex-based differential treatment is not the view that the man is the norm for being (fully) human, but only the view that women are "different but equal"—different from men but equal to them in moral worth. There is a serious impediment to crediting that claim, which some supporters of sex-based differential treatment no doubt sincerely embrace: "Whatever the articulated beliefs regarding 'different but equal' roles of women and men, women's gender-assigned roles have invariably been subordinate, passive, and/or restricted to the private sphere."[77]

Given the practical difficulty sometimes of discerning if a particular instance of governmental action singling out women or men for worse treatment is predicated on the view that sex is relevant to a person's status as a human being—and given, too, the prevalance of sexist ideology even in contemporary American culture[78] and the importance, therefore, of a healthy suspicion about the real (versus the asserted) predicate of governmental action singling out women or men for worse treatment—it makes sense for the Court to do what it does: rule that such action will be adjudged unconstitutional unless the Court is persuaded that the case for the singling out—the case for drawing a line based on sex rather than on some other, less suspicious basis—satisfies a strict standard of justification. As the Court, per Justice Sandra Day O'Connor, put it in *Mississippi University for Women v. Hogan*, "The burden is met only by showing at least that the [sex-based singling out] serves 'important governmental objectives and . . . [is] substantially related to the achievement of those objectives.'"[79] A governmental objective is not constitutionally legitimate, much less "important", if it presupposes that sex is relevant to a person's status as a human being: "Although the test for determining the validity of a gender-based classification is straightforward, it must be applied free of fixed notions concerning the roles and abilities of males and females. Care must be taken in ascertaining whether the statutory objective itself reflects archaic and stereotypic notions. Thus, if the statutory objctive is to exclude or 'protect' members of one gender because they are presumed to suffer from an inherent handicap or to be innately inferior, the objective itself is illegitimate."[80]

Even if the basic shape of modern constitutional doctrine is, as I am suggesting here, consistent with the originalist approach to constitutional interpretation, is it consistent with the normative-minimalist, or Thayerian, approach to constitutional adjudication? I argue in the next chapter that a judge should not pursue the normative-minimalist approach to the specification of the antidiscrimination directive.[81] But let us assume, for the sake of argument, that a judge should pursue the minimalist approach. Does modern constitutional doctrine regarding sex-based discrimination run afoul of normative minimalism? Not unless there is room for reasonable disagreement about whether sex is relevant to a person's status, to her worth, as a human being—in particular, not unless one can reasonably conclude that "a man is the norm for being human", that "the male sex is superior to the female in the very order of creation or by the very nature of things". The crucial question for the Thayerian judge, therefore, is whether one may reasonably conclude that sex is relevant to a person's worth as a human being? (In the next chapter, I do what is now overdue, namely, elaborate on the notion of "reasonably" implicit in that Thayerian question.[82])

Note, by way of comparison, that the analogous question regarding race—"can one reasonably conclude that race is relevant to a person's worth as a human being?"—does not, or at least should not, even arise for the Thayerian judge. A specific aspect of the complex antidiscrimination directive represented by section 1 of the Fourteenth Amendment proscribes political choices based on the view that race is relevant to a person's worth as a human being. Therefore, for the Court to rule that political choices may not be based on that view is not for the Court to specify, to shape, the antidiscrimination directive represented by section 1; it is only for the Court to accept a specific, concrete (determinate) aspect of that directive.[83] Therefore, modern constitutional doctrine regarding race-based differential treatment does not even implicate normative minimalism. However, there is no specific aspect of the complex antidiscrimination represented by section 1 according to which sex is irrelevant to a person's worth as a human being. (Again, the folks who gave us the Fourteenth Amendment simply did not believe that sex was irrelevant to a person's worth or status as a human being.) For the Court to rule that political choices may not be based on the view that sex is relevant to a person's moral worth *is* for the Court to specify, to shape, a general, indeterminate aspect of the complex antidiscrimination directive represented by section 1; according to that general, indeterminate aspect, political choices may not be based on the view that the members of a group are inferior, as human beings, to persons not members of the group, if the group is defined in terms of a trait irrelevant to their status as human beings. Modern constitutional doctrine regarding sex-based differential treatment, therefore, does implicate normative minimalism.

According to modern Fourteenth Amendment doctrine, govermental action singling out the "illegitimate" offspring of a parent for worse treatment than the parent's "legitimate" offspring receive is unconstitutional unless the Court is persuaded that the singling out "is substantially related to an important governmental objective."[84] The originalist case for this approach to illegitimacy-based differential treatment is fully analogous to the originalist case for the Court's approach to sex-based differential treatment. Moreover, even a Thayerian judge, a judge committed to normative minimalism, can support the attack on illegitimacy-based differential treatment"—*unless* she believes that one can reasonably conclude that a child's (legal) status as "legitimate" is relevant to his or her (moral) status as a human being, that the "illegitimate" offspring of a parent are inferior, as human beings, to the parent's "legitimate" offspring, that they are less worthy, less deserving of concern and respect.[85] Again, in the next chapter I develop the notion of "reasonably" implicit in the Thayerian approach and then argue that the judiciary should not pursue that approach to the specification of (the general, indeterminate aspect of) the (complex) antidiscrimination directive represented by section 1.

Many laws and other governmental actions that single out the members of one group (or groups) for worse treatment than persons not members of the disfavored group—differential treatment based, not on race, sex, illegitimacy, or national origin,[86] but on any of a multitude of other possible traits or factors, such as being a "doctor," "lawyer," "farmer," or "fisherman"—cannot fairly be thought to implicate, much less violate, the antidiscrimination directive represented by section 1 of the Fourteenth Amendment (as originally understood).[87] Yet, according to established Fourteenth Amendment doctrine, no instance of governmental action singling out the members of one group for worse treatment—no matter what, or how unsuspicious, the basis of the singling out ("doctor," "farmer," etc.)—is consistent with section 1 unless the singling out has a "rational basis", in the sense that one could reasonably conclude that the singling out serves, to some extent at least, a legitimate governmental interest.[88] As the Court recently put it, the singling out—the "classification"—must "rationally further a legitimate state interest."[89] (Governmental action that singles out the members of one group for *better* treatment than other persons is necessarily action that singles out the members of one group—namely, all persons not members of the favored group—for *worse* treatment than others, the members of the favored group.)

Can an originalist judge accept this doctrinal state of affairs? The antidiscrimination directive represented by section 1 (as originally understood) has two dimensions, as I explained in the preceding chapter: One of the dimensions proscribes, as a predicate for governmental action, the view that the members of a group are inferior, as human beings, to persons not members of the group, *if the group is defined, explicitly or implicitly, in terms of a trait irrelevant to their status as human beings*; the other dimension proscribes, as a predicate for governmental action, hostility towards the members of a group, *if the group is defined in terms of an activity, a way of life, or a set of beliefs—whether religious, political, cultural, and so on—toward which no state may, as a constitutional matter, express hostility*.[90] Neither dimension requires, however, every instance of governmental action singling out the members of one group for worse treatment than others receive to have a "rational basis": That a particular instance of such singling out lacks a rational basis does not entail that the singling out violates either dimension of the antidiscrimination directive. A regulatory regime that singles out "opticians" for worse treatment than "ophthalmologists" and "optometrists" receive,[91] for example, may well represent venal politics, but it is not even plausible to suppose that such a regime is predicated, either on the view that persons who are opticians are inferior, as human beings, to persons who are ophthalmologists or optometrists, or on any religious, etc., hostility to opticians. The rule that no law or other governmental action singling out some persons for worse treatment than others is consistent with section 1 unless it has a rational basis, probably cannot be grounded on the particular antidiscrimination directive represented by section 1.

But that rule *can* be grounded on a different directive arguably represented by section 1 (as originally understood). As I explained in the preceding chapter, an originalist judge can plausibly reach either of two conclusions about the original meaning of the privileges or immunities clause: first, that the clause was meant to protect against only legislation that discriminates on certain prohibited bases; second, that it was meant to protect, not only against such legislation, but also against some other legislation, namely, legislation that, although it may not discriminate on any prohibited basis, nonetheless fails to regulate for the public good in a reasonable fashion.[92] According to the first conclusion, the privileges or immunities clause represents only an antidiscrimination directive, but according to the second conclusion, it represents both an antidiscrimination directive and what we might call a reasonableness directive; according to the second conclusion, the clause governs, not only (some) legislation that discriminates, but also (some) legislation that *otherwise* unreasonably regulates protected privileges or immunities (by failing to regulate them for the public good in a reasonable fashion). According to the second conclusion, denying protected privileges or immunities to persons on certain prohibited bases is one way—and, for purposes of the Fourteenth Amendment, the exemplary way—of unreasonably regulating protected privileges or immunities, but it is not the only way.

The rule that no law is consistent with section 1 that singles out some for worse treatment than others receive unless, minimally, the singling out has a rational basis can be grounded on the reasonableness directive. After all, no singling out of persons for worse treatment—no matter what, or how innocent, the basis of the singling out—can be said to be a reasonable regulation, a regulation "for the public good in a reasonable fashion", if the singling out lacks even a rational basis, if, that is, no one could reasonably conclude that the singling out serves, to any extent, a legitimate governmental interest. In *Cleburne v. Cleburne Living Center, Inc.*, the Court ruled that, in requiring a special use permit for the operation of a group home for the mentally retarded, a municipal ordinance violated section 1 of the Fourteenth Amendment. After scrutinizing the municipality's reasons for requiring the permit (which the municipality refused to issue), the Court concluded: "[In] our view the record does not reveal any rational basis for believing that the . . . home would pose any special threat [any threat not posed by other group homes not subject to the permit requirement] to the city's legitimate interests. . . ."[93] Even *if* the governmental action at issue in *Cleburne* did not implicate the particular antidiscrimination directive represented by section 1 of the Fourteenth Amendment,[94] it did implicate, and violate, the reasonableness directive, and an originalist who accepts the broader version of the original meaning of the privileges or immunities clause can accept the Court's ruling in *Cleburne* on that basis. It is doubtful, however, that an originalist judge who rejects the broader version—and, with it, the reasonableness directive—can endorse the requirement of a rational basis. As I suggested earlier, standing alone, the antidiscrimination directive represented by section 1—at least, as I have (re)constructed the directive in the preceding chapter—probably cannot, given the directive's particular shape, ground the rational basis requirement.

Even an originalist who is also a committed normative minimalist can sign on to the Court's rational basis requirement: A minimalist approach is an inherent part of the requirement. The inquiry is not whether "we, the members of this Court" believe that the singling out of one group for worse treatment than others receive serves a legitimate governmental interest; the inquiry, rather, is whether there is room for a reasonable difference of opinion about whether the singling out serves, to some extent, such an interest. In the case of legislation, the test is whether a legislator could reasonably conclude that the singling out serves a legitimate governmental interest.[95] (I argue, in the next chapter, that although the judiciary should not pursue the minimalist approach to the specification of the antidiscrimination directive represented by section 1, it *should* pursue the minimalist approach to the specification of the reasonableness directive.)[96]

V. Affirmative Action

We now come to one of the two most controversial issues with which the Supreme Court has recently struggled in the name of the Fourteenth Amendment: affirmative action. (The other of the two issues is, of course, abortion, which I discuss in the next chapter.) By "affirmative action", I mean, in this context, governmental action singling out nonwhites, not for worse treatment than whites receive, but for better treatment,[97] whether to ameliorate the effects of past discrimination against nonwhites or to achieve greater racial diversity in an area in which such diversity would be salutary—among the personnel of an urban police department, for example, or on the faculty of an urban public school system.[98]

The question of the constitutionality of affirmative action has sharply divided the Court ever since 1974, when the Court first addressed the issue.[99] The position of a majority of the present Supreme Court is unclear. When it last addressed the question in 1990, the Court, in a five-to-four decision, concluded that the affirmative action in question was constitutional.[100] But two members of the five-man majority have since resigned (William Brennan and Thurgood Marshall), every member of the four-person minority is still sitting, and the two newest members of the Court (David Souter, who replaced Justice Brennan, and Clarence Thomas, who replaced Justice Marshall), have not yet had an opportunity, as Justices of the Court, to address the question of affirmative action. My aim, in any event, is not to predict how the present Court will resolve the issue, only to suggest how an originalist judge should approach the issue under section 1 of the Fourteenth Amendment.

Governmental action singling out nonwhites for worse treatment than whites is, at the very minimum, properly suspected of being predicated on the view that nonwhites are inferior, as human beings, to whites; such "suspect" action is therefore properly presumed to be illicitly predicated and, so, adjudged unconstitutional unless the Court is persuaded that the action, because "necessary" to serve a "compelling" governmental interest, is not so predicated. However, it does not seem to make sense, as a real-world matter, to suspect that governmental action singling out nonwhites, not for worse treatment than whites, but for better treatment, is predicated on the view, either that the favored nonwhites are inferior (as human beings) to whites, or (much less) that the disfavored whites are inferior to the favored nonwhites. At least, it does not make sense to suspect that such governmental action is illicitly predicated if the action is, as in the contemporary United States such action invariably is, either the action of a political authority still largely white or, if the action of a largely nonwhite political authority—for example, an urban city council[101]—tolerated by a political hierarchy (in particular, by a state legislature) still largely white. Unless affirmative action is illicitly predicated, however, it does not violate the antidiscrimination directive represented by section 1, as that section was originally understood.[102] It is difficult to see, therefore, the basis on which an originalist judge could conclude that affirmative action is unconstitutional.

In particular, it is difficult to see the basis on which Justice Scalia, as an originalist, can justify his conclusion that no instance of affirmative action is constitutional that seeks either to compensate nonwhites for past societal discrimination against them or to achieve racial diversity in an area in which such diversity would be salutary. (In Scalia's view, an instance of affirmative action is constitutional if, and only if, it "is necessary to elimi-

nate [government's] own maintenance of a system of unlawful racial classification."[103]) Justice Scalia might try to defend his approach by insisting
that section 1 of the Fourteenth Amendment was meant to forbid states to
single out any racial group, white as well as nonwhite, for worse treatment
than any other racial group receives (except as "necessary to eliminate a
state's own maintenance of a system of unlawful racial classification"),
period, thus rejecting the position that section 1 was meant to forbid states
to single out a racial group, or any other group, for worse treatment on the
ground that its members are inferior, as human beings, to other persons.

The problem with the former reading of the original meaning of section 1, however, is that it is demonstrably less faithful to the relevant historical materials than is the latter reading. Indeed, the former reading
seems ad hoc, conjured up for no better reason than to attack the constitutionality of affirmative action. As I explained in the preceding chapter,
the folks who gave us the Fourteenth Amendment were focused on the
problem of *racist* discrimination against nonwhites: discrimination, against
nonwhites, predicated on an ideology of "white supremacy". Section 1 of
the Fourteenth Amendment was meant to forbid states to practice such
discrimination or, more broadly, any discrimination predicated on an
analogous ideology.

Let me rehearse a few relevant points from the preceding chapter.
There is no question that state action singling out nonwhites for worse
treatment than whites receive was meant to be the principal focus of section 1. But there is no question, either, that "the singling out of nonwhites
for worse treatment" was not meant to be the sole focus of the section: Section 1 was meant to govern the singling out of *any* group for worse treatment. It was certainly not meant, however, to forbid states *ever* to single
out any group for worse treatment. (States must sometimes single out
groups for worse treatment.) It was meant, rather, to forbid such singling
out *only on certain prohibited bases*.[104] That there is room for reasonable disagreement about the precise shape or contours of the bases section 1 was
meant to prohibit does not mean that it is plausible to believe that the
folks who gave us the Fourteenth Amendment meant section 1 to forbid
the singling out of any group for worse treatment on certain prohibited
bases *except for the singling out of nonwhites or whites for worse treatment, which
was meant to be prohibited whether or not the singling out was on any prohibited
basis*.[105] If an originalist judge should not think that a law singling out
women (for example) for worse treatment than men *necessarily* violates the
antidiscrimination directive represented by section 1—if he should not
think that the law violates the antidiscrimination directive *unless* the singling out is predicated on the view that women are inferior, as human
beings, to men—then why should he think that a law singling out whites
for worse treatment than nonwhites violates the antidiscrimination directive even if the singling out is not predicated on the view that the disfavored whites (or the favored nonwhites) are inferior? Surely it is not Justice Scalia's position that a law singling out women for worse treatment

violates the antidiscrimination directive represented by section 1 even if the singling out is not predicated on the view that women are inferior. (But then, Justice Scalia may believe that a law singling out women for worse treatment does not even implicate, much less violate, section 1 as originally understood.)

Of course, if an originalist judge's conception of proper judicial role, or his political morality, or both, can influence his choice between two plausible readings of the original meaning of a constitutional provision, it is similarly the case that he can be influenced to choose an implausible reading. Justice Scalia seems to have been influenced, whether by his conception of judicial role, or by his political morality, or—more likely—by both, to choose, if only implicitly, an implausible reading of the original meaning of section 1.[106]

With respect to Justice Scalia's conception of judicial role: It is not surprising, given his minimalist originalist approach (which I discussed in chapter 6[107]), that Scalia prefers the directive "states may not single out any racial group for worse treatment than any other racial group receives" to "states may not single out any racial group for worse treatment on the ground that its members are inferior to other persons". The former directive is more determinate than the latter, in this sense: In at least some cases the latter directive leaves at least some room for judges to disagree about whether a particular instance of singling out for worse treatment is in fact predicated on the illicit ground. Moreover, the latter directive is often implemented by the "compelling governmental interest" test, which is itself somewhat indeterminate; one can easily imagine Scalia decrying the test for leaving too much room for "subjective" judicial judgments about whether a particular instance of singling out for worse treatment is necessary ("how necessary?") to serve a compelling ("how compelling?") governmental interest.[108]

The possibility that Justice Scalia's politics has influenced his handling of the question of affirmative action should be at least as apparent as the possibility that his conception of proper judicial role—his minimalist originalism—has influenced his handling of the question. It bears emphasis, therefore, that whatever reasons there may be for one to oppose a particular instance of affirmative action—or, indeed, to oppose affirmative action generally—there is no good *constitutional* reason for an originalist judge, like Scalia, to oppose a particular instance of race-based affirmative action unless the judge concludes that the instance is the yield of a racist ideology. That, in the judge's view, the instance is the yield of a politically misguided and perhaps even dangerous judgment is not, for an originalist, a good constitutional reason. I am inclined to agree with David Chang that "[p]olitical conservatism, rather than judicial conservatism," has more to do with the "restrictions on legislative discretion to redress the effects of past racial discrimination" that Justice Scalia and several of his colleagues mean to impose in the name of the Fourteenth Amendment.[109] Note, in that regard, that Justice Scalia's minimalist originalist approach—according to which, given a choice between two or more plausible readings of the original meaning of a constitutional provision, the Court should opt for the reading according to which the constitutional provision represents a relatively determinate directive rather than a relatively indeterminate one[110]—can serve, and in the context of affirmative action does serve, not to reduce the political power of the Court on which Scalia sits, but to augment it at the expense of the political power of the Congress and of state legislatures. As Frank Easterbrook has observed, "[Justice Scalia's approach to the question of the constitutionality of affirmative action] reduces judicial *discretion* but increases judicial *power* relative to the other branches." Judge Easterbrook continues: "It is the claim of judicial power that must be justified; although a reduction in judicial discretion is desirable, we do not get there unless the scope of the authority has first been established."[111]

We ought not to overlook the possibility that a particular instance of affirmative action is nothing more than what Justice O'Connor has called "a form of racial politics":[112] a divvying up of the political spoils along racial lines. If so, the instance of affirmative action—like, arguably, a regulatory policy that favors optometrists over opticians[113]—does not constitute "a regulation for the public good in a reasonable fashion" and therefore violates the reasonableness directive represented by section 1. The principal point of the (meager) requirement of a "rational basis"—which, again, is grounded on the reasonableness directive—is to rule out legislation and policies that fail to regulate for the public good in a reasonable fashion because they are nothing more than the yield of a to-the-political-victor(s)-belong-the-spoils form of politics. However difficult the distinction may be to administer or, for a court, to enforce, a "to the political victor belong the spoils" justification for legislation and a "public good" justification are different. Recall, in that regard, Senator Howard's comment, quoted in the preceding chapter: "[The protected privileges and immunities are] subject . . . to such restraints as the Government may justly prescribe *for the general good of the whole*."[114] Indeed, "to the political victor belong the spoils" is less a justification than an explanation—an explanation that, as I said in chapter 6, offends the ideal of the rule of law.[115]

There is, in any event, no reason why the rational basis requirement should govern the singling out of nonwhites for better treatment any less than it governs the singling out of any group for better, or for worse, treatment than any other group. The difficult question is whether there are good reasons—and not merely good reasons, but good reasons on which an originalist judge may appropriately rely—for subjecting any instance of affirmative action to a standard of justification *stricter* than the rational basis standard, if no instance of affirmative action in the contemporary United States is properly suspected of being illicitly predicated. John Ely has argued that "[w]hen the group that controls the decision making process classifies so as to advantage a minority and disadvantage itself, the reasons for being unusually suspicious, and, consequently, employing a stringent brand of review are lacking."[116] But that one rationale—indeed, the principal rationale—for strict scrutiny is absent does not entail that no other rationale for strict scrutiny is present. What other rationale might be present in this context? The Court might believe that the constitutional costs of affirmative action are so substantial—in particular, costs in the form of fomenting racial resentment and of reinforcing, to nonwhites as well as to whites, negative stereotypes about the relevant abilities of nonwhites—that more than a mere rational basis should be established if an affirmative action program is to be sustained.[117] And, indeed, even so staunch a judicial friend of affirmative action as Justice Brennan subjected affirmative action programs to a stricter than "rational basis" standard: In 1990, speaking for five members of the Supreme Court (only three of whom remain on the Court), Brennan ruled that "benign race-conscious measures mandated by Congress . . . [must] serve important governmental objectives . . . and [be] substantially related to the achievement of those objectives."[118]

But may an *originalist* judge undertake such an inquiry—a "proportionality" inquiry—and, depending on the outcome of the inquiry, invalidate an affirmative action program that, notwithstanding its costs, is not (in the judge's view) predicated on the supposed moral inferiority of one racial group to another? May an originalist judge *with minimalist inclinations* do so?[119] I explain, in the next chapter, how the reasonableness directive necessitates a proportionality inquiry—and why the Court should conduct that inquiry deferentially.[120]

9

The Supreme Court and the
Fourteenth Amendment, II:
Substantive Due Process

In the preceding chapter, we considered mainly issues the Supreme Court has addressed and doctrinal developments it has fashioned in the name of "equal protection". I now want to turn to issues addressed and developments fashioned in the name of "substantive due process". To what extent is modern substantive due process doctrine consistent with the originalist approach to constitutional interpretation? To what extent is it consistent with the minimalist (Thayerian) approach to constitutional specification? (As I emphasized at the beginning of the preceding chapter, that the Court has traditionally invoked the due process clause to support decisions that are supported, if at all, by the privileges or immunities clause presents a minor formal problem, not a major substantive one.)

I. The "Old" Substantive Due Process

As I explained in chapter 7, one can plausibly reach either of two conclusions about the (relevant aspect of the) original meaning of the privileges or immunities clause. Originalist judges may reasonably disagree among themselves about which of the two following conclusions is sounder: (1) The protected privileges and immunities—that is, those that do not derive from the Bill of Rights or from any other federal source—were meant to be protected from, and only from, legislation that discriminates on certain prohibited bases; (2) they were meant to be protected, not only from such legislation, but also from some nondiscriminatory legislation, namely, legislation that fails to regulate for the public good in a reasonable fashion.

On the basis of the second, broader reading, the privileges or immunities clause represents not just an antidiscrimination directive, but both an antidiscrimination directive and a reasonableness directive. The clause forbids states to enact or enforce laws that "abridge" protected privileges or immunities in either of two ways: first, by denying protected privileges or immunities (or by otherwise diminishing the enjoyment of protected privileges or immunities) on certain prohibited bases; or, second, by otherwise unreasonably regulating protected privileges or immunities—that is, by failing to regulate them "for the public good in a reasonable fashion". Denying protected privileges or immunities on certain prohibited bases is one way—and, for purposes of the Fourteenth Amendment, the exemplary way—of unreasonably regulating protected privileges or immunities, but, according to the broader reading, it is not the only way.

What counts, or should count, as an "otherwise unreasonable" regulation of a protected privilege or immunity—as a regulation for the public good in a "unreasonable" fashion. To say that a state law regulating a protected privilege or immunity is not reasonable must mean (because it is difficult to discern what else it could possibly mean) either: (1) that the law lacks a "rational basis", in the sense that the law does not actually succeed—or, if it once did, no longer actually succeeds—in securing, to any extent, the public good or benefit that the law was meant to secure[1] (or, at least, that those charged with defending the law from constitutional challenge affirm it as securing[2]); or, if it has a rational basis, or (2) that the law lacks "proportionality", in the sense that the magnitude of the public benefit (or benefits) the law succeeds in securing is not proportionate to—not commensurate with—the magnitude of the cost (or costs) entailed by the law. (The magnitude of the public benefit secured by a law depends, of course, both on the importance of the public benefit secured by the law and on the extent to which the law actually succeeds in securing that benefit.)

There is a constitutional warrant—a constitutional major premise—for the Supreme Court's evaluation of state legislation in the (so-called) substantive due process cases, but it is not the due process clause of section 1, which governs mainly a state's prosecutorial and adjudicatory practices and procedures; it is, rather, the privileges or immunities clause, which governs state legislation. In particular, it is the broader reading of the original meaning of the privileges or immunities clause. The results decreed by the Court in those cases—results invalidating state legislation—are supported, not by the antidiscrimination directive, but, if at all, by the reasonableness directive. In particular, they are supported either by the "rational basis" aspect of the reasonabless directive or by the "proportionality" aspect. The (in)famous case of *Lochner v. New York*[3] is a useful context in which to illustrate how both aspects of the reasonableness directive can be, and often are, implicated in a substantive due process case.

The "old" substantive due process review was focused principally, though not exclusively, on regulation of economic relationships.[4] *Lochner* is typical—indeed, exemplary—in that regard. At issue in *Lochner* was a New York law limiting the number of hours employees were free to work in bakeries to ten a day and sixty a week—and limiting, too, therefore, the freedom of employers and employees to contract for hours of work longer than the prescribed maximum. The privilege—the citizen freedom—regulated by the law is certainly protected by section 1 of the Fourteenth Amendment,[5] as the Court in *Lochner* understood. In mistakenly invoking the due process clause, however, the Court put the point in terms of the "liberty" protected against deprivation without due process of law by the due process clause of section 1 rather than in terms of the privileges (and immunities) protected against abridgment by the privileges or immunities clause of section 1: "The statute necessarily interferes with the right of contract between the employer and [employees]. . . . The general right to make a contract in relation to his business is a part of the liberty of the individual protected by the Fourteenth Amendment. . . . The right to purchase or to sell labor is part of the liberty protected by this amendment. . . ."[6]

The Court recognized, however, that not every regulation of a protected freedom ("liberty") is prohibited by section 1: In addition to certain discriminatory regulations, only "otherwise unreasonable" regulations are prohibited. The Court asked whether the regulation was a "reasonable" exercise of the the police power—the power "to conserve the morals, the health or the safety of the people"—or whether, instead, it was an "unreasonable . . . interference with the right of the individual to his personal liberty or to enter into those contracts in relation to labor which may seem to him appropriate or necessary for the support of himself and his family".[7]

The Court struck down the law on two distinct grounds. First, the Court concluded that one objective the law was meant to secure—fewer hours of work for bakery employees, understood not merely as conducive to an employee's well-being but indeed as a constituent of it, and of his family's well-being as well—was not a "public" benefit: "There is no contention that bakers . . . are not able to assert their rights and care for themselves without the protecting arm of the State, interfering with their independence of judgment and of action. They are in no sense wards of the State. Viewed in the light of a purely labor law, with no reference whatever to the question of health, we think that a law like the one before us involves neither the safety, the morals nor the welfare of the public, and that the interest of the public is not in the slightest degree affected by such an act."[8] The Court ruled, in effect, that because the law, vis à vis the "labor" objective, was all cost and no "public" benefit, the law was not a "reasonable" exercise of the police power—a regulation for the public good in a "reasonable" fashion. There are two ways in which a law can fail to secure a public benefit and therefore lack a rational basis: Although the benefit the law was meant to secure may be "public", the law may fail to secure the benefit; or although the law may succeed in securing the benefit it was meant to secure, the benefit may not be "public". Although the law at issue in *Lochner*, "viewed in the light of a purely labor law," suc-

ceeded in securing the (labor) benefit it was meant to secure, in the
Court's view that benefit was not really "public".

The Court next evaluated the law vis à vis another objective the law was
claimed to secure: protecting the physical health of employees from the dan-
gers of long hours of work in bakeries. It was obviously not open to the
Court to challenge the status of that "health" objective as a "public" benefit.[9]
Rather, the Court concluded that the law, vis à vis the health objective,
secured too slight a public benefit, and that the law was therefore not a "reasonable" exercise of the police power. "We think that there can be no fair
doubt that the trade of a baker, in and of itself, is not an unhealthy one to
that degree which would authorize the legislature to interfere with the right
to labor, and with the right of free contract on the part of the individual,
either as employer or as [employee]. . . . There must be more than the mere
fact of the possible existence of some small amount of unhealthiness to warrant legislative interference with liberty."[10] Here the Court was saying, in
effect, not that the law was "all cost and no public benefit", but that is was
"too insubstantial a public benefit, given the magnitude of the cost". The
problem was not the lack of a rational basis, but the lack of proportionality.

The Court's decision in *Lochner* is widely regarded as one of the great
negative examples of the Court's constitutional decision making. Justifiably
so. First, there is no adequate justification—least of all from the perspective of normative minimalism, which, I am about to argue, is the appropriate perspective under the reasonableness directive—for the Court's
excessively narrow reading of the category of benefits (what I am calling
"public" benefits) a state may try to secure. Certainly there is no justification based on premises derived from the Constitution (i.e., from the Constitution as originally understood). There is no good reason, constitutionally derived or otherwise, for decreeing that shorter hours of work is not
a "public" benefit—and that therefore a state may not seek to secure
shorter hours of work—any more than there is a constitutional reason for
decreeing that higher pay, or any of a multitude of other political-eco-
nomic arrangements, is not a public benefit: The physical health of persons—including workers—has traditionally been understood to be a
public benefit, but well-being has dimensions or constituents in addition
to purely physical ones. If the health of workers is a public benefit—a
benefit the state may seek to secure—as it indisputably is, other aspects of
a worker's well-being are public benefits too. (Whether a legislature
should try to secure this or that aspect of a worker's well-being, all things
considered—or even whether it should presume to know very much
about the requirements of a worker's, or of anyone else's, well-being—is a
separate question.) Bruce Ackerman has made the point from a contemporary perspective:

> For the overwhelming majority of today's Americans, *Lochner*'s constitu-
> tional denunciation of a maximum-hours law, limiting bakers to a sixty
> (!) hour work week, speaks in an alien voice. We still place a high value
> on each American's right to make basic occupational choices. Fifty years

after the New Deal, however, we believe there are some things workers shouldn't be forced to bargain about—like an employer's demand that he or she endure racial or sexual subordination, let alone the grinding indecencies of the sweatshop. Most of us don't think that employers should be allowed to put such humiliating demands on the bargaining table. We support legal guarantees to workers of certain basic rights before they can bargain in a self-respecting way on other conditions of employment. While the proper scope of these guaranteed rights remains an endless subject for democratic debate, the *Lochner* effort to take the issue off the agenda of normal politics seems an ideologically extreme solution to a multifaceted problem. Though some libertarians may believe that laissez faire remains the best approach to labor relations, very few fail to recognize that others may reasonably and responsibly come to different views.[11]

According to Ackerman, however, the majority's decision in *Lochner* was a plausible constitutional-interpretive effort in the context of its day— certainly more plausible than it would be in our day. It only seems so implausible, argues Ackerman, when viewed from the other side of the various sea changes forged during the period of the New Deal.[12] But there is a serious question, at least, whether Justice Holmes's dissenting opinion in *Lochner* wasn't more much plausible than the majority opinion *even in the context of 1905*. (Indeed, Terrance Sandalow has written that "[i]n the most charitable terms I can muster, Ackerman's defense of *Lochner* fails, utterly and completely."[13]) Holmes wrote:

> The Fourteenth Amendment does not enact Mr. Herbert Spencer's Social Statics. . . . [A] constitution is not intended to embody a particular economic theory, whether of paternalism and of the organic relation of the citizen to the State or of *laissez faire*. It is made for people of fundamentally differing views, and the accident of our finding certain opinions natural and familiar or novel and even shocking ought not to conclude our judgment upon the question whether statutes embodying them conflict with the Constitution of the United States. . . . Men whom I certainly could not pronounce unreasonable would uphold [the law] as a first installment of a general regulation of the hours of work.[14]

In any event, when, a generation after *Lochner*, the Court finally began its retreat from the decisions of "the *Lochner* era",[15] one of the two principal paths along which it did so consisted of an appropriately broad—which is to say, deferential—reading of the category of ("public") benefits a state may try to secure.[16]

The second basic reason the Court's decision in *Lochner* is widely regarded as one of the great negative examples of judicial review is that in evaluating the law—that is, the law now understood not as "a purely labor law" but simply as a health measure—the Court asked the wrong question. The Court implicitly inquired if in the Court's own view the magnitude of the health benefit secured by the law (if any) was proportionate to the magnitude of the cost entailed by the law. (The Court answered in the negative.) The Court should have asked, instead, if a legislator could reasonably have concluded that the health benefit secured by the law was proportionate to the cost entailed by the law. As Justice Harlan wrote in dissent: "It is enough for the determination of this case, and it is enough for this court to know, that *the question is one about which there is room for debate and for an honest difference of opinion*. There are many reasons of a weighty, substantial character, based upon the experience of mankind, in support of the theory that, all things considered, more than ten hours' steady work each day, from week to week, in a bakery or confectionery establishment, may endanger the health, and shorten the lives of the workmen, thereby diminishing their physical and mental capacity . . . to provide for those dependent upon them. If such reasons exist that ought to be the end of this case. . . ."[17] Justice Holmes, in dissent, sounded a similar note: "A reasonable man might think [the law] a proper measure on the score of health."[18] When, in the 1930s, the Court retreated from its decisions in *Lochner* et al., the second principal path along which it did so consisted of an appropriately deferential approach to the question whether a challenged law regulates for the public good in a reasonable fashion.

Why should the majority in *Lochner* have pursued, with Justices Harlan and Holmes, the deferential, or Thayerian, approach to the reasonableness inquiry? (I disaggregate the reasonableness inquiry, which subsumes several questions, later in this chapter, and I amplify the deferential approach to the inquiry.) There are not merely the general, context-independent reasons for Thayerian deference, which I discussed in chapter 6. There is also a context-specific reason, and it is powerful. Whether or not it is compelling in any other context, the case for the minimalist approach to the judicial specification of constitutional indeterminacy is compelling in the context of the reasonableness directive represented, or arguably represented, by section 1.[19] The reasonableness directive (arguably) represented by the privileges or immunities clause insists that virtually *every* law regulate for the public good in a reasonable fashion, because, given the breadth of the category of privileges and immunities—including citizen freedoms—protected by the privileges or immunities clause, virtually *every* law regulates a protected privilege or immunity. For the Court to ask of every law—or to stand ready to ask in a case properly before it—if "we, the members of this Court" believe that the law regulates for the public good in a reasonable fashion is for the Court largely to collapse, with respect to the evaluation of virtually any law, any meaningful distinction between the legislative function and the judicial function; in particular, it is for the Court to set itself up as a superlegislature, evaluating, de novo, legislative judgments, about the requirements of the public good, made by those with the principal authority for making them: the elected, and electorally accountable, representatives of the people, whose main charge (office, responsibility), after all, is to secure the public good.[20]

For some judges, moreover, there are additional reasons to enforce the reasonableness directive deferentially. Imagine a judge who, although she believes that the reasonableness directive is probably a part of the original meaning of section 1, thinks that the folks who gave us the Fourteenth Amendment probably should not have constitutionalized the directive—and thereby, in effect, charged the judiciary with enforcing it—because in doing so they came perilously close to constituting the courts, especially the federal courts, as a kind of superlegislature over the legislatures of the states. Such a judge has good reason to enforce the directive deferentially. Or imagine a judge who, like some scholars,[21] strongly doubts that the reasonableness directive is any part of the original meaning of section 1: If, because she believes that precedent has its claims, she accepts the reasonableness directive, at least provisionally, as a relatively fixed, if implicit, feature of the American constitutional tradition, she nonetheless has good reason to enforce the directive deferentially.

Let me try to forestall a misunderstanding. To specify a contextually indeterminate directive is one thing. To enforce ("apply") a contextually determinate directive—a directive already specified in the relevant context—is something else.[22] Normative (Thayerian) minimalism is a position about the judicial specification of constitutional directives in contexts in which the directives are indeterminate and therefore require specification. It is not a position about the judicial enforcement (application) of directives in contexts in which the directives are determinate, because they have already been specified, and now require enforcement. To contend for the deferential, or minimalist, approach to the judicial *specification* of the reasonableness directive, as I am doing here, is not to suggest that the deferential approach to the judicial *enforcement* of every aspect of the privileges or immunities clause, or of every aspect of section 1 generally, is appropriate. In particular, it is not to suggest that a deferential approach to the judicial enforcement of the antidiscrimination directive—to its enforcement in a context in which it has already been specified—is appropriate.

For example, the Court has already specified the antidiscrimination directive in the context of race in the sense that the Court has already concluded that race is not relevant to a person's status as a human being. If a case arises in which the Court strongly suspects a law—for example, a law singling out nonwhites for worse treatment than whites—of being illicitly predicated on the view that race is relevant to a person's status as a human being, the Court should not let go its suspicion, and will not, unless the Court *itself* becomes persuaded that the law is not illicitly predicated. The Court will not become persuaded unless the party defending the law convinces the Court that the law is necessary to serve a compelling governmental interest.[23] If the Court is to let go *its* suspicion, it is not enough for the Court to think that perhaps *someone else*—perhaps someone less vigilant—could reasonably become persuaded to let go *his* or *her* suspicion, could reasonably become convinced that the law bears the requisite relation to a weighty governmental interest.

With respect, not to the judicial specification of the reasonableness directive, but to the judicial enforcement of the antidiscrimination directive, the Court's responsibility is primary, not secondary: The deferential approach is out of place. (I argue later in this chapter that even with respect to the judicial *specification* of the antidiscrimination directive, the minimalist approach is out of place.[24] But the question at the moment is the propriety of the deferential approach, not to the judicial specification of the antidiscrimination directive, but to the judicial enforcement of the directive—to its enforcement in a context in which it has already been specified.) My conclusion in that regard tracks a virtual consensus in modern constitutional commentary: A deferential judicial posture is inappropriate if and when the Court is engaged in a task that, institutionally, in consequence of its relative insularity from the exigencies of ordinary politics, it is uniquely well suited to perform, namely, guarding against, and ferreting out, illicit discrimination.[25] Although ordinary politics can sometimes perform that task, it cannot invariably be relied on to perform it well or disinterestedly. Moreover, there can be no reasonable doubt that an antidiscrimination directive is a central part of the original meaning of section 1, even if, as I said before, there is room for reasonable disagreement about the precise shape or contours of the antidiscrimination directive section 1, as originally understood, represents. (I return to the important issue of aggressive judicial enforcement of the antidiscrimination directive later, in discussing abortion and the Fourteenth Amendment.[26])

But, again, in the different context of judicial specification of the reasonableness directive, a *non*deferential approach is out of place: As I said, the approach of the majority in *Lochner*, in contrast to the approach of Justices Harlan and Holmes, collapses the distinction between the legislative function and the judicial function with respect to the evaluation, not just of some laws—for example, laws appropriately suspected of being illicitly predicated—but of virtually any law, since, again, virtually every law regulates a protected privilege or immunity. (Moreover, it is open to reasonable doubt that the reasonableness directive is a part of the original meaning of section 1.)

The retreat from *Lochner* and its progeny—the decline and fall of the "old" substantive due process—began in the mid-1930s during the Great Depression, with the Court's decisions in cases like *Nebbia v. New York*,[27] in which the Court rejected a constitutional challenge to a state law fixing the price at which milk could be sold, and *West Coast Hotel v. Parrish*,[28] in which the Court rejected a constitutional challenge to a state law setting a minimum wage for women.[29] The modern Court has not abandoned the reasonableness directive that grounds the constitutional inquiry in *Lochner* and in allied cases. (Indeed, that directive, as I explained in the preceding chapter, grounds the the modern Court's rational basis inquiry in equal protection cases. It also grounds, as I am about to explain, the inquiry the Court has pursued in the "new" substantive due process cases.) In the context of constitutional challenges to economic-regulatory legislation, however, the modern Court has habitually enforced the directive so deferentially[30] that some commentators have concluded, sometimes critically, that as a practical matter, if not as a rhetorical one, the modern Court has abandoned the directive in the context of challenges to such legislation.[31] If the Court is going to enforce the reasonableness directive in the context of constitutional challenges to *some* legislation,[32] the Court should enforce the directive in the context of constitutional challenges to *any* legislation, including economic-regulatory legislation.[33] Nonetheless, imperially delimiting the category of ("public") benefits a state may seek to secure, and otherwise specifying the reasonableness directive nondeferentially—both of which the Court did in *Lochner* and in many other cases thereafter—are judicial practices difficult to justify. The Court's abandonment of each of those two practices, in the 1930s, made good sense.

None of this is to deny that some laws invalidated during the *Lochner* era would not have had all the political support needed to get enacted but for economically self-interested, rather than public-regarding, motives on the part of some relatively well-off and influential political constituencies. (No doubt, many laws then as now could not get enacted but for economically self-interested motives on the part of some such groups.) Consider, for example, the law invalidated in *Lochner* itself, which was supported by large bakeries in an effort to drive small bakeries out of business. The baking process spanned two shifts. The small bakeries, unlike the large bakeries, could not afford to hire two shifts of workers, so they had been getting by with workers who, though on the premises for a double shift, were permitted to sleep while the bread (etc.) baked.[34] The question why large bakeries supported the legislation is an interesting one. But the ultimately dispositive question, under the reasonableness directive, is not what motives animate this or that constituency to support a law but whether the law is a reasonable regulation for the public good (or, in Thayerian terms, whether a legislator can reasonably conclude that it is such a regulation). That a law would not have been enacted but for economically self-interested motives does not mean that the law *necessarily* fails to regulate for the public good in a reasonable fashion. Of course, that a particular law would not have been enacted but for economically self-interested motives may well be, in some contexts, a good reason for suspecting that, and therefore for inquiring if, the law in fact fails to regulate for the public good in a reasonable fashion.

Participating in a debate, in 1977, among members of the Court about the proper judicial approach or methodology in substantive due process cases, and acutely aware that substantive due process review was, during the *Lochner* era, the very embodiment of judicial imperialism, Justice Powell said (echoing Justice Harlan before him): "Appropriate limits on substantive due process [review] come not from drawing arbitrary lines but rather from 'careful respect for the teachings of history [and] solid recognition of the basic values that underlie our society.'"[35] As a maxim for constraining substantive due process review—for constraining, that is, judicial enforcement of the reasonableness directive—Justice Powell's test is quite indeterminate, as indeed Justice White insisted in the very case in which Powell spoke.[36] A much better test—though, of course, no test is immune to manipulation—is for the Court, in enforcing the reasonableness directive, to ask, pace James Bradley Thayer, not whether the challenged law is in the Court's own view a reasonable regulation for the public good, but only whether there is room for a reasonable difference of opinion about the matter—whether a legislator can reasonably conclude that it is such a regulation.

II. The Emergence of the "New" Substantive Due Process: *Griswold v. Connecticut*

Whereas the "old" substantive due process review, as I said, was focused principally on regulation of economic relationships, the "new" substantive due process review has been focused primarily, though not exclusively, on regulation of intimate, often sexual, relationships.[37] The rise of modern substantive due process began in 1965, about a generation after *Nebbia* and *West Coast Hotel*, with the Supreme Court's decision in *Griswold v. Connecticut*.[38] At issue in *Griswold* was the constitutionality, under section 1 of the Fourteenth Amendment, of a statute that proscribed the use of contraceptives "for the purpose of preventing conception".[39] (Use of contraceptives for the purpose of preventing disease was not proscribed.) The statute was challenged "as applied" to married couples. Because the statute did not single out some persons for worse treatment than others but applied equally to all persons, including married couples, there was no question whether the statute implicated, much less violated, the antidiscrimination directive represented by section 1 of the Fourteenth Amendment. The serious question was whether the statute violated the reasonableness directive: Was Connecticut's regulation of the freedom of married couples to use contraceptives a regulation "for the public good in a reasonable fashion"? The precise question, in an appropriately deferential mode, was this: Can a legislator reasonably conclude that the statute actually succeeds in securing a public benefit—namely, the putatively public benefit the official charged with defending the statute from constitutional challenge (let us call that official "the Attorney General") affirms it as securing—and, if so, that the magnitude of the benefit is proportionate to the magnitude of the cost or costs entailed by the statute?

Why should the relevant public benefit be the one the Attorney General affirms the statute as securing rather than the one the statute was actually enacted to secure (assuming the two are different)? It is not always clear what public benefit (or benefits) a statute was enacted to secure: The legislative history may be indeterminate; or, indeed, there may be no legislative history. But even where there is or may be a determinate legislative history, there is no reason for the Court the plumb it, because there is no reason for the Court *not* to credit the Attorney General's statement that the rationale of the statute is such-and-such— unless there is some reason for the Court to suspect that the real story of the statute is darker than the Attorney General's story. (For example, the Attorney General's tale may conceal the central role played by racial animus in the real story.) What if the Attorney General disserves the state he represents by telling an inaccurate story (about the rationale of the statute) on the basis of which the Court concludes that the statute violates the reasonableness directive? It is not the job of the Court to protect the state from the mistakes of the Attorney General elected to represent it.[40] Moreover, if the Attorney General disserves the state in that way, the people of the state, through their representatives, may reenact the statute, making it crystal clear what the rationale of the statute is— making it clear, that is, what public benefit the statute is being enacted to secure.

In *Griswold*, the party charged with defending the statute—the Connecticut Attorney General—did not argue that the statute expressed Connecticut's judgment that the use of contraceptives (even by married persons) was in and of itself immoral. Rather, he argued that the statute "serve[s] the State's policy against all forms of promiscuous or illicit sexual relationships, be they premarital or extramarital".[41] Justice Goldberg, in a concurring opinion joined by Chief Justice Warren and Justice Brennan, observed: "[Connecticut] says that preventing the use of birth-control devices by married persons helps prevent the indulgence by some in . . . extra-marital relations. The rationality of this justification is dubious, particularly in light of the admitted widespread availability to all persons [in] Connecticut, unmarried as well as married, of birth-control devices for the prevention of disease, as distinguished from the prevention of conception. . . ."[42] In short, it was simply implausible to believe that the Connecticut statute, insofar as it regulated the use of contraceptives by married persons, did anything of consequence to diminish the incidence of "illicit sexual relationships". As Justice White put it in his concurring opinion: "At most the broad ban is of marginal utility to the declared objective. A statute limiting its prohibition on use to persons engaging in the prohibited relationship would serve the end posited by Connecticut in the same way, and with the same effectiveness, or ineffectiveness, as the broad anti-use statute under attack in this case. I find nothing in this record justifying the sweeping scope of this statute, with its telling effect on the freedoms of married persons. . . ."[43] In short: The asserted goal of the statute at issue in *Griswold* was to diminish the incidence of sex outside of marriage; because this the statute plainly did not do, it failed utterly as a means to an end. (Moreover, no legislator could reasonably have concluded otherwise.) The statute therefore lacked a rational basis in violation of the reasonableness directive.

It is relatively easy to justify invalidating Connecticut's anticontraception statute, even from the perspective of normative minimalism, principally because the Connecticut Attorney General declined to defend the law as a legal expression or embodiment of the view that the use of "artificial" contraceptives to prevent pregnancy is, in and of itself, an immoral act. (As Justice White wrote: "There is no serious contention that Connecticut thinks the use of artificial or external methods of contraception immoral or unwise in itself. . . ."[44]) Yet, the Connecticut law, which proscribed the use of contraceptives even by married couples, represented, when it was originally enacted, just that view.[45] The decision not to defend the law as expressing the view that contraceptive use is itself immoral is understandable: The position that the use of contraceptives is immoral has now largely been abandoned in the United States.[46]

It is exceedingly unlikely that today a state legislature would enact an anticontraception statute in order to express the view that the use of contraceptives is immoral (and to try to deter the conduct). But "what if"? Three points bear emphasis. First, the Court cannot plausibly declare that the "morals" objective of expressing disapproval for conduct deemed immoral and of trying to deter the conduct falls outside the category of ("public") benefits a state may seek to secure.[47] Paraphrasing Holmes's dissent in *Lochner*, we might say that the Constitution does not enact Mr. John Stuart Mill's *On Liberty*. As Justice Scalia has emphasized, "Our society prohibits, and all human societies have prohibited, certain activities not because they harm others but because they are considered, in the traditional phrase, '*contra bonos mores*,' *i.e.*, immoral. In American society, such prohibitions have included, for example, sadomasochism, cockfighting, bestiality, suicide, drug use, prostitution, and sodomy. While there may be great diversity of views on whether various of these prohibitions should exist . . . there is no doubt that, absent specific constitutional protection for the conduct involved, the Constitution does not prohibit them simply because they regulate 'morality.'"[48]

Second, the conclusion is always perilous—especially for a Supreme Court appropriately wary about acting imperially—that no legislator can reasonably deem particular conduct immoral. As Justice Harlan wrote in 1961, in *Poe v. Ullman*, the moral judgment represented by anticontraception statutes "are no more demonstrably correct or incorrect than are the varieties of judgment, expressed in law, on marriage and divorce, on adult consensual homosexuality, abortion, and sterilization, or euthanasia and suicide."[49] Third, if anticontraception legislation were enacted today, the Court should think long and hard before concluding—which is not to say that it should never finally conclude—that no legislator can reasonably think that the public benefit secured by the law is proportionate to the costs: After all, a critical mass of legislators would just have concluded that the public benefit secured by the law *is* proportionate to the costs—unless, of course, they were oblivious to the costs, which, though possible, is unlikely, given the debate that would surely have surrounded enactment of the law.

If there is no constitutional impediment to a state enacting a fornication statute to express the view that sex outside of marriage is immoral (and to try to deter it), it seems to follow that the state may also enact a statute expressing the view that the distribution of contraceptives (or contraceptives for the purpose of preventing pregnancy) is immoral too; after all, such distribution serves only to facilitate the primary conduct deemed immoral. Moreover, it seems a fair assumption that a legislator could reasonably conclude that the latter statute satisfies the requirement of proportionality. (Responding to the argument that if an anticontraception statute "does deter any fornication, it will do so at a disproportionate cost, because there will be more pregnancies and more unwanted children", Judge Posner has written: "Although a higher percentage of premarital intercourse will end in pregnancy, there will be less such intercourse; for all one knows, the effects may cancel out and the number of pregnancies and unwanted children remain the same. . . ."[50]) Given that assumption, *Eisenstadt v. Baird*[51] was probably wrongly decided. In *Eisenstadt*, decided seven years after *Griswold* and one year before the 1973 abortion case discussed later in this chapter (*Roe v. Wade*[52]), the Court struck down a Mas-sachusetts law that forbade, inter alia, the distribution of contraceptives (for the purpose of preventing pregnancy) to unmarried persons.

As defended by the Connecticut Attorney General, the law at issue in *Griswold* was a wholly "strategic" or "instrumental" law, and, again, the law failed utterly as a means to its (asserted) end—and therefore lacked a rational basis. By contrast, the law at issue in *Eisenstadt* was principally "expressive": The law expressed Massachusetts's judgment that the prohibited conduct—distributing contraceptives to unmarried persons—is in and of itself immoral. Therefore, the Massachusetts law did not, because it could not, fail as a means to an end: The law achieved its principal end simply in virtue of being enacted, and it achieved that end whether or not the law succeeded to any particular extent in achieving the additional goal of deterring the prohibited conduct. Indeed, as I have already suggested, if the Connecticut Attorney General had defended the law in *Griswold* as an "expressive" law—a law principally expressing the state's judgment that the prohibited conduct (use of contraceptives by anyone, including married persons) is in and of itself immoral—the law would/could not then have failed as a means to its principal end; it would be much more difficult to justify the Court's invalidation of the law.

Of course, if *Roe v. Wade* was rightly decided, then a fortiori both *Griswold* and *Eisenstadt* were rightly decided: If, as the Court ruled in *Roe*, a state is constitutionally disabled from forbidding persons, married or unmarried, to have abortions, then surely it is disabled from forbidding them to use contraceptives to prevent pregnancy in the first place. But it is not obvious that *Roe* was rightly decided. If *Roe* was wrongly decided, it does not follow that either *Griswold* or *Eisenstadt* was wrongly decided—though either or both may have been wrongly decided. I have argued in this chapter that *Griswold* (but probably not *Eisenstadt*) was rightly decided—rightly decided *assuming* the reasonableness directive—whether or not *Roe* was rightly decided. Later in this chapter I address the question whether *Roe* was rightly decided.

Griswold v. Connecticut introduced, in 1965, the modern era of substantive due process. Two of the most important and controversial subjects addressed by the Supreme Court in its modern substantive due process cases—indeed, perhaps the two most important and controversial subjects—are sexual orientation and abortion. I now want to consider, mainly from an originalist perspective but also from a normative-minimalist perspective, the adequacy of what the Court has said about the constitutionality both of laws that criminalize homosexual sexual activity and of laws that criminalize abortion.

III. Sexual Orientation and the Fourteenth Amendment

It is rather unlikely that today many state legislatures would enact an anti-contraception law. But it is not so unlikely that today some state legislatures would enact a law, *or at least would reject any effort to remove an existing law from the books, even a little-enforced one,* that expressed the view that homosexual sexual activity is immoral. The reasonableness directive (arguably) represented by section 1 of the Fourteenth Amendment is probably not a strong basis for ruling that a law criminalizing homosexual sexual activity is unconstitutional. As I said near the end of the preceding section, it is always perilous for the Court to conclude that no legislator can reasonably deem immoral conduct a legislature does in fact deem immoral; moreover, it may be no less perilous to conclude that no legislator can reasonably think that the public benefit of a "morals" law is proportionate to the law's cost when a legislature does in fact think that the benefit of the law is proportionate to its cost. But even if the reasonableness directive is a weak basis for such a ruling, the other directive (unarguably) represented by section 1—the antidiscrimination directive—may well be a strong basis.

The Georgia criminal statute upheld (against a "substantive due process" challenge) by a bare majority of the Supreme Court in *Bowers v. Hardwick* outlawed "sodomy", which it defined as "any sexual act involving the sex organs of one person and the mouth or anus of another."[53] As written, the statute proscribed sodomy not merely when practiced by persons of the same sex, but also when practiced by a man and a woman, even by a married couple. Perhaps wincing at the possibility that a state might apply such a statute to marital sodomy, Justice White wrote, for the five-person majority, that the "only claim properly before the Court [is] Hardwick's challenge to the Georgia statute as applied to consensual homosexual sodomy. We express no opinion on the constitutionality of the Georgia statute as applied to other acts of sodomy."[54] It is unlikely the Court will ever have to "express an opinion" about the constitutionality of such a statute as applied to marital sodomy, because it is unlikely that any state with a law like Georgia's will now or hereafter apply it to marital sodomy—principally because no state with such a law will likely deem it immoral for a *married couple* to engage in whatever kind of sexual intercourse the husband and wife want to engage in, whether vaginal, oral, or anal. While a legislature may well deem immoral *any* sexual activity between a man and a woman not married to each another, it is unlikely that a legislature will believe that the immorality of sexual contact between a man and a woman not married to one another derives from the fact that it is oral or anal rather than vaginal; it is almost certainly the case that the legislature would claim that the immorality of the sexual contact derives from the fact that the man and the woman are not married to each another. (If one or both of them is married to someone else, the immorality of their sexual contact derives from the fact—or so a legislature would likely claim—that one or both of them is married to someone else, even if it also derives, independently, from the fact that they are not married to each other. Just as a single act can violate two laws, a single act can violate two moral norms.) But it is not at all unlikely that some legislature will believe that the immorality of sexual contact between a man and a man (or between a woman and a woman) derives from the fact that they are a man and a man (even if, in the legislature's view, it also derives independently from the fact that their sexual activity is nonmarital). Surely it is the view that homosexual sexual activity is immoral qua homosexual (and not only qua nonmarital) that underlies both (1) statutes that as written apply only to homosexual sexual activity and (2) statutes, like Georgia's, that, though as written apply to sexual activity without regard to whether it is practiced maritally or heterosexually or homosexually, are today applied, if at all, only to homosexual sexual activity.

That a state may regulate some activity does not entail that it may regulate the activity in a discriminatory way. That a state may outlaw nonmarital sexual activity does not entail that it may take the separate step of outlawing interracial nonmarital sexual activity. A state may not, consistently with the antidiscrimination directive represented by section 1, outlaw interracial nonmarital sexual activity. It may not do so because the predicate of such a law is conspicuously that nonwhites are inferior, as human beings, to whites. Similarly, that a state may outlaw nonmarital sexual activity does not entail that it may take the separate step of outlawing homosexual sexual activity—nonmarital sexual activity between persons of the same sex—any more than it entails that it may take the separate step of outlawing nonmarital sexual activity between a white person and a nonwhite person. May a state, consistently with the antidiscrimination directive, outlaw—not sex outside of marriage, or certain sexual activity (outside marriage) without regard to whether the activity is prac-

ticed heterosexually or homosexually—but homosexual sexual activity?
(That a state outlaws homosexual sexual activity by means of selective
enforcement, or the threat thereof, under a statute directed at sexual
activity without regard to whether it is practiced heterosexually or homosexually, rather than by means of a statute directed specifically at homosexual sexual activity, is constitutionally irrelevant, just as it would be constitutionally irrelevant that a state outlawed interracial sexual activity, not
under a statute directed specifically at interracial sexual activity, but under
a statute directed at sexual activity without regard to whether it was practiced interracially or not.) In a recent case striking down, on the basis of
the state constitution, a state statute directed specifically at homosexual
sexual activity, the Kentucky Supreme Court said: "Certainly, the practice
of [sodomy] violates traditional morality. But so does the same act between
heterosexuals, which activity is decriminalized. Going one step further, all
sexual activity between consenting adults outside of marriage violates our
traditional morality." The Court then put what I want to suggest is the
central constitutional question in this area today: "The issue here is not
whether sexual activity traditionally viewed as immoral can be punished
by society, *but whether it can be punished solely on the basis of sexual preference.
. . .* The question is whether a society that no longer criminalizes adultery,
fornication, or [sodomy] between heterosexuals, has a rational basis to single out homosexual acts for different treatment."[55]

Some people have thought that to be black is to be, not merely different, but defective, it is to be a defective human being—less than fully
human—because being white is normative. (By contrast, to have blue
eyes, or red hair, is to be merely different.) Some people have thought
that to be female is to be a defective human being, because being male is
normative. And some people have thought—and think—that to be
homosexual, to have a homosexual sexual orientation, is to be a defective
human being, because being heterosexual ("straight") is normative. Judge
Posner has observed that "[homosexuals,] like Jews, are despised more
for who they are than for what they do. . . ."[56] (In *Bowers*, Justice Stevens,
in a dissenting opinion joined by Justices Brennan and Marshall, decried
"the habitual dislike for, or ignorance about," homosexuals.[57]) If a law
banning homosexual sexual activity is indeed predicated on the view that
to be homosexual is somehow to be not merely different but defective—
the view that a person's sexual orientation is relevant to his or her status
or worth as a human being—then a state may not, consistently with the
antidiscrimination directive represented by section 1, outlaw homosexual
sexual activity.[58] A state may not, consistently with the antidiscrimination
directive, base a political choice on the view that a person's sexual orientation is relevant to his or her status as a human being. May not, that is,
unless a person's sexual orientation *is* relevant to his or her status as a
human being. Those who want to defend the result in *Bowers* as consistent
with the originalist approach to constitutional interpretation,[59] need to
meet the central argument here, namely, that a person's sexual orienta-

tion is, like a person's race or sex, simply irrelevant to his or her status as a human being.

As a real-world matter, it certainly seems that the predicate of a law outlawing homosexual sexual activity, and the predicate of applying a facially nondiscriminatory "sodomy" law only to homosexual sexual activity, is that persons of homosexual sexual orientation are somehow defective, as human beings, to persons of heterosexual sexual orientation: they are inferior human beings; they are less worthy of respect and concern, in the sense that their fulfillment and their suffering—in particular, their sexual fulfillment and their sexual suffering—count for less than the sexual fulfillment/suffering of persons of heterosexual sexual orientation (who are legally free, even if not married, to engage in sexual intercourse, even oral and anal intercourse). What other predicate could there be? In the recent Kentucky case, the Kentucky Supreme Court wrote:

> The Commonwealth [of Kentucky] has tried hard to demonstrate a legitimate governmental interest justifying a distinction [between homosexuals and heterosexuals], but it has failed. Many of the claimed justifications are simply outrageous: that "homosexuals are more promiscuous than heterosexuals, . . . that homosexuals enjoy the company of children, and that homosexuals are more prone to engage in sex acts in public." The only proffered justification with superficial validity is that "infectious diseases are more readily transmitted by anal sodomy than by other forms of sexual copulation." But this statute is not limited to anal copulation, and this reasoning would apply to male-female anal intercourse the same as it applies to male-male anal intercourse.[60]

I said that those who want to defend the result in *Bowers* as consistent with the originalist approach to constitutional interpretation need to argue that a person's sexual orientation is relevant to his or her status as a human being. However, pursuant to the minimalist approach to the judicial specification of the antidiscrimination directive, they need argue only that one could reasonably believe that a person's sexual orientation is relevant to his or her status as a human being. Is the minimalist (Thayerian) approach to the judicial specification of the antidiscrimination directive the right approach?

The proper issue for the Court under the reasonableness directive, as I have explained, is what a legislator can reasonably conclude. What a legislator can reasonably conclude depends, of course, on the society or culture in which the legislator is acting. A conclusion may be reasonable in the context of one society, given its characteristic assumptions about the world, values, and priorities, but unreasonable in the context of another society, with very different characteristic assumptions, values, and priorities. The relevant society, for purposes of the reasonableness directive represented by section 1, is, of course, the society governed by the Fourteenth Amendment: American society, which, because it is morally and religiously pluralistic—and excluding inevitable, but uncharacteristic, extremes—contains a broad range of competing assumptions, values, and priorities, each shared by a significant number of citizens but none the object of consensus.

The proper issue for the Court under the antidiscrimination directive, however, is not what one can reasonably conclude. Again excluding inevitable but uncharacteristic extremes, there may be some not insignificant number of citizens, perhaps many, who, given where they stand in the religiously and morally pluralistic American political community, believe that a particular trait—sex, for example—is relevant to a person's status as a human being. They may believe something to the effect that "the man is the 'norm' for being human while the woman is an 'auxiliary,' someone defined exclusively by her relationships to men"—that "'the [male] sex . . . is superior to the other in the very order of creation or by the very nature of things'".[61] Moreover, their belief in that regard may be reasonable—that is, reasonable for them whose belief it is, reasonable in the context of their (sub)culture—in the sense that the belief is supported by much else that they believe, much else that is a part of their overall, culturally shared web of beliefs.[62] (At one time, it was not unreasonable for many Americans, given what else they believed, to embrace even slavery: "The history of the pre-civil war debates in the United States Congress demonstrates that reasonable people did indeed differ on [slavery]."[63]) But that such a belief may be reasonable in that sense cannot be determinative. The issue must be whether the trait is *in the Court's own view* relevant to one's status as a human being.

This is the heart of the matter: Whereas the judicial specification of the reasonableness directive operates, or should operate, within the context of the competitor assumptions, values, and priorities of pluralistic American society, the judicial specification of the antidiscrimination directive must be grounded in a critical stance toward some of those assumptions, namely, assumptions about the relevance, to a person's status as a human being, of particular traits, including race, sex, illegitimacy, and—yes—sexual orientation. Under the reasonableness directive, the (pluralistic) moral shape of American society is largely taken for granted, but under the antidiscrimination directive, some aspect of the moral shape of American society must be, for the Court, in question. ("[The purpose of the equal protection clause] is not to protect traditional values and practices, but to call into question such values and practices when they operate to burden disadvantaged minorities."[64]) Given the range of the competing assumptions, values, and priorities characteristic of pluralistic American society—some of which are racist, some of which are sexist, some of which are homophobic, and so on—to counsel the minimalist approach to the judicial specification of the antidiscrimination directive is, in effect if not in intent, to counsel a radical marginalization of the directive. While true that to counsel the minimalist approach to the judicial specification of the reasonableness directive is to counsel a marginalization of that directive, too, there is, as I indicated, a good reason to marginalize the reasonableness directive: The nonminimalist approach to the judicial specification of the reasonableness directive tends to collapse the distinction between the legislative function and the judicial function with respect to virtually all legislation. Moreover, one may reasonably doubt that the reasonableness directive is even a part of the original meaning of the privileges or immunities clause. But there is no good reason to counsel marginalization of the antidiscrimination directive. To the contrary, there is this good reason for resisting its marginalization: Our historical experience—which, after all, is our best teacher—suggests that *our ordinary politics has been particularly ill suited to decide what traits are relevant to a person's status or worth as a human being.* (Consider the extent to which ordinary politics has been— and remains—racist and sexist.) Moreover, there is simply no good reason to doubt that an antidiscrimination directive is a central part of the original meaning of the privileges or immunities clause and of section 1 generally. If there is any indeterminate constitutional directive (regarding rights or liberties) the judiciary should have the primary responsibility for specifying, and not merely a secondary responsibility, the antidiscrimination directive of section 1 of the Fourteenth Amendment is such a directive.[65]

It is not difficult to identify the aspect of the moral shape of American society that should have been in question in *Bowers v. Hardwick*. Judge Posner has already done so:

> Perhaps the strongest argument for Michael Hardwick was that statutes which criminalize homosexual behavior express *an irrational fear and loathing of a group that has been subjected to discrimination, much like that directed against the Jews, with whom indeed homosexuals—who, like Jews, are despised more for who they are than for what they do—were frequently bracketed in medieval persecutions.* The statutes thus have a quality of invidiousness missing from statutes prohibiting abortion or contraception. The position of the homosexual is difficult at best, even in a tolerant society, which our society is not quite; and it is made worse, though probably not much worse, by statutes that condemn the homosexual's characteristic methods of sexual expression as vile crimes (the Georgia statute carried a maximum punishment of twenty years in prison). There is a gratuitousness, an egregiousness, a cruelty, and a meanness about the Georgia statute. . . .[66]

IV. Abortion and the Fourteenth Amendment

Now we come to the case—*Roe v. Wade*[67]—and the issue—abortion— around which constitutional theory has swirled for the last twenty years. No constitutional decision by the Supreme Court in the modern period of American constitutional law has been more controversial than—or as persistently controversial as—the Court's ruling in *Roe*.

Robert Cover wrote that "[e]ach constitutional generation organizes itself about paradigmatic events. . . . For my generation it is clear that the events are *Brown v. Board of Education*[68] and the Civil Rights Movement."[69] The Supreme Court's decision in *Brown v. Board of Education*—"the decision that opened our era of judicial activity"[70]—was the principal text of constitutional theory, or at least its principal subtext, for the twenty years or so after *Brown.* The Court's ruling in *Brown*, though once at the center of a storm of controversy—constitutional-theoretical controversy[71] as well as political[72]—is now widely regarded as a legitimate exercise of the power of judicial review.[73] (Of course, that a ruling by the Court is widely embraced as legitimate does not entail that the particular justification the Court happened to give in support of the ruling is widely accepted.) I have myself argued, in the preceding chapter of this book, that the Court's ruling in *Brown* is easily justifiable on an originalist basis. Many even regard the Court's ruling in *Brown* as such an exemplary exercise of the power of judicial review that no constitutional theory that fails to accomodate the ruling can be talken seriously. "The acid test of originalism, as indeed of any theory of constitutional adjudication, is its capacity to justify what is now almost universally regarded as the Supreme Court's finest hour: its decision in *Brown v. Board of Education*."[74]

Roe v. Wade has been the principal text (or subtext) of constitutional theory for the last twenty years. But the Court's ruling in *Roe*, in contrast to its ruling in *Brown*, is still widely regarded, after all these years, as of seriously questionable legitimacy. Gerald Gunther's comment is indicative: "In my view, *Brown v. Board of Education* was an entirely legitimate decision. . . . By contrast, I have not yet found a satisfying rationale to justify *Roe v. Wade* . . . on the basis of modes of constitutional interpretation I consider legitimate."[75] Can the central ruling in *Roe*—the ruling that laws forbidding a woman to have an abortion in the first or the second trimester of her pregnancy are unconstitutional—be justified on the basis of "a legitimate mode of constitutional interpretation"? (The constitutionality of laws that forbid a woman to have an abortion in the third trimester of her pregnancy are not seriously at issue, so long as such laws provide an exception for an abortion necessary to save the life of the mother or to protect her basic physical health from a serious threat of grave and irreparable damage.)

In what is probably the most powerful critique of the Court's ruling in *Roe*, John Ely has argued that the ruling cannot be so justified.[76] (Ely's book *Democracy and Distrust*,[77] the most important contribution to constitutional theory in the twenty years since *Roe*,[78] is essentially an elaboration—a careful, eloquent elaboration—of the theoretical basis of his critique of *Roe*.) Ely's argument is that restrictive abortion legislation of the sort invalidated by the Court in *Roe* does not seriously implicate, much less violate, any constitutional norm. I disagree. As I am about to argue, such legislation does seriously implicate a constitutional norm—indeed, *two* constitutional norms: the reasonableness directive and the antidiscrimination directive. To implicate a constitutional norm, however, is not necessarily to violate it. In my view, restrictive abortion legislation like that invalidated in *Roe* does not violate the reasonableness directive. But such legislation—some aspects of it, at least—may defensibly be adjudged to violate the antidiscrimination directive. Or so I want to argue.

Anticontraception laws are a thing of the past: No state would today enact one, even if the relevant constitutional doctrine permitted a state to do so. (By the 1960s, only two states had them: Massachusetts and Connecticut.[79]) Laws criminalizing homosexual sexual activity, too, may be largely a thing of the past, at least in this sense: Few states today enforce such laws, even though the relevant constitutional doctrine permits a state to do so. But antiabortion laws are certainly not a thing of the past: Many states would today enact and enforce such laws, in one form or another, if the relevant constitutional doctrine permitted them to do so. Many states are today poised to do so, if the relevant constitutional doctrine is revised, or relaxed, to permit some such laws. Indeed, one state, Louisiana, has already enacted (over the Republican governor's veto) an extremely restrictive abortion law—tolerating only abortions necessary to save the life of the mother and abortions in the case of rape or incest *if the woman has reported the rape or incest within five days of its occurrence*—in anticipation of the demise of *Roe v. Wade*. "Louisiana's criminal abortion statute reflected the first time in the twentieth century that a state had passed an antiabortion measure that did not even contain an exception for a pregnant woman's *health*."[80] (In conjunction, two events in 1992 make it very unlikely that the relevant doctrine will be, at any time in the foreseeable future, revised or even much relaxed: The five-to-four decision of the Supreme Court in *Planned Parenthood of Southeastern Pennsylvania v. Casey*, which reaffirmed "the essential holding of *Roe v. Wade*",[81] and the election of Bill Clinton to the presidency of the United States.)

Do antiabortion laws—in particular, laws criminalizing abortion in the first or the second trimester of pregnancy—violate section 1 of the Fourteenth Amendment? Before it gets to that question, the Court must determine if such legislation even implicates section 1. It does not implicate section 1—in particular, it does not implicate the clause of section 1 that governs legislation: the privileges or immunities clause—unless the legislation "abridges" a protected freedom, whether a freedom *to* ("privilege") or a freedom *from* ("immunity"). The freedom to decide if and when to become a parent is, of course, such a freedom. As I argued in the preceding chapter: If one wants to limit the jurisdiction of section 1 of the Fourteenth Amendment over the kinds of laws states may enact and enforce, one probably may not do so, consistently with the originalist approach to constitutional interpretation, by construing the category of protected privileges and immunities—of protected citizen freedoms—narrowly. Restrictive abortion legislation does implicate section 1.[82] The serious question is whether any such legislation violates section 1.

Can the Court's decision in *Roe* that the restrictive abortion legislation in question there violates section 1 be justified on the basis of the reasonabless directive? In enforcing the reasonableness directive, the relevant question, as I explained in the course of commenting on the Court's misadventure in *Lochner v. New York*, is what a legislator can reasonably conclude. In this context, the relevant question is whether a legislator can reasonably conclude that restrictive abortion legislation—say, legislation outlawing all abortions except those necessary to save the life of the mother—is a reasonable regulation for the public good: in particular, that the legislation serves a public benefit the magnitude of which is proportionate to the magnitude of the various costs entailed by the legislation, especially the costs visited by the legislation on those whose reproductive freedom the legislation restricts. To answer that question, we must disaggregate the reasonableness inquiry.

First, can a legislator reasonably believe that the benefit the legislation aims to secure—saving fetal life—is a "public" benefit? If a legislator can reasonably believe that protecting the lives of Alaskan wolves, for example, is a public benefit, it is certainly reasonable for a legislator to believe that saving fetal life is a public benefit. Indeed, no one can reasonably believe that saving fetal life is not a public benefit. Relatedly, a legislator can reasonably believe that the legislation actually succeeds, to some extent at least, in saving fetal life. (To say that a legislator cannot reasonably believe that the benefit a law aims to secure is a public benefit—or that a legislator cannot reasonably believe that the law actually succeeds in securing, to any extent, the public benefit it aims to secure—is to say that the law lacks a "rational basis", in which case the proportionality question does not even arise.)

Second, can a legislator reasonably believe that the principal costs of the legislation—the costs visited on pregnant women who would otherwise choose to abort their pregnancies—are small? (Those are not the only costs, but surely they are the principal ones.) Those costs are undeniably great. The Court in *Roe* emphasized the magnitude of the costs[83]—but only to a point. As Judge Posner reports, commenting critically on Justice Blackmun's opinion for the majority in *Roe*: "No effort is made to dramatize the hardships to a woman forced to carry her fetus to term against her will. The opinion does point out that 'maternity, or additional offspring, may force upon the woman a distressful life and future,' and it elaborates on the point for a few more sentences. But there is no mention of the woman who is raped, who is poor, or whose fetus is deformed. There is no reference to the death of women from illegal abortions."[84]

Third, because the magnitude of the costs are great, the magnitude of the public benefit secured by the legislation must be great, too: The latter must be proportionate to—commensurate with—the former. The Court in *Roe* indicated that the public benefit must be great when it insisted that restrictive abortion legislation "may be justified only by a 'compelling state interest,' . . . [and] that the legislative enactment must be narrowly drawn to express only the legitimate state interests at stake."[85] (It is worth noting that whereas under the antidiscrimination directive, the "compelling state interest" test functions to vindicate or dissipate suspicion—*the Court's own suspicion*—about the real predicate of a law,[86] under the reasonableness directive, the test serves a different function: to establish the presence or absence of the proportionality that is an essential ingredient of "reasonable" regulation.) The Court erred, however, in asking if in its own view the public benefit secured by the legislation was proportionate to the costs of the legislation. The right question: Can a legislator reasonably conclude that the public benefit secured by the legislation is proportionate to the costs? In the vocabulary of the compelling-state-interest test, the right question is whether a legislator can reasonably conclude that the law serves a compelling state interest (and is narrowly drawn, etc.). There is no reason that the compelling-state-interest test cannot be applied in a deferential, or Thayerian, fashion. The serious question is whether it should be applied in that fashion. As I have explained, the reasonableness directive (but not the antidiscrimination directive) should be enforced—and, therefore, the proportionality inquiry, as a constituent of judicial enforcement of the reasonableness directive, should be pursued—in a Thayerian fashion. The compelling-state-interest test is, in this context, a way of structuring the proportionality inquiry. Therefore, where, given the magnitude of the costs, application of the compelling-state-interests test is appropriate, the test should be applied in a Thayerian fashion. The nondeferential approach to the reasonableness inquiry that was wrong in *Lochner* was no less wrong in *Roe*.

Now we are at the crux of the matter. To rule that there is no room for reasonable, and indeed conscientious, differences of opinion—that no legislator can reasonably conclude that in saving fetal life to the extent it does, restrictive abortion legislation is proportionate to the (great) costs of the legislation—is, in a word, ridiculous. (The point is not that one cannot reasonably conclude that restrictive abortion legislation does not satisfy the proportionality requirement; the point, rather, is that one cannot reasonably think that it is unreasonable to believe that the legislation *does* satisfy the requirement.) There are, in contemporary American society, very great differences of opinion about whether the (public) benefit secured by restrictive abortion legislation is proportionate to the (great) costs of the legislation, and those differences of opinion—of belief, of conviction—divide persons of reason and conscience on the one side from persons of reason and conscience on the other. (Not that everyone who supports restrictive abortion legislation—or, for that matter, everyone who opposes it—is a person of reason and conscience.) Recall that under the reasonableness directive, as I explained in the preceding section of this chapter, the moral shape of American society is largely taken for granted: Judicial enforcement of the reasonableness directive should operate within the context of the competing assumptions, values, and priorities characteristic of pluralistic American society. The (sometimes very great) differences of opinion about restrictive abortion legislation are among the central or core moral differences that today constitute the pluralistic character of American moral (including religious-moral) culture. To deny that the differences about restrictive abortion legislation are often reasonable differences—that is, reasonable differences *within the context of pluralistic American moral culture*—is to be blinded by the polemical crudities that surround and sometimes overwhelm the abortion controversy. (Such crudities abound on *all* sides of the controversy.)

Therefore, the Court's decision in *Roe* probably cannot be justified on the basis of the reasonableness directive. But that is not the end of the matter. Earlier I said that even if laws criminalizing homosexual sexual activity do not violate the reasonableness directive of section 1, they may well violate the antidiscrimination directive. Similarly, restrictive abortion legislation—or some instances of it—may well violate the antidiscrimination directive: The failure of the law to permit a pregnant woman to have an abortion may well be, depending on certain features of her pregnancy, a species of discrimination based on sex in violation of the section 1. My argument in that regard should be of particular interest to those who believe that, as originally understood, the privileges or immunities clause does not represent the reasonableness directive, but only the antidiscrimination directive.[87]

To develop the argument—a version of which I first sketched in 1988[88]—I need to rehearse an earlier point.[89] It is not always obvious whether a law claimed to single out some persons (e.g., nonwhites) for worse treatment than others (whites) in fact does so. That a law whose adverse effect is visited mainly on nonwhites sweeps up some whites in its net may suggest that the law does not single out nonwhites for worse treatment than whites, but it does not preclude that possibility. If a decision against funding research aimed at finding a cure for sickle-cell anemia would not have been made—if, instead, a decision to fund such research would have been made—but for the fact that the disease afflicts primarily nonwhites, the decision singles out nonwhites for worse treatment than whites (would) receive, notwithstanding that some whites are victimized by the decision, namely, those who have, or will have, sickle-cell anemia. Now, imagine an analogous decision not to permit women to abort pregnancies that are, for example, a consequence of rape or incest. If that decision would not have been made—if, instead, a decision to allow such abortions would have been made—but for the fact that the condition (pregnancy caused by rape or incest) afflicts only women, the decision singles out women for worse treatment than men.

It scarcely seems controversial to insist that a law violates section 1 of the Fourteenth Amendment if is an expression of "racially selective sympathy and indifference"[90]—as, for example, laws whose adverse effect is visited only or mainly on nonwhites are surely an expression of racially selective sympathy and indifference if they would not have been enacted were their adverse effect visited only or mainly or even equally on whites.

But if such laws violate section 1, it is difficult to understand why laws that are an expression of "selective sympathy and indifference" based on sex do not violate section 1. (A law whose adverse effect is visited only or mainly on women and that would not have been enacted were its adverse effect visited equally on men is, of course, an expression of sex-selective sympathy and indifference.) After all, selective sympathy and indifference, whether based on race or on sex, is rooted in—and is an expression of—an imputation to some persons, to (some) nonwhites or to women, not merely of a different but of a lesser humanity. Such sympathy and indifference represents, therefore, the very racist or sexist ideology that may not, consistent with the antidiscrimination directive represented by the privileges or immunities clause and by section 1 generally, be a predicate for state laws or other state action.

In *Personnel Administrator of Massachusetts v. Feeney*, the Court wrote: "'Discriminatory purpose,' however, implies more than intent as volition or intent as awareness of consequences. . . . It implies that the decision-maker . . . selected or reaffirmed a particular course of action at least in part 'because of,' not merely 'in spite of,' its adverse effects upon an identifiable group. Yet nothing in the record demonstrates that this preference for veterans was originally devised or subsequently re-enacted because it would accomplish the collateral goal of keeping women in a stereotypic and predefined place in the Massachusetts Civil Service."[91] However, that a law was enacted, not because of its adverse effect on women, but in spite of it, does not preclude the possibility that the law would not have been enacted (or maintained) were the law's adverse effect visited equally on men. It does not preclude the possibility that the law would not have been enacted "in spite of its adverse effect" were the law's adverse effect visited equally on men. That a law was enacted in spite of its adverse effect on women, not because of it, cannot conclude the matter, therefore: However difficult the inquiry, the Court should ask if the law would have been enacted were its adverse effect visited equally on men: If the law would not have been enacted were its adverse effect visited equally on men, the law is an expression of sex-selective sympathy and indifference in violation of the antidiscrimination directive of section 1.

To conclude that a legal restriction on abortion law would not have been enacted were its adverse effect visited equally on men and that the restriction is therefore an expression of sex-selective sympathy and indifference does not presuppose or entail that each and every person who supports the restriction—a group that may include more women than men[92]—would not do so but for sex-selective sympathy and indifference. But to acknowledge, as we should, that some people who support restrictive abortion legislation are not in the grip of sex-selective sympathy and indifference[93] is not to deny that legal restrictions on at least some categories of abortions would be virtually inconceivable in a world in which sex-selective sympathy and indifference was absent—or in which the costs of the restrictions were visited equally on men. With respect to restrictions

on at least some categories of abortions, take away the support of the legislators whose support for the restrictions is an expression of sex-selective
sympathy and indifference, and there is almost certainly insufficient support to enact the restrictions or even to maintain them on the books.[94]

Michael McConnell has observed that "[g]iven the inconvenience
(albeit unequal) of unintended parenthood to both men and women, it is
inconceivable that even the most sexist of legislatures would pass an antiabortion law if it were not for a good faith concern for fetal life."[95] But
McConnell's observation misses the point: That "a good faith concern for
fetal life" is a *necessary* condition for enactment of legal restrictions on
abortions does not entail that it is *sufficient* condition for enactment of
every such restriction; there is good reason to believe that sex-selective
sympathy and indifference is a necessary (though, by itself, not sufficient)
condition for enactment of restrictions on at least some categories of abortions.[96] At any rate, a judge can reasonably conclude that in a world happily bereft of sex-selective sympathy and indifference, there would not be
a critical mass of political support for enacting or maintaining legislation
forbidding a woman to abort, for example, a pregnancy caused by rape or
incest; a pregnancy that, although not life threatening, nonetheless poses
a serious threat of grievous and irreparable harm to her physical health;
or a pregnancy that, if it proceeds, will yield a severely deformed infant
destined to live a short and painful life. As I draft this chapter, delegates
to the national legislative convention of the Presbyterian Church (U.S.A.)
have voted to take a more "conservative" position on abortion. It is significant, I think, that in doing so, both the majority report (which calls
abortion "an option of last resort" and was adopted by a vote of 434 to
121) and the minority report (which calls abortion "unjustified and a sin
before God") "would permit abortion in circumstances such as rape,
incest, a threat to the mother's life or threat of a serious fetal deformity."[97]

A judge who takes the time to inform herself and who conscientiously
concludes that a legal restriction on a particular category (or categories) of
abortions—whether abortions of pregnancies that are a consequence of
rape or incest or some other category of abortions—would almost certainly not have been enacted if the adverse effect of the restriction were
visited on men equally with women, must conclude as well that the restriction is rooted in, that it would not exist but for, sex-selective sympathy
and indifference, and, therefore, that the restriction violates section 1 of
the Fourteenth Amendment: It is simply not possible to discern any explanation, much less justification, for what we are assuming the judge has
found to be true—namely, that were its adverse effect visited equally on
men, the restriction would not have been enacted—other than sex-selective sympathy and indifference. Richard Posner misconceives the point,
which is not that judges should strike down laws "just because *some* of the
supporters of [the] laws . . . had bad motives."[98] "Some" supporters is not
enough. A judge must conclude, not merely that some political support
for the law, but a critical mass of such support, is rooted in sex-selective

sympathy and indifference. A judge should strike down a law, as a violation of the antidiscrimination directive of section 1, only if she concludes that but for sex-selective sympathy and indifference, the law would not exist—that the law, in that sense, represents/expresses/embodies such sympathy and indifference.

Admittedly, such counterfactual judgments—"this law would not exist were its adverse effect visited equally on [whites, men, etc.]"—are difficult to make, and no court should make them casually. But that is not to say that the inquiry should not be undertaken.[99] Such judgments are not impossible to make, after all. (Michael McConnell has conceded that the pregnancy exclusion upheld by the Court in *Geduldig v. Aiello*[100] was probably an expression of sex-selective sympathy and indifference.[101]) Of course, not every judge will agree that a legal restriction on a particular category of abortions—or, indeed, a restriction on *any* category of abortions, other than the abortions no sane person wants to restrict anyhow, namely, those necessary to save the mother's life—is an expression of sex-selective sympathy and indifference. (Professor McConnell does not agree that such restrictions are an expression of sex-selective sympathy and indifference.[102]) But it seems disingenuous to deny that a judge can conclude, in good faith and with good reason, that a restriction on one or more categories of abortions is an expression of such sympathy and indifference. So, although the Court's decision in *Roe* probably cannot be justified on the basis of the reasonableness directive, a decision striking down restrictions on some categories of abortions *can* be justified on the basis of the antidiscrimination directive: restrictions defensibly judged to be expressions of sex-selective sympathy and indifference.

One might be tempted to suggest, at this point, that the relevant inquiry under the antidiscrimination directive is not whether the judge herself believes that a restriction on a particular category of abortions is an expression of sex-selective sympathy and indifference, but only whether one could reasonably *disbelieve* that proposition. However, that suggestion neglects the fundamental difference between the judicial enforcement (application) of the antidiscrimination directive, which should not be deferential, and the judicial specification of the reasonableness directive, which should be. As I emphasized earlier in this chapter, normative (Thayerian) minimalism is a position about the judicial specification of constitutional directives in contexts in which the directives are indeterminate and therefore require specification; it is not a position about the judicial enforcement of directives in contexts in which the directives are determinate (either because they were never indeterminate in any real context or because they have already been specified in the relevant context) and now require enforcement. Although I have argued in this chapter that the judicial specification of the antidiscrimination directive, unlike the judicial specification of the reasonableness directive, should not be Thayerian, the relevant point at the moment is simply that the deferential approach to the judicial enforcement of the antidiscrimination directive—its enforcement in a context in which it has already been specified[103]—does not make sense. As I remarked earlier, there is a virtual consensus in modern constitutional commentary that a deferential judicial posture is inappropriate if and when the Court is engaged in a task that, institutionally, it is uniquely well suited to perform: guarding against and ferreting out illicit discrimination.[104] Although ordinary politics can sometimes perform that task, it cannot invariably be relied on to perform it well or disinterestedly. The task of guarding against and ferreting out illicit discrimination is not one the judiciary alone should or does perform, to be sure. But it is a task that, when the courts are called upon to perform it, they should perform aggressively, not deferentially. In the performance of that constitutional task perhaps more than in the performance of any other, the judiciary is the principal jury, the principal guardian of the conscience, of the American political community.

Perhaps least of all in the context of the deeply divisive and often hysterical abortion controversy, where both deep convictions and self-interested (career-preserving) political strategizing loom large, can individual legislators sensibly be relied on to perform the difficult task of discerning if a proposed restriction on one or another category of abortions would not be enacted but for sex-selective sympathy and indifference. After all, such a legislator may himself be committed to the proposed restriction—even if not on the basis of sex-selective sympathy and indifference—whether out of deep conviction, political self-interest, or, most likely, some mixture of both. How then can he be expected to see with any clarity at all whether the restriction would not be enacted but for sex-selective sympathy and indifference, much less to oppose the legislation—legislation he supports—on the ground that it would not be enacted but for such sympathy and indifference?

The modern consensus is correct: In enforcing the antidiscrimination directive—in guarding against and ferreting out illicit discrimination—the courts, and the Court, should act, not deferentially, but aggressively. The question for a judge who suspects that challenged governmental action has a racist predicate is whether, in the judge's own view, it in fact does so, not whether someone else—perhaps someone less sensitive to, or less concerned about, the continuing malignancy of racism—could reasonably conclude otherwise. Similarly, the question for a judge suspicious that challenged governmental action (e.g., restrictive abortion legislation) has a sexist predicate is whether, in the judge's own view, it in fact does so, not whether someone else—perhaps someone less sensitive, or less concerned about, to the extent to which sexism infects our sensibilities and, therefore, our judgments—could reasonably conclude otherwise.

That a state may not, consistently with the antidiscrimination directive of section 1, disallow *all* abortions in a particular category does not entail that it may not disallow *any* abortions in the category; nor am I suggesting that a state may not regulate abortions it may not disallow.

Even if disallowing all abortions in a particular category (e.g., rape or incest) is an expression of sex-selective sympathy and indifference, it does not necessarily follow that disallowing some abortions in that category (e.g., abortions late in a pregnancy) or regulating abortions it may not disallow (e.g., by insisting that a woman seeking an abortion be provided with information about available alternatives before the abortion may be performed) is an expression of sex-selective sympathy and indifference.[105]

I have argued that some restrictions on abortion—in particular, the failure to tolerate abortions in the three situations to which I have referred—may defensibly be adjudged to violate the antidiscrimination directive of section 1 of the Fourteenth Amendment.[106] But I have also acknowledged that a judge can reasonably reject the conclusion that such restrictions violate the antidiscrimination directive. Many critics of the Court's ruling in *Roe* will reject my argument on the ground that the counterfactual inquiry I would have the Court conduct is simply beyond anyone's ability to conduct. ("We cannot possibly know what kind of abortion legislation we would have in a world in which there was no sex-selective sympathy and indifference. Judges pretending to know are almost certainly ending up where their policy preferences lead them.") And many defenders of the Court's ruling will reject my argument as insufficiently enthusiastic about the breadth of the Court's decree in *Roe*, according to which a state must tolerate, not just some abortions, but all abortions before the beginning of the third trimester of pregnancy. To the first group I say that although the counterfactual inquiry I would have the Court conduct is undeniably difficult, it is not impossible—and that given the gravity of what is at stake, it is more irresponsible for the Court to run away from the inquiry than for it to pursue the inquiry as well as it can. To the second group I say that I have not seen nor can I imagine any argument stronger than an antidiscrimination argument of the sort I have offered here—any stronger argument, that is, under the Constitution we actually have as distinct from the constitution some persons fantasize us to have.[107]

V. Judicial Imperialism?

According to Robert Bork, section 1 of the Fourteenth Amendment has been, in the hands of the modern Supreme Court, an instrument of "judicial imperialism".[108] Now, people can mean different things by "judicial imperialism", but it seems clear enough, in the context of Bork's book, that to call a constitutional decision or doctrine an instance of judicial imperialism is to claim that the decision/doctrine is, *from the perspective of originalism,* beyond the pale. Bork and many others have spent their most vigorous criticism of the modern Court on the way the Court has handled two issues under the Fourteenth Amendment: affirmative action and abortion.[109] Bork has also been quite wary about the modern Court's attack on sex-based discrimination.[110] By contrast, Bork has applauded the Court's refusal to move against laws criminalizing homosexual sexual activity.[111] Affirmative action, sex-based discrimination, homosexuality, and abortion are certainly four of most controversial issues with which the Court has recently struggled in the name of the Fourteenth Amendment.

As I explained in the preceding chapter, it is Bork's own position on affirmative action that, from the perspective of originalism, is defective—his position, shared by Justice Scalia, that government-sponsored affirmative action programs violate the Fourteenth Amendment. Similarly, Bork's wariness about the Court's attack on sex-based discrimination—his inclination to constitutional indifference about sex-based discrimination—is deeply problematic. Even Bork's position—and the present Court's—that legislation outlawing homosexual sexual activity does not violate the Fourteenth Amendment is quite troublesome from an originalist perspective—unless, as I said, one believes either that a person's sexual orientation is relevant to the question of his or her worth or status as a human being or that the proper approach to the specification of the antidiscrimination directive is minimalist.

The charge of judicial imperialism is finally credible only with respect to the Court's handling of the abortion issue in *Roe v. Wade*—for a reason having to do, however, not with originalism, but with normative minimalism: In pursuing the proportionality inquiry, the Court in *Roe* failed to adopt an appropriately deferential (Thayerian) stance. That charge of imperialism is considerably blunted, however, if, as I have argued in this chapter, the result decreed in *Roe* (as distinct from the Court's articulated justification for the result) can be defended, *to an extent,* on the basis of the antidiscrimination directive of section 1—which, as I have emphasized, should be aggressively, not deferentially, enforced. (Note that if my argument is sound, the result decreed in *Roe* can be defended, to an extent, even if we assume that the reasonableness directive is no part of the original meaning of section 1.) While it is a controversial question whether my "counterfactual" approach to the issue of the constitutionality of restrictive abortion legislation is manageable, the question does not divide originalists from nonoriginalists; it divides originalists from one another. Originalists can and should agree that sex-selective sympathy and indifference is a constitutionally offensive basis of political choice even if they disagree that my counterfactual approach is, in the context of restrictive abortion legislation, a sensible way of trying to ferret out such sympathy and indifference.

Bork's charge of judicial imperialism—his charge that the modern Court has acted beyond the pale, from point of view of originalism—is thus greatly overstated. In chapter 1, I commented on the excessively polemical character of much writing—too much—about constitutional adjudication. Robert Bork's critique of the modern Supreme Court's Fourteenth Amendment work product—a critique endorsed by many others, including many scholars—can now be seen for what it is: a vigorous and engaging polemic, but ultimately a shallow effort, clarifying little, obscuring much, and likely to mislead the underinformed.[112] All of which is very regrettable. Constitutional law is much too important—the real-world, flesh-and-blood stakes are much too high—for us to acquiesce in the polemicization of constitutional debate. (As I noted at the beginning of this book, such polemicization is a problem on the "left" side—the "liberal" or "progressive" side—of constitutional studies as well as on the "right" side—the "conservative" side.)

Robert Bork & Co. to the contrary notwithstanding, the modern Court's Fourteenth Amendment work product has been, in the main, much more originalist than imperialist. The results of our inquiry in both this and the preceding chapter are a substantial vindication of Lawrence Solum's claim, which I quoted in chapter 1, that the victory of originalism over nonoriginalism represents, for many originalist critics of the modern Court, only a Pyrrhic victory.[113] The originalist approach to constitutional interpretation either supports much that those critics criticize or it underdetermines the outcome of many of the most important constitutional controversies that engage and divide us. As I suggested at the beginning of chapter 4, and as I hope I have by now illustrated, originalism is an inadequate basis for challenging the legitimacy of the allegedly "imperialist" decisions that have so exercised some of the Court's fiercest critics (like Bork). There are real differences, to be sure, between conservative constitutional commentators and liberal or progressive commentators. But it is a basic mistake—a fundamental confusion—to think that the question of originalism is any longer the real or at least the principal divide between the former and the latter.[114]

10

Constitutional Adjudication:
Law *and* Politics

I

I left a question hanging at the end of chapter 6: With respect to which indeterminate constitutional directives regarding rights or liberties, if any, does the minimalist approach to the specification of constitutional indeterminacy make sense? In chapter 9, in partial response to that question, I suggested that although the minimalist approach to the specification of the reasonableness directive represented, or arguably represented, by section 1 of the Fourteenth Amendment makes good sense, the minimalist approach to the specification of the antidiscrimination directive of section 1 is ill advised: The proper question for the Court is not whether, depending on where one stands in the religiously and morally pluralistic American political community, one can reasonably conclude that this or that trait is relevant to a person's status or worth as a human being, but whether the trait is, in the Court's own view, relevant.

Does the minimalist approach to the specification of any indeterminate constitutional directives, other than the reasonableness directive, make sense—either any right- or liberty-regarding directives or, at least, any directives regarding the allocation of governmental power, whether the vertical allocation of power between the national government and the governments of the states or the horizontal allocation of power among the three basic institutions (legislative, executive, and judicial) of the national government?[1] Does the nonminimalist approach to the specification of any indeterminate constitutional directives regarding rights or liberties, other than the antidiscrimination directive, make sense—for example, the directives concerning the freedoms of religion, speech, and press?

Minimalism *vel non* is a problem in the allocation of competences. In deciding whether to pursue the minimalist approach to the specification of this or that indeterminate constitutional directive, individual judges and justices encounter issues like those I tried to articulate in chapter 6, where I used James Bradley Thayer's work as the principal point of departure. They must inquire into the character of the "ordinary politics" of the American political community and also into the capacity, not merely of themselves, but of other judges and justices, to deliberate well about fundamental issues of constitutional value and policy. That the judicial capacity to deliberate about constitutional issues of certain sorts is, at least as a general matter, comparatively good—good compared to the alternative loci of deliberation about the issues—does not entail that the judicial capacity 'o deliberate about constitutional issues of *every* sort is comparatively good. In assessing comparative judicial capacity, one must distinguish among the different species of indeterminate constitutional directives: directives regarding rights or liberties, directives regarding the horizontal allocation of governmental power, and directives regarding the vertical allocation of governmental power.[2] One must distinguish—as I have done with respect to the reasonableness directive and the antidiscrimination directive—even among the different directives in a single species. In responding to the question of normative minimalism, judges and justices should heed the now famous admonition issued by Alexander Bickel in the course of his own struggle with Thayer's work[3]—an admonition that, in its very phrasing, bears traces of that struggle.[4] (I quoted the admonition at the beginning of chapter 6.)

I suggested in the preceding chapter that John Ely's *Democracy and Distrust*[5] is the most important work in American constitutional theory in the post–*Roe v. Wade* era. In the book, Ely does not address the question whether to pursue the "minimalist" approach (as I am calling it here) to the specification of constitutional indeterminacy. Ely's concern is mainly with the different question of what unenumerated constitutional rights, if any, the judiciary—in particular, the Supreme Court—may legitimately enforce.[6] But Ely's argument is nonetheless relevant to the question of the role the Court should play—primary or secondary, large or small, active or passive—in enforcing the indeterminate constitutional rights, *whether enumerated or not*, it may or must enforce.

As Ely has recently characterized the essential argument of *Democracy and Distrust*, "[P]ublic issues generally should be settled by a majority vote of [sane adults] or their representatives. . . ."[7] But, Ely continues, public issues of three sorts are sensibly resolved—resolved as *constitutional* issues—principally by the judiciary: (1) the question whether, "where a majority of such persons [sane adults or their representatives] votes to exclude other such persons from the [political] process or otherwise to dilute their influence on it", it may do so; (2) the question whether, "where such a majority enacts one regulatory regime for itself and another, less favorable one, for one or another minority", it may do so; and (3) the question whether, where such a majority makes a political choice that implicates a "side constraint" with a certain pedigree, the choice violates the side constraint: a side constraint that, because it is "sufficiently important (and vulnerable to majority sentiment)", was designated by a super-majority "in a constitutional document and thereby render[ed] . . . immune to displacement by anything short of a similar supermajority vote in the future."[8]

Ely then explains: "[P]recisely because of their tenure, courts are the appropriate guardians of at least exceptions (1) and (2)".[9] As he elaborated the point in *Democracy and Distrust,*

> Obviously our elected representatives are the last persons we should trust with [exceptions (1) and (2)]. Appointed judges, however, are comparative outsiders in our governmental system, and need worry about continuance in office only very obliquely. This does not give them some special pipeline to the genuine values of the American people: in fact it goes far to insure that they won't have one. It does, however, put them in a position objectively to assess claims—though no one could suppose the evaluation won't be full of judgment calls—that either by clogging the channels of change or by acting as accessories to majority tyranny, our elected representatives in fact are not representing the interests of those whom the system presupposes they are.[10]

Ely adds, with respect to exception (3)—which, unlike exceptions (1) and (2), concerns enumerated rights, not unenumerated ones—that on "the supposition that no right is to be thus designated *unless it is unusually vulnerable to majority sentiment*", courts are the appropriate guardians of exception (3) as well.[11] Finally, Ely writes: "What does not follow from anything said above, or in my opinion from anything sensible said ever, is that judges are also to be given a license to create or 'discover' further rights, not justified by exceptions (1) or (2) nor ever constitutionalized by a supermajority, and protect them as if they had been."[12]

One could agree with Ely's position about the rights the Court may enforce—both the enumerated rights (exception (3)) and the unenumerated ones (exceptions (1) and (2))—and yet insist that if and to the extent any such right is indeterminate, the Court should play only a secondary role—a Thayerian role—in specifying it. One could say, in that regard, that answering the question of the best or optimal specification of an indeterminate constitutional right requires many "judgment calls" (as Ely describes them),[13] and that so long as the judgment calls implicit in the challenged governmental action are not unreasonable, the Court should defer to them.

Nonetheless, Ely's argument lends support to the position that as a comparative matter, as an issue in the allocation of competences, the judiciary—not least, the federal judiciary—is institutionally well suited to play the primary role in specifying any right- or liberty-regarding directive it is charged with enforcing *if our historical experience suggests that the directive is, like the antidiscrimination directive, "unusually vulnerable to majority sentiment"*. ("Like the antidiscrimination directive", because, as I noted in chapter 9, our historical experience attests that our ordinary politics has often been ill suited to decide what traits are relevant to a person's status or worth as a human being.) The First Amendment directive protecting the free exercise of religion (which I discussed in chapter 4) is surely one example—even a conspicuous one—of a right- or liberty-regarding directive unusually vulnerable to majority sentiment. To settle for our elected representatives, and not the judiciary, playing the primary role in specifying such a directive is probably to settle for many specifications that, while "not unreasonable" for purposes of Thayer's minimalist approach to constitutional adjudication, are nonetheless suboptimal: specifications that fail to give the important constitutional value at stake—the value privileged by the directive[14]—its full due.

Of course, that the Supreme Court chooses to exercise the principal responsibility for specifying one or another indeterminate constitutional directive—the antidiscrimination directive, say, or the free exercise clause—does not preclude the possibility that in exercising that responsibility the Court will, on occasion, act too timidly, or with insufficient sensitivity or vigilance, thereby failing to give the constitutional value at stake its full due.[15] But that possibility does not begin to support the argument that the Court should exercise only a secondary responsibility, that it should pursue only the Thayerian approach to the specification of the directive. Even if in exercising the principal responsibility the Court occasionally acts too timidly, the American political community is no worse off than it would be if the Court were to exercise a secondary responsibility *as a matter of course*, habitually deferring to political judgments that, while arguably reasonable for purposes of Thayer's approach, nonetheless give the constitutional value less than its full due. Indeed, the community is better off, so long as the Court acts too timidly only occasionally.

For a depressing example of the kind of suboptimal specification the Thayerian approach might well affirm, consider the political judgment to which Thayer's most prominent judicial disciple, Felix Frankfurter, deferred in *West Virginia State Board of Education v. Barnette*,[16] where he, and he alone, dissented from the Supreme Court's decision striking down a public school regulation that compelled students, including Jehovah's Witnesses who conscientiously objected on religious grounds, to salute the American flag and recite the Pledge of Allegiance. It was, insisted Frankurter, a judgment "upon which men might reasonably differ. . . . And since men may so reasonably differ, I deem it beyond my constitutional power to assert my view of the wisdom of this law against the view of the State of West Virginia."[17] One may fairly think that if the Thayerian approach to the specification of the relevant directive (or directives[18]) plausibly yields Frankfurter's position in *Barnette*, so much the worse for the Thayerian approach to the specification of the directive.

As Frankfurter's Thayerian performance in *Barnette* illustrates: Because legislatures so rarely make political choices about whose constitutionality men and women may *not* reasonably differ, the Thayerian approach to the specification of any constitutional directive effectively marginalizes the directive—virtually to the point of eliminating it—insofar as constitutional adjudication is concerned. It is not obvious, therefore, why one would advocate the minimalist approach to the specification of a directive unless one thought that the directive *should be* marginalized. Now, one might plausibly think that some directives should be marginalized because mechanisms other than constitutional adjudication—political as distinct from judicial mechanisms—are adequate, more or less, to the protection of the directives: namely, directives regarding the allocation of power, whether between the national government and the governments of the states or among the three branches of the national government.[19] One might also plausibly think that some right- or liberty-regarding directives—the reasonableness directive, say—are relatively unimportant, or at least inappropriate to a constitution that is to be judicially enforced, and should therefore be marginalized. But it is not obvious why one would want to marginalize any right- or liberty-regarding directive—that is, why one would support the Thayerian approach to the specification of any such directive—that one thought was relatively important, and appropriate to a constitution, unless one concluded that, overall, political mechanisms are somehow better suited than constitutional adjudication to protect the directive. But surely such a conclusion is seriously questionable with respect to many important right- or liberty-regarding directives.[20]

II

The Preamble to the Constitution speaks of "We the people of the United States . . . [who] do ordain and establish this Constitution for the United States of America." What about "We the people" *now living*—we who do maintain this Constitution for the United States of America, and who do, from time to time, have to consider revising it? Where do *we* go from here?

There are reasonable differences about how large or small a role the Court should play, about how active or passive a role, in bringing the interpreted Constitution to bear—that is, in specifying constitutional indeterminacy. The question of originalism versus nonoriginalism (and, even more so, the question of textualism versus nontextualism) is, if not easy, at least *relatively* easy: easy as compared to the question of normative minimalism. But rather than chew on the question of normative minimalism again, I want to try, for now, to deflect the question: Whether or not one is, as a general matter, skeptical about the Thayerian, minimalist approach to the specification of constitutional indeterminacy, one should be able to take seriously the possibility of modifying the practice of judicial review in ways that make it at least somewhat more responsive to "We the people" now living, who, after all, unlike our dead political ancestors, are supposed to be politically sovereign.[21] Even if, because we do not tend to alter basic aspects of our governmental practice except in response to a crisis, we are not likely to make any modifications in the practice of judicial review ("Where's the crisis?"), two modifications, one relatively small, one relatively large, are worth considering.

First, the relatively small modification. It may make sense to appoint federal judges, including, or especially, Supreme Court justices, not for life ("during good behaviour"[22]), but for a term of years. It is far from clear why anyone should be a Supreme Court justice for more than, say, ten years—which is, after all, longer than one may be president.[23] Moreover, life tenure for federal judges and justices makes the stakes in the judicial appointments process much higher than they need be, with the unsavory consequence, in our time, that the process has become increasingly ideologized and debased.[24] The idea is hardly radical. The judges of the German Constitutional Court, for example, are appointed for a term of twelve years and are ineligible for reappointment.[25] Moreover, the idea may be timely, since the kindred idea of term limits for our representatives in both Houses of the Congress engages us today (and, in engaging us, divides us) as it never has before.[26] Note, in that regard, that one of the principal arguments against congressional term limits—namely, that they are undemocratic, that we ought to be able to vote for whomever we want, including someone who has already represented us for a lengthy period—has no force against term limits for Supreme Court justices (for whom, of course, we do not vote). Indeed, term limits for Supreme Court justices are *more* democratic than the status quo, in the sense that such limits empower the present to exert more political influence over the Court than does life tenure for Supreme Court justices.[27]

Now, the relatively large modification. It may even make sense—especially if we are skeptical *both* about the capacity of ordinary politics to specify constitutional indeterminacy *and* about the capacity of many of our judges and justices to do so—to subject judicial specifications of certain indeterminate constitutional values to the possibility of political control in the way, or something like it, some constitutional specifications are subject to political control under the Canadian Charter of Rights and Freedoms, adopted in 1982. Under section 33 of the Canadian Charter, "Parliament or the legislature of a province may expressly declare in an Act of Parliament or of the legislature, as the case may be, that the Act or a provision thereof shall operate notwithstanding a provision included in section 2 [the provision regarding 'fundamental freedoms'] or sections 7 to 15 of this Charter [the provisions regarding 'legal rights' and 'equality rights']."[28] Such a declaration becomes inoperative if not restated at least every five years. (The provisions in sections 3 to 6, regarding "democratic rights" and "mobility rights", are not subject to section 33.) As Paul Weiler has suggested, commenting on section 33 of the Canadian Charter:

> One cannot choose . . . between formal [constitutional] amendment and legislative override as the preferred method for revising judge-

made constitutional policy simply by a priori reasoning about rights and democracy. One must make a practical judgment about the relative competence of two imperfect institutions in the context of a particular nation. The premise of the Charter is that the optimal arrangement for Canada is a new partnership between court and legislature. Under this approach judges will be on the front lines; they will possess both the responsibility and the legal clout necessary to tackle "rights" issues as they regularly arise. At the same time, however, the Charter reserves for the legislature the final say to be used sparingly in the exceptional case where the judiciary has gone awry. This institutional division of labor rests on the assumption that the chief threat to rights in Canada comes from legislative thoughtlessness about particular intrusions, a fault that can be cured by thoroughly airing the issues of principle in a judicial forum. The Charter contemplates no serious danger of outright legislative oppression; certainly none sufficient to concede ultimate authority to Canadian judges and lawyers.[29]

Professor Weiler has addressed the question of the exportability of this Canadian innovation—which Professor Weiler played an important role in designing[30]—to the United States:

> I suspect that this arrangement would not be unthinkable in the United States . . . if it were translated into a *congressional* override of the Supreme Court. Any measure that could be navigated through all the branches of the national legislative process, each reflecting a variety of constituencies and points of view, might well be considered a more sensible approach to the problem than would a verdict from a bare majority of five on the Supreme Court. But almost all American scholars would have grave qualms about conferring any such power on the state legislatures, both from general disenchantment with the deliberative capacities of state governments and because of the fear that certain state legislatures would respond to majorities that do not necessarily adhere to the values spelled out in the national constitution. For many people, reflection on what might have happened after *Brown v. Board of Education* had Mississippi had a legislative override on fourteenth amendment issues is sobering enough to discredit the entire notion.[31]

Perhaps now, early in the third century of our Republic, we Americans should take seriously the possibility of importing the Canadian innovation, or of fashioning an Americanized version, as "an intrinsically sound solution to the dilemma of rights and courts."[32]

Imagine, for a moment, that the United States Constitution contains a provision like the Japanese Constitution's Article 9: "[T]he Japanese people forever renounce war as a sovereign right of the nation and the threat or use of force as means of settling international disputes. [Accordingly,] land, sea, and air forces, as well as other war potential, will never be maintained. The right of belligerency of the state will not be recognized." Imagine further that the issue has arisen in the United States (as it has in Japan)—and that the issue is extremely controversial and deeply divisive in the United States (as it is in Japan)—whether, under the antiwar provision of the Constitution, Congress may enact a law permitting the dispatch of military personnel abroad to play a strictly limited role in international peacekeeping operations.[33] One may reasonably believe that the Supreme Court should address the issue. One may even reasonably believe that the Court should address the issue vigorously, not deferentially, on the theory that the Court has an indispensable role to play both in focusing the people's discussion of the issue and in giving the people the benefit of its own best judgment. But it does not seem to me reasonable that (absent a constitutional amendment) a majority of the Court—five justices—should have the *final* say (or even the final say about who has the final say) about the constitutionality of the law under the antiwar provision of the Constitution. In a society committed to the sovereignty of "We the people" now living, surely it makes much more sense that, given both the sheer gravity of the matter and the contextual indeterminacy of the antiwar provision, a majority of the Congress acting in concert with the president—or, without the president, a supermajority of the Congress acting alone—should have the final say.

In the past I have been among those suggesting that, contra Thayer,[34] nonminimalist judicial review can energize rather than enervate popular political deliberation about fundamental constitutional matters. In his Hart Lecture at Oxford, Justice Brennan said that "an active judiciary seems to me . . . as the calmer, cooler party to a dialogue from which the community benefits over time. Michael Perry has written that 'what the majority comes to believe in the long-term, after having been rebuffed by the electorally unaccountable Supreme Court in the short-term, is more likely to be morally correct than are established but untested, unreflective moral conventions'. To the extent that reason and reflection have any role to play in moral judgment and constitutional adjudication . . . the dialogue in which the courts and the legislature engage is a salutary one."[35] Such statements about a salutary dialogic relation between (nonminimalist) judicial review and ordinary politics—about a political-moral dialogue between the courts and the nonjudicial departments and agencies of government—would be much more credible, they would be much easier to take seriously, were we Americans to adopt the Canadian innovation (or something like it).[36] (Such statements have been widespread in the modern period of American constitutional law.[37])

Consider Bickel's suggestion—perhaps an expression more of what Bickel hoped than of what he thought he saw—that "courts have certain capacities for dealing with matters of principle that legislatures and executives do not possess. Judges have, or should have, the leisure, the training, and the insulation to follow the ways of the scholar in pursuing the ends of government. This is crucial in sorting out the enduring values of a society, and it is not something that institutions can do well occasionally, while operating for the most part with a different set of gears. It calls for a habit of mind, and for undeviating institutional customs."[38] The Canadian innovation has a great advantage over normative (Thayerian) minimalism: One the one hand, and unlike normative minimalism, the Canadian innovation preserves an active, vigorous judicial role—a role that, at its best, is special, and perhaps even indispensable, in just the way Bickel suggested—in the discourse about constitutional meaning, the discourse about how best to specify indeterminate constitutional values, about how best to "interpret" the constitutional tradition. On the other hand, and unlike the present state of affairs, the Canadian innovation does not so privilege the judicial voice in that discourse that there is, realistically, no opportunity for effective political response. The Canadian innovation represents an effort to have the best of two worlds: an opportunity for a deliberative judicial consideration of a difficult and perhaps divisive constitutional issue *and* an opportunity for electorally accountable officials to respond, in the course of ordinary politics, in an effective way. At least, it represents such an effort on the assumption that, as has been powerfully argued, Canada's "notwithstanding clause should only be employed in a remedial way, *after* legislation has already been considered by the courts and struck down; it should not be used preemptively, to block anticipated judicial review altogether. . . . [S]ection 33 is intended to allow a further stage in the dialogue between courts and legislatures as to the meaning of *Charter* rights, not to prevent such dialogue altogether."[39]

Bickel's statement in the preceding paragraph conspicuously presupposes that, in the main at least, we have judges and justices with certain admirable capacities. I asked in chapter 6, however, whether we should be any more sanguine about the relevant capacities of our judges and justices—the judges and justices we actually have, and are likely to have, rather than those we would like to have—than we are about the relevant capacities of our political representatives.[40] But given something like the Canadian innovation, it might be easier, as a real-world political matter, to appoint truly exemplary judicial figures to the Supreme Court—the sort of persons who inhabit Bickel's hopeful statement—since the power of judicial review would then be less fearsome, less threatening, to the politicians and others now so exercised and angered by what they perceive to be the excesses of "judicial imperialism". How wonderful it would be to have a better chance than present political circumstances now permit of getting great rather than mediocre jurists—or, worse, mediocre ideologues—appointed to the United States Supreme Court. (Again, abolishing life tenure for federal judges—or at least for Supreme Court justices—might help, too.)

Even a Thayerian—a normative minimalist—should find adopting the Canadian innovation an attractive way of modifying the American practice of judicial review. Recall Thayer's claim that "the exercise of judicial review, even when unavoidable, is always attended with a serious evil, namely, that the correction of legislative mistakes comes from the outside, and the people thus lose the political experience, and the moral education and stimulus that comes from fighting the question out in the ordinary way, and correcting their own errors. The tendency of a common and easy resort to this great function, now lamentably too common, is to dwarf the political capacity of the people, and to deaden its sense of moral responsibility."[41] Adopting the Canadian innovation would significantly enhance, not diminish, the constitutional and moral responsibility of the people. Were it adopted, the Canadian innovation would present the people—or the people's political representatives in the Congress and the White House—with more rather than fewer opportunities to exercise their constitutional and moral responsibility (which is not to say that in exercising it, the political representatives of the people ultimately would or even should often decide to reverse what the Court had done). Therefore, those who, like Sanford Levinson, want to deprivilege the judicial voice in constitutional discourse should find the Canadian innovation attractive. According to Levinson, "[T]he United States Constitution can meaningfully structure our polity if and only if *every* public official—and ultimately *every* citizen—becomes a participant in the conversation about constitutional meaning, as opposed to the pernicious practice of identifying the Constitution with the decisions of the United States Supreme Court or even of courts and judges more generally."[42] Adopting the Canadian innovation would certainly encourage greater citizen participation "in the conversation about constitutional meaning".[43]

I said in chapter 1 that I share the "hope for newly reinvigorated deliberation about constitutional commitments—deliberation that will occasionally take place in the courtroom, but more often, and far more fundamentally, through democratic channels."[44] My suggestion, perhaps utopian, is that the Canadian innovation might help us both to multiply the occasions and to enhance the quality of political deliberations about matters of constitutional morality.

Where do "We the people" now living go from here? We should begin to take seriously proposals for modifying the practice of judicial review in ways that make it somewhat more responsive to our putative sovereignty. It is not written in stone that the present practice of judicial review is beyond modification. We should take some such proposals seriously, like the proposal to adopt an Americanized version of the Canadian innovation.[45] We should put some such proposals on our political agenda, we should deliberate about them—even if, absent a crisis, we are likely to modify nothing.

III

It is now time to return to the issue with which this book began. We can now see—if we couldn't already, which is doubtful—that the choice Bork presents in *The Tempting of America*, between constitutional adjudication as "law" and constitutional adjudication as "politics", is a false choice. Of

course, at its worst, constitutional adjudication is little more than politics
in a debased sense of "politics": willful rather than deliberate, monologic
rather than dialogic, and so forth. But the serious issue, for normative
constitutional theory, is not what constitutional adjudication is at its worst,
its most debased, but what constitutional adjudication can be at its best.
Even at its best constitutional adjudication is, in part, a species of politics—as, indeed, all adjudication is a species of politics—although, now,
not in the debased sense of the term:[46] "[T]he juristic job both is and is not
political. It is not like setting up a committee or pressure group to change
the law in some way. Indeed, it is not remotely like that kind of politics. It
is, on the other hand, highly judgmental, and the value judgments
involved in the ordering of legal materials include judgments of moral
and political value."[47] (Moreover, as I explained in chapter 5, constitutional adjudication is a species of "constitutive" rather than merely of
"instrumental" or "technocratic" politics.[48]) Constitutional adjudication—
the judicial specification of constitutional indeterminacy—does not stand
apart from politics (even though the extraordinary politics of constitutional adjudication does stand above ordinary politics). Rather, constitutional adjudication is a part of the overall politics of the American political
community. Of course, the precise extent to which "the juristic job" is
political depends on whether a judge, in pursuing the normative
inquiry—in specifying the relevant, indeterminate legal materials—is or
is not following the minimalist approach.

The ways in which constitutional adjudication is a part of the overall
politics of the American political community—in particular, the ways in
which it complements ordinary politics—bear emphasis.

Many constitutional directives—especially those regarding rights or
liberties—can be understood as constituents of a particular conception of
human good: the American political community's conception of how it is
good or fitting for it to live its collective life, its life in common, especially
of how it is good or fitting for the political community, acting through the
various institutions and agencies of its state and federal governments, to
treat "the people", both individually and collectively.[49] Indeed, their
shared commitment to that conception of human good—to those directives, which serve as standards, as criteria, of political-moral judgment—is
a major part of what constitutes the American people as a political community: a community of political-moral judgment.[50] Although it may be a
matter of controversy whether a particular constitutional provision represents an indeterminate directive—or how indeterminate a directive a
particular provision represents—it is difficult to deny that indeterminacy
is a significant feature of at least some basic aspects of the American political community's constitutional conception of human good, of its standards of political-moral (constitutional) judgment, just as indeterminacy is
a feature of aspects of any large, historically extended community's conception of human good. It is not in the nature of a conception of human
good to be highly determinate in all its basic aspects; relatedly, there is

often a plurality of plausible instantiations or specifications of a (partially indeterminate) conception of human good.[51]

Because, and to the extent, the American political community's constitutional conception of human good is (partially) indeterminate, *and* because the American political community is an historically extended community—because it is, in that sense, a "tradition"—the community must constantly bring the relevant past of the tradition to bear in and for the present. The relevant past the community must bring to bear consists of the indeterminate aspects of the conception of human good to which the tradition, in its present embodiment, remains committed—a commitment that is the yield of the tradition's lived experience, especially in certain critical, formative moments.[52] The community must constantly "interpret" the tradition. Because, and to the extent, the tradition's conception of human good is indeterminate, the community must constantly establish the meaning of the tradition's conception of human good in and for the present; more precisely, it must establish the meaning, in and for the present, of some aspect of the tradition, of one or another standard of political-moral judgment, one or another constitutional directive.

Because the American political community is a human community— "all too human"—it must struggle to remain faithful to (the relevant past of) the tradition even as it is tempted by various exigencies to break faith with the tradition. The practice of judicial review—as I remarked in chapter 2—is one important way the American political community struggles to remain faithful to its ongoing (if sometimes merely provisional) commitment to various constitutional directives. In exercising judicial review, the courts, and especially the Supreme Court, serve a representative function. In constitutional adjudication, the courts represent the political community by testing various policies and practices of the community's governments against the community's fundamental political-moral directives. Moreover, and relatedly, the courts represent the political community in constitutional adjudication by specifying constitutional directives in contexts to which they are relevant but in which they are indeterminate— novel contexts that constantly emerge in the ongoing life of the historically extended community. The courts, representing the political community, "interpret" the indeterminate tradition. Through the process of specification they establish the meaning, in and for the present, of one or another aspect of the tradition's indeterminate conception of human good; they bring the relevant past of the tradition to bear in and for the present. In that sense, constitutional adjudication—the judicial specification of indeterminate constitutional principles—is one of the primary institutionalizations of the self-critical rationality of the American political community;[53] it is "an institutional forum for the advancement of arguments (narratives) about how we are to live"[54]—about how we are to live, that is, *given* the tradition's conception of human good, its commitment to certain standards of political-moral judgment, to certain constitutional principles. The fundamental aim of constitutional adjudication is the good of the American political community *as that good is conceived by the American political—that is, constitutional—tradition*. Because the tradition's conception of the good is indeterminate, however, that aim can be achieved only through the process of specifying the indeterminacy and thereby developing the conception.

There is no denying the creative and even constitutive character of constitutional adjudication, involving, as it does, decisions to establish one rather than another meaning of one or another aspect of the tradition's conception of human good, decisions to lead, or coax, the community along one rather than another path of political-moral development; decisions, in that sense, to develop the indeterminate tradition in one rather than another direction. Constitutional adjudication, then, is not only a principal institutionalization of the self-critical rationality of the American political community. It is a principal institutional matrix for the development of the American political/constitutional tradition. Constitutional adjudication serves two essential, interrelated functions: In helping the political community maintain fidelity to the indeterminate political tradition, constitutional adjudication serves a conservative and (self-)critical function; in participating in the development of the tradition, it serves a creative and constitutive function. (To say that constitutional adjudication serves, and even that it should serve, those two functions is not to say that no other institutions or practices serve or should serve them; it is not even to deny that some other institution(s) or practice(s) should bear the principal responsibility.) At its best, constitutional adjudication looks in two directions: backward, toward the past, for the constitutional principles— the directives—to which fidelity is to be maintained,[55] and forward, toward the future, for the likely shape of the world in which the principles are to function and for which, therefore, they must be specified (if they are indeterminate, as some of them are). Because, and to the extent, it looks backward, constitutional adjudication is "authoritarian" (though I do not use the term in the pejorative sense Frank Michelman and others have used it[56]); but because, and to the extent, it looks forward, constitutional adjudication is "pragmatic".[57] To conceive of constitutional adjudication as *either* authoritarian *or* pragmatic is to misconceive it.[58]

Constitutional adjudication, properly conceived and practiced, is neither just law nor just politics. Conjunction makes much more sense here than disjunction: both/and, not either/or. The polemical disjunction "law *or* politics" obscures the fact that constitutional adjudication, at its best, is *both* law *and* politics. It is *both* authoritarian *and* pragmatic, *both* backward-looking *and* present-oriented and future-looking.

NOTES

Chapter 1

1. See pp. 122–23.

2. See R. Bork, The Tempting of America: The Political Seduction of the Law (1989).

3. 347 U.S. 483 (1954).

4. See C. Black, Decision According to Law 33 (1981) (describing *Brown* as "the decision that opened our era of judicial activity"); W. Brennan, Jr., "Why Have a Bill of Rights?" 9 Oxford J. Legal Studies 425, 430–31 (1989). Cf. J. Ely, Democracy and Distrust: A Theory of Judicial Review 48 (1980): "[T]he Court's power . . . probably has never been greater than it has been over the past two decades."

5. The literature constituting "critical legal studies" (CLS) is voluminous—as is the literature commenting on CLS. For a critical comment on the mainline CLS position on the nature of adjudication—or at least on what at the time seemed to be the mainline position—see J. Stick, "Can Nihilism Be Pragmatic?" 100 Harvard L. Rev. 332 (1986).

6. Bork, note 2, at 1.

7. Id. In the passage, where I have put the ellipsis, Bork writes: "in a statute or". Bork's subject, however, is constitutional, not statutory, adjudication. Constitutional adjudication poses a political-theoretical problem not posed by either statutory adjudication or common law adjudication. "Nor will it do to liken judicial review to the general lawmaking function of judges. In the latter aspect, judges are indeed something like administrative officials, for their decisions are also reversible by any legislative majority—and not infrequently they are reversed. Judicial review, however, is the power to apply and construe the Constitution, in matters of the greatest moment, against the wishes of a legislative majority, which is, in turn, powerless to affect the judicial decision." A. Bickel, The Least Dangerous Branch: The Supreme Court at the Bar of Politics 29 (1962). I amplify the point in chapter 6. See pp. 93–94.

8. Bork, note 2, at 1–2.

9. Id. at 2.

10. Later in the introduction Bork refers to "[t]he orthodoxy of original understanding, and the political neutrality of judging it requires. . . ." Id. at 7. I explain in this book why "the orthodoxy of original understanding" often does not, indeed cannot, require "political neutrality of judging".

11. Id. at 3.

12. Id. at 1.

13. Id. at 351. See id. at 136: "Some [constitutional theorists] are quite explicit about their intention to convert the Constitution from law to politics, and judges from magistrates to politicians. Others have no such conscious intent, but their prescriptions would have the same effect."

14. Id. at 2.

15. Id.

16. Id. at 5 (emphasis added).

17. Id. at 4.

18. Id. at 5.

19. Id.

20. "Comments by President on His Choice of Justice," New York Times, July 24, 1990, at A8.

21. R. Bork, "At Last, An End to Supreme Court Activism," New York Times, Aug. 29, 1990, at A15.

22. See note 19 and accompanying text.

23. A related challenge is to understand the sense of "legal" in which constitutional adjudication should be a legal process and the sense of "political" in which it must be a political process.

24. Cf. T. Sandalow, "The Supreme Court in Politics," 88 Michigan L. Rev. 1300, 1325 (1990) (reviewing E. Bonner, Battle for Justice: How the Bork Nomination Shook America (1989)): "As the public and its leaders increasingly come to see the [Supreme Court] justices as political actors, whose function is not markedly different from that of other political actors, both the processes and bases of [judicial] selection are likely to approximate, more and more closely, those for the selection of other political actors. If that occurs, no one—on either side of the debate over Judge Bork—will be very happy with the outcome." An aim of this book is to explain the sense in which the justices are indeed "political" (as well as "legal") actors, but political actors whose function *is* "markedly different from that of other political actors". We may hope that if, and to the extent, that difference in function—*political* function—is understood and affirmed, "the processes and bases of [judicial] selection" will not "approximate, more and more closely, those for the selection of other political actors."

25. Bork's book has been widely reviewed by constitutional scholars. Among the best of those reviews, in my opinion, are these: G. Bradley, "Probing Bork's Judicial Philosophy," 52 Rev. Politics 491 (1990); R. Dworkin, "Bork's Jurisprudence," 57 U. Chicago L. Rev. 657 (1990); R. Kay, "The Bork Nomination and the Definition of 'The Constitution'," 84 Northwestern U. L. Rev. 1190 (1990); R. Nagel, "Meeting the Enemy," 57 U. Chicago L. Rev. 633 (1990); G. Nichol, "Bork's Dilemma," 76 Virginia L. Rev. 337 (1990); R. Posner, "Bork and Beethoven," 42 Stanford L. Rev. 1365 (1990). See also Sandalow, note 24; Symposium, "Confirmation Controversy: The Selection of a Supreme Court Justice," 84 Northwestern U. L. Rev. 832 (1990).

26. See p. 37.

27. See G. Stone & D. Strauss, "Bush's Losing Judicial Philosophy," Chicago Tribune, Oct. 28, 1992, 1, p. 19.

28. See chapter 8, note 1 and accompanying text.

29. I comment on Justice Scalia's work, in addition to Bork's, at several points in this book.

30. L. Solum, "Originalism as Tranformative Politics," 63 Tulane L. Rev. 1599, 1602 (1989).

31. The first volume of the project has been published: B. Ackerman, We the People: Foundations (1991). Two more volumes are to follow.

32. 347 U.S. 483 (1954).

33. 381 U.S. 479 (1965).

34. Cass Sunstein develops the general point in his review of Ackerman's book. See C. Sunstein, "New Deals," New Republic, Jan. 20, 1992, at 32, 34–35.

35. See id. See also W. Fisher III, "The Defects of Dualism," 59 U. Chicago L. Rev. 955 (1992); M. Klarman, "Constitutional Fact/Constitutional Fiction: A Critique of Bruce Ackerman's Theory of Constitutional Moments," 44 Stanford L. Rev. 759 (1992); T. Sandalow, "Abstract Democracy: A Review of Ackerman's *We the People*," 9 Constitutional Commentary 309 (1992).

36. In Volume 1, at least. See note 31.

37. J. Waldron, Book Review, 90 J. Philosophy 149, 153 (1993).

38. See Sunstein, note 34, at 34: "At least in America, a Constitution is a written text. . . . Unwritten amendments simply are not amendments."

39. See pp. 29–31.

40. C. Sunstein, The Partial Constitution 9 (1993).

41. See R. McCloskey, The Modern Supreme Court 290–91 (1972):

> American constitutional history has been in large part a spasmodic running debate over the behavior of the Supreme Court, but in a hundred seventy years we have made curiously little progress toward establishing the terms of this war of words, much less toward achieving concord. . . . [T]hese recurring constitutional debates resemble an endless series of re-matches between two club-boxers who have long since stopped developing their crafts autonomously and have nothing further to learn from each other. The same generalizations are launched from either side, to be met by the same evasions and parries. Familiar old ambiguities fog the controversy, and the contestants flounder among them for a while until history calls a close and it is time to retire from the arena and await the next installment. In the exchange of assertions and counter-assertions no one can be said to have won a decision on the merits, for small attempt has been made to arrive at an understanding of what the merits are.

42. Sunstein, note 40, at 354.

43. See pp. 197–201.

44. Professor Sherry's plea concluded her comments on the paper I presented to the symposium on James Bradley Thayer held at the Northwestern University Law School in April, 1993. For the various papers presented to the symposium and the critical comments on the papers, see 88 Northwestern U. L. Rev. (forthcoming, 1993).

Chapter 2

1. See note 40.

2. See M. Tushnet, Red, White, and Blue: A Critical Analysis of Constitutional Law 4 (1988): "Judicial review is an institution designed to meet some difficulties that arise when one tries to develop political institutions forceful enough to accomplish valued goals and yet not so powerful as to threaten the liberties of the citizenry." See also G. Calabresi, "Foreword: Antidiscrimination and Constitu-

tional Accountability (What the Bork-Brennan Debate Ignores)," 105 Harvard L. Rev. 80, 81 (1991): "The general power of courts to keep legislatures and executives from violating fundamental rights is what many people, including myself, mean by the power of judicial review."

On the origins of the term "judicial review", see R. Clinton, *Marbury v. Madison and Judicial Review* 7 (1989): "'Judicial review,' as a term used to describe the constitutional power of a court to overturn statutes, regulations, and other governmental activities, apparently was an invention of law writers in the early twentieth century. Edward S. Corwin may have been the first to coin the phrase, in the title of an article in the 1910 *Michigan Law Review*." Clinton's reference is to E. Corwin, "The Establishment of Judicial Review," 9 Michigan L. Rev. 102 (1910).

3. A. Bickel, The Least Dangerous Branch: The Supreme Court at the Bar of Politics 16–17 (1962).

4. Id. at 17.

5. Id. at 18–19.

6. Id. at 17–18, 19.

7. Article 96 continues: "and shall thereupon be submitted to the people for ratification, which shall require the affirmative vote of a majority of all votes cast thereon, at a special referendum or at such elections as the Diet shall specify."

8. Similarly, Article 98 provides: "The fundamental human rights by this Constitution guaranteed to the people of Japan are fruits of the age-old struggle of man to be free; they have survived the many exacting tests for durability and are conferred upon this and future generations in trust, to be held for all time inviolate." It has been suggested that the Constitution of Germany, because it "declares that certain fundamental principles are immune to constitutional amendment," exemplifies "absolute entrenchment". A. Chander, "Sovereignty, Referenda, and the Entrenchment of a United Kingdom Bill of Rights," 101 Yale L. J. 457, 462 & n. 30 (1991). See B. Ackerman, The Future of Liberal Revolution 110–11 (1992) (commenting on the German practice of absolute entrenchment).

9. See note 27 and accompanying text. Cf. Chander, note 8, at 462: "An absolutely entrenched [constitutional provision] is . . . (as are all other parts of an existing legal regime) vulnerable to revolution."

10. Article VI of the U.S. Constitution provides that "[t]his Constitution . . . shall be the supreme law of the land. . . ." Article 98 of the Japanese Constitution provides: "This Constitution shall be the supreme law of the nation and no law, ordinance, imperial rescript or other act of government, or part thereof, contrary to the provisions hereof, shall have legal force or validity."

11. See Chander, note 8, at 463: "One common type of manner and form entrenchment requires that all contrary legislation contain an explicit declaration of its intent to override the entrenched rule." Canada has pursued, in its Constitution, such a strategy. See chapter 10, pp. 197–98.

12. See generally J. Eule, "Temporal Limits on the Legislative Mandate: Entrenchment and Retroactivity," 1987 American Bar Foundation Research J. 379.

13. For a thoughtful discussion of such reasons, see D. Chang, "A Critique of Judicial Supremacy," 36 Villanova L. Rev. 281, 290–302 (1981).

14. For a helpful "outline of some of the reasons for entrenching institutional arrangements and substantive rights", see C. Sunstein, "Constitutionalism and Secession," 58 U. Chicago L. Rev. 633, 636–43 (1991).

15. See W. Brennan, Jr., "Why Have a Bill of Rights?," 9 Oxford J. Legal Stud-

ies 425, 426 (1989): "The genius of the Magna Carta, as well as its longevity, lay partly in its creation of a device for resolving grievances and compelling the Crown to abide by the committee of barons' decision. Paper promises whose enforcement depends wholly on the promisor's goodwill have rarely been worth the parchment on which they were inked."

16. Indeed, even if one is *more* skeptical about the capacity of constitutional adjudication adequately to protect a right than about the capacity of ordinary politics to do so, one may opt for the constitutional strategy for protecting the right in an effort to secure a margin of additional protection for the right—protection above and beyond what ordinary politics will likely give—but only if one believes that the availability of judicial protection for the right (which is an aspect of the constitutional strategy for protecting the right) will not make ordinary politics somehow less committed to, or effective in, protecting the right. I am grateful to Kent Greenawalt for this point.

17. See L. Sager, "The Incorrigible Constitution," 65 New York U. L. Rev. 893, 925 (1990): "The rhetorical flourish of 'We the people' cannot obscure the simple fact that it is *they*—the drafters, ratifiers, voters, and judges whose mortality has deprived them of an ongoing stake in political affairs—not *we*, who have made most of the decisions embodied in our constitutional tradition."

18. I say "as it has come down to us" because the modern practice of judicial review may not be identical to the original practice. See p. 26.

19. Sunstein, note 14, at 367.

20. Cf. Sager, note 17, at 901: "The question is whether expressions of will by historical majorities—by persons who lived a century or two ago—can legitimately bind contemporary social majorities who disagree."

21. Brennan, note 15, at 426–27.

22. It simply will not work to say that we, the living, have "consented" to the Constitution: Few of us have consented. Arguments based on "hypothetical", not actual, consent are, at bottom, arguments about what we have reason to accept (or no reason to reject): What reasons do we have for accepting, and therefore for protecting, the various constitutional directives issued by our political ancestors? That is simply a verbal variation on the question I am addressing.

23. Excerpts from the Charter appeared in the *New York Times* on November 22, 1990.

24. See chapter 3. There can be disagreement, too, about whether a right or a liberty as constitutionalized by our political ancestors is a right or a liberty against only the national government or, instead, against both the national government and the governments of the states. See pp. 126–27.

25. See pp. 106–8.

26. The problem is not just that the Court, unlike the Congress and the president, is not electorally accountable. Neither is a president in his second term. The problem is the extreme political unaccountability of the Supreme Court, and of the federal judiciary generally, which inheres in the fact, *not* that the justices are appointed rather than elected—a person who is appointed by the governor of a state to the United States Senate to fill an unexpired term is not thereby politically unaccountable—but that he or she is appointed for life and so, unlike the appointed senator, doesn't have to worry about eventually losing his or her position because of one or more unpopular decisions.

27. "No matter how far they transgress existing rules, successful constitutional conventions, like those of 1787–89, are unlikely to be perceived as outlaws. If

they prosper, they will be founders." R. Kay, Book Review, 7 Constitutional Commentary 434, 440–41 (1990) (reviewing R. Caplan, Constitutional Brinkmanship: Amending the Constitution by National Convention (1988)). See R. Kay, "Comparative Constitutional Fundamentals," 6 Connecticut J. International L. 445 (1991). But cf. R. Hardin, "Why a Constitution?" in The Federalist Papers and the New Institutionalism 100, 102, 113 (B. Grofman & D. Wittman eds., 1989): "Contracts are generally backed by external sanctions; constitutions are more nearly backed by default, by the difficulty of recoordinating on an alternative arrangement. . . . [O]nce we have settled on a constitutional arrangement, it is not likely to be in the interest of some of us then to try to renege on the arrangement. And this is generally true not because we will be coerced to abide if we choose not to but because we generally cannot do better than to abide. To do better, we would have to carry enough others with us to set up an alternative, and that will typically be too costly to be worth the effort."

28. See A. Amar, "Philadelphia Revisited: Amending the Constitution outside Article V," 55 U. Chicago L. Rev. 1043 (1988). In a subsequent, unpublished addendum (1990), Professor Amar argues: "Only if a current majority of deliberate citizens can, if they desire, amend our Constitution can the document truly be said to derive from 'We the People of the United States,' here and now, rather than from the hands of a small group of white men ruling us from their graves. Any contrary reading of Article V would violate the Preamble's promise that the framers' 'Posterity' would continue to enjoy 'the Blessings of Liberty'—most importantly, the liberty of popular self-governance." Bruce Ackerman, too, has offered an extra-Article V theory of constitutional amendment. See B. Ackerman, "The Storrs Lectures: Discovering the Constitution," 93 Yale L. J. 1013 (1984); B. Ackerman, "Constitutional Politics/Constitutional Law," 99 Yale L. J. 553 (1990). David Dow rejects "these recent and novel claims." See D. Dow, "When Words Mean What We Believe They Say: The Case of Article V," 76 Iowa L. Rev. 1 (1990) (arguing "that the only way to amend the Constitution is in accordance with the mechanism outlined in article V"). (The quoted language appears at p. 4.)

29. See pp. 197–201.

30. See B. Ackerman, We the People: Foundations 54–55 (1992). Cf. Sager, note 17, at 906: "In no meaningful sense do persons control their destiny as to matters that are understood to be the object of constitutional fiat if they are unable, short of meeting the extraordinary conditions of constitutional amendment, to make political choices contrary to those stipulated in the Constitution."

31. Bickel, note 3, at 13.

32. See M. Perry, The Constitution, the Courts, and Human Rights 13–14 (1982).

33. See id. at 14–15.

34. See id. at 15–17. Cf. C. Black, Structure and Relationship in Constitutional Law, chap. 3 (1969).

35. See C. Rossiter, "Introduction," The Federalist Papers viii (C. Rossiter ed., 1961).

36. J. Choper, Judicial Review and the National Political Process: A Functional Reconsideration of the Role of the Supreme Court 66 (1980) (quoting 1 Annals of Congress 457 (1834)).

37. See Clinton, note 2. For a recent, revisionist view of the emergence of the modern practice of judicial review—a view that offers a different perspective

from Clinton's—see S. Snowiss, Judicial Review and the Law of the Constitution (1990).

38. Clinton, note 2, at ix.

39. Id. at x. "A close reading of *Marbury* [*v. Madison* (1803)] itself supports no more than this narrow view. Subsequent decisions of the Supreme Court lend additional support." Id.

> When the framers undertook to place formal limitations on the legislative power, they left little room for doubt as to what they had done. First, they provided for executive review of policy by instituting the veto power. Second, they provided for legislative review through the override capacity. Third, they provided for limited judicial review in cases of a judiciary nature.
>
> This kind of coordinate review bears little resemblance to the famous Jeffersonian idea which sometimes carries a similar label. His central point seems to be that all the agencies of national government possess a similar capacity to pass judgment on constitutional questions, no matter what the question involved. . . .
>
>   . . . .
>
> [Under t]he "Marshallian" variant [of coordinate review] . . . , the decision as to where power to make a final authoritative determination of constitutionality lies depends upon the type of case involved; and specifying the type of case in turn depends upon functional relations which stem from the system of balanced government established in the Constitution.

Id. at 25–26. For an informative review of Clinton's argument, see K. Newmyer, Book Review, 7 Constitutional Commentary 380 (1990). See also M. Franck, "Origins and Limits of Judicial Review," 52 Rev. Politics 485 (1990).

40. See Black, note 34, at 71: "[J]udicial review of Acts of Congress for federal constitutionality . . . rests also on the visible, active, and long-continued acquiescence of Congress in the Court's performance of this function. The Court now confronts not a neutral Congress nor a Congress bent on using its own constitutional powers to evade the Court's mandates, as some state legislatures have tried (and as Congress very clearly could succeed in doing, in many cases, if it were so minded), but rather a Congress which has accepted, and which by the passage of jurisdictional and other legislation has facilitated, this work of the Court." See also S. Freeman, "Original Meaning, Democratic Interpretation, and the Constitution," 21 Philosophy & Public Affairs 3, 7 (1992) (judicial review "is primary among . . . the many significant practices, institutions, and procedures that are part of our constitution . . . that are not set forth in the document bearing the name 'the Constitution'"). Cf. Snowiss, note 37, at x: "I do not offer this [historical] reinterpretation as a way of attacking or defending the [modern] institution of judicial review. I share the prevailing view that judicial authority over legislation has by now generated sufficient support to be unaffected by assessments of original intent."

41. See note 31 and accompanying text.

Chapter 3

1. Steven Smith has asked a "fundamental, and ultimately ontological, question: What *is* a principle? Where, or in what form, can a principle be said to exist,

or to be real?" S. Smith, "Idolatry in Constitutional Interpretation," 79 Virginia L. Rev. 583, 621 (1993). If we talk, as I think we should, not in terms of constitutional "principles", but in terms of constitutional "directives"—the directives constitution makers issue—Smith's ontological inquiry seems puzzling. "What is a directive?" In its central case, a directive is simply a direction, an imperative, issued by one person (or persons) to another: for example, "Don't abridge the freedom of speech." With respect to such imperatives, the serious question is not "Where can a directive be said to exist?" A serious question is: Did P in fact issue the directive she is claimed to have issued, or did she issue a different directive (or perhaps no directive)? Another serious question: What does the directive require us to do in *this* context, in which the directive is, as directives sometimes are, indeterminate?

2. Article VI of the Constitution provides that "[t]his Constitution . . . shall be the supreme law of the land. . . ."

3. But not as a moral matter. See chapter 2, note 27 and accompanying text.

4. Or arguably except. See chapter 2, note 28 and accompanying text.

5. The Twenty-seventh Amendment provides: "No law, varying the compensation for the services of the Senators and Representatives, shall take effect, until an election of Representatives shall have intervened." See "With Little Fanfare, Amendment Is Signed," New York Times, May 19, 1992, at A14.

6. See Marbury v. Madison, 5 U.S. (1 Cranch) 137, 177 (1803).

7. M. Moore, "Do We Have an Unwritten Constitution?," 63 Southern California L. Rev. 107, 122, 123 (1989). See id. at 121–23. See also L. Solum, "Originalism as Transformative Politics," 63 Tulane L. Rev. 1599, 1601 (1989).

8. S. Freeman, "Constitutional Democracy and the Legitimacy of Judicial Review," 9 L. & Philosophy 327, 369 (1990–91).

9. S. Freeman, "Original Meaning, Democratic Interpretation, and the Constitution," 21 Philosophy & Public Affairs 3, 6 (1992).

10. Nontextualism ought not to be confused with a different position, which Gary Jacobsohn has articulated. According to Jacobsohn,

> [T]he written Constitution was meant to embody the natural rights commitments of the framers. Therefore, judicial appeals to "higher law" are not justifiable when they lead to a distinction between written and unwritten constitutions, but they are justifiable insofar as they help explicate and illuminate the written words of the Constitution itself. From this perspective the positivists are correct in their insistence upon the exclusive authority of the written document, but fundamentally misguided in their understanding of the nature of this document, since, as we have seen, the written words do not preclude a natural rights content. Judges who accept the intermediate position stated above will not feel free to invoke ideas of natural justice that are not grounded in the constitutional text. Yet neither will they read the text as if it were a business contract or, worse, as an "unprincipled" document. If the Constitution is a set of rules and procedures, it is so in part because it flows out of a coherent and knowable, not arbitrary or ever-mutable, set of philosophic presuppositions.

G. Jacobsohn, The Supreme Court and the Decline of Constitutional Aspiration 75 (1986). To reject nontextualism, therefore, is not necessarily to reject "judicial appeals to 'higher law'".

11. I am grateful to Larry Solum for this point.

12. For an argument that at the time of the founding of the United States, courts sometimes followed the nontextualist approach to constitutional adjudication, see S. Sherry, "The Founders' Unwritten Constitution," 54 U. Chicago L. Rev. 1127 (1987). But see H. Michael, "The Role of Natural Law in Early American Constitutionalism: Did the Founders Contemplate Judicial Enforcement of 'Unwritten' Individual Rights?" 69 North Carolina L. Rev. 421 (1991) (arguing against Sherry). My claim is that it is difficult to justify the nontextualist approach in the context of modern American political-legal culture. Cf. Sherry, this note, at 1176: "By approximately 1820, . . . the reliance on natural law was waning, disappearing entirely within a few years. It is this nineteenth century rejection of the notions of natural rights that has most influenced modern constitutional law. After two brief flirtations with decisionmaking on the basis of natural law, the Supreme Court since 1937 has made a consistent and at least partially successful attempt to link all of its decisions to specific clauses of the Constitution, even when doing so stretches the language to the limits of credibility."

13. At least, the originalism I defend in this chapter is a species of textualism. For a position that is originalist but partly nontextualist, see B. Ackerman, We the People: Foundations (1992). I suggested in chapter 1 that Ackerman does not need the nontextualism to defend the Supreme Court cases he wants to defend. See p. 11.

14. A. Rapaczynski, "The Ninth Amendment and the Unwritten Constitution: The Problems of Constitutional Interpretation," 64 Chicago-Kent L. Rev. 177, 192 (1988).

15. W. Brennan, Jr., "Why Have a Bill of Rights?" 9 Oxford J. Legal Studies 425, 432 (1989). However activist his approach to constitutional adjudication may have been, Justice Brennan is best understood not only as a textualist, but as an originalist, in the sense of originalism presented and defended in this chapter. See M. McConnell, "A Moral Realist Defense of Constitutional Democracy," 64 Chicago-Kent L. Rev. 89, 92 n. 16 (1988). (Professor McConnell, a prominent originalist, served as a law clerk to Justice Brennan.) Cf. id. at 100: "Traditional constitutionalism is not hostile to judicial enforcement of aspirational principles— if they can fairly be discovered in the text, structure, and purposes of the Constitution."

16. To reject nontextualism is not to deny that extraordinary circumstances might arise in which a judge would act admirably were she to engage in a kind of civil disobedience, resolving a constitutional issue against government even when, in her view, there is no good textual basis for doing do, but pretending that there is such a basis. To allow for that possibility, however—the possibility of morally extraordinary circumstances—is not to embrace nontextualism as a legitimate judicial option for morally ordinary circumstances. John Ely has made a point that is relevant here: "It is an entirely legitimate response to the gall bladder law [a hypothetical "statute making it a crime for any person to remove another person's gall bladder, except to save that person's life"] to note that it couldn't pass and refuse to play any further. In fact it can only deform our constitutional jurisprudence to tailor it to laws that couldn't be enacted, since constitutional law appropriately exists for those situations where representative government cannot be trusted, not those where we know it can." J. Ely, Democracy and Distrust: A Theory of Judicial Review 183 (1980). On what Justice Ely might be tempted to do in morally extraordinary circumstances, see Ely, this note, at 183 (contemplating the

possibility of "staying on the bench and engaging in a little judicial civil disobedience"). On what Justice Ackerman would do in such circumstances, see Ackerman, note 13, at 10–16 (rejecting "rights foundationalism").

17. See R. Bork, The Tempting of America: The Political Seduction of the Law
144 (1989):

> Though I have written of the understanding of the ratifiers of the Con-
> stitution, since they enacted it and made it law, that is actually a short-
> hand formulation, because what the ratifiers understood themselves to
> be enacting must be taken to be what the public of that time would
> have understood the words to mean. It is important to be clear about
> this. The search is not for a subjective intention. If someone found a
> letter from George Washington to Martha telling her that what he
> meant by the power to lay taxes was not what other people meant, that
> would not change our reading of the Constitution in the slightest. Nor
> would the subjective intentions of all the members of a ratifying con-
> vention alter anything. When lawmakers use words, the law that results
> is what those words ordinarily mean. If Congress enacted a statute out-
> lawing the sale of automatic rifles and did so in the Senate by a vote of
> 51 to 49, no court would overturn a conviction because two senators in
> the majority testified that they really had intended only to prohibit the
> *use* of such rifles. They said "sale" and "sale" it is. Thus, the common
> objection to the philosophy of original understanding—that Madison
> kept his notes of the convention at Philadelphia secret for many
> years—is off the mark. He knew that what mattered was public under-
> standing, not subjective intentions. Madison himself said that what
> mattered was the intention of the ratifying conventions. His notes of
> the discussions at Philadelphia are merely evidence of what informed
> public men of the time thought the words of the Constitution meant.
> Since many of them were also delegates to the various state ratifying
> conventions, their understanding informed the debates in those con-
> ventions. . . . [W]hat counts is what the public understood. Law is a
> public act. Secret reservations or intentions count for nothing. All that
> counts is how the words used in the Constitution would have been
> understood at the time. The original understanding is thus manifested
> in the words used and in secondary materials, such as debates at the
> convention, public discussion, newspaper articles, dictionaries in use at
> the time, and the like.

Bork's statement echoes Thomas Cooley, who wrote more than a hundred years
before Bork:

> [A]s the constitution does not derive its force from the convention which
> framed, but from the people who ratified it, the intent to be arrived at is
> that of the people, and it is not to be supposed that they have looked for
> any dark or abstruse meaning in the words employed, but rather that
> they have accepted them in the sense most obvious to the common
> understanding, and ratified the instrument in the belief that that was the
> sense designed to be conveyed. These proceedings therefore are less
> conclusive of the proper construction of the instrument than are legisla-
> tive proceedings of the proper construction of a statute; since in the lat-
> ter case it is the intent of the legislature we seek, while in the former we

are endeavoring to arrive at the intent of the people through the discussions and deliberations of their representatives.

T. Cooley, A Treatise on the Constitutional Limitations *66–67 (2d ed. 1871) (quoted in Ely, note 16, at 17–18).

By "the public of that time", does Bork mean not the whole public but that particular public—namely, the enfranchised—on whose behalf the provision was ratified? Or does he mean a public larger than the enfranchised, on the theory that at least some of those who were not enfranchised were being virtually, though not actually, represented by the ratifiers? On "virtual representation", see Ely, note 16, at 82–87.

18. Whose understanding of a statutory provision, as distinct from a constitutional provision, should be privileged for purposes of statutory adjudication? The understanding of the people at the time the provision was legislated? Or the understanding of the people's representatives, who legislated the provision? The passage by Thomas Cooley, quoted in the preceding note, is relevant here. Statutes, unlike the Constitution, do not typically begin with "We the people", and the process of legislating a statutory provision is often much less public than the process of ratifying a constitutional provision.

19. For the text of Article V of the Constitution, which concerns the amendment process, see pp. 17–18.

20. A. Bickel, Politics and the Warren Court 214 (1965).

21. Kent Greenawalt has sketched a version of the "combination of different groups" approach. See K. Greenawalt, Speech, Crime, and the Uses of Language, chap. 10 (1989).

22. A. Scalia, "Originalism: The Lesser Evil," 57 Cincinnati L. Rev. 849, 862–63 (1989).

23. See pp. 59–60.

24. See pp. 131–33.

25. R. Dworkin, "Bork's Jurisprudence," 57 U. Chicago L. Rev. 657, 668 n. 9 (1990).

26. On the contemporary debate about the original meaning of the free exercise clause, see pp. 59–60.

27. Ely, note 16, at 16. Steven Smith has suggested, in discussion, this way of making the point: "Suppose that the Constitution is written in Latin but that none of the current justices understands Latin. Then of course they would first need to translate a constitutional provision into English (step one) before they could specify its meaning in a particular case (step two). The same would be true if the Constitution were written in the English of Chaucer's time, or in some special current dialect of English. For various reasons, in other words, a text may need to be 'translated' before we can work with it, and this can be true of some constitutional provisions and not others." Perhaps we should say, not that the current justices don't understand Latin (or Chaucer's English)—for then, strictly speaking, *they* could not translate Latin into English but would have to rely on someone else to do it for them—but that they cannot understand Latin without a strenuous effort at translating it (consulting appropriate dictionaries, etc.).

28. Because there are competing understandings of the meaning of the free exercise clause, of what directive the clause represents—competing understandings both in the present and also between past and present, in particular, between the time the clause was ratified and the present—the question "What does the clause mean?" is incomplete: What does (did) the clause mean *to whom*, how is

(was) is understood *by whom?* Some of the most important constitutional provisions—in particular, some constitutional provisions regarding rights or liberties—are like the free exercise clause in that there is not only no widely shared understanding of the meaning of the provisions (i.e., of what directives they represent), but there are, in the American political community, competing understandings, both intratemporally and intertemporally.

29. H.-G. Gadamer, Truth and Method 275 (Eng. tran., 1975). For the complete passage, see chapter 5, note 15 and accompanying text. I am grateful to Larry Solum for pressing this objection.

30. I am grateful to Steven Smith for formulating this objection.

31. 16 Wall. (83 U.S.) 36, 72 (1872).

32. Id. at 67, 71.

33. Id. at 72.

34. Strauder v. West Virginia, 100 U.S. 303, 308 (1880).

35. The four dissenting justices in the *Slaughter-House Cases*, but not the *Slaughter-House* majority, thought that section 1 of the Fourteenth Amendment was meant to deal with discrimination beyond just racial discrimination.

36. Bork, note 17, at 166.

37. Id. at 166–67.

38. See R. Dworkin, "The Bork Nomination," New York Rev. of Books, Aug. 13, 1987, at 6:

> History alone might be able to show that some particular concrete opinion, like the opinion that school segregation was not unconstitutional, was widely shared within the group of legislators and others mainly responsible for a constitutional amendment. But it can never determine precisely which general principle or value it would be right to attribute to them. This is so not because we might fail to gather enough evidence, but for the more fundamental reason that people's convictions do not divide themselves neatly into general principles and concrete applications. Rather they take the form of a more complex structure of layers of generality, so that people regard most of their convictions as applications of further principles or values more general still. That means that a judge will have a choice among more or less abstract descriptions of the principle that he regards the framers as having entrusted to his safekeeping, and the actual decisions he makes, in the exercise of that responsibility, will critically depend on which description he chooses.

39. Bork, note 17, at 149–50.

40. See M. Perry, Morality, Politics, and Law 126–27 (1988).

41. See Bork, note 17, at 216–17.

42. Id. at 187.

43. For the language of the second sentence of section 1 of the Fourteenth Amendment, see p. 116.

44. See p. 77.

45. Ely, note 16, at 16 (emphasis in original).

46. D. Laycock, "Text, Intent, and the Religion Clauses," 4 Notre Dame J. L., Ethics & Public Policy 683, 687 (1990). Recall Bork's statement, quoted in the text accompanying note 39, that "a judge should state the principle at the level of generality that the text and historical evidence warrant." Just two pages earlier in

his book, however, Bork said: "The Constitution states its principles in majestic generalities that we know cannot be taken as sweepingly as the words alone might suggest." Bork, note 17, at 147. I wonder how Bork would reconcile the two statements. (I wonder, too, how he would reconcile the latter statement with the statement quoted in the text accompanying note 39.) Bork seems to assume that "historical evidence" warrants a construal of original meaning narrower than the construal warranted by textual language alone. As a generalization about *all* constitutional provisions, that assumption is surely a perilous one (even if it is true of *some* provisions that historical evidence warrants a construal of original meaning narrower than that warranted by text alone). If that is indeed Bork's assumption/generalization—how else might the two statements be reconciled?—then Bork has fallen prey to wishful thinking.

47. See T. McAffee, "The Original Meaning of the Ninth Amendment," 90 Columbia L. Rev. 1215, 1224–25, 1238–39 (1990).

48. R. Kay, "Adherence to the Original Intentions in Constitutional Adjudication: Three Objections and Responses," 82 Northwestern U. L. Rev. 226, 235 (1988). See M. McConnell, "Free Exercise Revisionism and the *Smith* Decision," 57 U. Chicago L. Rev. 1109, 1115–16 (1990) (discussing the free exercise clause of the First Amendment): "While we cannot rule out the possibility that the term 'prohibiting' might impliedly be limited to laws that prohibit the exercise of religion in a particular way—that is, in a discriminatory fashion—we should at least begin with the presumption that the words carry as broad a meaning as their natural usage."

49. The problem, of course, is that there will often be available a range of historically plausible readings—some more general, some less so—of the original meaning. In that sense, the historical inquiry constitutive of the originalist approach to constitutional interpretation is often indeterminate. I discuss the indeterminacy of originalism in chapter 4, though there I am concerned with the choice, not between more general and less general readings of the original meaning, but between more determinate and less determinate readings. (Particularity/generality should not be confused with determinacy/indeterminacy. See pp. 77–78.)

50. See Bork, note 17, at 218 (criticizing Leonard Levy's "highly oversimplified version of the philosophy of original understanding that bears little resemblance to the theory set out in this book. . . . No even moderately sophisticated originalist holds the view Levy refutes [in his *Original Intent and the Framers' Constitution* (1988)].") The "intentionalist" approach to constitutional interpretation James Boyd White criticizes in his new book bears little resemblance to the originalist approach presented in this chapter. See J. White, Justice as Translation: An Essay in Cultural and Legal Criticism, chap. 5 (1990).

51. See D. Richards, "Originalism without Foundations," 65 New York U. L. Rev. 1373, 1380 (1990): "[Raoul] Berger's originalism is a kind of appeal to what I call Founders' denotations. He holds that the meaning of a constitutional provision is to be understood in terms of the things in the world to which the relevant Founders would have applied the term at the time the constitutional provision was adopted authoritatively. A provision should be interpreted to include certain things only if those things would have been included within the meaning of the clause by the Founders. According to Berger, then, the equal protection clause properly cannot be interpreted to invalidate state-sponsored racial segregation because the relevant Founders (the Reconstruction Congress and ratifying

state legislatures) would not have regarded such segregation as violative of equal protection."

52. Bork, note 17, at 162–63. See also R. Bork, "Original Intent and the Constitution," Humanities, Feb. 1986, at 22, 26 ("The objection that we can never know what the [ratifiers] would have done about specific modern situations is entirely beside the point. The originalist attempts to discern [and then enforce] the principles the [ratifiers] enacted, the values they sought to protect."); R. Bork, "The Constitution, Original Intent, and Economic Rights," 23 San Diego L. Rev. 823, 826–27 (1986) (arguing that his originalist theory does not require "judges . . . invariably to decide cases the way the [ratifiers] would if they were here today", but does require them to "confine themselves to the principles the [ratifiers] put into the Constitution"). Cf. Dworkin, note 25, at 670 (commenting on the passage quoted in the text accompanying this note): "We should pause to note what an amazing passage this is. It could have been written by almost any of the people Bork takes to be members of the academic conspiracy against him and the nation." For a vision of the Constitution substantially the same as Bork's, see E. Meese III, Speech before the D.C. Chapter of the Federalist Society Lawyers Division, Nov. 15, 1985, Washington, D.C., reprinted in The Great Debate: Interpreting Our Written Constitution 31, 33 (1986):

> Our approach does not view the Constitution as some kind of super-municipal code, designed to address merely the problems of a particular era—whether those of 1787, 1789, or 1868. There is no question that the Constitutional Convention grew out of widespread dissatisfaction with the Articles of Confederation. But the delegates at Philadelphia moved beyond the job of patching that document to write a *Constitution*. Their intention was to write a document not just for their time but for posterity.
>
> The language they employed clearly reflects this. For example, they addressed *commerce*, not simply shipping or barter. Later the Bill of Rights spoke, through the Fourth Amendment, to "unreasonable searches and seizures," not merely the regulation of specific law enforcement practices in 1789. Still later, the Framers of the 14th Amendment were concerned not simply about the rights of black citizens to personal security, but also about the equal protection of the laws for all persons within the states. The Constitution is not a legislative code bound to the time in which it was written.

Meese added: "Neither, however, is [the Constitution] a mirror that simply reflects the thoughts and ideas of those who stand before it." Id.

53. Bork, note 17, at 167–68.

54. Id. at 352.

55. 347 U.S. 483 (1954).

56. Bork, note 17, at 169.

57. Bork is admirably frank in acknowledging such movement. See id. at 352: "The concept of original understanding itself gains in solidity, in articulation and sophistication, as we investigate its meanings, implications, and requirements, and as we are forced to defend its truths from the constitutional heresies with which we are continually tempted." Cf. Solum, note 7, at 1601: "As originalism has been modified and defined in response to nonoriginalist critiques, the originalist's position has become more and more plausible as a theory of constitutional interpre-

tation. . . . [Originalism] provide[s] an accurate description of the phenomenology of constitutional practice."

58. G. Bassham, Original Intent and the Constitution: A Philosophical Study 55–56 (1992).

59. Id. at 56.

60. Id. ("In short, by adopting moderate intentionalism, conservatives could admit that the framers had sometimes wrought more wisely than they had known, yet deny that they had wrought half so wisely as nonoriginalists often claimed." Id.) For an argument similar to Bassham's, see E. Simien, Jr., "It Is a Constitution We Are Expounding," 18 Hastings Constitutional L. Q. 67, 86–108 (1990).

61. Ely, note 16, at 1.

62. McAffee's reference is to R. Berger, Congress v. the Supreme Court (1969).

63. T. McAffee, "Reed Dickerson's Originalism—What It Contributes to Contemporary Constitutional Debate," 16 Southern Illinois U. L. J. 617, 647 (1992).

64. In R. Berger, Government by Judiciary: The Transformation of the Fourteenth Amendment (1977).

65. See McAffee, note 63, at 648. In fairness to Berger, it should be noted that he does not seem unaware of the distinction on which McAffee (and countless others) insists. See R. Berger, "Original Intent: The Rage of Hans Baade," 71 North Carolina L. Rev. 1151, 1169 (1993): "We are not . . . to assimilate the *application to changing facts* of a basic principle . . . to judicial *change of the principle* itself. . . . Should the people desire to change [the] principles [of the Constitution], Article V provides the exclusive machinery for amendment. It is not for the judges to usurp that function. *That* is the issue."

66. See pp. 79–81.

67. See Bork, note 17, at 213–14. See also Scalia, note 22, at 863.

68. If a judge is what Michael Moore calls a "moral realist", one would expect the judge, if an adherent of originalism, to be an adherent of "a morally realist originalism". According to Moore, "such . . . originalism would develop theories about the nature of equality, liberty, liberties of speech and of worship, cruel punishment, and the like, in a never completed quest to discover the true nature of such things. To seek such theories is to conform to the original understanding, just as to seek to apply the word 'tiger' by the best theory of what tigers are is to conform to the usual authorial intention in the use of that word." Moore, note 7, at 135.

Contrary to Sotirios Barber's and Graham Walker's criticisms of my work, I am *not* a moral conventionalist. See S. Barber, "Michael Perry and the Future of Constitutional Theory," 63 Tulane L. Rev. 1289 (1989); G. Walker, Moral Foundations of Constitutional Thought 16–17, 36–38, 124–25, 144 n. 106 (1990). I am a moral realist—as my book, *Love and Power: The Role of Religion and Morality in American Politics* (1991), makes amply clear. (Walker includes John Courtney Murray among those "contemporary thinkers . . . [who] have attempted 'moral realist' approaches to constitutional theory. . . ." Id. at 17, 46. *Love and Power* is partly a retrieval of Murray's work, especially his *We Hold These Truths: Catholic Reflections on the American Proposition* (1960).) I am, however, an epistemological holist: My conception of justification is holistic. See M. Perry, Love and Power, chap. 4; cf. pp. 96–101. In his book Walker correctly understands Michael Moore to be a moral realist who is also an epistemological holist (or coherentist), and Walker criticizes, in part on the basis of the moral-realist position, Moore's epistemology. Although the epistemological differences between, on the one side, Moore and me, and, on the other, Walker (and Barber?) are real differences (see E. Santurri, "Nihilism Revisited," 71 J. Religion 67 (1991)), I doubt the differences have much cash value, if indeed they have any, insofar as constitutional adjudication is concerned.

69. Cf. W. Twining, "Talk about Realism," 60 New York U. L. Rev. 329, 337 (1985): "It should be a working precept of all jurisprudential criticism and polemics that before launching an attack one should first identify worthy opponents and attribute to them what one considers to be the least vulnerable interpretation of their views that the relevant texts will sustain. Intellectual debate is impoverished when one attacks caricatures; soft targets generally only suit weapons with correspondingly low firepower."

70. See Simien, note 60, at 93–94: "Much of the criticism [of originalism] . . . spills over from a critique of strict originalism and a failure either to perceive or to admit the differences between strict and moderate originalism."

71. See Kay, note 48, at 236–59. Note that my reference is to Kay's response to the "It's Impossible" objection, not to his reponses to the "It's Self-Contradictory" and "It's Wrong" objections (id. at 259–92). Kay's response to the "It's Wrong" objection seems to me basically sound, but, for reasons I develop later in this book, his response to the "It's Self-Contradictory" objection—in particular, his reading of the original meaning both of the Ninth Amendment and of the privileges or immunities clause of the Fourteenth Amendment—seems to me problematic. See pp. 63–68 (on the Ninth Amendment), and pp. 124–27 (on the privileges or immunities clause).

72. So far as I am aware, Ronald Dworkin, who seems to have a continuing interest in challenging Borkean originalism, has never cited, much less discussed, Kay's important work. See Dworkin, note 25; Dworkin, note 38. In the relevant chapter of his book, where he briefly recites, in the form of questions, the claims to which Kay has responded, James Boyd White fails to notice Kay's work. See J. White, note 50, chap. 5.

73. Richard Kay is not alone. Gregory Bassham's recent book is excellent in rebutting "three misconceived objections to originalism". See Bassham, note 58, 67–90. Other useful discussions include: G. Bradley, "The Bill of Rights and Originalism," 1991 U. Illinois L. Rev. 417; E. Maltz, "Foreword: The Appeal of Originalism," 1987 Utah L. Rev. 773; E. Maltz, "The Failure of Attacks on Originalist Theory," 4 Constitutional Commentary 43 (1987); McAffee, note 63; Simien, note 60; Scalia, note 22.

74. Some constitutional provisions limit the power of the national government to protect the power of state government, and some limit the power of state government to protect the power of the national government. Some constitutional provisions limit the power of government—whether the national government, state government, or both—to protect some aspect of the well-being or of the autonomy of persons, whether persons as citizens or persons simple as human beings.

75. Cf. R. Kay, "The Bork Nomination and the Definition of 'The Constitution'," 84 Northwestern U. L. Rev. 1190, 1193 (1990): "The influence of the Constitution is the consequence of continuing regard not for a particular assortment of words, but for the authority and sense of a certain constituent act."

76. Kay, note 48, at 234.

77. R. Kay, "Original Intentions, Standard Meanings, and the Legal Character of the Constitution," 6 Constitutional Commentary 39, 50 (1989).

78. Kay, note 75, at 1193.

79. S. Smith, "Law Without Mind," 88 Michigan L. Rev. 104, 119 (1989). (For an interesting response to aspects of Smith's essay, see L. Alexander, "Of Two Minds about Law and Minds," 88 Michigan L. Rev. 2444 (1990).) See also M. McConnell, "The Role of Democratic Politics in Transforming Moral Convictions into Law," 98 Yale L. Journal 1501, 1526–29 (1989). Agreeing that the original meaning of the constitutional text is authoritative, Tom Merrill suggested to me in conversation that a different rule might apply if we had a practice of reratifying the Constitution every generation.

80. C. Sunstein, After the Rights Revolution: Reconceiving the Regulatory State 129 (1990). I suspect it misses the point to make that observation of statutes (federal or otherwise) as well.

81. Cf. id. at 129 ("courts might well conclude that what is controlling is the contemporary meaning of the statute").

82. Id.

83. See Freeman, note 9, at 13. I don't mean to suggest that Burkean political philosophy is, in every version, nothing more than ancestor worship.

84. See pp. 23–24.

85. See Freeman, note 9, at 17: "Public reason requires, at a minimum, that the Constitution's meaning be comprehensible and affirmable without appeals to external authority. The absence of others' authority (that of our ancestors, of God, or of anyone else) follows from democratic sovereignty. Therefore, affirming the Constitution as sovereign citizens, and not as subjects of someone else's will, requires that we reject the doctrine of original meaning."

86. In at least one passage in his book Bork seems to come close to making the question-begging originalist argument for originalism. See Bork, note 17, at 177. In the main, however, Bork seems to understand that any valid argument for originalism cannot be originalist. See id. at 150.

87. See H. Jefferson Powell, "The Original Understanding of Original Intent," 98 Harvard L. Rev. 885 (1985). (The strict intentionalism/moderate intentionalism language is Gregory Bassham's. See pp. 44–45.)

88. G. Bassham, note 58, at 68. See id. at 67–71. For important critical comments on Powell's famous article, note 87, see Bassham, note 58, at 67–71; C. Lofgren, "The Original Understanding of Original Intent," 5 Constitutional Commentary 77 (1988); McAffee, note 63, at 630–45; Simien, note 60, at 99–102.

In a recent essay, Powell does not attend to anything like the distinction between the project of translating/decoding the constitutional text (when it needs translation/decoding) and the project of specifying indeterminate norms represented by the interpreted text. See H. Jefferson Powell, "The Political Grammar of Early Constitutional Law," 71 North Carolina L. Rev. 949 (1993). Perhaps Powell will, on reflection, conclude that any such distinction is deeply flawed. If, however, he concludes that some such distinction is sound, it would be interesting to see the use to which Powell would put such a distinction both in describing the founding period of American constitutional law and in prescribing an approach to constitutional adjudication.

89. See R. Bork, "Foreword," G. McDowell, The Constitution and Contemporary Constitutional Theory v, xi (1985): "[E]ven a judge purporting to be [an originalist] can manipulate the levels of generality at which he states the [ratifiers'] principles. . . . [E]ven under [originalism] there are no safeguards against that except the intellectual honesty of the judge and the scrutiny of an informed pro-

fession that accepts the premises of [originalism]." See also S. Sherry, "Original Sin," 84 Northwestern U. L. Rev. 1215, 1222 (1990) ("originalism leaves . . . much room for . . . manipulation").

90. On judicial "discretion", see chaps. 5 and 6.

91. See Smith, note 79, at 111–12: "To be sure, the words of the enacted law may continue to constrain the judge. But the essential fact that made *those words* (and not a science fiction novel, or even a law review article) efficacious to bind the judge—*i.e.*, the fact that the words express a specific collective decision made by the designated political authority—is now de-emphasized or dismissed. The legal text is methodically dissociated from the phenomenon upon which its power to constrain depends. The important question that emerges from this new perspective is not whether the statute, so viewed, *could* constrain judicial choice. Perhaps it could. But the critical question is why a statute, so understood, *should* constrain judges."

92. See Bork, note 17, at 150: "Even if evidence of what the founders thought about the judicial role were unavailable, we would have to adopt the rule that judges must stick to the original meaning of the Constitution's words. If that method of interpretation were not common in the law, if James Madison and Justice Joseph Story had never endorsed it, if Chief Justice John Marshall had rejected it, we would have to invent the approach of original understanding in order to save the constitutional design. No other method of constitutional adjudication can confine courts to a defined sphere of authority and thus prevent them from assuming powers whose exercise alters, perhaps radically, the design of the American republic. The philosophy of original understanding is thus a necessary inference from the structure of government apparent on the face of the Constitution." For a critical comment on Bork's argument—and here I quote Richard Posner's construal of Bork's argument—that "the judiciary should embrace originalism . . . [because] it is implicit in our democratic form of government. Originalism is necessary in order to curb judicial discretion, and curbs on judicial discretion are necessary in order to keep the handful of unelected federal judges from seizing the reins of power from the people's representatives", see R. Posner, "Bork and Beethoven," 42 Stanford L. Rev. 1365, 1369–70 (1990). For a vigorous reply to Posner's critical review, see L. Graglia, "'Interpreting' the Constitution: Posner on Bork," 44 Stanford L. Rev. 1019 (1992).

93. See E. Meese III, "The Battle for the Constitution," 35 Policy Rev. 32 (1985); E. Meese III, "Toward a Jurisprudence of Original Intention," 2 Benchmark 1 (1986); E. Meese III, "The Supreme Court of the United States: Bulwark of a Limited Constitution," 27 South Texas L. J. 455 (1986). (In his better moments, Meese contended for "moderate intentionalism" originalism. See note 52.) See also W. Rehnquist, "The Notion of a Living Constitution," 54 Texas L. Rev. 693 (1976).

94. See F. Michelman, "Law's Republic," 97 Yale L. J. 1493, 1521–23 (1988).

95. Consider, for example, the free exercise clause of the First Amendment. See pp. 59–61.

96. In particular, let us assume that as originally understood the provision represents only the directive that government is not to prevent the accused from having a lawyer.

97. I am grateful to Kent Greenawalt for suggesting both this particular example and the general state of affairs it exemplifies.

98. John Ely's presentation of "two significant (and iterrelated) comparative attractions of an [originalist] approach" is relevant here. See Ely, note 16, at 3–5.

An interesting recent argument in support of a nonoriginalist approach comes from Samuel Freeman. According to Freeman, the written Constitution should be interpreted to represent, not the directives the provisions were originally understood to represent, but "the principles *we* could reasonably intend in endorsing [the Constitution] as our public charter. . . . Against originalism's proposal that the Constitution be interpreted by asking what values or principles our ancestors intended, I have suggested an alternative inquiry: What principles could we, as sovereign citizens, mutually acknowledge as interpretive of the Constitution in the free and public use of democratic reason?" Freeman, note 9, at 17 & 20.

In responding to Freeman's proposal, I want to consider several possibilities:

1. *The principle (or, as I prefer, the directive) "we could reasonably intend" in endorsing, as a part of our public charter, a particular provision is the principle the provision was originally understood to establish.* In that case, the practical difference between the originalist approach and Freeman's is nil.

2. *There is more than one principle we could reasonably intend in endorsing (as a part of our public charter) a particular provision, only one of which is the principle the provision was originally understood to establish.* But in that case, why should we want to concede to a judicial elite—the nine members of the Supreme Court, or a majority of them—the power to privilege, in the name of the provision, any principle other than the one the provision was originally understood to establish, which, *ex hypothesi*, is one of the principles, though not the only one, we could reasonably intend in endorsing the provision? Why, that is, should we want to make that concession unless we are inclined to romanticize the Supreme Court (something that it is becoming increasingly difficult to do)?

3. *The principle a particular provision was originally understood to establish is not one we could reasonably intend in endorsing the provision.* . . . However we may evaluate it as a matter of political theory, Freeman's proposal is, at the end of the day, of little practical consequence except to the extent it is the case that the principles the Constitution was originally understood to establish are not ones we could reasonably intend in endorsing, as our public charter, the Constitution. What reason do we have for supposing that any, much less many, of the principles the Constitution was originally understood to establish are not ones we could reasonably intend in endorsing the Constitution? The challenge to Freeman is to identify those provisions about which it is the case that the principles they were originally understood to establish are not ones we could reasonably intend in endorsing the provisions. (What if a particular constitutional provision will bear only one reading, and, thus read, the principle represented by the provision is not one that as free and equal citizens we could reasonably constitutionalize? Freeman's position: "[W]hen the inherited Constitution contains provisions deviating from equal sovereignty, the Court is in no position to contravene it by declaring them invalid." Id. at 37.)

3(a). The principle a particular provision was originally understood to establish is not one we could reasonably intend in endorsing the provision, *but the provision can be understood to represent a principle we could reasonably intend in endorsing the provision.* What existing constitutional provisions fit that description? Again, for any right- or liberty-regarding provision of the Constitution the subject of a significant amount of litigation—for example, the free exercise clause of the First

Amendment, the assistance of counsel clause of the Sixth Amendment, and the privileges or immunities clause of the Fourteenth Amendment—there is almost certainly a significant dissensus, among those citizens who think about such matters, about whether the provision represents this or that directive: Such a provision is almost certainly understood, by different citizens, to represent different directives. Perhaps, therefore, such a provision can be understood to represent, not just one principle we could reasonably intend in endorsing the provision, but more than one such principle.

3(b). The principle a particular provision was originally understood to establish is not one we could reasonably intend in endorsing the provision, *but the provision can be understood to represent more than one principle we could reasonably intend in endorsing the provision.* Why should we concede to the Court the power, not merely to decline to enforce the principle the provision was originally understood to represent—which, *ex hypothesi*, we could not reasonably intend in endorsing the provision—but also to choose which of the two or more principles we *could* reasonably intend, shall be privileged?

99. Of course, this imaginary scenario is based, albeit loosely, on the constitutional experience of post–World War II Japan. See K. Inoue, MacArthur's Japanese Constitution: A Linguistic and Cultural Study of Its Making (1991). Relatively few citizens of contemporary Japan seem to oppose the Japanese Constitution; most seem to embrace it. The party that ruled Japan for almost all of the postwar period—the Liberal Democratic Party (which, as it is sometimes said in Japan, is neither liberal nor particularly democratic)—is understood by many citizens of Japan, however, and certainly by many Japanese constitutional scholars, to be anticonstitutional.

100. Scalia, note 22, at 856.

Chapter 4

1. R. Bork, The Tempting of America: The Political Seduction of the Law 318 (1989).

2. See R. Posner, The Problems of Jurisprudence 131 (1990): "In many cases the conventional materials will lean so strongly in one direction that it would be unreasonable for the judge to go in any other. But in some they will merely narrow the range of permissible decision, leaving an open area within which the judge must perforce attempt to decide the case in accordance with sound policy—in those grand symbolic cases that well out of the generalities and ambiguities of the Constitution, in accordance with a vision of the good society—while paying due heed to the imprudence of trying to foist an idiosyncratic policy conception or social vision on a recalcitrant citizenry."

3. Important and interesting questions lurk here about "the total *weight* or *magnitude* of evidence needed to establish the meaning of a given text in a given context." See generally G. Lawson, "Proving the Law," 86 Northwestern U. L. Rev. 859 (1992).

4. See note 19 and accompanying text.

5. I omit here the possibility that a law forbidding the drinking of wine in any and all circumstances is a covert discriminatory prohibition on free exercise. Imagine, for example, that the but-for reason for enactment of a law forbidding anyone to drink wine is a desire to hammer Catholics.

6. See A. Scalia, "Originalism: The Lesser Evil," 57 Cincinnati L. Rev. 849 (1989).

7. See M. McConnell, "The Role of Democratic Politics in Transforming Moral Convictions into Law," 98 Yale L. J. 1501 (1989); M. McConnell, "A Moral Realist Defense of Constitutional Democracy," 64 Chicago-Kent L. Rev. 89 (1988).

8. See M. McConnell, "The Origins and Historical Understanding of Free Exercise of Religion," 103 Harvard L. Rev. 1409 (1990); M. McConnell, "Free Exercise Revisionism and the *Smith* Decision," 57 U. Chicago L. Rev. 1109 (1990).

9. See McConnell, "The Origins and Historical Understanding of Free Exercise of Religion," note 8, at 1511–13; M. McConnell, "Free Exercise Revisionism and the *Smith* Decision," note 8, at 1117.

10. See, e.g., W. Marshall, "The Case against the Constitutionally Compelled Free Exercise Exemption," 40 Case Western Reserve L. Rev. 357, 375–79 (1989–90); G. Bradley, "Beguiled: Free Exercise Exemptions and the Siren Song of Liberalism," 20 Hofstra L. Rev. 245 (1991); P. Hamburger, "A Constitutional Right of Religious Exemption: An Historical Perspective," 60 George Washington L. Rev. 915 (1992). Professors McConnell and Marshall have debated the question of "constitutionally compelled free exercise exemptions", with particular reference to the *Employment Division v. Smith*, 110 S. Ct. 1595 (1990), in the *University of Chicago L. Review*: McConnell, "Free Exercise Revisionism and the *Smith* Decision," note 8; W. Marshall, "In Defense of *Smith* and Free Exercise Revisionism," 58 U. Chicago L. Rev. 308 (1991); M. McConnell, "A Response to Professor Marshall," 58 U. Chicago L. Rev. 329 (1991).

11. See A. Scalia, "The Rule of Law as the Law of Rules," 56 U. Chicago L. Rev. 1175 (1989).

12. See Employment Division v. Smith, 110 S. Ct. 1595 (1990). McConnell—who, as an effective proponent of originalism, should have some credibility with Justice Scalia—responded to Scalia's judicial-role concerns in McConnell, "Free Exercise Revisionism and the *Smith* Decision," note 8, at 1141–49.

13. Id. at 1116–17.

14. See note 11.

15. Scalia, note 11, at 1185.

16. See K. Sullivan, "Foreword: The Justices of Rules and Standards," 106 Harvard L. Rev. 22, 82–83 (1992) (arguing that Justice Scalia's "commitment to textualism, originalism, and historical positivism is contingent and secondary" to his commitment to minimizing judicial discretion).

17. Or: a more particular reading, or a more general one. See p. 77.

18. See note 20 and accompanying text.

19. R. Posner, "What Am I? A Potted Plant?" New Republic, Sept. 28, 1987, at 23, 24–25. See Posner, note 2, at 291–92.

20. F. Michelman, "Conceptions of Democracy in American Constitutional Argument: The Case of Pornography Regulation," 56 Tennessee L. Rev. 291, 297–98 (1989).

21. The literature on the Ninth Amendment is voluminous. See R. Barnett, ed., The Rights Retained by the People: The History and Meaning of the Ninth Amendment (1989); R. Barnett, ed., The Rights Retained by the People: The History and Meaning of the Ninth Amendment, Volume 2 (1993).

22. See Barron v. Mayor & City Council of Baltimore, 32 U.S. (7 Pet.) 243 (1833).

23. "The people" to whom the Ninth Amendment refers—like the First, Second, and Fourth, and Tenth Amendments—are presumably the same people who are the beneficiaries, either collectively or individually or both, of the various other rights [and privileges] enumerated in the Bill of Rights.

24. See C. Black, "On Reading and Using the Ninth Amendment," in R. Barnett, ed., The Rights Retained by the People: The History and Meaning of the Ninth Amendment 337, 338 (1989).

25. For a compilation of "[t]he most prominent recent works" supporting that conclusion, see T. McAffee, "The Original Meaning of the Ninth Amendment," 90 Columbia L. Rev. 1215, 1217 n. 12 (1990).

26. See id. See also T. McAffee, "The Bill of Rights, Social Contract Theory, and the Rights 'Retained' by the People," 16 Southern Illinois U. L. J. 267 (1992); T. McAffee, "Prolegomena to a Meaningful Debate on the 'Unwritten Constitution' Thesis," 61 U. Cincinnati L. Rev. 107 (1992).

27. McAffee, note 25, at 1221–22. According to Leonard Levy, the unenumerated rights the Ninth Amendment was meant to protect, as constitutional rights against the national government, were of two species: "natural"—the rights Madison called "the pre-existent rights of nature"—and "positive" in Madison's sense of rights "resulting from a social compact". See L. Levy, Original Intent and the Framers' Constitution 274, 278–79 (1988). McAffee's claim about the character of the unenumerated rights the Ninth Amendment was meant to protect—that they were "residual" and not "affirmative" in character—does not negate Levy's claim about the two species of unenumerated rights—"natural" and "positive"—the Ninth Amendment was meant to protect. McAffee's claim negates, rather, the claim, made by Levy and others, that the rights meant to be protected were "affirmative". Indeed, McAffee allows for the possibility that a "residual" right can also be a "natural" one. See McAffee, note 25, at 1221: "The conception of [residual] 'rights' . . . is inclusive enough to extend to a broad range of privileges and prerogatives that modern thinkers would not typically identify as moral or legal rights, as well as collective rights held by the people as a whole, rights held under state law, and those individual rights that we might call 'fundamental' and which the framers might have called 'natural'."

28. For a citation to several "recent works that endorse" the reading McAffee defends—all of which predate McAffee's own essay by one to three years—see T. McAffee, "The Bill of Rights, Social Contract Theory, and the Rights 'Retained' by the People," note 26, at 268 n. 3.

29. McAffee, note 25, at 1226.

30. In his essay McAffee suggests that "[a]s a general reserved powers provision, the tenth amendment does not address this problem [of powers being inferred from the very existence of an inevitably incomplete enumeration] at all, though it conceivably makes the feared inference more difficult to justify." Id. at 1302. McAffee then acknowledges the possibility that Madison or others "determined at some point that the tenth amendment was an adequate safeguard against any untoward implication of enlarged powers." Id. at 1302 n. 331.

One who accepts McAffee's reading might demur that the Ninth and Tenth Amendments are each amendments "for the sake of emphasis", so to speak, and then point out that whereas the Tenth Amendment emphasizes the principle of reserved *powers* and the two beneficiaries of that principle, "the States" and "the people", the Ninth Amendment emphasizes the principle of residual *rights* and the sole beneficiaries of that principle, "the people". This seems to be the gist of McAffee's response to the charge that his reading of the Ninth Amendment makes it functionally equivalent to the Tenth. See id. at 1305–7. Such a response seems less to deny the charge of functional equivalence, however, than to evade it: The question remains, What more is protected, if indeed anything more is protected, by the Ninth Amendment, given McAffee's reading, than by the Tenth Amendment's reservation of nondelegated powers "to the States" or "to the people"?

31. Charles Black has presented a powerful argument that the "others [i.e., other rights] retained by the people" under the Ninth Amendment include the "certain unalienable Rights" with which, according to the Declaration of Independence, "all men . . . are endowed by their Creator. . . . [A]mong these are Life, Liberty, and the Pursuit of Happiness." See C. Black, "'One Nation Indivisible': Unnamed Human Rights in the States," 65 St. John's L. Rev. 17 (1991). "We must go back to the Declaration of Independence, in its capacity as an obvious precursor of the ninth amendment, operating *in pari materia* with that amendment, and thus as an aid to the interpretation of the latter." Id. at 26.

32. McAffee, note 25, at 1306. (McAffee does admit, however, that "the multiplication of redundancies would raise questions." Id.) According to Richard Kay, "[R]edundancy in legal documents is not particularly odd. And, in this case, the drafting history of the Bill of Rights explains the presence of both provisions [the Ninth and Tenth Amendments]." Kay, "Adherence to the Original Intentions in Constitutional Adjudication: Three Objections and Responses," 82 Northwestern U. L. Rev. 226, 271 (1988). (Kay recounts the relevant history at pp. 271–73.)

33. See, e.g., R. Barnett, "Foreword: Unenumerated Constitutional Rights and the Rule of Law," 14 Harvard J. L. & Public Policy 615, 638–40 (1991); D. Mayer, "The Natural Rights Basis of the Ninth Amendment: A Reply to Professor McAffee," 16 Southern Illinois U. L. J. 313 (1992); S. Heyman, "Natural Rights, Positivism and the Ninth Amendment: A Response to Professor McAffee," 16 Southern Illinois U. L. J. 327 (1992); S. Sherry, "Natural Law in the States," 61 U. Cincinnati L. Rev. 171, 179–92 (1992).

34. But not as plausible, in my view, as the conclusion that the unenumerated rights meant to be protected by the Ninth Amendment include both "residual" rights and "affirmative" rights, rather than just residual rights. See J. Ely, Democracy and Distrust: A Theory of Judicial Review 34–35 (1980):

> It is true that there was fear, no matter how strained it may seem to a contemporary observer, that the addition of a bill of rights might be taken to imply the existence of congressional powers beyond those stated in the body of the Constitution. It is also true that the alleviation of this fear was one reason Madison gave for adding the Ninth Amendment to the Bill of Rights. The conclusion that that was the *only* reason for its inclusion does not follow, however, and in fact it seems wrong. The Tenth Amendment, submitted and ratified as the same time, completely fulfills the function that is here being proffered as all the Ninth Amendment was about. . . . [The Tenth Amendment] says—in language as clearly to the point as the language of the Ninth Amendment is not—that the addition of the Bill of Rights is not to be taken to have changed the fact that powers not delegated are not delegated. It does seem that a similar thought was part of what animated the Ninth Amendment, but if that were *all* that amendment has been calculated to say, it would have been redundant.

See also Mayer, note 33, at 317 et seq.

35. Cf. M. Arnold, "Doing More Than Remembering the Ninth Amendment," 64 Chicago-Kent L. Rev. 265, 266 (1988): "[T]he revolutionary generation had not completely thought through what the [ninth] amendment meant because the practice of judicial review was not all that firmly established. It is certain, of course, that that generation would not have asked itself immediately, as we would, what a court would do with a proposed constitutional text, because the Constitution was not thought of as belonging exclusively or even primarily to one branch of the government, and, moreover, the power of courts to transform society had not yet been experienced."

36. See pp. 146–48. John Ely has provided us with a list of ways *not* to identify Ninth Amenmdment rights, including reliance on "natural law", "tradition", or "consensus". See Ely, note 34, chap. 3. Happily, the ways I suggest, in chapter 8, are not on Ely's hit list.

37. Cf. id. at 40: "It would be a cheap shot to note that there is no legislative history specifically indicating an intention that the Ninth Amendment was to receive judicial enforcement. There was at the time of the original Constitution little legislative history indicating that *any* particular provision was to receive judicial enforcement: the Ninth Amendment was not singled out one way or another." For Robert Bork's version of the "cheap shot", see Bork, note 1, at 183–84. Bruce Ackerman volleys Bork's shot in B. Ackerman, "Robert Bork's Grand Inquisition," 99 Yale L. J. 1419, 1431 (1990).

38. Ely, note 34, at 38.

39. Arnold, note 35, at 268 (quoting S. Macedo, The New Right v. The New Constitution 27 (1986)).

40. McAffee, note 25, at 1316.

41. Id. at 1317. In correspondence McAffee has emphasized that his point is not that historical inquiry into the original meaning of the Ninth Amendment is in fact indeterminate, but only that the residual rights reading of the original meaning is *at least as* strong as the affirmative rights reading, and that Bork and Meese are therefore not vulnerable to the charge of inconsistency. McAffee believes that his residual rights reading is not merely at least as strong but is actually stronger than the affirmative rights reading. "The ninth amendment, at least, provides an area in which originalist methodology can supply a reason to accept one answer as authoritative. The combination of text, context and historical consensus here establishes the meaning of the ninth amendment as conclusively as it can be for any constitutional provision whose meaning is not self-evident on its face." Id. at 1318. In a recent essay, in which he responds to some criticism of his position, McAffee is, if anything, even more confident that his reading of the original meaning of the Ninth Amendment is the only plausible one. See McAffee, "The Bill of Rights, Social Contract Theory, and the Rights 'Retained' by the People," note 26.

42. See McAffee, note 25, at 1317: "This Article should at least demonstrate that the affirmative rights reading of the ninth amendment cannot be firmly established as its original meaning. The residual rights reading more than adequately accounts for the most clearly relevant textual and historical materials. Moreover, a number of the advocates of the affirmative rights reading have conceded that the originally intended meaning of the amendment is less than clear. . . ."

43. See note 34.

Chapter 5

1. H.-G. Gadamer, Truth and Method 275 (Eng. trans., 1975).

2. See p. 37. For the relevant passage from Gadamer, see this chapter, note 15 and accompanying text.

3. Cf. P. Brest, "Constitutional Citizenship," 34 Cleveland State L. Rev. 175, 179 (1986): "[T]he Constitution both reflects and shapes public morality, [and] it delegates to its interpreters no small amount of responsibility to engage in moral decisionmaking themselves. This [is what] makes it [so] crucial to ask *who* the decisionmakers shall be."

4. For a kindred discussion, see K. Sullivan, "Foreword: The Justices of Rules and Standards," 106 Harvard L. Rev. 22, 57–62 (1992).

5. My concern is with the determinacy/indeterminacy of legal materials from the perspective of a judge who must reach a judgment based on the materials. See K. Greenawalt, "How Law Can Be Determinate," 31 UCLA L. Rev. 1, 54 (1990).

6. See id. at 55: "No absolute general principle of morality bars [a judge's] deciding contrary to her understanding of the law's provisions. However, strong reasons oppose that course. In taking office, [the judge] has sworn to uphold the law. She has agreed to perform a job as conceived in a certain way. If she wanders too far from the widely understood job description, she has failed to keep her promise to perform *that* job." See also D. Kennedy, "Freedom and Constraint in Adjudication: A Critical Phenomenology," 36 J. Legal Education 518, 527 (1986): "I see myself as having promised some diffuse public that I will 'decide according to law,' and it is clear to me that a minimum meaning of this pledge is that I won't do things for which I don't have a good legal argument."

7. Greenawalt, note 5, at 85. Cf. Kennedy, note 6, at 523: "What would betray legality would be to adopt the wrong attitude at the *end* of the reasoning process, when I've reached a conclusion about 'what the law requires' and found it still conflicts with how-I-want-to-come-out."

8. See Greenawalt, note 5, at 29: "Few, if any, writers have asserted the most extreme thesis about indeterminacy—that no legal questions have determinate answers—in clear terms, and almost no one may actually believe that thesis . . ." See also B. Cardozo, The Nature of the Judicial Process 129 (1921): "In countless litigations, the law is so clear that judges have no discretion. They have the right to legislate within gaps, but often there are no gaps. We shall have a false view of the landscape if we look at the waste spaces only, and refuse to see the acres already sown and fruitful." In his compelling phenomenology of adjudication, Duncan Kennedy has acknowledged that the relevant legal materials are sometimes irresistibly determinate. See Kennedy, note 6.

9. See Greenawalt, note 5, at 29: "The most ambitious claim of determinacy is that the law provides an answer to every legal question, but that claim has few modern defenders, and I am not one of them."

10. Or, more precisely, "underdeterminate". See L. Solum, "On the Indeterminacy Crisis: Critiquing Critical Dogma," 54 U. Chicago L. Rev. 462 (1987).

Greenawalt's exhaustive discussion of the determinacy/indeterminacy of legal and other norms is excellent. See Greenawalt, note 5.

11. Cf. G. Currie, "Work and Text," 100 Mind 325, 339 (1991) (arguing that "[i]nterpreting [literary] works and interpreting [literary] texts, where there is the opportunity for [the latter], are quite different kinds of activities").

12. Basic Law: Human Dignity and Freedom, enacted by the Knesset on 12th

Adar B 5752 (17 March 1992). The bill and explanatory comments were published in *Hatza'ot Hok* 2086, of 6th Kislev 5752 (Nov. 13, 1991), p. 60.

13. Cf. B. Cardozo, The Nature of the Judicial Process 67 (1921): "[W]hen
[judges] are called upon to say how far existing rules are to be extended or
restricted, they must let the welfare of society fix the path, its direction and its dis-
tance."

14. The Federalist Papers 229 (C. Rossiter ed., 1961). See K. Scheppele, Legal
Secrets 94–95 (1988): "Generally in the literature on interpretation the question
being posed is, What does a particular text (or social practice) *mean*? Posed this
way, the interpretive question gives rise to an embarassing multitude of possible
answers, a cacophony of theories of interpretation. . . . [The] question that (in
practice) is the one actually asked in the course of lawyering and judging [is]:
what . . . does a particular text mean *for the specific case at hand?*"

15. H.-G. Gadamer, note 1, at 275.

16. N. MacCormick, "Reconstruction after Deconstruction: A Response to
CLS," 10 Oxford J. Legal Studies 539, 548 (1990). Where I have used the term
"specification", MacCormick uses the Latin term *determinatio*, borrowing it from
John Finnis. "John Finnis has to good effect re-deployed St Thomas' concept of
determinatio; Hans Kelsen's translators used the term 'concretization' to much the
same effect." Id. (citing J. Finnis, "On the Critical Legal Studies Movement," 30
American J. Jurisprudence 21, 23–25 (1985), and H. Kelsen, The Pure Theory of
Law 230 [M. Knight trans., 1967]).

17. A. Kronman, "Living in the Law," 54 U. Chicago L. Rev. 835, 847–48
(1987). Of course, there can be cases in which it is difficult to administer the appli-
cation/specification distinction, but for present purposes that problem need not
detain us.

18. See note 16 and accompanying text.

19. Cf. R. Pildes & E. Anderson, "Slinging Arrows at Democracy: Social Choice
Theory, Value Pluralism, and Democratic Politics," 20 Columbia L. Rev. 2121,
2194–95 (1990): "Past choices change our *evaluations* of future possibilities not
just instrumentally but constitutively: past choices often alter a political community's self-understanding. By committing itself to certain choices, a political community may move provisionally toward a more articulate definition of itself, of
what it stands for, of how it defines its problems, and of how solutions to its problems might be viewed. This self-definition creates possibilities for articulating *new
kinds of reasons* for action, reasons that take on their compelling character against
a background of previous justifications for action that has already been accepted."

20. R. Posner, "What Am I? A Potted Plant?" New Republic, Sept. 28, 1987, at
23, 24.

21. H.L.A. Hart, The Concept of Law 125 (1961).

22. Id.

23. Id. at 126.

24. This is not to say that determinacy ought never to be a goal: "To escape
this oscillation between extremes we need to remind ourselves that human inability to anticipate the future, which is at the root of this indeterminacy, varies in
degree in different fields of conduct. . . ." Id. at 127. See id. at 127–32.

25. Id. at 126.

26. J. Schneewind, "Moral Knowledge and Moral Principles," in Revisions 113,
113 (S. Hauerwas & A. MacIntyre eds., 1983). "[U]nlike [the principle that] 'One
ought to help old ladies crossing busy streets,' which is relevant only to a relatively

limited set of situations, 'One ought to help people in need' is applicable to an indefinitely large number of kinds of cases." Id.

27. B. Cardozo, note 8, at 83–84. Contrary to what Steven Smith has suggested, it seems quite unremarkable that fidelity to a directive—a directive to privilege some value (that is, some *valued* state of affairs)—necessitates (in a context in which, because the value is indeterminate, the directive is indeterminate) that those to whom the directive is issued instantiate the value, that they "embody" or "concretize" it, in a way not foreseen, and perhaps not even foreseeable, by those who issued the directive. See S. Smith, "Idolatry in Constitutional Interpretation," 79 Virginia L. Rev. 583 (1993). Why might such a directive—a directive necessitating such unforeseen/unforeseeable choices—be issued? Because, as Hart's comments suggest, it may make sense to issue a directive—and, thereby, to offer some guidance—but not one that "blindly prejudges what is to be done in a range of future cases, about whose composition [the issuers of the directive] are ignorant." See note 25 and accompanying text. But why, or to what extent, might a later generation choose to abide an earlier generation's directives, whether determinate or indeterminate—in particular, their *constitutional* directives? That is the question to which chapter 2, on the legitimacy of judicial review, is largely addressed.

28. See pp. 93–94.

29. Cf. T. Sandalow, "Constitutional Interpretation," 79 Michigan L. Rev. 1033, 1046 (1981): "[O]ur understanding of the framers' intentions is necessarily distorted if we focus solely upon their larger purposes, ignoring the particular judgments they made in expressing those purposes. Intentions do not exist in the abstract; they are forged in response to particular circumstances and in the collision of multiple purposes which impose bounds upon one another. . . . [B]y wrenching the framers' 'larger purposes' from the particular judgments that reveal them, we incur a loss of perspective, a perspective that might better enable us to see that the particular judgments they made were not imperfect expressions of a larger purpose but a particular accommodation of competing purposes." But cf. note 33 and accompanying text.

30. One might want to argue, on that basis, that the *Minnesota Mortgage Moratorium Case—Home Building & Loan Association v. Blaisdell*, 290 U.S. 398 (1934)—was wrongly decided. (For a discussion of the case, see C. Miller, The Supreme Court and the Uses of History 39–51 (1969).) On the other hand, one might respond to an argument of that sort by insisting that the relevant description of the practice they who issued the relevant directive specifically meant to disallow is not P but P *at time T*, or P *in context C*, whereas the practice the court is being asked to invalidate in the name of the directive is P *at time U*, or P *in context D*. However, such a response may seriously underestimate the intertemporal continuities in the historically extended American political community. For an argument that "*Blaisdell* was rightly decided only if an interpreter may legitimately pay no heed to positive law", see C. Bieneman, "Legal Interpretation and a Constitutional Case: *Home Building & Loan Association v. Blaisdell*," 90 Michigan L. Rev. 2534 (1992). (The quoted language is at p. 2564.) Cf. Maryland v. Craig, 110 S. Ct. 3157, 3172 (1990) (Scalia, J., joined by Brennan, Marshall, and Stevens, JJ., dissenting):

> According to the Court, "we cannot say that [face-to-face] confrontation [with witnesses appearing at trial] is an indispensable element of the Sixth Amendment's guarantee of the right to confront one's accusers."
> . . That is rather like saying "we cannot say that being tried before a jury

is an indispensable element of the Sixth Amendment's guarantee of the right to jury trial." The Court makes the impossible plausible by recharacterizing the Confrontation Clause, so that confrontation (redesignated "face-to-face confrontation") becomes only one of many "elements of confrontation." . . . The reasoning is as follows: The Confrontation Clause guarantees not only what it explicitly provides for—"face-to-face" confrontation—but also implied and collateral rights such as cross-examination, oath, and observation of demeanor (TRUE); the purpose of this entire cluster of rights is to ensure the reliability of evidence (TRUE); the Maryland procedures preserves the implied and collateral rights (TRUE), which adequately ensure the reliability of evidence (perhaps TRUE); therefore the Confrontation Clause is not violated by denying what it explicitly provides for—"face-to-face" confrontation (unquestionably FALSE). This reasoning abstracts from the right to its purposes, and then eliminates the right. It is wrong because the Confrontation Clause does not guarantee reliable evidence; it guarantees specific trial procedures that were thought to *assure* reliable evidence, undeniably among which was "face-to-face" confrontation. Whatever else it may mean in addition, the defendant's constitutional right "to be confronted with the witnesses against him" means, always and everywhere, at least what it explicitly says: the "'right to meet face to face all those who appear and give evidence at trial.'"

31. See pp. 149–50.

32. Cf. L. Tribe, American Constitutional Law 1164–65 (2d ed. 1988) (discussing the establishment clause of the First Amendment): "Where the original intent *not* to outlaw a practice is clear, a judge ought to view the history as evidence that the practice does not violate the Constitution. The showing should not, however, settle the question entirely—particularly if the context has changed. . . . To prevail, the opponent ought to demonstrate that, history notwithstanding, the practice offends the fundamental concepts . . . that underlie the constitutional language."

33. P. Brest, "The Misconceived Quest for the Original Understanding," 60 Boston U. L. Rev. 204, 217 (1980). Brest adds: "To the [originalist] interpreter falls the unenviable task of ascertaining, for each provision, how much more or less." Id.

34. See chapter 3, notes 59–60.

35. See pp. 45–46.

36. See pp. 149–52.

37. Cf. A. Bickel, The Least Dangerous Branch: The Supreme Court at the Bar of Politics 102–3 (1962): "[T]o seek in historical materials relevant to the framing of the Constitution . . . specific answers to specific present problems is to ask the wrong questions. With adequate scholarship, the answer that must emerge in the vast majority of cases is no answer. . . . It is not true that the Framers intended the Fourteenth Amendment to outlaw segregation or to make applicable to the state all restrictions on government that may be evolved under the Bill of Rights; but they did not foreclose them and may indeed have invited them."

38. Bob Nagel has suggested, in correspondence, that "proponents' speeches might sometimes indicate an intention to allow a practice, as might their subsequent behavior. Moreover, an inference might be drawn from the failure to discuss (or even imagine) the possibility that a certain practice would not continue to

be legal. Now, of course, you might say that you are looking for direct evidence, not inferences, but this would be to insist on the kind of certain evidence you know judges often have to operate without."

Chapter 6

1. A. Bickel, The Least Dangerous Branch: The Supreme Court at the Bar of Politics 24 (1962).

2. Nor is to defend minimalism to defend originalism.

3. See pp. 59–61.

4. See pp. 66–68.

5. See pp. 131–33.

6. See pp. 128–29.

7. See A. Scalia, "Originalism: The Lesser Evil," 57 Cincinnati L. Rev. 849, 862–63 (1989).

8. A. Scalia, "The Rule of Law as the Law of Rules," 56 U. Chicago L. Rev. 1175, 1179–80 (1989). See id. at 1180: "While announcing a firm rule of decision can thus inhibit courts, strangely enough it can embolden them as well. Judges are sometimes called upon to be courageous, because they must sometimes stand up to what is generally supreme in a democracy: the popular will. . . . The chances that frail men and women will stand up to their unpleasant duty are greatly increased if they can stand behind the solid shield of a firm, clear principle enunciated in earlier cases."

9. L. Levy, "Editorial Note," in Judicial Review and the Supreme Court: Selected Essays 43 (L. Levy ed., 1967). (Levy reprints Thayer's article, which was originally published in 7 *Harvard Law Review* 129 (1893), at pp. 43–63. My citations are to the article as reprinted by Levy.) See P. Kahn, Legitimacy and History: Self-Government in American Constitutional Theory 84 (1992):

> Thayer was a friend and professional colleague of Oliver Wendell Holmes, first in law practice and then at Harvard, where Thayer taught for thirty years. Louis Brandeis was a student of Thayer's, and Felix Frankfurter, who just missed Thayer at Harvard, acknowledged Thayer's substantial influence. Of Thayer's most famous essay in constitutional law, "The Origin and Scope of the American Doctrine of Constitutional Law," Holmes wrote, "I agree with it heartily and it makes explicit the point of view from which implicitly I have approached the constitutional questions upon which I have differed from some other judges.

Thayer presented his essay in Chicago on August 9, 1893, to the World's Congresses on Jurisprudence and Law Reform, which was one of a number of such conferences held from May to October during the World's Columbian Expedition. The conferences were planned and organized by the World's Congress Auxiliary of the World's Columbian Expedition, an organization authorized and supported by the Exposition corporation. I am grateful to Ellen Bentsen for this information.

10. Thayer, note 9, at 54, 59.

11. West Virginia State Board of Education v. Barnette, 319 U.S. 624, 661–62, 666–67 (1943). According to Thayer, the minimalist approach is fitting when a federal court reviews, for federal constitutionality, federal action or when a state court reviews, either for federal constitutionality or for state constitutionality, state

action, but not when a federal court reviews, for federal constitutionality, state action, in which case (according to Thayer) the non-minimalist approach is fitting. See Thayer, note 9, at 62–63. Limiting the minimalist approach in the way Thayer did makes little sense, however, and most commentators who discuss Thayer's conception of proper judicial role fail even to note the limitation. See, e.g., Bickel, note 1, at 35–46; W. Mendelson, "The Influence of James B. Thayer upon the Work of Holmes, Brandeis, and Frankfurter," 31 Vanderbilt L. Rev. 71 (1978); but see C. Black, Decision According to Law 34–35 (1981). Even Felix Frankfurter failed to note, much less to heed, the limitation—as the text accompanying this note indicates. (Sanford Gabin has explicitly argued that "the reasonable doubt test should be applied not just to all national legislation but, contrary to Thayer's prescription, to all state legislation as well." S. Gabin, Judicial Review and the Reasonable Doubt Test 5 (1980).) I am in good company, therefore, in thinking that the limitation is not a sensible aspect of the minimalist conception of proper judicial role.

12. Gabin, note 11, at 45–46.

13. See W. Brennan, Jr., "Why Have a Bill of Rights?" 9 Oxford J. Legal Studies 425, 433 (1989).

14. If one believes that wrongly denying a right or a liberty to a person is a worse wrong than wrongly granting the right or liberty to her, one might even argue that in the improbable event the Court is, at the end of the day, in equipoise between two specifications of the relevant rights-regarding directive, the Court should resolve the benefit of the doubt *against* the law or other governmental action whose constitutionality is in question.

15. I develop the point in chapter 9.

16. For the classic argument that the minimalist approach is fitting with respect to the adjudication of such claims, see H. Wechsler, "The Political Safeguards of Federalism," in H. Wechsler, Principles, Politics, and Fundamental Law 49 (1960); cf. J. Choper, Judicial Review and the National Political Process: A Functional Reconsideration of the Supreme Court, chap. 4 (1980) (arguing that the Court should decline even to adjudicate such claims). See also M. Perry, The Constitution, the Courts, and Human Rights 41–49 (1982) (endorsing Wechsler's position and commenting critically on Choper's more extreme thesis). Wechsler's position has been substantially endorsed by a bare majority of the Supreme Court. See Garcia v. San Antonio Metropolitan Transit Authority, 469 U.S. 528 (1985).

17. See M. Perry, note 16, at 49–60. The minimalist approach is fitting, in my view, if both the Congress and the president support the same (reasonable) specification of the relevant directive(s).

18. If Wechsler's position (see note 16) is sound with respect to claims that the Congress, to the detriment of the states, has exceeded its (delegated) power, for example, "to regulate commerce . . . among the several states" (U.S. Const., art. I, § 1, par. 3), then it is sound too with respect to claims that the Congress, to the detriment of the states, has exceeded its (delegated) power, under section 5 of the Fourteenth Amendment, "to enforce, by appropriate legislation, the provisions of [the Fourteenth Amendment]." Let me emphasize that nothing in this book is meant to call into question the minimalist approach to the adjudication of such claims: "federalism" claims, claims about whether the Congress has exceeded a delegated power to the detriment of the states. This book is mainly about the proper judicial approach to the adjudication of claims that government—whether

the national government or a state government—has transgressed, to the detriment of an individual qua citizen or simply qua person, a constitutional provision limiting its power. Cf. M. Pawa, "When the Supreme Court Restricts Constitutional Rights, Can Congress Save Us? An Examination of Section 5 of the Fourteenth Amendment," 141 U. Pennsylvania L. Rev. 1049 (1993).

19. R. Bork, The Tempting of America: The Political Seduction of the Law 5 (1989). On how "[t]he picture of the judge as an interstitial legislator is both unedifying and, on a realistic view of the legislative process, misleading", see R. Posner, The Problems of Jurisprudence 130–31 (1990).

20. Bork, note 19, at 252.

21. Brennan, note 13, at 426. In a footnote Justice Brennan explained that the Brandeis statement is "[q]uoted in A. Bickel, *The Least Dangerous Branch* (1962) 107. This passage was part of Brandeis' draft dissent in *United States v. Moreland*, 258 U.S. 433, 441 (1922). At Chief Justice Taft's behest he withdrew it prior to publication." Id. at 426 n. 1.

22. R. Posner, "What Am I? A Potted Plant?" New Republic, Sept. 28, 1987, at 23, 24. Compare American Jewish Congress v. City of Chicago, 827 F.2d 120, 137–40 (7th Cir. 1987) (Easterbrook, J., dissenting).

23. Kahn, note 9, at 85 (quoting Thayer, note 9).

24. Kahn, note 9, at 86–87.

25. J. Thayer, John Marshall 106–7, 109–10 (1901). (For a commentary on Thayer's position, see Kahn, note 9, at 85–89.) But cf. Choper, note 16, at 66: "[O]n the one hand, it is impossible convincingly to refuse the propositions that lawmaking would be more sensitive to individual liberties if it were conducted with the knowledge that its resolutions were final, and that the ever present potential of judicial disapproval actually encourages popular irresponsibility and stultifies the people's sense of moral and constitutional obligation. On the other hand, it is equally impracticable to reject the contention that, without the threat of judicial invalidation in the background, majoritarian excesses in respect to minority rights would be all the less restrained."

26. Hutchinson's reference is to the Canadian Charter of Rights and Freedoms.

27. A. Hutchinson, "Waiting for Coraf (or the Beatification of the Charter)," 41 U. Toronto L. J. 332, 358 (1991).

28. Thayer, note 9, quoted in Kahn, note 9, at 87.

29. Id.

30. A more extreme claim would deny even that there is such a thing as an unreasonable answer to the question of how such a directive should be specified.

31. To reject the noncognitivist conception of the process of specifying indeterminate constitutional materials—that is, the conception of the process as a fundamentally "not rational" one—is not necessarily to accept that the Court should have the primary responsibility for specifying constitutional indeterminacy. See M. McConnell, "A Moral Realist Defense of Constitutional Democracy," 64 Chicago-Kent L. Rev. 89 (1988).

32. The problem is not just that the Court, unlike the Congress and the president, is not electorally accountable. (Neither is a president in his second term.) The problem is the extreme political unaccountability of the Supreme Court (and of the federal judiciary generally), which inheres in the fact, *not* that a Supreme Court justice is appointed rather than elected—a person appointed by a governor to the United States Senate to fill an unexpired term is not thereby politically unaccountable—but that he or she is appointed for life and so, unlike the

appointed senator, doesn't have to worry about eventually losing his or her position because of one or more unpopular decisions.

33. See pp. 16–17.

34. J. Ely, Democracy and Distrust: A Theory of Judicial Review 4 (1980). See also id. at 67–68. Cf. C. Auerbach, "A Revival of Some Ancient Learning: A Critique of Eisenberg's *The Nature of the Common Law*," 75 Minnesota L. Rev. 539, 557 (1991): "The legitimacy of lawmaking by common law courts lies in the legislature's power to undo the courts' work."

35. It is a mistake to think that the argument for the practice of judicial review is also an argument for the minimalist approach to the practice. (For an apparent instance of the mistake, see Gabin, note 11, at 38 & 45.) The argument for the practice of judicial review is an argument that, notwithstanding the countermajoritarian difficulty, we should support the judicial protection of constitutional directives. The argument underdetermines the answer to the question whether in protecting indeterminate constitutional directives, the judiciary should exercise the primary responsibility, or only a secondary one, for specifying the directives—or for specifying some of them. To accept the argument for the practice of judicial review is not necessarily to accept—nor is it necessarily to reject—the proposition that, because of the countermajoritarian difficulty or for some other reason, the judiciary should play only a secondary role in specifying constitutional indeterminacy.

36. G. Rosenberg, The Hollow Hope: Can Courts Bring about Social Change? 343 (1991). For a somewhat different view, see B. Canon, "The Supreme Court as a Cheerleader in Politico-Moral Disputes," 54 J. Politics 637 (1992).

37. Is Rosenberg right? See Canon, note 36, at 647 n. 8: "In my judgment, Rosenberg makes a strong case against concluding that *Brown* and *Roe* had a positive catalytic impact, but I think that his evidence is too selective and indirect to justify the opposite conclusion—that these decisions had little if any catalytic impact." See also N. Devins, "Judicial Matters," 80 California L. Rev. 1027, 1069 (1992): "Through a combination of incomplete analysis, questionable presumptions, and indirection, *The Hollow Hope* underestimates the sweep of the judiciary's contribution to social reform."

38. B. Cardozo, "Jurisprudence" (Address before the New York State Bar Association Meeting, Jan. 22, 1932), in B. Cardozo, Selected Writings 7, 43–44 (M. Hall ed., 1947).

39. M. Nussbaum, "Rosenthal Lecture 3: It Has Nothing to Do with the Law," unpublished ms. (1991). Nussbaum, in the quoted passage, is reporting a position, not embracing it. Indeed, in her lecture she criticizes the position. Cf. Posner, note 19, at 148–49 ("Often the choice will be made on the basis of deeply held personal values, and often these values will be impervious to argument. Persuasion will figure in some cases, but it will be persuasion by rhetoric rather than by the coolest forms of reasoned exposition."), 423 ("Lawyers and judges . . . muddl[e] through, struggling with questions that often cannot be resolved other than by the lights of the decision maker's personal values and preferences, constituting a social vision that may be in irreconcilable conflict with other people's equally plausible social vision."), & 456 ("Many changes of legal doctrine . . . are the result of gestalt switches or religious-type conversions.").

40. See note 19 and accompanying text.

41. See M. Perry, Love and Power: The Role of Religion and Morality in American Politics, chap. 4 (1991).

42. B. Williams, Ethics and the Limits of Philosophy 113 (1985).

43. C. Elgin, "The Relativity of Fact and the Objectivity of Value," in Relativism: Interpretation and Confrontation 86, 91 (M. Krausz ed., 1989).

44. J. Stout, "Holism and Comparative Ethics," J. Religious Ethics 301, 312 (1983).

45. See Perry, note 41.

46. See chapter 5, note 14 and accompanying text.

47. See chapter 5, note 15 and accompanying text.

48. Cf. Cardozo, note 38, at 18: "I prefer to give the label law to a much larger assembly of social facts than would have that label affixed to them by many of the neo-realists. I find lying around loose, and ready to be embodied into a judgment according to some process of selection to be practiced by a judge, a vast conglomeration of principles and rules and customs and usages and moralities. If these are so established as to justify a prediction with reasonable certainty that they will have the backing of the courts in the event that their authority is challenged, I say that they are law . . ., though I am not disposed to quarrel with others who would call them something else."

49. On reliance on "common sense" in adjudication, see D. Van Zandt, "An Alternative Theory of Practical Reason in Judicial Decisions," 65 Tulane L. Rev. 901 (1990).

50. Brennan, note 13, at 435 (emphasis added).

51. Cf. Posner, note 19, at 456–57: "[Law] is better, though not fully, described as the activity of the licensed professionals we call judges, the scope of their license being limited only by the diffuse outer bounds of professional propriety and moral consensus."

52. J. Buckley, "The Catholic Public Servant," First Things, Feb. 1992, at 18, 19.

53. Cf. Posner, note 19, at 94–95: "Even if judges should not feel limited to previous cases in seeking guidance in deciding novel ones, it can be argued that they should not stray outside the bounds of conventional moral and political opinion in their society—and therefore that an American judge is not to decide cases on the basis of the ethics of Marx or Nietzsche, but is to stay within the circle marked out by the values that have already gained a footing in our legal traditions. I wonder. How does a new value get into the legal tradition? By legislation or constitutional enactment only? Can a judge never be the first person to bring a new value, a new political or ethical insight, into the law?"

54. Brennan, note 13, at 435.

55. Id.

56. See D. Tracy, Dialogue with the Other 6 (1990) (commenting critically on "monological forms of rationality").

57. Id. at 41.

58. Cf. S. Smith, "The Pursuit of Pragmatism," 100 Yale L. J. 409, 435 (1990) ("'dialogue' seems to have become the all-purpose elixir of our time").

59. Nussbaum, note 39.

60. Posner, note 19, at 110.

61. See note 39 and accompanying text.

62. Posner, note 19, at 30.

63. M. Krygier, "Marxism and the Rule of Law: Reflections after the Collapse of Communism," 15 L. & Social Inquiry 633, 640 (1991).

64. See id. Krygier's essay is followed by several, often critical, sometimes quite critical. commentaries, to which Krygier responds—eloquently, in my view—in a rejoinder. See 15 L. & Social Inquiry 707 et seq.

65. J. Raz, "The Politics of the Rule of Law," 3 Ratio Juris 331, 331 (1990).

66. Id.

67. Cf. D. Kennedy, "Freedom and Constraint in Adjudication: A Critical Phenomenology," 36 J. Legal Education 518, 527 (1986): "I see myself as having promised some diffuse public that I will 'decide according to law,' and it is clear to me that a minimum of meaning of this pledge is that I won't do things for which I don't have a good legal argument."

68. This is not to deny that in a particular case in which the relevant law has been established judicially there may be other, compelling reasons for not overruling precedent.

69. On "traditional formalism and the rule of law", see M. Radin, "Reconsidering the Rule of Law," 69 Boston U. L. Rev. 781, 792 et seq. (1989).

70. Id. at 796.

71. F. Schauer, "Rules and the Rule of Law," 14 Harvard J. L. & Public Policy 645, 657 (1991).

72. Id.

73. W. Brennan, Jr., "The Constitution of the United States: Contemporary Ratification," 27 South Texas L. J. 433, 434 (1986).

74. See G. Miller, "Rights and Structure in Constitutional Theory," 8 Social Philosophy & Policy 196, 221 (1991); C. Sunstein, "Naked Preferences and the Constitution," 84 Columbia L. Rev. 1689 (1984).

75. Cf. Radin, note 69, at 812–13.

76. Raz, note 65, at 331.

77. Id. at 332.

78. Nussbaum, note 39.

79. Cf. D. Mayhew, Congress: The Electoral Connection 101–2 (1974) ("[L]eaders in both houses [of the Congress] have a habit of counselling their members to 'vote their constituencies.'"); R. Dahl, Pluralist Democracy in the United States: Conflict and Consent 131 (1967): "[C]ongressional leaders rely mainly on persuasion, party loyalty, expectations of reciprocal treatment, and, occasionally, special inducements such as patronage or public works. But none of these is likely to be adequate if a member is persuaded that a vote to support his party will cost him votes among his constituents. . . . Fortunately, for him, the mores of Congress, accepted by the leaders themselves, are perfectly clear on this point: His own election comes first."

80. "The World of Congress," Newsweek, Apr. 24, 1989, at 28.

81. "Congress: It Doesn't Work. Let's Fix It," Business Week, Apr. 16, 1990, at 54, 56.

82. E. Rubin, "Beyond Public Choice: Comprehensive Rationality in the Writing and Reading of Statutes," 66 New York U. L. Rev. 1, 32 (1991).

83. Id. at 33. Cf. D. Farber & P. Frickey, Law and Public Choice: A Critical Introduction 21 (1991): "[A] legislator's primary goal may be obtaining policy-making influence, not reelection for its own sake—but of course the former requires the latter."

84. Rubin, note 82, at 33–34. Cf. id. at 4: "Those who do not share the public choice perspective tend to attack the theory on empirical grounds. They argue that legislators have motivations other than the desire to be re-elected, that voters have motivations other than self-interest, and that even interest groups often organize around broad policy perspectives that bear little relationship to the personal well-being of their members."

85. See Farber & Frickey, note 83, at 20: "Responsiveness to broad constituencies is not only an important aspect of representation, it also helps ameliorate the influence of special interests. . . . Yet fixation on re-election has its drawbacks. It may lead legislators to spend their time on pork barrel legislation for their districts and on personal contact with voters and casework for constituents, rather than on addressing hard policy issues."

86. M. Glendon, Rights Talk: The Impoverishment of Political Discourse x (1991).

87. Id. at x.

88. Id. at xii.

89. See G. Will, Restoration: Congress, Term Limits, and the Recovery of Deliberative Democracy (1992).

90. Cf. "TV Holds Power in Politics," Chicago Tribune, Nov. 19, 1990, at sec. 1, p. 1.

91. "America's Politics Loses Way as Its Vision Changes World," New York Times, March 18, 1990, at sec. 1, p. 1, 22 (quoting "Representative David R. Obey, Democrat of Wisconsin, a veteran legislator respected in both parties as a student of the institutions of government").

92. See, e.g., "The Trouble with Politics," New York Times, Mar. 18, 19, 20, & 21, 1990; "We the People . . . ," Chicago Tribune, Nov. 18, 19, 20, 21, & 25, 1990.

93. As I write the first draft of this chapter, it is June 1991. The congressional debate about a civil rights bill is prominent. Michael Kinsley writes: "The Republican marketing of the quota issue has been brilliant and despicable. It is Willy Hortonism redux. . . . Hortonism is the cynical concoction of a divisive issue in the political laboratory for narrow electoral advantage." M. Kinsley, "TRB from Washington — Hortonism Redux," New Republic, June 24, 1991, at 4. Kinsley goes on to delineate Hortonism's "certain familiar features". Id.

94. The quoted language is John Ely's. See chapter 10, note 8 and accompanying text.

95. Brennan, note 13, at 434.

96. P. Bator, P. Mishkin, D. Shapiro & H. Wechsler, Hart & Wechsler's The Federal Courts and the Federal System 82 (2d ed. 1973). See S. Freeman, "Constitutional Democracy and the Legitimacy of Judicial Review," 9 L. & Philosophy 327, 365 (1990–91).

97. A. Bickel, note 1, at 26.

98. For a recent argument along these lines, see L. Sager, "The Incorrigible Constitution," 65 New York U. L. Rev. 893, 958–59 (1990).

99. A. Bickel, note 1, at 24–25.

100. Sager, note 98, at 957.

101. A. Kronman, "Living in the Law," 54 U. Chicago L. Rev. 835, 873 (1987).

102. D. Tracy, note 56, at 4. Steven Smith, commenting wryly that "'dialogue' seems to have become the all-purpose elixir of our time", has suggested that "[t]he hard question is not whether people should talk, but rather what they should say and what (among the various ideas communicated) they should believe." Smith, note 58, at 434–35. As David Tracy's observation suggests, however, there is yet another "hard" question, which Smith's suggestion tends to obscure: Not whether but *how* people should talk; what qualities of character and mind they should bring, or try to bring, to the task.

103. Guido Calabresi apparently thinks that mediocre ideologues *now* sit on the Court. Writing in equivocal support of President Bush's nomination of

Clarence Thomas to the Supreme Court, Dean Calabresi writes that the present
Court

> is outrageously homogeneous. It is overwhelmingly made up of gray
> Republican political hangers-on of virtually identical backgrounds. They
> all bring to the Court the same life experience and lack thereof. How can
> they know what discrimination *really* means? How can they understand
> what fear of police, prosecutorial or state abuse and brutality is? When
> they babble that coerced confessions need not make trials unfair, that
> discrimination must be proved in individual cases and not through sta-
> tistics, or that a single appeal is adequate even if a defendant is served by
> a lousy lawyer, they sound like what they are: people who neither
> through personal experience nor academic thought could ever imagine
> themselves erroneously crushed by the power of the state. . . . I despise
> the current Supreme Court and find its aggressive, willful, statist behav-
> ior disgusting—the very opposite of what a judicious moderate, or even
> conservative, judicial body should do.

G. Calabresi, "What Clarence Thomas Knows," New York Times, July 28, 1991,
§ 4, at 15 (passages rearranged).

104. Dean Calabresi was asking more of the Court in his comments supporting
(albeit equivocally) Clarence Thomas: "I would much rather have someone who
does stand out, who holds his or her *own* views, with which I deeply disagree but
who has somewhere, some time, experienced life and has been willing to stand up
against the pack. Better such a one than someone who will readily blend in and be
another anonymous vote for the activist and virulent views now so dominant on
the Court. For there is just a chance that such a one may stand up to the pack
again, and remind us all what it is like to be poor and friendless and to be facing
a hostile state." Id.

105. See Symposium, "Approaching Democracy: A New Legal Order for Eastern Europe," 58 U. Chicago L. Rev. 439–670 (1991).

106. Cf. Sager, note 98, at 955–56. "[W]henever I learn of great abuses of citizens at the hands of their state, I find myself wishing that a courageous and independent judiciary, with enough respect and authority to alter the course of events,
were in place, and I think our national experience justifies the optimism in the
judicial process implicit in that wish." Id. at 956. For a different, competing perspective, see G. Spann, "Pure Politics," 88 Michigan L. Rev. 1971 (1990) (arguing
that constitutional adjudication is majoritarian, not counter-majoritarian).

107. Posner, note 19, at 458. For a discussion of "the danger of intellectual
homogeneity on the [Supreme] Court", see D. Strauss & C. Sunstein, "The Senate, the Constitution, and the Confirmation Process," 101 Yale L. J. 1491, 1510–12
(1992). For a debate about the proper criteria for appointment to the Supreme
Court, compare S. Carter, "It Demeans the Court," New York Times, Apr. 28,
1993, at A13, to P. Gewirtz, "Legal Views Do Matter," New York Times, Apr. 28,
1993, at A13.

108. E. Burke, "Speech to the Electors of Bristol at the Conclusion of the Poll,
Nov. 3, 1774," in Edmund Burke on Government, Politics, and Society 157 (B.
Hill ed., 1976).

109. M. Shapiro, "Morality and the Politics of Judging," 63 Tulane L. Rev.
1555, 1585–86, 1588 (1989). (Professor Shapiro was commenting on chapter 6 of
my *Morality, Politics, and Law* (1988).)

Chapter 7

1. For a recent recounting, see J. Harrison, "Reconstructing the Privileges or Immunities Clause," 101 Yale L. J. 1385, 1401–10 (1992).

2. 12 Statutes 1268 (1863).

3. For an important recent discussion of the Thirteenth Amendment, see A. Amar & D. Wildawsky, "Child Abuse as Slavery: A Thirteenth Amendment Response to *DeShaney*," 105 Harvard L. Rev. 1359, 1364–72 (1992).

4. Laws of Mississippi, 1865, 82, 84, 166–67. This provision is quoted in E. Barrett, W. Cohen, & J. Varat, eds., Constitutional Law: Cases and Materials 22 (8th ed. 1989).

5. Id. at 23.

6. 16 Wall. (83 U.S.) 36, 70 (1872).

7. 14 Statutes 27.

8. See Harrison, note 1, at 1404.

9. However, removing doubt about the Congress's constitutional power to enact the 1866 Act was apparently not the only reason for proposing the Fourteenth Amendment. According to Earl Maltz, "the Fourteenth Amendment presented 'terms for the South' and was in essence both a peace treaty and part and parcel of the Republican political platform for the elections of 1866." Letter from E. Maltz to M. Perry, May 29, 1991.

10. Slaughter-House Cases, 16 Wall. (83 U.S.) 36, 73 (1872). In *Dred Scott v. Sandford*, 19 How. (60 U.S.) 393 (1857)—surely the single most infamous case in American constitutional law—the Supreme Court ruled, inter alia, that no "freeman" of African ancestry was a citizen of the United States within the meaning of the Constitution.

11. Raoul Berger has argued that, as originally understood, the second sentence does nothing but constitutionalize the 1866 Act. See R. Berger, Government by Judiciary: The Transformation of the Fourteenth Amendment (1977).

12. See chapter 3, note 48 and accompanying text.

13. See Harrison, note 1.

14. See pp. 128–29.

15. See Harrison, note 1, at 1433–51.

16. R. West, "Toward an Abolitionist Interpretation of the Fourteenth Amendment," 94 West Virginia L. Rev. 111, 139 (1991). See also Harrison, note 1, at 1437 & 1448.

17. See Yick Wo v. Hopkins, 118 U.S. 356, 369 (1886). For Harrison's argument against that construal, see Harrison, note 1, at 1390. But cf. id. at 1450: "The Equal Protection Clause . . . probably also imposes the equality requirement on the substance of a category of laws [i.e., "laws that protect conventional rights"] that was, in the nineteenth century, of fundamental importance. If [so], then the Equal Protection Clause overlaps the Privileges or Immunities Clause to a significant extent."

18. Speech of Senator Howard, May 23, 1866, Congressional Globe, 39th Congress, 1st Session, 2766 (1866).

19. However, even if the privileges or immunities clause and the equal protection clause overlap in governing discriminatory legislation, section 1 of the Fourteenth Amendment, as I explain below, was arguably meant to permit the states to discriminate between citizens and aliens in allocating *some* privileges—in particular, the privilege of owning property. See pp. 122–23.

20. Cf. Murray's Lessee v. Hoboken Land & Improvement Co., 59 U.S. 272,

276 (1856): "[The due process clause of the Fifth Amendment] is a restraint on the legislative as well as on the executive and judicial powers of the government. . . ."

21. See Harrison, note 1, at 1454.

22. J. Ely, Democracy and Distrust: A Theory of Judicial Review 25 (1980).

23. Id. Ely's position is strengthened if, as Kenneth Karst has noted, the framers of the Fourteenth Amendment made "no serious effort to differentiate the functions of the various clauses [of section 1]." K. Karst, "The Supreme Court, 1976 Term—Foreword: Equal Citizenship under the Fourteenth Amendment," 91 Harvard L. Rev. 1, 15 (1977). Cf. Berger, note 11, at 18: "The three clauses of [section 1] were three facets of one and the same concern. . . ."

24. Ely, note 22, at 25.

25. See, e.g., E. Maltz, Civil Rights, the Constitution, and Congress, 1863–69, 96–102 (1990) (clause meant to be limited to citizens). Cf. W. Nelson, The Fourteenth Amendment: From Political Principle to Judicial Doctrine (1988) (noting an interpretation according to which "what ultimately became section 1 was designed to give constitutional stature to a basic distinction in mid-nineteenth-century American law between the rights of aliens and the rights of citizens"). But see Berger, note 11, at 216–20 (clause not meant to be limited to citizens); compare E. Maltz, "The Constitution and Nonracial Discrimination: Alienage, Sex, and the Framers' Ideal of Equality," 7 Constitutional Commentary 251, 262 (1990) (disputing Berger's position).

26. See id. at 257–65; Harrison, note 1, at 1442–46.

27. Maltz, "The Constitution and Nonracial Discrimination," note 25, at 264 & 271.

28. See chapter 8, note 86.

29. For an affirmative answer, at least with respect to privileges and immunities that derive from state law (including state common law), see Harrison, note 1; see also note 60.

30. I do not mean to exclude the possibility that the equal protection clause was meant, like the privileges or immunities clause, to govern discriminatory legislation.

31. 16 Wall. (83 U.S.) 36 (1872).

32. See M. Curtis, No State Shall Abridge: The Fourteenth Amendment and the Bill of Rights 75 (1986) (quoting Blackstone). Incarceration is the paradigmatic deprivation of Blackstonian liberty.

33. Nelson, note 25, at 163.

34. See Harrison, note 1, at 1416–20.

35. 4 Wash. C.C. 371, 6 F. Cas. 546 (C.C.E.D. Pa. 1823).

36. Speech of Senator Howard, May 23, 1866, Congressional Globe, 39th Congress, 1st Session, 2765 (1866) (emphasis added). Cf. Ely, note 22, at 19: "The phrase 'life, liberty, and property' was [until recently] read as a unit [by the Court] and given an open-ended, functional interpretation, which meant that the government couldn't seriously hurt you without due process of law."

37. Quoted in the Slaughter-House Cases, 16 Wall. (83 U.S.) 36, 111 n. * (1872) (dissenting op'n).

38. See 16 Wall. (83 U.S.) 36, 79 (1872).

39. See Barron v. Mayor & City Council of Baltimore, 7 Pet. (32 U.S.) 243 (1833).

40. See generally A. Amar, "The Bill of Rights and the Fourteenth Amendment," 101 Yale L. J. 1193 (1992). Amar's argument in that regard builds on his

argument in an earlier essay: A. Amar, "The Bill of Rights as a Constitution," 100 Yale L. J. 1131 (1991). See also A. Amar, "The Creation and Reconstruction of the Bill of Rights," 16 Southern Illinois U. L. J. 337 (1992). Amar's argument about "the Bill of Rights as a Constitution" has been vigorously attacked. See P. Finkelman, "The Ten Amendments as a Declaration of Rights," 16 Southern Illinois U. L. J. 351 (1992); R. Palmer, "Akhil Amar: Elitist Populist and Anti-Textual Textualist," 16 Southern Illinois U. L. J. 397 (1992).

The establishment clause of the First Amendment ("Congress shall make no law respecting an establishment of religion"), unlike the free exercise clause discussed earlier in this book (see pp. 59–60), was arguably meant to be, not a privileges-or-immunities provision, the beneficiaries of which are individual citizens, but only a federalism provision—a provision allocating power between the national government and the governments of the states—the beneficiaries of which are the states, some of which had established churches, or might later want to establish them, and therefore feared congressional interference. Thus understood, the establishment clause, like the Tenth Amendment (and, if McAffee is right, like the Ninth; see pp. 63–66), only makes explicit a disability of the national government vis à vis the governments of the states; it does not establish or protect any privilege or immunity of individual citizens against the national government. For an impressive argument to that effect, see D. Conkle, "Toward a General Theory of the Establishment Clause," 82 Northwestern U. L. Rev. 1115, 1136–42 (1988). See also Note, "Rethinking the Incorporation of the Establishment Clause: A Federalist View," 105 Harvard L. Rev. 1700 (1992). Richard Aynes is skeptical of the position. See R. Aynes, "Charles Fairman and John Bingham's Not-So-'Singular' View of the Fourteenth Amendment and the Bill of Rights," 103 Yale L. J. (forthcoming, 1993).

41. U.S. Const., art. I, sec. 10, par. 1.

42. But not superfluous in another respect: Even with respect to federal constitutional privileges and immunities that exist independently of the Fourteenth Amendment—a category that includes some privileges and immunities against state government as well as several against the national government—section 5 of the Amendment makes explicit a congressional power to protect, against state government, a citizen's exercise of any of those privileges or her invocation of any of those immunities: "Congress shall have power to enforce by appropriate legislation the provisions of this article."

In the *Slaughter-House Cases*, the four dissenting Justices complained: "If [the privileges or immunities clause] . . . only refers, as held by [the majority], to such privileges and immunities as were before its adoption specifically designated in the Constitution or necessarily implied as belonging to citizens of the United States, it was a vain and idle enactment, which accomplished [nothing]. With privileges and immunities thus designated or implied no State could ever have interfered by its laws, and no new constitutional inhibition was required to inhibit such interference." 16 Wall. (83 U.S.) 36, 96 (1872). This complaint has force, however, only if we impute to the majority the view that the privileges or immunities clause merely forbids the states to interfere with a citizen's exercise of a federal constitutional privilege against the national government. The clause does not "accomplish nothing" on the majority's view of the clause if it was an element of the majority's view that the clause transformed the Bill of Rights privileges and immunities into privileges and immunities against state government. It is not clear, however, what the majority's position was in that regard. For opposing views of the *Slaughter-House* majority's position, compare G. Gunther, Constitutional Law 410 (12th ed. 1991), with Ely, note 22, at 196–97.

43. Amar, "The Bill of Rights and the Constitution," note 40, at 1237.

44. See Curtis, note 32. See also J. Baer, Equality under the Constitution: Reclaiming the Fourteenth Amendment (1983). Akhil Amar's recent work is powerfully confirmatory. See Amar, "The Bill of Rights and the Constitution," note 40. For additional recent confirmation, see Aynes, note 40. In a recent study, Earl Maltz has concluded:

> [T]here can be little doubt that the privileges and immunities clause was [meant] to [protect] *some* of the Bill of Rights. Republicans had constantly complained that slave-state governments had denied opponents of slavery freedom of speech, and both [Representative John A.] Bingham [of Ohio] and Governor Jacob Cox of Ohio referred directly to these concerns during arguments over ratification. Bingham also mentioned the right to teach the Bible—a clear appeal to the religion clauses. [Actually, a clear appeal not to the religion clauses, but to the free exercise clause. The other religion clause of the First Amendment— the establishment clause—presents a problem. See note 40.] Thus, the evidence impressively demonstrates that the basic guarantees of the First Amendment were understood to be included in the concept of privileges and immunities.

Maltz, Civil Rights, the Constitution, and Congress, 1863–69, note 25, at 117. Maltz continues that "[o]ther values from the Bill of Rights also figured prominently in the Reconstruction-era debates", including the Fifth Amendment's "no taking of property without just compensation", the Second Amendment's "right to keep and bear arms" ("Alabama and other rebellious states had denied blacks the right to bear arms" [Curtis, note 32, at 53]), the Eighth Amendment's "no cruel or unusual punishments". Maltz, Civil Rights, the Constitution, and Congress, 1863–69, note 25, at 117. "In short, one can only conclude that contemporaries must have understood the privileges and immunities clause to embody most of the Bill of Rights, and they probably viewed the first eight amendments as incorporated in their entirety." Id. at 117–18.

For the most prominent skeptical position on the question whether section 1 of the Fourteenth Amendment was meant to transform the Bill of Rights privileges and immunities into privileges and immunities against state government, see C. Fairman, "Does the Fourteenth Amendment Incorporate the Bill of Rights? The Original Understanding," 2 Stanford L. Rev. 5 (1949). Fairman was criticizing Justice Black's position, first articulated in his dissenting opinion in *Adamson v. California*, 332 U.S. 46, 105–7 (1977), that section 1 was meant to transform the Bill of Rights privileges and immunities into privileges and immunities against state government. Fairman provoked critics of his own. See W. Crosskey, "Charles Fairman, 'Legislative History,' and the Constitutional Limitations on State Authority," 22 U. Chicago L. Rev. 1 (1954); A. Kelly, "Clio and the Court: An Illicit Love Affair," 1965 Supreme Court Rev. 119. Fairman responded to Crosskey: "A Reply to Professor Crosskey," 22 U. Chicago L. Rev. 144 (1954). As Ely has pointed out, Fairman's argument has been, but ought not to be, confused with the distinct argument, which Fairman did not make, that section 1 was not meant to transform the Bill of Rights privileges and immunities into privileges and immunities against state government. Ely, note 22, at 195 n. 56. For a prominent skeptical position in addition to and more recent than Fairman's, see Berger, note 11, chap. 8. For one of Berger's many responses to one of his many critics, see R. Berger, "Incoporation and the Bill of Rights: A Response to Michael Zuckert," 26 Georgia L. Rev. 1 (1991).

It is sometimes claimed that Justice Black's position makes the due process clause of section 1 of the Fourteenth Amendment "superfluous" because the Fifth Amendment of the Bill of Rights contains a due process clause. See Ely, note 22, at 27; R. Posner, "Bork and Beethoven," 42 Stanford L. Rev. 1365, 1374 (1990). (Ely is nonetheless sympathetic to an affirmative answer: Ely, note 22, at 196–97 n. 59. Posner, however, is not: Posner, this note, at 1374.) For an effective response to the claim, see T. Bishop, "The Privileges or Immunities Clause of the Fourteenth Amendment: The Original Intent," 79 Northwestern U. L. Rev. 142, 166 n. 141 (1984). See also Amar, "The Bill of Rights and the Fourteenth Amendment," note 40, at 1224–26.

For an argument—by someone who rejects the position that the Ninth Amendment is merely a federalism provision—that the privileges and immunities of citizens protected against the national government by the Ninth Amendment should be understood as protected against state government by the Fourteenth, see L. Sager, "You Can Raise the First, Hide behind the Fourth, and Plead the Fifth. But What on Earth Can You Do with the Ninth Amendment?" 64 Chicago-Kent L. Rev. 239, 253–54 (1988). But cf. E. Maltz, "The Role of the Framers' Political Theory in Constitutional Adjudication," unpublished ms. at 22–23 (1991): "In modern parlance, 'Bill of Rights' does refer to the first ten amendments to the Constitution. During the Reconstruction era, by contrast, the understanding of the phrase seems to have been somewhat more limited. Both Representative John A. Bingham of Ohio and Senator Jacob Howard of Michigan—the two authorities relied upon most heavily by supporters of the incorporation theory—state that section 1 [of the Fourteenth Amendment] incorporated the first *eight* amendments. Thus incorporation theory would not seem to support the application of the ninth amendment to the states." For references to the Ninth Amendment in the legislative history of the Fourteenth Amendment, see Curtis, note 32, at 53 & 165.

Under well-settled constitutional doctrine, the most important Bill of Rights privileges and immunities are transformed by section 1 of the Fourteenth Amendment into privileges and immunities against state government. See Barrett et al., note 4, at 548–50.

45. Amar, "The Bill of Rights and the Fourteenth Amendment," note 40, at 1265–66. Amar continues: "An argument can also be made that major aspects of current Seventh Amendment doctrine may be driven by federalism concerns that should not be imposed on the states. If so, refined incorporation can offer a more principled basis for retaining one of the widely hailed pragmatic virtues of [Justice] Brennan's approach: namely, the refusal to require state courts in the late twentieth century to follow English civil jury rules circa 1791." Id. (Amar's argument about the "the Bill of Rights as a Constitution" has been vigorously criticized, however. See note 40.)

46. Slaughter-House Cases, 16 Wall. (83 U.S.) 36, 72 (1872).

47. See p. 118.

48. For John Ely's brief but effective critique of Raoul Berger's argument to the contrary, see Ely, note 22, at 199 n. 66.

49. See Nelson, note 25, at 138–39.

50. Id. at 163. The four dissenting Justices in the *Slaughter-House Cases*, but not the *Slaughter-House* majority, believed that the protected privileges and immunities were meant to be protected from discriminatory legislation beyond just racial discrimination. They did not think, however, that discrimination based on sex was constitutionally problematic. See 16 Wall. (83 U.S.) 36, 110 (1872): "To [citizens of the United States], everywhere, all pursuits, all professions, all avocations are open without other restrictions than such are imposed equally upon all others of the same age, sex, and condition." See also Strauder v. West Virginia, 100 U.S. 303, 310 (1880): "[A state] may confine the selection [of jurors] to males, to freeholders, to citizens, to persons within certain ages, or to persons having educational qualifications. We do not believe the Fourteenth Amendment was ever intended to prohibit this. Looking at its history, it is clear it had no such purpose. Its aim was against discrimination because of race or color. . . . We are not now called upon to affirm or deny that it had other purposes." In the next chapter, I present the originalist case for concluding that discrimination based on sex implicates, and sometimes violates, section 1 of the Fourteenth Amendment.

51. Congressional Globe, 39th Congress, 1st Session, 516 (1866) (statement of Rep. Eliot).

52. A. Avins, "Fourteenth Amendment Limitations on Banning Racial Discrimination: The Original Understanding," 8 Arizona L. Rev. 236, 246 (1967). Cf. M. Belknap, *Federal Law and Southern Order: Racial Violence and Constitutional Conflict in the Post-Brown South* 11 (1987): "Congress had written the Fourteenth Amendment following hearings at which its Joint Committee on Reconstruction took extensive testimony about the refusal of southern states to punish private wrongs against blacks, carpetbaggers, and unionists."

53. J. Baer, "Making Moderation an End in Itself: William Nelson's *Fourteenth Amendment*," 15 L. & Social Inquiry 321, 335 (1990).

54. Nelson, note 25, at 138–39. Cf. id. at 80: "Americans in 1866, like Americans of today, could all agree upon the rightfulness of equality only because they did not agree on its meaning, and their political leaders, unlike the managers of the modern bureaucratic state, were content to enact the general principle rather than its specific applications into law."

55. Cf. Dred Scott v. Sanford, 19 How. (60 U.S.) 393, 405, 407, 409 (1857): "[The negroes] were at that time considered as a subordinate and inferior class of beings, who . . . had no rights or privileges but such as those who held the power and the Government might choose to grant them. . . . They had for more than a century before been regarded as beings of an inferior order, and altogether unfit to associate with the white race . . . ; and so far inferior, that they had no rights which the white man was bound to respect; and that the negro might justly and lawfully be reduced to slavery for [the white man's] benefit. . . . [Whites]. . . looked upon [negroes] as so far below them in the scale of created beings, that intermarriages between white persons and negroes or mulattoes were regarded as unnatural and immoral, and punished as crimes. . . ."

56. The quoted words (without the emphasis) are those of the 1866 Act. See p. 118.

57. See id.

58. Nelson, note 25, at 150 (emphasis added).

59. Id. at 123.

60. This is Harrison's position—that is, his position with respect to the protected privileges and immunities we are presently discussing: those that do not

derive from the Bill of Rights or from any other federal source. See Harrison, note 1. Professor Amar has characterized Harrison's principal argument as follows: "[W]here a privilege or immunity derives not from the federal Constitution or Bill of Rights, but from common law or state law, the privileges or immunities clause prohibits only irrational discrimination in defining and enforcing these rights." Amar, "The Bill of Rights and the Fourteenth Amendment," note 40, at 1231. Amar then continues, in a footnote: "The language of the privileges or immunities clause can be understood as . . . two-tiered. Harrison's central textual argument is that the word 'abridge' can be read to prohibit mere discrimination in the allocation of state-created rights. . . . Where only state-law-created rights are at stake, this is a plausible—perhaps the most plausible—reading of the word 'abridge.' But where rights specified and declared by We the People in Our Constitution are at stake, the best understanding of the word 'abridge' in section 1 surely comes from its fundamental rights counterpart in the First Amendment, whose language section 1 so carefully tracks." Id. at 1231 n. 174. For Harrison's brief comments on the question of "incorporation of the Bill of Rights", see Harrison, note 1, at 1465–66; see also Nelson, note 25, at 115–19.

61. Ely, note 22, at 23.

62. See note 36 and accompanying text (emphasis added).

63. The Fifth Amendment provides, in relevant part: "No person shall . . . be deprived of life, liberty, or property, without due process of law. . . ."

64. See Harrison, note 1, at 1453: "[I]f, as seems likely, it derives from the 'law of the land' provision of Magna Carta, the Due Process Clause also refers to the principle of legality itself: the requirement that the government act only pursuant to law—the 'due process of law'—and not according to the whim of some official."

65. Note, however, that if the intended beneficiaries of the due process clause of the Fifth Amendment, which limits the national government, are only citizens, the intended beneficiaries of the due process clause of the Fourteenth Amendment, which limits state government, are all persons, noncitizens included. See Amar, "The Bill of Rights and the Fourteenth Amendment," note 40, at 1222–26.

What about "substantive", as distinct from "procedural", due process? See pp. 136–37.

66. If the available historical materials compelled the conclusion, John Harrison (for example) would have reached the conclusion, but they don't and he didn't. See Harrison, note 1.

67. Baer, note 53, at 324. Professor Baer cites, "on the right", Raoul Berger's *Government by Judiciary* (1977) and Chester J. Antieau's *The Original Understanding of the Fourteenth Amendment* (1981) and, "on the left", Michael Kent Curtis's *No State Shall Abridge: The Fourteenth Amendment and the Bill of Rights* (1986) and her own *Equality under the Constitution: Reclaiming the Fourteenth Amendment* (1983). Id.

68. Baer, note 53, at 341. For a fuller statement of Professor Baer's position about the difficulty of retrieving the original understanding of a constitutional provision, see J. Baer, "The Fruitless Search for Original Intent," in Judging the Constitution: Critical Essays on Judicial Lawmaking 49 (M. McCann & G. Houseman eds., 1989).

Chapter 8

1. R. Bork, The Tempting of America: The Political Seduction of the Law 180 (1989).

2. See pp. 121–22.

3. I am referring here to legislation other than legislation prescribing rules for the investigation, prosecution, or adjudication of cases, which is governed principally by the due process clause. See chapter 7, note 20 and accompanying text.

4. See pp. 120–22.

5. Notice that for one whose position is that only the privileges or immunities clause governs discriminatory legislation, there is a strong practical incentive to construe broadly, rather than narrowly, the category of privileges and immunities protected by the privileges or immunities clause: To construe them narrowly is to accept that there is much discriminatory legislation, including much racially discriminatory legislation, that does not implicate, much less violate, the clause, namely, discriminatory legislation that abridges a privilege or immunity not protected by the privileges of immunities clause. (Not that an originalist judge needs such an incentive. I argue below that an originalist judge should construe the category of protected privileges and immunities broadly rather than narrowly. See pp. 140–43.

6. See generally A. Amar, "The Bill of Rights and the Fourteenth Amendment," 101 Yale L. J. 1193 (1992). As I reported in chapter 7, Amar's argument about "the Bill of Rights as a Constitution" has been vigorously attacked. See chapter 7, note 40.

7. See Penn Central Transportation Co. v. New York City, 438 U.S. 104, 122 (1978) (in which the Court said that "of course" the takings clause of the Fifth Amendment ["nor shall private property be taken for public use, without just compensation"] "is made applicable to the States through the Fourteenth Amendment", citing Chicago, B. & Q. R. Co. v. Chicago, 166 U.S. 226 (1897)).

8. For a concise overview, see E. Barrett, W. Cohen, & J. Varat, eds., Constitutional Law: Cases and Materials 548–50 (8th ed. 1989).

9. See Amar, note 6.

10. See pp. 126–27.

11. C. Black, "'One Nation Indivisible': Unnamed Human Rights in the States," 65 St. John's L. Rev. 17, 55 (1991).

12. See pp. 84–86.

13. As I explained in the preceding chapter, the establishment clause of the First Amendment poses a special problem. See chapter 7, note 40.

14. Allgeyer v. Louisana, 165 U.S. 578, 589 (1897).

15. Meyer v. Nebraska, 262 U.S. 390, 399 (1923).

16. Poe v. Ullman, 367 U.S. 497, 543 (1961) (Harlan, J., dissenting).

17. See chapter 7, note 36.

18. See chapter 7, note 37.

19. See Speech of Senator Howard, May 23, 1866, Congressional Globe, 39th Congress, 1st Session, 2766 (1866): "The right of suffrage is not, in law, one of the privileges or immunities thus secured by the Constitution. It is merely the creature of law. It has always been regarded in this country as the result of positive local law. . . ." (Not that Howard did not want to extend the right of suffrage to freedmen. He did—passionately. But he despaired that a constitutional provision to that effect would be ratified. See id.) See also T. Bishop, "The Privileges or Immunities Clause of the Fourteenth Amendment: The Original Intent," 79 Northwestern U. L. Rev. 142, 151–57 (1984); E. Maltz, Civil Rights, the Constitution, and Congress, 1863–69, 118–20 (1990).

20. 377 U.S. 533 (1964).

21. 383 U.S. 663 (1966).

22. 395 U.S. 621 (1969).

23. 393 U.S. 23 (1968).

24. And, according to the Twenty-fourth Amendment, "The right of citizens of the United States to vote in any primary or other election for President or Vice-President, or for Senator or Representative in Congress, shall not be denied or abridged by the United States or by any State by reason of failure to pay any poll tax or other tax."

25. See J. Ely, Democracy and Distrust: A Theory of Judicial Review 7 (1980).

26. Cf. Cruzan v. Director, Missouri Department of Health, 497 U.S. 261, 300 (1990) (Scalia, J., concurring): "Are there, then, no reasonable and humane limits that ought not to be exceeded in requiring an individual to preserve his own life? There obviously are. . . . What assures us that those limits will not be exceeded is the same constitutional guarantee that is the source of most of our protection. . . . Our salvation is the Equal Protection Clause, which requires the democratic majority to accept for themselves and their loved ones what they impose on you and me. This Court need not, and has no authority to, inject itself into every field of human activity where irrationality and oppression may theoretically occur, and if it tries to do so it will destroy itself."

Justice Scalia's "equal protection" point restates (but does not cite) the central point of the "Conclusion" to John Ely's *Democracy and Distrust*. See Ely, note 25, at 181–83. For a critical response to Scalia's point, see L. Tribe & M. Dorf, "Levels of Generality in the Definition of Rights," 57 U. Chicago L. Rev. 1057, 1093–94 (1990).

27. See Michael H. v. Gerald D., 491 U.S. 110, 127 n. 6 (1989) (op'n of Scalia, J.). See also Cruzan v. Director, Missouri Department of Health, 497 U.S. 261, 300 (1990) (Scalia, J. concurring).

28. See, e.g., Moore v. City of East Cleveland, Ohio, 431 U.S. 494, 537 (1977) (Stewart, J., dissenting, joined by Rehnquist, J.).

29. In *Moore v. City of East Cleveland, Ohio,* Justice White commented critically on what he called Justice Stewart's "crabbed construction" of the freedoms protected by section 1. See 431 U.S. 494, 544–47 (White, J., dissenting).

30. See pp. 84–86.

31. For other examples, see pp. 59–61 (free exercise clause); pp. 156–59 (affirmative action).

32. The quoted words (without the emphasis) are those of the 1866 Civil Rights Act. See p. 118.

33. See Hirabayashi v. United States, 320 U.S. 81, 100 et seq. (1943); Korematsu v. United States, 323 U.S. 214, 216 (1944).

34. See In re Griffiths, 413 U.S. 717, 721–22 (1973): "The Court has consistently emphasized that a State which adopts a suspect classification 'bears a heavy burden of justification', a burden which, variously formulated, requires the State to meet certain standards of proof. In order to justify the use of a suspect classification, a State must show that its interest or purpose is both constitutionally permissible and substantial, and that its use of the classification is 'necessary [to] the accomplishment' of its purpose or the safeguarding of its interest." In a footnote attached to the word "substantial", the Court wrote: "The state interest required has been characterized as 'overriding', 'compelling', 'important', or 'substantial'. We attribute no particular significance to these variations in diction." Id. at 722 n. 9.

35. When the Court, in *Plessy v. Ferguson*, said, incredibly, that "[l]aws permit-

ting, and even requiring, [the] separation [of the races] in places where they are liable to be brought into contact do not necessarily imply the inferiority of either race to the other" (163 U.S. 537, 544 (1896)), the Court in effect acknowledged that laws that *do* "imply" racial inferiority are unconstitutional. See also 163 U.S. at 551: "We consider the underlying fallacy of the plaintiff's argument to consist in the assumption that the enforced separation of the two races stamps the colored race with a badge of inferiority."

36. Loving v. Virginia, 388 U.S. 1, 10 (1967).

37. 100 U.S. 303, 308 (1880).

38. The Court first made this point during World War II, in *Hirabayashi v. United States*. See 320 U.S. 81, 100 et seq. (1943).

39. Concurring in the judgment of the Court in *McLaughlin v. Florida*, Justice Stewart, joined by Justice Douglas, wrote: "[T]he Court implies that a criminal law of the kind here involved might be constitutionally valid if a State could show 'some overriding statutory purpose.' This is an implication in which I cannot [join]. [I] think it is simply not possible for a state law to be valid under our Constitution which makes the criminality of an act depend upon the race of the actor. Discrimination of that kind is invidious per se." 379 U.S. 184, 198 (1964).

40. See C. Madigan, "Racism Retains Its Malignant Hold: After Three Decades, Progress is Elusive," Chicago Tribune, May 10, 1992, 1, p. 1 (writing, in the wake of the Los Angeles riots of 1992, that "racism remains the nation's incurable malignancy"); C. Madigan, "Racial Stereotyping: An Old, Virulent Virus," Chicago Tribune, May 13, 1992, § 1, p. 1. See also A. Aleinikoff, "The Constitution in Context: The Continuing Significance of Racism," 63 U. Colorado L. Rev. 325 (1992); cf. R. Delgado, "A Comment on Aleinikoff," 62 U. Colorado L. Rev. 383 (1992).

41. 232 U.S. 214 (1944).

42. See also Hirabayashi v. United States, note 33.

43. 347 U.S. 483 (1954).

44. 388 U.S. 1.

45. R. Burt, The Constitution in Conflict 11–12 (1992).

46. See also pp. 42–46.

47. Cf. G. Bassham, Original Intent and the Constitution: A Philosophical Study 105 (1992): "The acid test of originalism, as indeed of any theory of constitutional adjudication, is its capacity to justify what is now almost universally regarded as the Supreme Court's finest hour: its decision in *Brown v. Board of Education*."

48. See G. Gunther, ed., Constitutional Law 652 n. 1 (12th ed. 1991).

49. 163 U.S. 537 (1896).

50. 163 U.S. at 562. See also id. at 569: "What can more certainly arouse race hate, what can more certainly create and perpetuate a feeling of distrust between these races, than state enactments, which, in fact, proceed on the ground that colored citizens are so inferior and degraded that they cannot be allowed to sit in public coaches occupied by white citizens?"

51. 388 U.S. at 11.

52. 347 U.S. 497 (1954).

53. 320 U.S. 81 (1943).

54. 323 U.S. 214 (1944). Justice Murphy's dissenting opinion argued that the military exclusion order at issue in *Korematsu* "goes over 'the very brink of constitutional power' and falls into the ugly abyss of racism." Id. at 233. Murphy then

claimed that in sustaining the order, the majority had participated in "the legalization of racism." Id. at 242.

55. See pp. 121–22.

56. See Bork, note 1, at 83–84.

57. See pp. 63–68.

58. Ely, note 25, at 33.

59. See chapter 4, note 39 and accompanying text.

60. Ely, note 25, at 105. Ely continues: "That theory has been the right one, that rights like these, whether or not they are explicitly mentioned, must nonetheless be protected, strenuously so, because they are critical to the functioning of an open and effective democratic process." Id.

61. Cf. Washington v. Davis, 426 U.S. 229 (1976).

62. Cf. Arlington Heights v. Metropolitan Housing Development Corp., 429 U.S. 252 (1977).

63. See pp. 149–52.

64. For the relevant materials, see G. Gunther, note 48, at 704–51.

65. See id. at 728–50. For the Court's most recent discourse in this area, see Freeman v. Pitts, 112 S. Ct. 1430 (1992).

66. I addressed aspects of the question years ago. See M. Perry, "Modern Equal Protection: A Conceptualization and Appraisal," 79 Columbia L. Rev. 1023, 1036–42 (1979). Cf. M. Perry, "The Disproportionate Impact Theory of Racial Discrimination," 125 U. Pennsylvania L. Rev. 540 (1976).

67. See Bork, note 1, at 326–31.

68. See Reed v. Reed, 404 U.S. 71 (1971).

69. The most important cases and other relevant materials are collected in all the constitutional law casebooks. See, e.g., Gunther, note 48, at 656–80 & 751–57.

70. 16 Wall. (83 U.S.) 36, 110 (1872) (emphasis added). For even more dramatic confirmation that distinctions based on sex were not thought constitutionally problematic by many persons in the generation that gave us the Fourteenth Amendment, see Justice Bradley's notorious opinion (joined by Justices Swayne and Field), which concurred in the Court's judgment (but not in the majority's reasoning) in *Bradwell v. Illinois*, 16 Wall. (83 U.S.) 130, 139–42 (1872). (*Bradwell* is the very next case in 16 Wall. (83 U.S.) after the *Slaughter-House Cases*.)

71. 100 U.S. 303, 310 (1880) (emphasis added).

72. United States Catholic Bishops, "Fourth Draft/Response to the Concerns of Women for Church and Society," 22 Origins 221, 224 (1992). Cf. P. Steinfels, "Pastoral Letter on Women's Role Fails in Vote of Catholic Bishops," New York Times, Nov. 19, 1992, at A1 (letter too liberal for some bishops, too conservative for others, failed to achieve required two-thirds support of bishops).

73. United States Catholic Bishops, note 72, at 224.

74. See id.: "This error and the sinful attitudes it generates represent, in fact, a radical distortion of the very order of creation. Unjust discrimination of this sort, whether subtle or overt, distorts interpersonal relations and adversely affects the social patterns and the modes of communication that influence day-to-day life in our world."

75. The amendment also provides that "Congress shall have the power to enforce this article by appropriate legislation."

76. See Frontiero v. Richardson, 411 U.S. 677, 682–88 (1973) (op'n of Brennan, J., joined by Douglas, White, & Marshall, JJ.).

77. M. Farley, "Sexism," New Catholic Encyclopedia (Supplement), vol. 17, 604 (1979).

78. See note 74.

79. 458 U.S. 718, 724 (1982).

80. Id. at 724–25. Thus, the modern Court's approach to governmental action that singles out women or men for worse treatment than the other receives is close to its approach to governmental action that singles out nonwhites for worse treatment than whites. While the standard of justification the Court employs in reviewing governmental action of the latter sort purports to be stricter than the standard it employs in reviewing governmental action of the former sort, the difference may be more rhetorical than real. It is doubtful, for example, that the distinction between governmental objectives that are "compelling" (as governmental objectives must be, under the strictest standard that governs discrimination against nonwhites) and those that are merely "important" (as they must be, under the so-called intermediate standard that governs discrimination against women or men) is administrable. Moreover, the Court does not even purport to administer the distinction. See note 34.

81. See pp. 177–79.

82. See pp. 177–79.

83. See pp. 79–80.

84. Clark v. Jeter, 486 U.S. 456, 461 (1988). See generally Gunther, note 48, at 688–93.

85. Cf. M. Stier, "Corruption of Blood and Equal Protection: Why the Sins of the Parents Should Not Matter," 44 Stanford L. Rev. 727 (1992).

86. The originalist case for the Court's practice of approaching differential treatment based on "national origin" just as it approaches race-based differential treatment (see, e.g., Hernandez v. Texas, 347 U.S. 475 (1974)) should be obvious. By contrast, the modern Court's approach to alienage-based differential treatment (see Gunther, note 48, at 680–88) cannot be justified on the basis of the originalist approach to the interpretation of section 1. But no matter, because the modern Court's solicitude for aliens *can* be justified on the basis of the supremacy clause of Article VI of the Constitution. See Perry, "Modern Equal Protection," note 66, at 1060–65. For more elaborate development of the point, see D. Levi, "The Equal Treatment of Aliens: Preemption or Equal Protection?," 31 Stanford L. Rev. 1069 (1979); R. Neff, "State Burdens on Resident Aliens: A New Preemption Analysis," 89 Yale L. J. 940 (1980).

87. Cannot fairly be understood to implicate, that is, either of the two basic dimensions of the antidiscrimination directive. See pp. 000–00.

88. See Gunther, note 48, at 608–35 & 694–701. For a more precise statement of the rational basis requirement, see note 95.

89. Nordlinger v. Hahn, 112 S. Ct. 2326, 2332 (1992).

90. See p. 131.

91. See Williamson v. Lee Optical Co., 348 U.S. 483 (1955).

92. See pp. 131–33.

93. 473 U.S. 432, 448 (1985). "[R]equiring the permit in this case appears to us to rest on an irrational prejudice against the mentally retarded. . . ." Id. at 450.

94. Given that it was mentally retarded persons who were singled out for worse treatment, the governmental action may have implicated, and violated, the antidiscrimination directive.

95. See Nordlinger v. Hahn, 112 S. Ct. 2326, 2332 (1992): "In general, [this test] is satisfied so long as there is a plausible policy reason for the classification, . . . the legislative facts on which the classification is apparently based rationally may have been considered to be true by the governmental decisionmaker, . . . and the relationship of the classification to its goal is not so attenuated as to render the distinction arbitrary or irrational."

96. It is a matter of controversy whether in cases in which discriminatory state action is challenged on the basis of section 1 of the Fourteenth Amendment the modern Court's rational basis inquiry has sometimes been so deferential as to constitute virtually no inquiry at all. For some relevant materials bearing on the question, see Gunther, note 48, at 617–22. The Court's decision in *Cleburne* indicates—as do many state court decisions (see, e.g., Stephenson v. Sugar Creek Packing, 250 Kan. 768 (Kansas Supreme Court, 1992))—that in such cases rational basis inquiry is alive and sometimes, though not always, well.

97. Or, from the other side: governmental action singling out whites for worse treatment than nonwhites.

98. "The public interest in broadcast diversity—like the interest in an integrated police force, diversity in the composition of a public school faculty or diversity in the student body of a professional school—is in my view unquestionably legitimate." Metro Broadcasting, Inc. v. FCC, 497 U.S. 547, 601–2 (1990) (Stevens, J., concurring).

99. See DeFunis v. Odegaard, 416 U.S. 312 (1974). For the relevant cases and other materials, see Gunther, note 48, at 757–819.

100. In *Metro Broadcasting, Inc. v. FCC* (1990), five members of the Court, in a opinion by Justice Brennan, upheld "certain minority preference policies of the Federal Communications Commission [FCC]" against a claim that the policies violated "the equal protection component of the Fifth Amendment". 497 U.S. 547, 552 (1990). (Formally, *Metro Broadcasting* was a Fifth Amendment decision; substantively, it was a Fourteenth Amendment decision. I have already explained why it would make more sense for the Court to base a decision like *Metro Broadcasting* on the Ninth Amendment rather than on the Fifth Amendment. See pp. 146–47.) "The policies in question", as described by the Court, were "(1) a program awarding an enhancement for minority ownership in comparative proceedings for new licenses, and (2) the minority 'distress sale' program, which permits a limited category of existing radio and television broadcast stations to be transferred only to minority-controlled firms." 497 U.S. at 552.

101. See Richmond v. J. A. Croson Co., 488 U.S. 469 (1989).

102. Affirmative action is certainly not predicated on any religious, political, cultural, etc., hostility either to the disfavored whites or to the favored nonwhites.

103. Richmond v. J. A. Croson Co., 488 U.S. 469, 524 (1989) (Scalia, J., concurring in judgment).

104. See pp. 130–31.

105. That the Civil Rights Act of 1866 prohibited several instances of the singling out of nonwhites for worse treatment than "white citizens" received without ever mentioning any prohibited bases is not to the contrary: As I explained both in the preceding chapter and earlier in this chapter, because the instances of singling out for worse treatment prohibited by the 1866 Act were all conspicuously based on white-supremacist ideology, there was no need to suggest that the instances were unlawful only if based on white-supremacist ideology.

106. This is not the only time Justice Scalia's originalism seems to have been trumped by his conception of judicial role or by his political morality. See pp. 59–61 and p. 143.

107. See pp. 84–86.

108. Cf. Employment Division, Oregon Department of Human Resources v. Smith, 494 U.S. 872, 886 n. 3 (1990) (op'n of Court, per Scalia, J.).

109. D. Chang, Discriminatory Impact, Affirmative Action, and Innocent Victims: Judicial Conservatism or Conservative Justices?," 91 Columbia L. Rev. 790, 831 (1991). See id.:

> Concern for the "innocent white victim" of affirmative action addressed explicitly in *Wygant* [*v. Jackson Board of Education*, 476 U.S. 267 (1986)] as a basis for invalidating an affirmative action program is implicitly reflected in the conditions that [several Justices] develop in [*Richmond v. J. A. Croson Co.*, 488 U.S. 469 (1989)] for restrictively defining when the purpose of redressing the effects of past racial discrimination is permissible. These conditions have nothing to do with determining whether the government acted because of impermissible racial animus, favoritism, or stereotype. They have everything to do with whether individual Justices views the state's redefinition of policies allocating public goods as wise or "fair." Political conservatism, rather than judicial conservatism, pervades the Court's restrictions on legislative discretion to redress the effects of past racial discrimination.

110. See pp. 84–86.

111. F. Easterbrook, "Abstraction and Authority," 59 U. Chicago L. Rev. 349, 377 (1992).

112. Richmond v. J. A. Croson Co., 488 U.S. 469, 493 (1989) (op'n of O'Connor, J., joined by Rehnquist, C.J., and White & Kennedy, JJ.).

113. See Williamson v. Lee Optical Co., 348 U.S. 483 (1955).

114. See chapter 7, note 36 and accompanying text.

115. See p. 105.

116. J. Ely, "The Constitutionality of Reverse Racial Discrimination," 41 U. Chicago L. Rev. 723, 735 (1974).

117. See Perry, "Modern Equal Protection," note 66, at 1043–50. See also Metro Broadcasting, Inc. v. FCC, 497 U.S. 547, 603–10 (1990) (O'Connor, J., dissenting, joined by Rehnquist, C.J., and Scalia & Kennedy, JJ.). Of course, if a particular affirmative action program is predicated on the supposed moral inferiority of one racial group to another, the program violates the antidiscrimination directive of section 1.

118. Metro Broadcasting, Inc. v. FCC, 497 U.S. 547, 564–65 (1990). Justice O'Connor, speaking for four members of the Court (all four of whom remain), argued that the strictest standard should govern—that "to be upheld, [even benign] racial classifications must be determined to be necessary and narrowly tailored to achieve a compelling state interest." Id. at 603 (dissenting op'n).

119. May an originalist judge, especially one with minimalist inclinations, proceed on the basis of what Alex Kozinski has called "pessimism"?

> Were racial discrimination always irrational, colorblindness wouldn't be very controversial. But there are times when the argument for color-consciousness is plausible: imposing colorblindness in those cases seems an extravagance. . . . [W]hy [in those cases] should an abstract principle

stand in the way? The answer to this question depends on whether you're an optimist or a pessimist. If you believe the branches of government, working together, can implement only (or mostly) the good race classifications and reject the bad ones, colorblindness will be at most an aspiration, a principle to be generally followed but scuttled when necessary. But if you're skeptical about the competence of lawmakers and judges in this area, you will choose colorblindness as a nearly ironclad prophylactic rule, to be breached only at great peril.

A. Kozinski, "Color and Caution," New Republic, Feb. 1, 1993, 72, 74 (reviewing A. Kull, The Color-Blind Constitution (1992)).

120. See pp. 166–67. My analysis of sex-based affirmative action, were I to articulate it here, would be analogous to my analysis of race-based affirmative action. For some relevant cases and other materials on sex-based affirmative action, see Gunther, note 48, at 751–57.

Chapter 9

1. Cf. Poe v. Ullman, 367 U.S. 497, 543 (1961) (Harlan, J., dissenting) (Fourteenth Amendment protects "a freedom from all substantial arbitrary impositions and purposeless restraints").

2. See pp. 170–71.

3. 198 U.S. 45 (1905).

4. Two important and related exceptions are *Meyer v. Nebraska*, 262 U.S. 390 (1923), and *Pierce v. Society of Sisters*, 268 U.S. 510 (1925).

5. See pp. 140–41.

6. 198 U.S. at 53.

7. Id. at 56.

8. Id. at 57.

9. See note 7 and accompanying text.

10. 198 U.S. at 59.

11. B. Ackerman, We the People: Foundations 64 (1991).

12. Ackerman develops the argument at various places in his book. See, e.g., id. at 100–101. See also P. Brest & S. Levinson, eds., Processes of Constitutional Decisionmaking 234 (2d ed. 1983):

> The received history tends to exaggerate the Court's perverseness [during the *Lochner* era], . . . just as it minimizes the facts that the Court sustained at least as many regulations as it invalidated, that it declined to review many others, and that Holmes and Brandeis—the progressive heroes of the period—did not invariably dissent from substantive due process invalidations or always agree with each other. The Court was considerably more constrained than some of the state supreme courts, and though it certainly never "judged social legislation on the basis of any consistent pattern of ideas which can properly bear the name of an economic theory," its decisions gain some coherence if one reads them in the context of the ideologies of the time.

(Quoting L. Friedman, "Freedom of Contract and Occupational Licensing: 1890–1920," 53 California L. Rev. 487, 525 (1965).)

13. T. Sandalow, "Abstract Democracy: A Review of Ackerman's *We the People*," 9 Constitutional Commentary 309, 333 (1992). See id. at 333–34. Cf. M. Klar-

man, "Constitutional Fact/Constitutional Fiction: A Critique of Bruce Ackerman's Theory of Constitutional Moments," 44 Stanford L. Rev. 759, 791–92 (1992) (Ackerman implausibly "portray[s] the *Lochner* era as one of unmitigated laissez-faire").

14. 198 U.S. at 75–76 (Holmes, J., dissenting).

15. See G. Gunther, ed., Constitutional Law 449–53 (12th ed. 1991).

16. See id. at 453–61.

17. 198 U.S. at 72 (emphasis added).

18. 198 U.S. at 76.

19. I am not referring here to judicial protection of a Bill of Rights privilege or immunity against a state. As I said in chapter 7, a state law regulating such a privilege or immunity—a privilege or immunity citizens have against the national government under the Bill of Rights, transformed by the privileges or immunities clause into a privilege or immunity citizens have against state government as well, and protected from the same threats from which it is protected (against the national government) by the Bill of Rights—is not reasonable if the law, were it a federal law, would be unconstitutional. See pp. 126–27. (There is, however, a proviso—as I noted earlier. See chapter 7, note 40 and accompanying text.) I am referring, rather, to judicial protection of a privilege or immunity other than those that derive from the Bill of Rights or from some other federal source.

20. Cf. A. Bickel, The Morality of Consent 26 (1975) (Court should be "mindful of the dominant role the political institutions are allowed, and always anxious . . . to invent compromises and accommodations").

21. See especially J. Harrison, "Reconstructing the Privileges or Immunities Clause," 101 Yale L. J. 1485 (1992).

22. See pp. 79–80.

23. See pp. 144–45.

24. See pp. 177–79.

25. See, e.g., J. Ely, Democracy and Distrust: A Theory of Judicial Review, chap. 6 (1980). See also G. Calabresi, "Foreword: Antidiscrimination and Constitutional Accountability (What the Bork-Brennan Debate Ignores)," 105 Harvard L. Rev. 80 (1991)

26. See pp. 187–88.

27. 291 U.S. 502 (1934).

28. 300 U.S. 379 (1937).

29. It is reported that during "the *Lochner* era" the Supreme Court invalidated approximately two hundred laws in the name of the due process clause of the Fourteenth Amendment. See G. Stone, L. Seidman, C. Sunstein, & M. Tushnet, eds., Constitutional Law 726 (1986).

30. See, e.g., Olsen v. Nebraska, 313 U.S. 236 (1941); Lincoln Federal Labor Union v. Northwestern Iron & Metal Co., 335 U.S. 525 (1949); Williamson v. Lee Optical Co., 348 U.S. 483 (1955).

31. See, e.g., R. McCloskey, "Economic Due Process and the Supreme Court: An Exhumation and Reburial," 1962 Supreme Court Rev. 34. For some relevant materials, see Gunther, note 15, at 457–65.

32. That is, some legislation that abridges a protected privilege or immunity, which, again, virtually all legislation does.

33. Cf. Note, "Resurrecting Economic Rights: The Doctrine of Economic Due Process Reconsidered," 103 Harvard L. Rev. 1363 (1990).

34. See R. Epstein, "The Mistakes of 1937," 11 George Mason U. L. Rev. 5, 17 (Winter 1988); see also Note, note 33, at 1373. I am grateful to my colleague Gary

Lawson for calling to my attention the point about the background of the law
invalidated in *Lochner*.

35. Moore v. City of East Cleveland, Ohio, 431 U.S. 494, 503 (1977) (plurality
op'n; Powell, J., joined by Brennan, Marshall, & Blackmun, JJ.) (quoting Griswold
v. Connecticut, 381 U.S. 479, 501 (1965) (Harlan, J., concurring)).

36. See 431 U.S. at 542–44 (White, J., dissenting).

37. For an important exception, see Cruzan v. Director, Missouri Department
of Health, 497 U.S. 261 (1990).

38. 381 U.S. 479 (1965).

39. Id. at 480.

40. Unless, of course, the mistakes violate the Constitution.

41. Id. at 505 (White, J., concurring in judgment).

42. Id. at 498.

43. Id. at 507.

44. Id. at 505.

45. See R. Posner, Sex and Reason 326 (1992).

46. Cf. id.: "Although most states placed some restrictions on contraceptives,
for example by permitting only licensed pharmacies to sell them to the consumer,
only Massachusetts had a statute like Connecticut's, attempting to ban the use of
contraceptives. These statutes owed their survival to the power of the Catholic
Church in Massachusetts and Connecticut. It is true that the statutes were not
Catholic in origin. Comstockery was not a Catholic movement; it was in fact anti-
Catholic. But by the 1960s most Protestants had swung around from opposition to
birth control to support for it. Now, among major sects at any rate, only the
Catholic Church and loyal Catholic parishioners supported the Connecticut
statute." It is not clear what Judge Posner means by "loyal Catholic parishioners".
In any event, notwithstanding that the "official" position of the Catholic
Church—that is, the position of the Vatican—still opposes "artificial" contraception, there is relatively little moral opposition to artificial contraception even
among churchgoing Catholics in the United States today.

47. There is, however, a serious question whether if the only reason for thinking that conduct is immoral is religious, government may, consistent with the
establishment clause of the First Amendment, outlaw the conduct. For a discussion, see M. Perry, Love and Power: The Role of Religion and Morality in American Politics 112–22 (1991).

48. Barnes v. Glen Theatre, Inc., 111 S. Ct. 2456, 2465 (1991) (concurring in
judgment).

49. 367 U.S. 497, 547 (1961) (dissenting).

50. Posner, note 45, at 300. However, even if a legislator could reasonably
believe that the effects probably cancel out, the proposition seems dubious. As
Posner himself reports, "the Swedish experience suggests otherwise." Id. And, as
Posner suggests just three lines later, "[Although there] are good reasons for
wanting to deter unwanted pregnancies, . . . that aim is *more likely* to be achieved
by encouraging rather than by discouraging the use of contraceptives." Id.
(emphasis added). Moreover, among teenagers and young adults it does not seem
likely that there would be significantly less sexual intercourse because of an anticontraception statute. Posner makes the point when, in commenting critically on
a Massachusetts ban on the distribution of contraceptives to minors, he writes:
"The law might deter some girls from engaging in intercourse, but to the extent
that deterrence failed, the adverse consequences would be more severe on the

whole under the Massachusetts ban. Moreover, deterrence was likely to fail. Teenagers are on average more impulsive, hence on average less responsive to incentives, than adults are. . . . They are less mature, and one badge of maturity or experience is the ability to reckon up the full consequences of a proposed course of action." Id. at 331–32.

51. 405 U.S. 238 (1972).

52. 410 U.S. 113 (1973)

53. 478 U.S. 186, 188 n. 1 (1986).

54. Id.

55. Commonwealth [of Kentucky] v. Wasson, 842 S.W.2d 487, 499–501 (Ky. 1992) (emphasis added). "With *Wasson*, the Kentucky Supreme Court became the highest state court to extend privacy protection to homosexual sodomy since *Bowers v. Hardwick*. More importantly, *Wasson* broke from the trend of other courts and recognized homosexuals as a 'separate and identifiable class' for equal protection purposes." Case Comment, 106 Harvard L. Rev. 1370, 1373 (1993).

56. See note 66 and accompanying text.

57. 478 U.S. at 219.

58. Unlike the United States Supreme Court, some state courts have been been willing to invalidate (on the basis of state constitutions) laws criminalizing homosexual sexual activity. For decisions by the highest appellate court of a state, see New York v. Onofre, 415 N.E.2d 936 (N.Y. 1980); Pennsylvania v. Bonadio, 415 A.2d 47 (Pa. 1980); Kentucky v. Wasson, 842 S.W.2d 487 (Ky. 1992). Recent decisions by a lower court of a state include: Texas v. Morales, 826 S.W.2d 201 (Tex. Ct. App., 3d Dist., 1992); Michigan Organization for Human Rights v. Kelley, No. 88–815820 (Wayne County Cir. Ct., July 9, 1990). Cf. Jantz v. Muci, 759 F. Supp. 1543 (D. Kan. 1991) (homosexuals are a suspect class for purposes of equal protection analysis). (Judge Posner cites *Jantz v. Muci* as a *counterexample* to his "generalization about judges' [lack of] knowledge [about things sexual]". Posner, note 45, at 347 n. 55.) See generally J. Morris, "Challenging Sodomy Statutes: State Constitutional Protections for Sexual Privacy," 66 Indiana L. J. 609 (1991).

Moreover, the European Court of Human Rights has ruled that legislation criminalizing homosexual sexual activity violates the European Convention on Human Rights. See Dudgeon v. United Kingdom, 45 Eur. Ct. H.R. (ser. A) (1981); Norris v. Ireland, 142 Eur. Ct. H.R. (ser. A) (1988). See also M. Dubber, "Homosexual Privacy Rights before the United States Supreme Court and the European Court of Human Rights: A Comparison of Methodologies," 27 Stanford J. International L. 189 (1990).

59. See G. Bradley, "Remaking the Constitution: A Critical Examination of the *Bowers v. Hardwick* Dissent," 25 Wake Forest L. Rev. 501 (1990); see also G. Bradley, "The Constitution and the Erotic Self," First Things, Oct. 1991, 28.

60. 842 S.W.2d at 501.

61. See chapter 8, note 72 and accompanying text.

62. See pp. 96–98 (on the "holistic" conception of rationality). Cf. J. Meiland & M. Krausz, eds., Relativism: Cognitive and Moral 4 (1982): "[J]ust as our ordinary conception of truth allows a person to hold beliefs which are false, so too the notion of relative truth must allow an individual to hold beliefs which are false *for him* or *her*. If it were not possible for an individual to hold beliefs which were false for him or her, then the notion of relative truth would be superfluous; for then to

say that a belief is true for Jones would only be a roundabout way of saying that it was one of Jones' beliefs. And we do not need a new way of saying *that*."

63. D. Greschner & K. Norman, "The Courts and Section 33," 12 Queen's L. J. 155, 171 (1987) (citing D. Fehrenbacher, Slavery, Law, and Politics 274 et seq. [1981]).

64. Watkins v. U. S., Army, 875 F.2d 699, 718 (9th Cir. 1989) (Norris, J., concurring in judgment).

65. I realize that the distinction between the normative and the factual poses deep problems—which I cannot pursue here. But it seems to me that, for present purposes, the least controversial move is to assume, as I've been doing, that the question whether a particular trait is relevant to one's status or worth as a human being is more a "normative" question than a "factual" (or "empirical") one: To say that a particular trait is not, or is, relevant to one's status or worth as a human being is to say how broadly, or how narrowly, we should draw the bounds of human community; it is to say what about persons and their lives should and should not matter to us—and how it should and should not matter. "Moral" and "religious" thought have traditionally addressed such matters more than has "science".

66. Posner, note 45, at 346 (emphasis added).

67. 410 U.S. 113 (1973).

68. 347 U.S. 483 (1954).

69. R. Cover, "The Origins of Judicial Activism in the Protection of Minorities," unpublished ms. (1979). See also G. Lynch, Book Review, 63 Cornell L. Rev. 1091, 1099 n. 32 (1983): "[T]o most lawyers of my generation, *Brown* is a touchstone for constitutional theory fully as powerful as *Lochner* was for a previous generation."

70. C. Black, Decision According to Law 33 (1981).

71. See, e.g., H. Wechsler, "Toward Neutral Principles of Constitutional Law," 73 Harvard L. Rev. 1 (1959).

72. See D. Bell, "*Brown v. Board of Education* and the Interest-Convergence Dilemma," 93 Harvard L. Rev. 518, 519 (1980).

73. See, e.g., M. Yudof, "School Desegregation: Legal Realism, Reasoned Elaboration, and Social Science Research in the Supreme Court," 42 L. & Contemporary Problems 57, 69–70 (1978).

74. G. Bassham, Original Intent and the Constitution: A Philosophical Study 105 (1992).

75. G. Gunther, "Some Reflections on the Judicial Role: Distinctions, Roots, and Prospects," 1979 Washington U. L. Q. 817, 819.

76. See J. Ely, "The Wages of Crying Wolf: A Comment on *Roe v. Wade*," 82 Yale L. J. 920 (1973).

77. Ely, note 25.

78. Just as Alexander Bickel's *The Least Dangerous Branch* (1962) was the most important contribution to constitutional theory in the twenty years after *Brown*.

79. See R. Posner, "Legal Reasoning from the Top Down and from the Bottom Up: The Question of Unenumerated Constitutional Rights," 59 U. Chicago L. Rev. 433, 448 (1991): "[S]tatutes forbidding contraceptives had been passed in a wave in the late nineteenth century but had been repealed in all but two states, Connecticut and Massachusetts, in both of which repeal, though repeatedly attempted, had been blocked by the vigorous lobbying of the Catholic Church working on the large Catholic population in both states."

80. R. Colker, Abortion & Dialogue: Pro-Choice, Pro-Life, and American Law

123 (1992) (emphasis in original). On the Louisiana statute, see id. at 123–24, 158–62, 163–75. Professor Colker's book is essential reading, in my view, for all who are interested in the problem of abortion.

81. 112 S. Ct. 2791, 2803 (1992).

82. Cf. Posner, note 45, at 336: "There is no problem with describing a prohibition against abortion as a deprivation of a pregnant woman's liberty. . . ."

83. See 410 U.S. at 153.

84. Posner, note 45, at 337.

85. 410 U.S. at 155.

86. See pp. 144–45.

87. See pp. 131–33.

88. See M. Perry, Morality, Politics, and Law 172–78 (1988). See also G. Calabresi, note 25, at 146–48; C. Sunstein, "Neutrality in Constitutional Law (With Special Reference to Pornography, Abortion, and Surrogacy)," 92 Columbia L. Rev. 1, 29–44 (1992).

89. See pp. 148–49.

90. See P. Brest, "Foreword: In Defense of the Antidiscrimination Principle," 90 Harvard L. Rev. 1 (1976).

91. 442 U.S. 256, 279 (1979).

92. See M. McConnell, "The Selective Funding Problem: Abortion and Religious Schools," 104 Harvard L. Rev. 989, 1042 (1991): "[W]omen . . . are more—not less—likely than men to support restrictions on abortion." (Citing H. Rodman et al., The Abortion Question 141–43 (1987).)

93. See Posner, note 79, at 443.

94. See Sunstein, note 88, at 37.

95. McConnell, note 92, at 1042.

96. According to Judge Posner, "For many opponents of abortion, opposition to abortion is part and parcel of opposition to a broader set of practices and values—call it feminism. . . . Should the Supreme Court take sides between feminism and antifeminism?" Posner, note 45, at 340. If by "antifeminism" we mean a constellation of beliefs, attitudes, etc., rooted in and representing the conviction or sensibility that a person's sex is relevant to her status as a human being, then yes, the Court *should* take sides—against antifeminism, i.e., against it *as a predicate for state action*—because, unless the Court accepts that a person's sex is relevant to her status as a human being, enforcement of the antidiscrimination directive requires that it do so. See p. 152. (Posner asks if we can rightly "call antiabortion laws even prima facie discriminatory against women if in fact they help some women and hurt others?" Posner, note 45, at 341. But even a law that "helps some women and hurts others" can be predicated on the view that a person's sex is relevant to her status as a human being.)

97. M. Hirsley, "Presbyterians Shift to Middle on Abortion," Chicago Tribune, June 9, 1992, § 1, p. 4.

98. Posner, note 79, at 443 (emphasis added).

99. Cf. Ely, note 77, at 138: "[I]t will be next to impossible for a court responsibly to conclude that a position was affected by an unconstitutional motivation whenever it is possible to articulate a plausible legitimate explanation for the action taken. But what does that prove? Only that it often will not be possible responsibly to conclude that the challenged action was the product of unconstitutional motivation, not that the inquiry should not be undertaken."

100. 417 U.S. 484 (1974).

101. See McConnell, note 92, at 1041–42.

102. Cf. note 95 and accompanying text.

103. The Court has already concluded that sex is not relevant to a person's status as a human being.

104. See note 25 and accompanying text.

105. The Court's decision in *Planned Parenthood of Southeastern Pennsylvania v. Casey*, 112 S. Ct. 2791 (1992)—which sustained several regulations of abortions that, under "the essential holding of *Roe v. Wade*" (reaffirmed by the Court in *Casey*, id. at 2803), no state may disallow—is consistent with the antidiscrimination argument I have offered here.

106. In the companion case to *Roe*—*Doe v. Bolton*, 410 U.S. 179 (1973)—the Supreme Court invalidated a modern Georgia abortion statute that, while restrictive, was nonetheless more moderate than the much older Texas legislation invalidated in *Roe*. The Texas legislation provided for only one exception: an abortion for the purpose of saving the life of the mother. The Georgia statute, by contrast—which was enacted in 1968 and "patterned upon the American Law Institute's Model Penal Code" (410 U.S. at 182)—provided for three exceptions: an abortion where "(1) [a] continuation of the pregnancy would endanger the life of the pregnant woman or would seriously and permanently injure her health; or (2) [t]he fetus would very likely be born with a grave, permanent, and irremediable mental or physical defect; or (3) [t]he pregnancy resulted from forcible or statutory rape." Id. at 183. (The Court "was assured by the State at reargument that . . . the statute's reference to 'rape' was intended to include incest." Id. at 183 n. 5.) It is much more difficult to conclude that restrictive abortion statutes like Georgia's would not exist but for sex selective sympathy and indifference, given the three exceptions for which such statutes provide. (In *Roe* the Court noted that "[f]ourteen states have adopted some form of the ALI statute." The Court also noted that "[b]y the end of 1970, four other states had repealed criminal penalties for abortions performed in early pregnancy by a licensed physician. . . ." 410 U.S. at 140 n. 37.) Thus, the Court's decision in *Doe* is more difficult to defend than would be a decision striking down restrictive abortion legislation only to the extent it failed to provide for one or more of the three exceptions.

107. Because it would require something I am not prepared to essay here—namely, an interpretation of the religion clauses of the First Amendment—I do not address Ronald Dworkin's recent argument that the Court's decision in *Roe* is required, *inter alia*, by the First Amendment (applicable to the states, Dworkin assumes, under the Fourteenth Amendment). See R. Dworkin, "Unenumerated Rights: Whether and How *Roe* Should Be Overruled," 59 U. Chicago L. Rev. 381 (1992). (Dworkin has elaborated the argument in his new book. See R. Dworkin, Life's Dominion: An Argument about Abortion, Euthanasia, and Individual Freedom (1993).) But I do want to indicate that I find the argument unpersuasive. It does not violate the religious liberty protected by the Constitution for the people of a state (a majority of them) to decide that because unborn human life, even at an early stage of development, is sacred, no one should be permitted to destroy it—except to save or to protect another human life. On no plausible construal of the establishment clause of the First Amendment does the clause disable government from predicating liberty-restricting laws on (and only on) the premise that human life is sacred. Cf. M. Perry, "Religious Morality and Political Choice: Further Thoughts—and Second Thoughts—on *Love and Power*," 9 U. San Diego L. Rev. (forthcoming, 1993). And on no plausible construal of the free exercise

clause of the First Amendment does the clause protect the liberty of persons to destroy a human life (for some reason other than to save or to protect another human life), the sacredness of which—if it is sacred—does not depend on whether the human life is yet "sentient" or not, or yet a bearer of "interests" in the way sentient creatures are bearers of interests. Cf. M. Perry, note 47, at 117–18.

108. See chapter 8, note 1 and accompanying text.

109. See R. Bork, The Tempting of America: The Political Seduction of the Law 101–10 (1989) (affirmative action); id. at 111–16 (abortion).

110. See id. at 329.

111. See id. at 116–26.

112. As it obviously misled the folks whose words of praise adorn the dust jacket of Bork's book, including Allan Bloom, Charles Krauthammer, and George F. Will.

113. See chapter 1, note 30 and accompanying text.

114. There is an important group of cases I have not discussed in either this or the preceding chapter, the cases usually collected, by authors of constitutional law casebooks, under a heading like "The Fundamental Rights and Interests Strand of Equal Protection". See, e.g., Gunther, note 15, at 819 et seq. In the main, the results in those cases are not problematic from the perspective of originalism. In particular:

1. The results in *Reynolds v. Sims*, 377 U.S. 533 (1964), *Harper v. Virginia Board of Elections*, 383 U.S. 663 (1967), and their progeny are best understood as resting on a proportionality analysis under the reasonableness directive of section 1. For a recent, clear statement by the Court that what I am calling a proportionality analysis governs "right to vote" cases, see Burdick v. Takushi, 112 S. Ct. 2059, 2062–64 (1992). Cf. pp. 141–42.

2. The same is true about the results in *Griffin v. Illinois*, 351 U.S. 12 (1956), *Boddie v. Connecticut*, 401 U.S. 371 (1971), and similar cases. (Thus, *Reynolds*, *Harper*, *Griffin*, and *Boddie* have more in common with "substantive due process" than with "equal protection" cases. Cf. Griffin, 351 U.S. at 34–39 (Harlan, J., dissenting, joined by Stewart, J.).) But the result in *Douglas v. California*, 372 U.S. 353 (1963)—a case usually allied with *Griffin*—is best understood as resting on a (generous) specification of the assistance of counsel directive of the Sixth Amendment, made applicable to the states by section 1 of the Fourteenth Amendment. (Thus, *Douglas* is better allied with *Gideon v. Wainwright*, 372 U.S. 335 (1963), than with *Griffin*. Indeed, *Gideon* and *Douglas*, both decided on March 18, 1963, were virtually companion cases.)

3. The results in *Shapiro v. Thompson*, 394 U.S. 618 (1969), and its progeny are best understood as resting, not on Fourteenth Amendment, but on the constitutional right of interstate migration, a right properly inferred from the structure of government ordained by the Constitution. Cf. Zobel v. Williams, 457 U.S. 55, 71 (1982) (O'Connor, J., concurring in judgment). On such inferences, see C. Black, Structure and Relationship in Constitutional Law (1969).

Of course, to say that the results in the cases cited in this note, or in any other cases, are not problematic from the perspective of originalism is not to say that the results are dictated by the originalist approach. It is simply to say only that one cannot fault those results, cannot delegitimate them, *on the basis of originalism.*

Chapter 10

1. See pp. 88–89.

2. See generally J. Choper, Judicial Review and the National Political Process (1980).

3. For Bickel on Thayer, see A. Bickel, The Least Dangerous Branch: The Supreme Court at the Bar of Politics 35–46 (1962).

4. Compare Bickel's admonition to the two passages from Thayer quoted in chapter 6, in the text accompanying notes 25 & 28.

5. J. Ely, Democracy and Distrust: A Theory of Judicial Review (1980).

6. I have addressed the question of the unenumerated constitutional rights the Court may enforce under the Ninth Amendment. See pp. 146–48.

7. J. Ely, "Another Such Victory: Constitutional Theory and Practice in a World Where Courts Are No Different from Legislatures," 77 Virginia L. Rev. 833, 834 n. 4 (1991).

8. Id.

9. Id.

10. Ely, note 5, at 103 (quoted in Ely, note 7, at 834 n. 4).

11. Id. at 834 n. 4 (emphasis added).

12. Id.

13. See note 10 and accompanying text.

14. See p. 74.

15. Cf. Bowers v. Hardwick, 478 U.S. 186 (1986). On *Bowers*, see pp. 174–79.

16. 319 U.S. 624 (1943).

17. 319 U.S. at 666–67 (1943).

18. The Court decided *Barnette* on the basis of the freedom of speech provision of the First Amendment (as "incorporated" against the states by the Fourteenth Amendment). But given that those who challenged the compulsory flag salute statute were Jehovah's Witnesses, and that they challenged it on the basis of religious conscience, the free exercise of religion clause of the First Amendment was also relevant (though, given its analysis, the Court did not have to address the free exercise issue).

19. See pp. 88–89.

20. But then, there's Martin Shapiro's warning. See chapter 6, note 109 and accompanying text.

21. For a thoughtful essay on the present unresponsiveness, to "We the people" now living, of the present practice of judicial review, see D. Chang, "A Critique of Judicial Supremacy," 36 Villanova L. Rev. 281 (1991).

22. According to section 1 of Article III of the Constitution, "The Judges, both of the supreme and of inferior Courts, shall hold their Offices during good Behaviour. . . ."

23. According to the Twenty-second Amendment, "No person shall be elected to the office of President more than twice, and no person who has held the office of President, or acted as President, for more than two years of a term to which some other person was elected President shall be elected to the office of President more than once."

24. For a helpful discussion, see G. Easterbrook, "Geritol Justice: Is the Supreme Court Senile?" New Republic, Aug. 19 & 26, 1991, at 17 (suggesting that Supreme Court justices should be limited to terms of about ten years).

25. Constitutional Court Act § 4(1) (1971); see D. Kommers, Judicial Politics in

Notes to pages 197–200

West Germany 88 (1976). For a sympathetic discussion of the German term limitation, see B. Ackerman, The Future of Liberal Revolution 105 (1992).

26. See, e.g., G. Will, Restoration: Congress, Term Limits, and the Recovery of Deliberative Democracy (1992). For a very critical review of Will's book, see N. Polsby, "Restoration Comedy," 102 Yale L. J. 1515 (1993).

27. It may make sense to consider combining term limits for Supreme Court justices with a requirement that no one is eligible to become a justice of the Supreme Court who has not yet attained the age of, say, fifty or fifty-five years. Such a requirement could help to forestall a scenario that might otherwise ensue, in which a relatively young Supreme Court justice would decide cases at least partly under the influence of the need to promote the career he or she would want or need to pursue after his or her tour of duty with the Court was up.

28. Can. Const. (Constitution Act, 1982), pt. I (Canadian Charter of Rights and Freedoms), § 33.

29. See P. Weiler, "Rights and Judges in a Democracy: A New Canadian Version," 18 J. L. Reform 51, 83–84 (1984). For more more recent discussions of Section 33, see B. Slattery, "A Theory of the Charter," 25 Osgoode Hall L. J. 701, 737–47 (1987); L. Weinrib, "Learning to Live with the Override," 35 McGill L. J. 541 (1990).

30. See Weiler, note 29, at 79–80.

31. Id. at 84–85.

32. Id. at 80. Weiler makes an impressive argument. See id. at 79–86. David Chang's similar agument, too, is impressive. See Chang, note 21.

33. On June 15, 1992, "[e]nding nearly two years of bitter debate, the Japanese Parliament approved a bill permitting the dispatch of military personnel abroad, for the first time since World War II, to play a limited role in international peacekeeping operations." D. Sanger, "Japan's Parliament Votes to End Ban on Sending Troops Abroad," New York Times, June 16, 1992, at A1.

34. See note 41 and accompanying text.

35. W. Brennan, Jr., "Why Have a Bill of Rights?" 9 Oxford J. Legal Studies 426, 433–34 (quoting M. Perry, The Constitution, the Courts, and Human Rights 111 (1982)).

36. For a critique of such talk, see E. Maltz, "The Supreme Court and the Quality of Political Dialogue," 5 Constitutional Commentary 375 (1988).

37. For examples, see M. Perry, note 35, at 111–13 (quoting statements by Eugene Rostow, Robert Jackson, and Alexander Bickel). In his Hart Lecture, Justice Brennan cited, in addition to my own work, work by Frank Michelman, Ronald Dworkin, and Alexander Bickel. See Brennan, note 35, at 434 n. 40. For a recent example, see L. Sager, "The Incorrigible Constitution," 65 New York U. L. Rev. 893, 960 (1990): "The process over time is one of dialogic collaboration, with the judiciary charged with carrying forward the project of constitutional justice upon which popular installation and periodic reshaping of the Constitution has embarked us. At times the dialogue may be adversarial: a Supreme Court that is widely perceived to have run off the rails can be redirected by the requisite Article V consensus, while a morally laggard society can be prodded into reflection and change. But collaboration, it is to be hoped, will be the more general tone."

38. Bickel, note 3, at 25–26.

39. This is Brian Slattery's accurate characterization (Slattery, note 29, at 742) of the position persuasively argued by Donna Greschner and Ken Norman in their important article: "The Courts and Section 33," 12 Queen's L. J. 155, 190 et seq. (1987).

40. See pp. 110–14.

41. See chapter 6, note 25 and accompanying text.

42. S. Levinson, "The Audience for Constitutional Meta-Theory (or, Why, and to Whom, Do I Write the Things I Do?)," 63 U. Colorado L. Rev. 389, 406–7 (1992).

43. See G. Calabresi, "Foreword: Antidiscrimination and Constitutional Accountability (What the Bork-Brennan Debate Ignores)," 105 Harvard L. Rev. 80, 124 (1991) (calling the Canadian Constitution, in consequence of section 33 of the Charter, "a wonderful example of an essentially Bickellian constitution").

My suggestion here is that perhaps the Congress and the president, acting together pursuant to something like the Canadian innovation, should play a larger role, not in amending the Constitution, but in giving shape, in particular contexts, to at least some indeterminate constitutional values. Perhaps they should play a larger role, too, in amending the Constitution, as Bruce Ackerman has recently suggested. See Ackerman, note 25, at 54–55.

44. C. Sunstein, The Partial Constitution 354 (1993).

45. Cf. Chang, note 21, at 397–99:

> [J]udicial supremacy and congressional supremacy are not the only options. Voters might consider, for example, (i) retaining judicial supremacy and abandoning life-tenure; (ii) adopting congressional supremacy while requiring a supermajority within Congress to override a court decision; (iii) adopting congressional supremacy while requiring Congress to wait one year (or two, or more) before it can enact responsive legislation; (iv) determining whether Congress' structure truly does provide optimal legislative accountability; (v) exercising Congress' power to curtail federal court jurisdiction; or (vi) determining whether article V [of the Constitution] provides the best procedures for constitutional amendment.

In a footnote accompanying item (iii), Chang writes: "This option would discourage a heated rush to judgment and create an opportunity for extended reflection and debate—as in constitutional politics itself. At the same time, however, it would extend the period during which a possibly erroneous judicial decision retains its status as governing law." Id. at 398 n. 361.

46. For an instructive comment on contemporary (mis)understandings of the term "politics", see M. Shapiro, "Morality and the Politics of Judging," 63 Tulane L. Rev. 1555, 1555–58 (1989).

47. N. MacCormick, "Reconstruction after Deconstruction: A Response to CLS," 10 Oxford J. Legal Studies 539, 558 (1990). (MacCormick adds: "Moreover, [the juristic job] is intensely political in its effects." Id.) Cf. R. Posner, The Problems of Jurisprudence 131 (1990):

> [T]here are important institutional and procedural differences between courts and legislators, and they impose bounds on the domain of the reasonable in judging that are not found in legislating. They differentiate the judicial product from that of a legislature but do not dictate the outcome of difficult cases—they may rule out some outcomes, but not all except one. The judge in the difficult case is more a policy maker than a conventional lawyer and within his domain of freedom or discretion may be as free-wheeling as a legislator. But neither is unconstrained, and, more to the point, the constraints are different.

48. See pp. 75–76.

49. Recall that the Bill of Rights speaks of and protects "the people" collectively as well as individually. See A. Amar, "The Bill of Rights as a Constitution," 100 Yale L. J. 1131 (1991).

50. I have discussed elsewhere the United States as a community of political-moral judgment. See M. Perry, Love and Power: The Role of Religion and Morality in American Politics, chap. 6 (1991).

51. See S. Hampshire, Two Theories of Morality 43, 48–49 (1977):

> The correct answer to the old question—'why should it be assumed, or be argued, that there is just one good for man, just one way of life that is best?'—is . . . an indirect one and it is not simple. One can coherently list all the ideally attainable human virtues and achievements, and all the desirable features of a perfect human existence; and one might count this as prescribing the good for man, the perfect realization of all that is desirable. But the best selection from this whole that could with luck be achieved in a particular historical situation by a particular person will be the supreme end for him, the ideal at which he should aim. It is obvious that supreme ends of this kind are immensely various and always will be various. There can be no single supreme end in this particularized sense, as both social orders and human capabilities change. . . .
>
> That there should be an abstract ethical ideal, the good for men in general, is not inconsistent with there being great diversity in preferred ways of life, even among men living at the same place at the same time. The good for man, as the common starting-point, marks an area within which arguments leading to divergent conclusions about moral priorities can be conducted. The conclusions are widely divergent, because they are determined by different subsidiary premises. Practical and theoretical reason, cleverness, intelligence and wisdom, justice, friendship, temperance in relation to passions, courage, a repugnance in the face of squalid or mean sentiments and actions; these are Aristotle's general and abstract terms, which do not by themselves distinguish a particular way of life, realizable in a particular historical situation. The forms that intelligence and friendship and love between persons, and that nobility of sentiment and motive, can take are at least as various as human cultures; and they are more various still, because within any one culture there will be varieties of individual temperament, providing distinct motives and priorities of interest, and also varieties of social groupings, restricting the choice of ways of life open to individuals.

52. The most important such moments, of course, are the founding, the post–Civil War reconstruction, and the 1930s. Cf. B. Ackerman, We the People: The Founding (1992).

53. For a discussion of "self-critical rationality", see M. Perry, note 50, chap. 4.

54. D. Patterson, "Law's Pragmatism: Law as Practice & Narrative," 76 Virginia L. Rev. 937, 995 (1990). Patterson's essay is addressed to law generally, not just constitutional law.

55. Cf. B. Ackerman, "Robert Bork's Grand Inquisition," 99 Yale L. J. 1419, 1419–20, 1438 (1990):

> Law isn't just politics. It isn't morals either. It's distinctive—and precisely in some of the ways Bork emphasizes. Judges begin by looking back-

wards—to the decisions of authorized lawmakers. They take interpretation seriously. Their job is to make sense of the legally relevant sources, recognizing that the messages they receive may prove inconsistent with their personal or political morality. . . . Bork is also right to suggest that much trendy 'theory' runs rough-shod over these distinctions. . . .
       . . . .
Reading and writing judicial opinions is not like reading and writing political philosophy. . . . The Supreme Court . . . speaks in the collective name of the People; it interprets the People's past achievements . . . ; it announces dogmas which may lead some to the electric chair, others to freedom.

56. See F. Michelman, "Law's Republic," 97 Yale L. J. 1493, 1496 (1988): "I will call . . . a looking backward jurisprudence *authoritarian* because it regards adjudicative actions as legitimate only insofar as dictated by prior normative utterance, express or implied, of extra-judicial authority." Compare Ackerman's statement, in the preceding footnote.

57. On "pragmatism" as a conception of adjudication, see Posner, note 47, chap. 15 ("A Pragmatist Manifesto"). For an effective, and often witty, critique of so-called "legal pragmatism", see S. Smith, "The Pursuit of Pragmatism," 100 Yale L. J. 409 (1990). (Smith comments specifically on Posner's brand of pragmatism at pp. 425–29.)

58. If Richard Posner conceives of constitutional adjudication as only "pragmatic", as he seems to, he misconceives it. See R. Posner, "Bork and Beethoven," 42 Stanford L. Rev. 1365 (1990).

INDEX

Abortion, 173, 190, 260n96, 261n106, 261–62n107. *See also* Roe v. Wade
  and the antidiscrimination directive, 184
  Louisiana's criminal statute, 181
  politics and, 188
  sex-selective sympathy and indifference, 185–89
Abridgement, 127, 128, 133, 247n60
Accusers, right to confront one's, 231–32n30
Ackerman, Bruce, 11–12, 164–65
Adamson v. California, 244n44
Affirmative action, 155–60, 190, 253n102, 254n109
  sex-based, 255n120
Amar, Akhil, 127–28, 245n45, 246–47n60
Antiwar provision, 198–99
Arms, right to bear, 244n44
Arnold, Morris, 67
Avins, Alfred, 128–29

Baer, Judith A., 135
Ballot, right to appear on, 142
Bassham, Gregory, 44–45
Berger, Raoul, 135, 217n51
  McAffee's criticism of originalism of, 45
Bickel, Alexander, 27, 193, 199, 200
  counter-majoritarian difficulty, 16–17
  on Fourteenth Amendment, 32–33
  on meaning of law, 95–96
  on politics and constitutional adjudication, 109–10
Bill of Rights, 245n44
  Fourteenth Amendment and, 137–40

history of, 25–26
national government
  limitations on, 64
  supremacy over state constitutions, 139
  privileges and immunities, 126–27, 244n44
Bingham, John A., 125, 244–45n44
Black, Charles, 139, 227n31
Black Codes, 117–18
Black, Hugo, 29
Blackstone, William, 125, 141
Bolling v. Sharpe, 146–47
Bork, Robert, 9, 34–35, 50
  on Bush's nomination of Souter, 6–7
  on constitutional adjudication, 205n7
  on the Fourteenth Amendment, 10, 136
  on "historical evidence", 217n46
  on "judicial imperialism" of Supreme Court, 189–91
  on limits put on legislative power, 211n39
  on morality, 54
  on originalism, 41–44, 222n92
  on provisional interpretation, lack of, 40
  sex-based discrimination, 149
  The Tempting of America, 4–7, 89–90, 201–2, 214n17
Bowers v. Hardwick, 174–75, 176, 179
Brandeis, Louis, 90, 233n9, 255n12
Brennan, William J., Jr., 99, 108, 156, 199, 213n15
  on affirmative action, 160
  on *Griswold*, 171
  on judicial review (Hart Lecture), 21–22

269

Printed in the United States
121635LV00008B/134/A